Decadent Plays: 18

Decadent Plays: 1890–1930

Salome

The Race of Leaves

The Orgy: A Dramatic Poem

Madame La Mort

Lilith

Ennoïa: A Triptych

The Black Maskers

La Gioconda

Ardiane and Barbe Bleue or, The Useless Deliverance

Kerria Japonica

The Dove

Edited by

ADAM ALSTON *and* JANE DESMARAIS

methuen | drama

LONDON • NEW YORK • OXFORD • NEW DELHI • SYDNEY

METHUEN DRAMA
Bloomsbury Publishing Plc
50 Bedford Square, London, WC1B 3DP, UK
1385 Broadway, New York, NY 10018, USA
29 Earlsfort Terrace, Dublin 2, Ireland

BLOOMSBURY, METHUEN DRAMA and the Methuen Drama logo are trademarks of
Bloomsbury Publishing Plc

First published in Great Britain 2024

A catalogue record for this book is available from the British Library.

A catalog record for this book is available from the Library of Congress.

ISBN: HB: 978-1-3501-7182-4
       PB: 978-1-3501-7183-1
       ePDF: 978-1-3501-7184-8
       eBook: 978-1-3501-7185-5

Series: Methuen Drama Play Collections

Typeset by RefineCatch Limited, Bungay, Suffolk
Printed and bound in Great Britain

To find out more about our authors and books visit www.bloomsbury.com
and sign up for our newsletters.

Contents

Acknowledgements

Compiling this anthology would not have been possible without the editorial wizardry of Jessica Gossling, who transcribed and formatted the texts, and offered valuable insight into their qualities and merits. Numerous colleagues also supported us in identifying plays for inclusion including Elaine Aston, Nathalie Coutelet, Jim Davis, Özen Nergis Dolcerocca, Sasha Dovzhyk, Melanie Hawthorne, Katharina Herold-Zanker, Jennifer Higgins, Isobel Hurst, Sandra Mayer, Ana Parejo Vadillo, M. Cody Poulton, Dan Rebellato, Anne Birgitte Rønning, Brian Stableford, and John Stokes. Works in progress of a selection of plays in this volume, including commissioned translations, were presented at the Albany Theatre, London, in a night of rehearsed readings on 10 November 2021. We would like to thank the director of that performance, Jonathan Meth, as well as the performers: Philip Arditti, Lauren John Joseph, Yuriri Naka, Georgia Sansom, and Sadao Ueda. We would also like to thank contributors to a focus group, who offered valuable feedback after the event – Shushma Malik, Neil McPherson, Blake Morrison, Owen Parry, Martin Sorrell, John Stokes, and Matthew Sweet – and Kevin Grant, Elizabeth Mylod and Christine Twite for their help in scouting out the meaning of esoteric references. This anthology was also made possible thanks to the generous support of Arts Council England (ACPG-00300552) and the Arts and Humanities Research Council (AH/T006994/1).

Finally, we have limited the number of footnotes in this volume as far as possible so as not to disrupt the flow of each text. Footnotes are by the editors, although Remy de Gourmont's *Lilith*, Jean Lorrain's *Ennoïa: A Triptych*, and Izumi Kyōka's *Kerria Japonica* include notes written by the translators as well as the editors.

Supported using public funding by

**ARTS COUNCIL
ENGLAND**

LOTTERY FUNDED

**Arts and
Humanities
Research Council**

Introduction

Adam Alston and Jane Desmarais

Theatre is resource-intensive, which is usually reflected in the cost of a ticket. Its costliness is partly the result of dependence on people both on and off stage who labour for the pleasure of those in the audience, and it is partly because many theatre performances require substantive material investment in sets and costumes that are only required for the course of a limited run. Commercial theatre auditoria built in the eighteenth and nineteenth centuries also tend to follow a stock design scheme that borders on rococo kitsch, with audiences sat beneath chandeliers watching a stage framed by a proscenium arch crowned with gilded scallop shells and cherubs blowing provocatively on trumpets. It is therefore unsurprising that the making and watching of theatre has been prone to derision as 'decadent'.

However, playwrights and theatre makers have also rebelled against the susceptibility of theatre to bourgeois taste ever since the bourgeoisie emerged as a social class with the rise of industrial modernity. Sometimes this has involved condemning theatre's commercialisation as a decadent symptom of an ailing institution – the Italian performer Eleonora Duse once pronounced that '[t]o save the Theatre, the Theatre must be destroyed, the actors and actresses must all die of the plague', while the British director Peter Brook sought to rid the theatre of a deadly inability to innovate[1] – and sometimes it has inspired playwrights and theatre makers to embrace decadence as a subversive and highly stylised art of decay and unconventional refinement at odds with the prevailing winds of social and economic 'progress'.

Decadence, in the period addressed in this anthology – 1890 to 1930 – has been harnessed as a rhetorical trope in the condemnation of theatre as an institution, and it has been embraced by playwrights as a reaction to a raft of cultural and societal changes that fall under the broad umbrella of modernity, and the progress that industrial modernity, especially, was seen to represent in the late nineteenth and early twentieth centuries. Decadence has also been used as a rhetorical trope in condemning playwrights who came to be associated with decadence because of their interest in countercultural themes and issues that went against the grain of propriety at the time, examples of which are addressed in each of this anthology's sections: subversive representations of empire and the ancient world, a fascination with oblivion and the occult, and probing explorations of eroticism and idolatry. The irony is that the very grounds on which theatre was condemned as decadent by the leading lights of modernism and the avant-gardes – a sclerotic inability to innovate – also prompted playwrights associated with decadence to embrace it as a stimulus for creative experimentation that subverted or at least troubled conformity with dominant styles and genres, like naturalism. Decadence also served as a petri dish for staging dissident genders and queer sexualities, and for experimenting with themes that presented a captivating and subversive retreat from the debilitating impact of industrial modernity on people and social environments. These

---

1 Eleonora Duse, qtd in Arthur Symons, 'Eleonora Duse', *The Contemporary Review, 1866–1900* 78 (August 1900), 196–202 (198); Peter Brook, *The Empty Space* (London: Penguin, 2008).

playwrights turned to the past in order to make sense of an evolving present, then, but they were also innovative authors concerned with enlivening tired tropes and styles.

This anthology is concerned with experimental and dissident playwrights, understood in the widest possible sense as *decadent*. Firstly, it is concerned with writers who embraced decadence in reacting against the influence of industrial modernity and the rise of bourgeois values on the writing and staging of plays, like Jean Lorrain (Paul Alexandre Martin Duval) and Remy de Gourmont. In its place they explored life's mysteries and excesses, ungovernable and unruly bodies and behaviours, and imprudent practices and salacious desires at odds with the delimitation of 'appropriate' and 'healthy' moral and behavioural tastes and codes. Secondly, it is concerned with playwrights, like Oscar Wilde and Djuna Barnes, whose homosexuality has since been vaunted in studies of queer cultures, as well as lesser-known but equally important figures like Michael Field (the pen name of Katherine Harris Bradley and her niece and lover Edith Emma Cooper), whose plays have drawn the attention of scholars inspired by their unconventional lesbianism. Thirdly, the volume features plays by playwrights whose dissidence is a world away from anything that could be thought of as 'progressive'. For instance, Gabriele D'Annunzio was a militant nationalist, and although his relationship to the fascist leader Benito Mussolini was complex – at times supportive, and at times threatening – he nonetheless participated, very actively, in the advancement of Italian nationalism and fascism. The French playwright Rachilde (Marguerite Vallette-Eymery) was also a vocal critic of feminism and universal suffrage, even though her plays and novels often feature dominant women who overpower men. Finally, several of the names in this anthology will be familiar to many readers – particularly its male, west-European contributors, like the Belgian Maurice Maeterlinck – although others may well be unfamiliar as they are yet to enter the west-European canon, like the Ukrainian poet and playwright Lesya Ukrainka, the Russian author Leonid Andreyev and the Japanese writer Izumi Kyōka (Kyōtarō Izumi).

The selection of plays in this volume, then, is intended to reflect the diversity of styles, themes, contexts and issues that playwrights associated with decadence explored in the period running from 1890 to 1930. We divide them into three thematic sections. In 'Empire and the Ancient World' the plays are filled with esoteric historical facts and myths, gods and goddesses, rituals and totems, some plucked from ancient chronicles, others from religious texts, but more often than not gleaned from or inspired by other historians, writers and artists, creating a complex intertextual web that Matthew Potolsky has aptly described as a 'decadent republic of letters'.[2] In 'Oblivion and the Occult', the playwrights seek to pierce the veil of the visible, probing deeper into a mysterious and unfathomable world of possibilities, often with profoundly morbid and unsettling results. In reacting against the influence of positivism on art and literature in the nineteenth century, especially as it came to manifest in naturalist literature and drama, playwrights associated with both symbolism and decadence frequently turned to, and embraced, a rising tide of interest in the occult. Theosophy was widely read, and many writers were associated with esoteric and occult organisations like Joséphin

---

2   Matthew Potolsky, *The Decadent Republic of Letters: Taste, Politics, and Cosmopolitan Community from Baudelaire to Beardsley* (Philadelphia: University of Pennsylvania Press, 2013).

Péladan's Salon de la Rose + Croix in France, and the Hermetic Order of the Golden Dawn in Britain. The final section, 'Eroticism and Idolatry', invites critical reflection on the representation of women in decadent plays. Women are frequently represented either as a threat, or as submissive playthings: at once persecuted, eroticised and idolised. A particularly illustrative example can be found in Gabriele D'Annunzio's play *La Gioconda*, which also invites reflection on another unsavoury aspect of the decadent sensibility in the hands of certain playwrights: the fact that a few playwrights who came to be associated with decadence ended up adhering not to countercultural anarchism, but nationalism and fascism. Women were idolised in the service of male fantasy in their hands, although they also presented their own cults of the personality as emblems fit for idolisation.

Despite the breadth of the present volume, it has of course been limited by the plays available to us within a bounded period. We chose this period because it is most closely associated with decadent poetics and aesthetics, and because it presents an illuminating snapshot of the range of styles and genres that might be appreciated and understood through a decadent frame. The 1890s is especially significant in the study of decadence – a decade that mapped the height of Oscar Wilde's fame and influence, as well as his imprisonment for acts of 'gross indecency' in 1895 – but so too are the first decades of the twentieth century beyond Paris and London, where Wilde largely resided. Many playwrights working outside of these cities were greatly influenced by the work that was produced within them, but that influence was less a determining factor than a stimulus for expanding and innovating the writing of idiosyncratic and experimental plays. This was the case in Russia, for instance, during its Silver Age (running roughly from the turn of the twentieth century to the Russian Revolution in 1917), as well as Japan during the Taishō period (1912–26). The period selected for this anthology enables us to offer a flavour of these decadent reverberations and legacies, although it only hints at the journey that decadence was to take in the hands of playwrights and theoreticians in the second half of the twentieth century – for instance, in the plays and essays of Derek Walcott, Wole Soyinka and Yukio Mishima.[3] As such, we hope that its temporal boundedness might spark other collections and studies that pick up where this volume leaves off.

In selecting texts for an anthology such as this, we face a double challenge. Not only, as Sos Eltis has remarked, are there 'only a tiny handful of plays [that] are widely identified as decadent' (these would include Maeterlinck's *La Princesse Maleine* (1889) and *Pelléas et Mélisande* (1892), and Wilde's *Salome* (1891)),[4] but decadence is notoriously hard to define. Our approach to the selection of plays makes any attempt to pin down the meaning of decadence all the more difficult. In fact, such a task is impossible given the myriad and often conflicting ways in which decadence was

---

3 For an illuminating study of the importance of decadence in the plays and critical essays of these writers, see Robert Stilling, *Beginning at the End: Decadence, Modernism, and Postcolonial Poetry* (Cambridge, MA, and London: Harvard University Press, 2018). For a study of Yukio Mishima's decadent drama, see Ikuho Amano, 'Visions of Phantasm: *Madame de Sade* in the Excess of Language and Imagination', *Volupté: Interdisciplinary Journal of Decadence Studies* 4, no. 2 (2021): 89–105.

4 Sos Eltis, 'Decadent Theater: New Women and "The Eye of the Beholder"', in *The Oxford Handbook of Decadence*, ed. Jane Desmarais and David Weir (Oxford: Oxford University Press, 2022), 318–34.

imagined in contexts ranging from Britain, France and Italy to Japan, Russia and Ukraine. Nonetheless, popular and scholarly understandings of decadence provide useful way markers in mapping its various lines of flight. In popular parlance, decadence is frequently used as a synonym for opulence and abundance – for instance, in describing the gilded scallop shells and cherubs adorning the upper recesses of theatre auditoria built in the nineteenth century, or the material resource and expense that is so often required to put on a show – but in the late nineteenth century decadence was more usually associated with decay and decline. The word 'decadence' derives from the Latin verb *decadēre* (de- 'down' + cadēre 'to fall'), meaning 'to decay' or fall down in quality. It is related to the word 'cadence' and was frequently used to describe a process of social, cultural, or moral decay, as well as declining artistic standards. Désiré Nisard was among the first to correlate the decay of the classical language of the third- and fourth-century Latin literature with the decline of contemporary French literature and an emergent cultural malaise in the nineteenth century with the publication of his *Études de Mœurs et de Critique sur les Poètes Latins de la Décadence* (Cultural-Critical Studies of the Latin Poets of the Decadence, 1834), but uses of the terms 'decadence' and 'decadent' to describe a set of stylistic and thematic preoccupations in art and literature only really gained traction after Théophile Gautier published an influential preface to the 1868 edition of Charles Baudelaire's *Les Fleurs du Mal* (1857). In the 1870s and 1880s, the poet and essayist Paul Bourget followed Gautier's example in turning to Baudelaire as a progenitor of a set of 'decadent' themes and motifs that reflected the spirit of the times, including pessimism, nervous and physical exhaustion, flight from the modern world, civic decline, hallucination, extraordinarily refined tastes and sensations, sadism, morbidity, a love of artifice, eclecticism and esotericism.[5] All of these themes can be found in Joris-Karl Huysmans's *À rebours* (1884), a book that proved influential in its stretching of the naturalist penchant for elaborate descriptions of people, places and things to points of exhaustive excess, causing some to consider the emergence of what Arthur Symons termed a 'decadent movement' in the 1880s and 1890s.[6]

It is tempting to trace a stylistic and thematic line from Baudelaire and Huysmans to the work of the playwrights included in this volume, several of whom acknowledged a debt to their influence. However, the importance of the playwrights themselves ought not to be underestimated. For instance, Wilde and Rachilde were establishing reputations around the same time as Huysmans – Wilde through his highly publicised wit and dandyism (his prose and society comedies gained recognition a little later, in the 1890s), and Rachilde with her fantastically scandalous novel *Monsieur Vénus*, which was

---

5   See Paul Bourget, 'Notes sur quelques poètes contemporains', *Le Siècle littéraire*, 1 April 1876, 266. Reprinted in André Guyaux, *Baudelaire: Un demi-siècle de lectures des* Fleurs du mal *(1855–1905)* (Paris: Presses de l'Université Paris-Sorbonne, 2007), 564. See also Bourget, 'The Example of Baudelaire', trans. Nancy O'Connor, *New England Review* 30, no. 2 (2009): 90–104, http://www.nereview.com/back-issues/2009-pages/vol-30-no-2-2009/. Accessed 22 Nov. 2016.

6   Arthur Symons, 'The Decadent Movement in Literature', *Harper's New Monthly Magazine* (November 1893), 858–67. Symons later rebranded what was essentially the same book as a study of symbolism rather than decadence, with very minor tweaks. See Symons, *The Symbolist Movement in Literature* (London: Archibald Constable & Co., Ltd., 1908).

published the same year as *À rebours* in 1884. Decadent style is also a contested area. Playwrights associated with decadence have often favoured historical verse dramas – Michael Field's *The Race of Leaves* (1901) is an example – although they also tested the boundaries of form, genre, and style. For instance, Gourmont's *Lilith* (1892) presents directors and performers with fascinating practical challenges that were not to be matched until Antonin Artaud penned his plays and theories some thirty years later. Other plays, like Barnes' *The Dove* (1923), bear little resemblance to such works at a formal or stylistic level, and yet its strange mix of Wildean dialogue and Ibsen-esque social commentary captures other stylistic and thematic characteristics of decadence that are more immediately legible and apparent from a contemporary standpoint, especially with regard to its depiction of suppressed lesbianism.

Playwrights sought or came to be associated with multiple styles and affiliations over the course of the fin de siècle, which in many cases makes their definitive association with 'naturalism', 'decadence', or 'symbolism' something of a fool's errand. This anthology takes the 1890s as its point of departure not just to mark a historical juncture at which playwrights picked up the baton of decadence from their poetic and novelistic forebears; rather, the selection of plays from this period – which you might also find in collections of symbolist drama, particularly plays by Maeterlinck and Rachilde, as well as Wilde's *Salome* – are intended to encourage readers to re-appraise taxonomies that neatly compartmentalise a work as 'symbolist' or 'naturalist'. There were literary circles that self-described as 'decadent',[7] and several literary reviews were associated with fin-de-siècle decadence in the 1880s and 1890s, like Anatole Baju's *Le Décadent* (1886–9), John Lane's *The Yellow Book* (1894–7), and Leonard Smithers's *The Savoy* (1896), but decadence is ultimately a vehicle for creative experimentation and moral provocation, and fails to coalesce into one coherent genre.[8] Instead, we might think of decadence as a lens that can help with focusing attention on aesthetic qualities and moral issues, which can lead to very different valuations of a work's merit once compared with established genres of the period.

A final word on the plays' performability. In most cases, and contrary to received wisdom, the playwrights who wrote the plays included in this volume intended, at least at some point in their professional careers, for their plays to be staged. More detailed substantiation is offered below, but one of the main reasons why these plays have been considered in some quarters to be unstageable is because of the coevolution of decadence and symbolism in the 1880s and 1890s and the stylistic bedhopping that many playwrights of the period embraced. The symbolist poet Stéphane Mallarmé played an especially important role in shaping opinion about the fleshy and unreliable presence of human bodies performing on a stage in front of other bodies. If disembodied symbolist poetry served as the literary ideal in the late 1880s and 1890s, then theatre was its intolerable perversion. Stage directions that dwell on evocative imagery also

---

7   Max Nordau describes how authors and artists meeting regularly at the Café Francois I on Boulevard St. Michel in Paris – including Jean Moréas, Laurent Tailhade and Charles Morice – called themselves 'Décadents'. Max Nordau, *Degeneration*, trans. from the second German edition by George L. Mosse (Lincoln and London: University of Nebraska Press, 1993), 100–1.

8   Sos Eltis makes a similar point. See 'Theatre and Decadence', in *Decadence: A Literary History*, ed. Alex Murray (Cambridge: Cambridge University Press, 2020), 201–17 (201).

present directors with extraordinary difficulties. For example, Gourmont offers this fantastic direction in *Lilith*:

> *The Heavens tear open. The veil of the Universe is torn away. The* **Sun** *rains burning fire down on Nature; the grass shrivels; the animals run frantically for the cover of trees – but the trees grow pale and, for the first time, the leaves fall. The* **Sun** *laughs.*

Did Gourmont really intend for these directions to be staged, or were they intended to raise a wry smile, poking fun at those who would demean poetic purity by contaminating it with the prospect of materialisation? As Dan Rebellato observes, '[s]uch directions go beyond "challenging" [. . . coming] close to demanding something incompatible with theatre [. . . But] it seems to me better to think of this play as one that is intended to be unperformable only in the conventions of the time and, by its very daring, to push theatre to reinvent its conventions as it also pushes a wider culture to reinvent its morality.'[9] The plays included in this anthology are offered in the same spirit. Taxonomically ambiguous, provocative, and ahead of their time, these plays demand reappraisal, and invite a new generation of theatre makers to realise their potential.

---

9   Dan Rebellato in Dan Rebellato and Jennifer Higgins, 'Decadent Plays: Jean Lorrain and Remy de Gourmont', *Staging Decadence Blog*, 14 December 2021, https://www.stagingdecadence.com/blog/decadent-plays-jean-lorrain-and-remy-de-gourmont. Accessed 5 October 2023.

EMPIRE AND THE ANCIENT WORLD

Salome

Oscar Wilde (1891)

Oscar Wilde's (1854–1900) landmark play *Salome* (1891) is an enigmatic work indebted to Maeterlinck and drawing inspiration from Gustave Flaubert's *Salammbô* (1862) and 'Hérodias' (from *Trois contes*, 1887), Stéphane Mallarmé's *Hérodiade* (1871), and Joris-Karl Huysmans's *À rebours* (1884), which features voluptuous descriptions of two paintings depicting Salome by Gustave Moreau. The influence of these texts on the style of Wilde's play, particularly Maeterlinck, suggests that it is a symbolist drama, although Sos Eltis describes it as '[t]he ultimate Decadent play of the nineteenth century', embracing 'a virtual checklist of Decadent tropes and styles. Soaked in perverse sensuality, set at the waning of an empire, and climaxing with a young girl kissing the severed head of the man she desires, the play openly advertised its multiple sources, giving it a deliberately artificial air of hybrid textuality.'[1]

Approached as a work '[s]oaked in perverse sensuality', it is easy to appreciate why this play was considered scandalous in England when rehearsals for an ill-fated 1892 production in London in the original French, starring Sarah Bernhardt, were called to a halt after the Lord Chamberlain's office banned public performances of the play in June of that year. The dramatization of scripture was forbidden at the time, which remained the case until 1931 (although private performances were permitted). However, Arthur Wing Pinero depicted a Bible being thrown into a fire in *The Notorious Mrs. Ebbsmith*, which was first produced in 1895, suggesting that the illicit depiction of scripture only scratched the surface of a more deep-seated unease about the play's content. *Salome* savours an overt taste for decadence, and it is this taste for the distasteful and an eroticisation of necrophiliac depravity that raised the hackles of the censor.

The first public staging of *Salome* was presented at Aurélien Lugné-Poe's Théâtre de l'Œuvre in Paris for one night only on 11 February 1896, starring Lina Munte as Salome and Lugné-Poe as Hérode, a year after Wilde was imprisoned for 'gross indecency' in 1895. As Erin Williams Hyman observes, 'not only was the staging of the banned work of an imprisoned author meant as an act of solidarity' among a community of anarchist artists associated with the theatre; the content of the play was also 'intended as an allegory of his predicament – Wilde, like Salome, was being brutally punished for the open expression of unruly sexual desire'.[2] Decadence had become dangerous, but that danger also made it more appealing to radical theatre makers on the other side of the channel.

Although Salome became a type in the art and literature of the fin de siècle – the ultimate femme fatale – Wilde's play proved particularly influential in developing twentieth-century modernism. Max Reinhardt's 1902 staging of the play in Berlin at the 'Schall und Rauch' ('Sound and Smoke') cabaret inspired Richard Strauss to compose his famous opera *Salome* in 1905, which helped with preserving Wilde's legacy in the years ahead. His play was also the most important stimulus for a 'Salomanian' dance craze at the turn of the century. Maud Allan's solo dance *Vision of*

---

1   Sos Eltis, 'Theatre and Decadence', in *Decadence: A Literary History*, ed. Alex Murray (Cambridge: Cambridge University Press, 2020), 201–17 (204).

2   Erin Williams Hyman, 'Salome as Bombshell, or How Oscar Wilde Became an Anarchist', in *Oscar Wilde and Modern Culture: The Making of a Legend*, ed. Joseph Bristow (Athens: Ohio University Press, 2008), 96–109 (103). See also Joseph Donohue, 'Distance, Death and Desire in Salome', in *The Cambridge Companion to Oscar Wilde*, ed. Peter Raby (Cambridge: Cambridge University Press, 1997), 118–42.

Salome (1906) is the most famous example, although Salome's 'dance of the seven veils' depicted in Wilde's play also furnished global majority performers with an inspiring platform for developing their craft. Examples range from Aida Overton Walker's *Salome* dance in 1912 at Oscar Hammerstein's Victoria Theater in New York, to the New Negro Art Theater's *Salome* (1928), starring the first African American modern dancer Hemsley Winfield as Salome when the original performer had fallen ill, and Mario Montez (René Rivera), famous for their collaborations with Jack Smith and Andy Warhol, performing a *Dance of the Seven Veils* (1966) that has fallen into obscurity.[3] These latter examples invite us to consider Salome not just as a figure prone to exoticization and the white gaze, but as an archetype that lends itself to subversive representations of gender, sexuality and race.

Wilde's emendations on the original rehearsal manuscript for the ill-fated 1892 production (the one that was meant to star Bernhardt in the title role) suggest that Salome was 'first and foremost imagined for the stage'.[4] The work implies scenographic austerity, and yet its climactic scene, in which Salome kisses the mouth of the severed head of Iokanaan, is also suggestive of an all-too-intimate encounter with scenographic materiality – however 'difficult' it may be to stage this moment in the context of such an ethereal work. The images that Salome conjures in the mind's eye are rich and evocative, alluring and disturbing, but we hope that Wilde's own intention to produce the play – a staging he was not able to witness while incarcerated, or in his lifetime – will be taken as encouragement for grappling with the challenges of staging one of the most notorious plays of the late nineteenth century.

---

3 Very little is known about Montez's performance, although it does receive a tantalising but cursory reference in David Kauffman's biography of Charles Ludlam. David Kaufman, *Ridiculous!: The Theatrical Life and Times of Charles Ludlam* (New York: Applause Theatre & Cinema Books, 2002), 55.

4 Ellen Crowell, 'The Ugly Things of *Salome*', in *Decadence in the Age of Modernism*, ed. Kate Hext and Alex Murray (Baltimore: Johns Hopkins University Press, 2019), 47–70 (52). See also Joseph Donohue, 'Wilde in France: The "*Salome*" Typescript, Sarah Bernhardt and the Production that Never Was', *Times Literary Supplement*, 11 Sept. 2015, 14–15.

To my Friend Lord Alfred Bruce Douglas the Translator of My Play[5]

Characters

Herod Antipas, *Tetrarch of Judaea*
Iokanaan, *the Prophet*
The Young Syrian, *Captain of the Guard*
Tigellinus, *a young Roman*
A Cappadocian
A Nubian
First Soldier
Second Soldier
The Page of Herodias
Jews, **Nazarenes**, *etc.*
A Slave
Naaman, *the Executioner*
Herodias, *wife of the Tetrarch*
Salome, *daughter of Herodias*
The Slaves of Salome

5   The version of the play selected for this volume is an amended revision of the first English translation
     by Lord Alfred Douglas, published in 1894. Douglas translated the text from Wilde's French with some
     input from Pierre Louÿs, although Wilde was displeased with his translation and undertook
     responsibility for the final version himself, appeasing Douglas with the dedication included here –
     which we draw from the Oxford World's Classics edition, inclusive of 'small emendations [. . .] mostly
     to correct obvious punctuation errors' and stage directions. See Peter Raby, 'Note on the Texts', in
     Oscar Wilde, *The Importance of Being Earnest and Other Plays*, ed. Peter Raby (Oxford: Oxford
     World's Classics, 2008 [1995]), pp. xxvi–xxvii (p. xxvii).

A great terrace in the palace of **Herod**, *set above the banqueting-hall. Some soldiers are leaning over the balcony. To the right there is a gigantic staircase, to the left, at the back, an old cistern surrounded by a wall of green bronze. The moon is shining very brightly.*

Present on stage are **Narraboth** *(the* **Young Syrian***) and the* **Page of Herodias**, *with four soldiers (first, second, the* **Nubian** *and the* **Cappadocian***) and, at one side,* **Naaman**, *the executioner.*

The Young Syrian   How beautiful is the Princess Salome tonight!

The Page of Herodias   Look at the moon. How strange the moon seems! She is like a woman rising from a tomb. She is like a dead woman. One might fancy she was looking for dead things.

The Young Syrian   She has a strange look. She is like a little princess who wears a yellow veil, and whose feet are of silver. She is like a princess who has little white doves for feet. One might fancy she was dancing.

The Page of Herodias   She is like a woman who is dead. She moves very slowly.

Noise in the banqueting-hall.

First Soldier   What an uproar! Who are those wild beasts howling?

Second Soldier   The Jews. They are always like that. They are disputing about their religion.

First Soldier   Why do they dispute about their religion?

Second Soldier   I cannot tell. They are always doing it. The Pharisees, for instance, say that there are angels, and the Sadducees declare that angels do not exist.[6]

First Soldier   I think it is ridiculous to dispute about such things.

The Young Syrian   How beautiful is the Princess Salome tonight!

The Page of Herodias   You are always looking at her. You look at her too much. It is dangerous to look at people in such fashion. Something terrible may happen.

The Young Syrian   She is very beautiful tonight.

First Soldier   The tetrarch has a sombre aspect.

Second Soldier   Yes; he has a sombre aspect.

First Soldier   He is looking at something.

Second Soldier   He is looking at someone.

First Soldier   At whom is he looking?

---

6   The Pharisees and Sadducees were leading politico-religious sects within Judaism. The Pharisees were the leading Jewish religious party, opposed by the Sadducees, which rejected the Pharisees' belief in the afterlife and the existence of angels and demons in a spiritual realm.

Second Soldier   I cannot tell.

The Young Syrian   How pale the Princess is! Never have I seen her so pale. She is like the shadow of a white rose in a mirror of silver.

The Page of Herodias   You must not look at her. You look too much at her.

First Soldier   Herodias has filled the cup of the Tetrarch.

The Cappadocian   Is that the Queen Herodias, she who wears a black mitre sewed with pearls, and whose hair is powdered with blue dust?

First Soldier   Yes; that is Herodias, the Tetrarch's wife.

Second Soldier   The Tetrarch is very fond of wine. He has wine of three sorts. One which is brought from the Island of Samothrace, and is purple like the cloak of Caesar.[7]

The Cappadocian   I have never seen Caesar.

Second Soldier   Another that comes from a town called Cyprus, and is as yellow as gold.

The Cappadocian   I love gold.

Second Soldier   And the third is a wine of Sicily. That wine is as red as blood.

The Nubian   The gods of my country are very fond of blood. Twice in the year we sacrifice to them young men and maidens: fifty young men and a hundred maidens. But I am afraid that we never give them quite enough, for they are very harsh to us.

The Cappadocian   In my country there are no gods left. The Romans have driven them out. There are some who say that they have hidden themselves in the mountains, but I do not believe it. Three nights I have been on the mountains seeking them everywhere. I did not find them, and at last I called them by their names, and they did not come. I think they are dead.

First Soldier   The Jews worship a God that you cannot see.

The Cappadocian   I cannot understand that.

First Soldier   In fact, they only believe in things that one cannot see.

The Cappadocian   That seems to me altogether ridiculous.

The Voice of Iokanaan (*from within the cistern*)   After me shall come another mightier than I. I am not worthy so much as to unloose the latchet of his shoes. When he cometh the solitary places shall be glad. They shall blossom like the rose. The eyes of the blind shall see the day, and the ears of the deaf shall be opened. The suckling child shall put his hand upon the dragon's lair, he shall lead the lions by their manes.

Second Soldier   Make him be silent. He is always saying ridiculous things.

---

7   Samothrace: an island in the northern Aegean Sea. Caesar: Tiberius, Roman Emperor AD 14–37.

First Soldier No, no. He is a holy man. He is very gentle, too. Every day when I give him to eat he thanks me.

The Cappadocian Who is he?

First Soldier A prophet.

The Cappadocian What is his name?

First Soldier Iokanaan.

The Cappadocian Whence comes he?

First Soldier From the desert, where he fed on locusts and wild honey. He was clothed in camel's hair, and round his loins he had a leathern belt. He was very terrible to look upon. A great multitude used to follow him. He even had disciples.

The Cappadocian What is he talking of?

First Soldier We can never tell. Sometimes he says things that affright one; but it is impossible to understand what he says.

The Cappadocian May one see him?

First Soldier No. The Tetrarch has forbidden it.

The Young Syrian The Princess has hidden her face behind her fan! Her little white hands are fluttering like doves that fly to their dove-cots. They are like white butterflies. They are just like white butterflies.

The Page of Herodias What is that to you? Why do you look at her? You must not look at her . . . Something terrible may happen.

The Cappadocian (*pointing to the cistern*) What a strange prison!

Second Soldier It is an old cistern.

The Cappadocian An old cistern! That must be a poisonous place in which to dwell!

Second Soldier Oh, no! For instance, the Tetrarch's brother, his elder brother, the first husband of Herodias the Queen, was imprisoned there for twelve years. It did not kill him. At the end of the twelve years he had to be strangled.

The Cappadocian Strangled? Who dared to do that?

Second Soldier (*pointing to the* **Executioner**, *a huge negro*) That man yonder, Naaman.

The Cappadocian He was not afraid?

Second Soldier Oh, no! The Tetrarch sent him the ring.

The Cappadocian What ring?

Second Soldier The death ring. So he was not afraid.

The Cappadocian Yet it is a terrible thing to strangle a king.

First Soldier   Why? Kings have but one neck, like other folk.

The Cappadocian   I think it terrible.

The Young Syrian   The Princess is getting up! She is leaving the table! She looks very troubled. Ah, she is coming this way. Yes, she is coming towards us. How pale she is! Never have I seen her so pale.

The Page of Herodias   Do not look at her. I pray you not to look at her.

The Young Syrian   She is like a dove that has strayed . . . She is like a narcissus trembling in the wind . . . She is like a silver flower.

Enter **Salome**.

Salome   I will not stay. I cannot stay. Why does the Tetrarch look at me all the while with his mole's eyes under his shaking eyelids? It is strange that the husband of my mother looks at me like that. I know not what it means. Of a truth I know it too well.

The Young Syrian   You have just left the feast, Princess?

Salome   How sweet is the air here! I can breathe here! Within there are Jews from Jerusalem who are tearing each other in pieces over their foolish ceremonies, and barbarians who drink and drink and spill their wine on the pavement, and Greeks from Smyrna,[8] with painted eyes and painted cheeks, and frizzed hair curled in columns, and Egyptians silent and subtle, with long nails of jade and russet cloaks, and Romans brutal and coarse, with their uncouth jargon. Ah! how I loathe the Romans! They are rough and common, and they give themselves the airs of noble lords.

The Young Syrian   Will you be seated, Princess?

The Page of Herodias   Why do you speak to her? Oh! something terrible will happen. Why do you look at her?

Salome   How good to see the moon! She is like a little piece of money, a little silver flower. She is cold and chaste. I am sure she is a virgin. She has the beauty of a virgin. Yes, she is a virgin. She has never defiled herself. She has never abandoned herself to men, like the other goddesses.

The Voice of Iokanaan   Behold! The Lord hath come. The Son of Man is at hand. The centaurs have hidden themselves in the rivers, and the nymphs have left the rivers, and are lying beneath the leaves in the forests.

Salome   Who was that who cried out?

Second Soldier   The prophet, Princess.

Salome   Ah, the prophet! He of whom the Tetrarch is afraid?

Second Soldier   We know nothing of that, Princess. It was the prophet Iokanaan who cried out.

---

8   Smyrna: a city on the Aegean coast of Asia Minor, modern Turkey.

The Young Syrian   Is it your pleasure that I bid them bring your litter, Princess? The night is fair in the garden.

Salome   He says terrible things about my mother, does he not?

Second Soldier   We never understand what he says, Princess.

Salome   Yes; he says terrible things about her.

Enter a **Slave**.

The Slave   Princess, the Tetrarch prays you to return to the feast.

Salome   I will not return.

The Young Syrian   Pardon me, Princess, but if you return not some misfortune may happen.

Salome   Is he an old man, this prophet?

The Young Syrian   Princess, it were better to return. Suffer me to lead you in.

Salome   This prophet . . . is he an old man?

First Soldier   No, Princess, he is quite young.

Second Soldier   One cannot be sure. There are those who say that he is Elias.

Salome   Who is Elias?

Second Soldier   A prophet of this country in bygone days, Princess.

The Slave   What answer may I give the Tetrarch from the Princess?

The Voice of Iokanaan   Rejoice not, O land of Palestine, because the rod of him who smote thee is broken. For from the seed of the serpent shall come a basilisk, and that which is born of it shall devour the birds.

Salome   What a strange voice! I would speak with him.

First Soldier   I fear it may not be, Princess. The Tetrarch does not suffer anyone to speak with him. He has even forbidden the high priest to speak with him.

Salome   I desire to speak with him.

First Soldier   It is impossible, Princess.

Salome   I will speak with him.

The Young Syrian   Would it not be better to return to the banquet?

Salome   Bring forth this prophet.

Exit the **Slave**.

First Soldier   We dare not, Princess.

Salome (*approaching the cistern and looking down into it*)   How black it is, down there! It must be terrible to be in so black a hole! It is like a tomb . . . (*To the*

Soldiers.) Did you not hear me? Bring out the prophet. I would look on him.

Second Soldier   Princess, I beg you, do not require this of us.

Salome   You are making me wait upon your pleasure.

First Soldier   Princess, our lives belong to you, but we cannot do what you have asked of us. And indeed, it is not of us that you should ask this thing.

Salome (*looking at* the **Young Syrian**)   Ah!

The Page of Herodias   Oh! what is going to happen? I am sure that something terrible will happen.

Salome (*going up to the* **Young Syrian**)   Thou wilt do this thing for me, will thou not, Narraboth? Thou wilt do this thing for me. I have ever been kind towards thee. Thou wilt do it for me. I would but look at him, this strange prophet. Men have talked so much of him. Often I have heard the Tetrarch talk of him. I think he is afraid of him, the Tetrarch. Art thou, even thou, also afraid of him, Narraboth?

The Young Syrian   I fear him not, Princess; there is no man I fear. But the Tetrarch has formally forbidden that any man should raise the cover of this well.

Salome   Thou wilt do this thing for me, Narraboth, and tomorrow when I pass in my litter beneath the gateway of the idol sellers, I will let fall for thee a little flower, a little green flower.

The Young Syrian   Princess, I cannot, I cannot.

Salome (*smiling*)   Thou wilt do this thing for me, Narraboth. Thou knowest that thou wilt do this thing for me. And on the morrow when I shall pass in my litter by the bridge of the idol-buyers, I will look at thee through the muslin veils, I will look at thee, Narraboth, it may be I will smile at you. Look at me, Narraboth, look at me. Ah! thou knowest that thou wilt do what I ask of thee. Thou knowest it . . . I know that thou wilt do this thing.

The Young Syrian (*signing to the* **Third Soldier**)   Let the prophet come forth . . . The Princess Salome desires to see him.

Salome   Ah!

The Page of Herodias   Oh! How strange the moon looks! Like the hand of a dead woman who is seeking to cover herself with a shroud.

The Young Syrian   She has a strange aspect! She is like a little princess, whose eyes are eyes of amber. Through the clouds of muslin she is smiling like a little princess.

The **Prophet** *comes out of the cistern;* **Salome** *looks at him and steps slowly back.*

Iokanaan   Where is he whose cup of abominations is now full? Where is he, who in a robe of silver shall one day die in the face of all the people? Bid him come forth, that he may hear the voice of him who hath cried in the waste places and in the houses of kings.

Salome   Of whom is he speaking?

The Young Syrian   No one can tell, Princess.

Iokanaan   Where is she who saw the images of men painted on the walls, even the images of the Chaldaeans painted with colours, and gave herself up unto the lust of her eyes, and sent ambassadors into the land of Chaldaea?

Salome   It is of my mother that he is speaking.

The Young Syrian   Oh, no, Princess.

Salome   Yes: it is of my mother that he is speaking.

Iokanaan   Where is she who gave herself unto the Captains of Assyria, who have baldricks on their loins, and crowns of many colours on their heads? Where is she who hath given herself to the young men of the Egyptians, who are clothed in fine linen and hyacinth, whose shields are of gold, whose helmets are of silver, whose bodies are mighty? Go, bid her rise up from the bed of her abominations, from the bed of her incestuousness, that she may hear the words of him who prepareth the way of the Lord, that she may repent her of her iniquities. Though she will not repent, but will stick fast in her abominations, go bid her come, for the fan of the Lord[9] is in His hand.

Salome   Ah, but he is terrible, he is terrible!

The Young Syrian   Do not stay here, Princess, I beseech you.

Salome   It is his eyes above all that are terrible. They are like black holes burned by torches in a tapestry of Tyre. They are like the black caverns where the dragons live, the black caverns of Egypt in which the dragons make their lairs. They are like black lakes troubled by fantastic moons . . . Do you think he will speak again?

The Young Syrian   Do not stay here, Princess. I pray you do not stay here.

Salome   How wasted he is! He is like a thin ivory statue. He is like an image of silver. I am sure he is chaste, as the moon is. He is like a moonbeam, like a shaft of silver. His flesh must be very cold, cold like ivory. I would look closer at him.

The Young Syrian   No, no, Princess!

Salome   I must look at him closer.

The Young Syrian   Princess! Princess!

Iokanaan   Who is this woman who is looking at me? I will not have her look at me. Wherefore doth she look at me, with her golden eyes, under her gilded eyelids? I know not who she is. I do not desire to know who she is. Bid her begone. It is not to her that I would speak.

Salome   I am Salome, daughter of Herodias, Princess of Judaea.

---

9   Winnowing fan. See Matthew 3.12: 'Whose fan is in his hand, and he will thoroughly cleanse his threshing-floor'.

Iokanaan   Back! daughter of Babylon! Come not near the chosen of the Lord. Thy mother hath filled the earth with the wine of her iniquities, and the cry of her sinning hath come up even to the ears of God.

Salome   Speak again, Iokanaan. Thy voice is as music to mine ear.

The Young Syrian   Princess! Princess! Princess!

Salome   Speak again! Speak again, Iokanaan, and tell me what I must do.

Iokanaan   Daughter of Sodom, come not near me! But cover thy face with a veil, and scatter ashes upon thine head, and get thee to the desert, and seek out the Son of Man.

Salome   Who is he, the Son of Man? Is he as beautiful as thou art, Iokanaan?

Iokanaan   Get thee behind me! I hear in the palace the beating of the wings of the angel of death.

The Young Syrian   Princess, I beseech thee to go within.

Iokanaan   Angel of the Lord God, what dost thou here with thy sword? Whom seekest thou in this palace? The day of him who shall die in a robe of silver has not yet come.

Salome   Iokanaan!

Iokanaan   Who speaketh!

Salome   I am amorous of thy body, Iokanaan! Thy body is white, like the lilies of a field that the mower hath never mowed. Thy body is white like the snows that lie on the mountains of Judaea, and come down into the valleys. The roses in the garden of the Queen of Arabia are not so white as thy body. Neither the roses of the garden of the Queen of Arabia, the garden of spices of the Queen of Arabia, nor the feet of the dawn when they light on the leaves, nor the breast of the moon when she lies on the breast of the sea . . . There is nothing in the world so white as thy body. Suffer me to touch thy body.

Iokanaan   Back! daughter of Babylon! By woman came evil into the world. Speak not to me. I will not listen to thee. I listen but to the voice of the Lord God.

Salome   Thy body is hideous. It is like the body of a leper. It is like a plastered wall, where vipers have crawled; like a plastered wall where the scorpions have made their nest. It is like a whited sepulchre, full of loathsome things. It is horrible, thy body is horrible. It is of thy hair that I am enamoured, Iokanaan. Thy hair is like clusters of grapes, like the clusters of black grapes that hang from the vine-trees of Edom[10] in the land of the Edomites. Thy hair is like the cedars of Lebanon, like the great cedars of Lebanon that give their shade to the lions and to the robbers who would hide them by day. The long black nights, when the moon hides her face, when the stars are afraid, are not so black as thy hair. The silence that dwells in the forest is not so black. There is nothing in the world that is so black as thy hair . . . Suffer me to touch thy hair.

---

10 Edom: a land bordering ancient Israel, modern southwest Jordan.

Iokanaan   Back, daughter of Sodom! Touch me not. Profane not the temple of the Lord God.

Salome   Thy hair is horrible. It is covered with mire and dust. It is like a crown of thorns placed on thy head. It is like a knot of serpents coiled round thy neck. I love not thy hair . . . It is thy mouth that I desire, Iokanaan. Thy mouth is like a band of scarlet on a tower of ivory. It is like a pomegranate cut in twain with a knife of ivory. The pomegranate flowers that blossom in the gardens of Tyre, and are redder than roses, are not so red. The red blasts of trumpets that herald the approach of kings, and make afraid the enemy, are not so red. Thy mouth is redder than the feet of those who tread the wine in the wine-press. Thy mouth is redder than the feet of the doves who inhabit the temples and are fed by the priests. It is redder than the feet of him who cometh from a forest where he hath slain a lion, and seen gilded tigers. Thy mouth is like a branch of coral that fishers have found in the twilight of the sea, the coral that they keep for the kings! . . . It is like the vermilion that the Moabites find in the mines of Moab,[11] the vermilion that the kings take from them. It is like the bow of the King of the Persians, that is painted with vermilion, and is tipped with coral. There is nothing in the world so red as thy mouth . . . Suffer me to kiss thy mouth.

Iokanaan   Never! daughter of Babylon! Daughter of Sodom! never.

Salome   I will kiss thy mouth, Iokanaan. I will kiss thy mouth.

The Young Syrian   Princess, Princess, thou who art like a garden of myrrh, thou who art the dove of all doves, look not at this man, look not at him! Do not speak such words to him. I cannot endure it . . . Princess, do not speak these things.

Salome   I will kiss thy mouth, Iokanaan.

The Young Syrian   Ah!

He kills himself, and falls between **Salome** *and* **Iokanaan**.

The Page of Herodias   The young Syrian has slain himself! The young captain has slain himself! He has slain himself who was my friend! I gave him a little box of perfumes and ear-rings wrought in silver, and now he has killed himself! Ah, did he not say that some misfortune would happen? I, too, said it, and it has come to pass. Well I knew that the moon was seeking a dead thing, but I knew not that it was he whom she sought. Ah! why did I not hide him from the moon? If I had hidden him in a cavern she would not have seen him.

First Soldier   Princess, the young captain has just slain himself.

Salome   Suffer me to kiss thy mouth, Iokanaan.

Iokanaan   Art thou not afraid, daughter of Herodias? Did I not tell thee that I had heard in the palace the beating of the wings of the angel of death, and hath he not come, the angel of death?

---

11 Moab: a kingdom bordering ancient Israel, east of the Dead Sea, in modern Jordan.

Salome   Suffer me to kiss thy mouth.

Iokanaan   Daughter of adultery, there is but one who can save thee. It is He of whom I spake. Go seek Him. He is in a boat on the sea of Galilee and He talketh with His disciples. Kneel down on the shore of the sea, and call unto Him by His name. When he cometh to thee, and to all who call on Him He cometh, bow thyself at His feet and ask of Him the remission of thy sins.

Salome   Suffer me to kiss thy mouth.

Iokanaan   Cursed be thou! daughter of an incestuous mother, be thou accursed!

Salome   I will kiss thy mouth, Iokanaan.

Iokanaan   I will not look at thee. Thou art accursed, Salome, thou art accursed.

He goes down into the cistern.

Salome   I will kiss thy mouth, Iokanaan; I will kiss thy mouth.

First Soldier   We must bear away the body to another place. The Tetrarch does not care to see dead bodies, save the bodies of those whom he himself has slain.

The Page of Herodias   He was my brother, and nearer to me than a brother. I gave him a little box full of perfumes, and a ring of agate that he wore always on his hand. In the evening we were wont to walk by the river, and among the almond trees, and he used to tell me of the things of his country. He spake ever very low. The sound of his voice was like the sound of the flute, of one who playeth upon the flute. Also he had much joy to gaze at himself in the river. I used to reproach him for that.

Second Soldier   You are right; we must hide the body. The Tetrarch must not see it.

First Soldier   The Tetrarch will not come to this place. He never comes on the terrace. He is too much afraid of the prophet.

Enter **Herod**, **Herodias** *and all the Court:* **Tigellinus** *(Caesar's ambassador) and one other Roman, five Jews, two Nazarenes, three Slaves (* **Manasseh**, **Issachar**, **Ozias** *), and Salome's* **Slaves**.

Herod   Where is Salome? Where is the Princess? Why did she not return to the banquet as I commanded her? Ah! there she is!

Herodias   You must not look at her! You are always looking at her!

Herod   The moon has a strange look tonight. Has she not a strange look? She is like a mad woman, a mad woman who is seeking everywhere for lovers. She is naked too. She is quite naked. The clouds are seeking to clothe her nakedness, but she will not let them. She shows herself naked in the sky. She reels through the clouds like a drunken woman . . . I am sure she is looking for lovers. Does she not reel like a drunken woman? She is like a mad woman, is she not?

Herodias   No; the moon is like the moon, that is all. Let us go within . . . You have nothing to do here.

Herod   I will stay here! Manesseh, lay carpets there. Light torches. Bring forth the ivory tables, and the tables of jasper. The air here is sweet. I will drink more wine with my guests. We must show all honours to the ambassadors of Caesar.

Herodias   It is not because of them that you remain.

Herod   Yes; the air is very sweet. Come, Herodias, our guests await us. Ah! I have slipped! I have slipped in blood! It is an ill omen. It is a very ill omen. Wherefore is there blood here? . . . and this body, what does this body here? Think you that I am like the King of Egypt, who gives no feast to his guests but that he shows them a corpse? Whose is it? I will not look on it.

First Soldier   It is our captain, sire. It is the young Syrian whom you made captain of the guard but three days gone.

Herod   I issued no order that he should be slain.

Second Soldier   He slew himself, sire.

Herod   For what reason? I had made him captain of my guard!

Second Soldier   We do not know, sire. But with his own hand he slew himself.

Herod   That seems strange to me. I thought it was but the Roman philosophers who slew themselves. Is it not true, Tigellinus, that the philosophers at Rome slay themselves?

Tigellinus   There be some who kill themselves, sire. They are the Stoics.[12] The Stoics are people of no cultivation. They are ridiculous people. I myself regard them as being perfectly ridiculous.

Herod   I also. It is ridiculous to kill one's self.

Tigellinus   Everybody at Rome laughs at them. The Emperor has written a satire against them. It is recited everywhere.

Herod   Ah! he has written a satire against them? Caesar is wonderful. He can do everything . . . It is strange that the young Syrian has slain himself. I am sorry he has slain himself. I am very sorry. For he was fair to look upon. He was even very fair. He had very languorous eyes. I remember that I saw that he looked languorously at Salome. Truly, I thought he looked too much at her.

Herodias   There are others who look too much at her.

Herod   His father was a king. I drove him from his kingdom. And of his mother, who was a queen, you made a slave, Herodias. So he was here as my guest, as it were, and for that reason I made him my captain. I am sorry he is dead. Ho! Why have you left the body here? It must be taken to some other place. I will not look at it, – away with it!

They take away the body.

---

12 Stoics: an austere school of philosophers, founded by Zeno (344–262 BC), who believed in moral excellence and the sufficiency of virtue for happiness.

It is cold here. There is a wind blowing. Is there not a wind blowing?

Herodias   No; there is no wind.

Herod   I tell you there is a wind that blows . . . And I hear in the air something that is like the beating of wings, like the beating of vast wings. Do you not hear it?

Herodias   I hear nothing.

Herod   I hear it no longer. But I heard it. It was the blowing of the wind. It has passed away. But no, I hear it again. Do you not hear it? It is just like a beating of wings.

Herodias   I tell you there is nothing. You are ill. Let us go within.

Herod   I am not ill. It is your daughter who is sick to death. Never have I seen her so pale.

Herodias   I have told you not to look at her.

Herod   Pour me forth wine. (*Wine is brought.*) Salome, come drink a little wine with me. I have here a wine that is exquisite. Caesar himself sent it me. Dip into it thy little red lips, that I may drain the cup.

Salome   I am not thirsty, Tetrarch.

Herod   You hear how she answers me, this daughter of yours?

Herodias   She does right. Why are you always gazing at her?

Herod   Bring me ripe fruits. (*Fruits are brought.*) Salome, come and eat fruits with me. I love to see in a fruit the mark of thy little teeth. Bite but a little of this fruit, that I may eat what is left.

Salome   I am not hungry, Tetrarch.

Herod (*to* **Herodias**)   You see how you have brought up this daughter of yours.

Herodias   My daughter and I come of a royal race. As for thee, thy father was a camel driver! He was a thief and a robber to boot!

Herod   Thou liest!

Herodias   Thou knowest well that it is true.

Herod   Salome, come and sit next to me. I will give thee the throne of thy mother.

Salome   I am not tired, Tetrarch.

Herodias   You see in what regard she holds you.

Herod   Bring me – What is it that I desire? I forget. Ah! ah! I remember.

The Voice of Iokanaan   Behold the time is come! That which I foretold has come to pass. The day that I spake of is at hand.

Herodias   Bid him be silent. I will not listen to his voice. This man is for ever hurling insults against me.

Herod   He has said nothing against you. Besides, he is a very great prophet.

Herodias   I do not believe in prophets. Can a man tell what will come to pass? No man knows it. Also he is for ever insulting me. But I think you are afraid of him . . . I know well that you are afraid of him.

Herod   I am not afraid of him. I am afraid of no man.

Herodias   I tell you you are afraid of him. If you are not afraid of him why do you not deliver him to the Jews who for these six months past have been clamouring for him?

A Jew   Truly, my lord, it were better to deliver him into our hands.

Herod   Enough on this subject. I have already given you my answer. I will not deliver him into your hands. He is a holy man. He is a man who has seen God.

A Jew   That cannot be. There is no man who hath seen God since the prophet Elias. He is the last man who saw God face to face. In these days God doth not show Himself. God hideth Himself. Therefore great evils have come upon the land.

Another Jew   Verily, no man knoweth if Elias the prophet did indeed see God. Peradventure it was but the shadow of God that he saw.

A Third Jew   God is at no time hidden. He showeth Himself at all times and in all places. God is in what is evil even as He is in what is good.

A Fourth Jew   Thou shouldst not say that. It is a very dangerous doctrine. It is a doctrine that cometh from Alexandria, where men teach the philosophy of the Greeks. And the Greeks are Gentiles.[13] They are not even circumcised.

A Fifth Jew   No one can tell how God worketh. His ways are very dark. It may be that the things which we call evil are good, and that the things which we call good are evil. There is no knowledge of anything. We can but bow our heads to His will, for God is very strong. He breaketh in pieces the strong together with the weak, for He regardeth not any man.

First Jew   Thou speakest truly. Verily, God is terrible. He breaketh in pieces the strong and the weak as men break corn in a mortar. But as for this man, he hath never seen God. No man hath seen God since the prophet Elias.

Herodias   Make them be silent. They weary me.

Herod   But I have heard it said that Iokanaan is in very truth your prophet Elias.

The Jew   That cannot be. It is more than three hundred years since the days of the prophet Elias.

Herod   There be some who say that this man is Elias the prophet.

A Nazarene   I am sure that he is Elias the prophet.

---

13 Gentiles: non-Jews.

The Jew   Nay, but he is not Elias the prophet.

The Voice of Iokanaan   Behold the day is at hand, the day of the Lord, and I hear upon the mountains the feet of Him who shall be the Saviour of the world.

Herod   What does that mean? The Saviour of the world.

Tigellinus   It is a title that Caesar adopts.

Herod   But Caesar is not coming into Judaea. Only yesterday I received letters from Rome. They contained nothing concerning this matter. And you, Tigellinus, who were at Rome during the winter, you heard nothing concerning this matter, did you?

Tigellinus   Sire, I heard nothing concerning the matter. I was but explaining the title. It is one of Caesar's titles.

Herod   But Caesar cannot come. He is too gouty. They say that his feet are like the feet of an elephant. Also there are reasons of state. He who leaves Rome loses Rome. He will not come. Howbeit, Caesar is lord, he will come if such be his pleasure. Nevertheless, I think he will not come.

First Nazarene   It was not concerning Caesar that the prophet spake these words, sire.

Herod   How? – it was not concerning Caesar?

First Nazarene   No, my lord.

Herod   Concerning whom then did he speak?

First Nazarene   Concerning Messias,[14] who hath come.

A Jew   Messias hath not come.

First Nazarene   He hath come, and everywhere He worketh miracles!

Herodias   Ho! ho! miracles! I do not believe in miracles. I have seen too many. (*To the* **Page**.) My fan.

First Nazarene   This man worketh true miracles. Thus, at a marriage which took place in a little town of Galilee, a town of some importance, He changed water into wine. Certain persons who were present related it to me. Also He healed two lepers that were seated before the Gate of Capernaum simply by touching them.

Second Nazarene   Nay; it was blind men that He healed at Capernaum.

First Nazarene   Nay; they were lepers. But He hath healed blind people also, and He was seen on a mountain talking with angels.

A Sadducee   Angels do not exist.

A Pharisee   Angels exist, but I do not believe that this Man has talked with them.

First Nazarene   He was seen by a great multitude of people talking with angels.

---

14 Jesus: the Messiah.

A Sadducee   Not with angels.

Herodias   How these men weary me! They are ridiculous! They are altogether ridiculous! (*To the* **Page**.) Well! my fan? (*The* **Page** *gives her the fan.*) You have a dreamer's look. You must not dream. It is only sick people who dream. (*She strikes the* **Page** *with her fan.*)

Second Nazarene   There is also the miracle of the daughter of Jairus.

First Nazarene   Yea, that is sure. No man can gainsay it.

Herodias   These men are mad. They have looked too long on the moon. Command them to be silent.

Herod   What is this miracle of the daughter of Jairus?

First Nazarene   The daughter of Jairus was dead. This Man raised her from the dead.

Herod   How! He raises people from the dead?

First Nazarene   Yea, sire; He raiseth the dead.

Herod   I do not wish Him to do that. I forbid Him to do that. I suffer no man to raise the dead. This Man must be found and told that I forbid Him to raise the dead. Where is this Man at present?

Second Nazarene   He is in every place, my lord, but it is hard to find Him.

First Nazarene   It is said that He is now in Samaria.[15]

A Jew   It is easy to see that this is not Messias, if He is in Samaria. It is not to the Samaritans that Messias shall come. The Samaritans are accursed. They bring no offerings to the Temple.

Second Nazarene   He left Samaria a few days since. I think that at the present moment He is in the neighbourhood of Jerusalem.

First Nazarene   No; He is not there. I have just come from Jerusalem. For two months they have had no tidings of Him.

Herod   No matter! But let them find Him, and tell Him, thus saith Herod the King, 'I will not suffer Thee to raise the dead.' To change water into wine, to heal the lepers and the blind . . . He may do these things if He will. I say nothing against these things. In truth I hold it a kindly deed to heal a leper. But no man shall raise the dead . . . It would be terrible if the dead came back.

The Voice of Iokanaan   Ah! The wanton one! The harlot! Ah! the daughter of Babylon with her golden eyes and her gilded eyelids! Thus saith the Lord God, Let there come against her a multitude of men. Let the people take stones and stone her . . .

---

15 Samaria: the central region of ancient Palestine.

Herodias   Command him to be silent!

The Voice of Iokanaan   Let the captains of the hosts pierce her with their swords, let them crush her beneath their shields.

Herodias   Nay, but it is infamous.

The Voice of Iokanaan   It is thus that I will wipe out all wickedness from the earth, and that all women shall learn not to imitate her abominations.

Herodias   You hear what he says against me? You suffer him to revile her who is your wife?

Herod   He did not speak your name.

Herodias   What does that matter? You know well that it is I whom he seeks to revile. And I am your wife, am I not?

Herod   Of a truth, dear and noble Herodias, you are my wife, and before that you were the wife of my brother.

Herodias   It was thou didst snatch me from his arms.

Herod   Of a truth I was stronger than he was . . . But let us not talk of that matter. I do not desire to talk of it. It is the cause of the terrible words that the prophet has spoken. Peradventure on account of it a misfortune will come. Let us not speak of this matter. Noble Herodias, we are not mindful of our guests. Fill thou my cup, my well-beloved. Ho! fill with wine the great goblets of silver, and the great goblets of glass. I will drink to Caesar. There are Romans here, we must drink to Caesar.

All   Caesar! Caesar!

Herod   Do you not see your daughter, how pale she is?

Herodias   What is it to you if she be pale or not?

Herod   Never have I seen her so pale.

Herodias   You must not look at her.

The Voice of Iokanaan   In that day the sun shall become black like sackcloth of hair, and the moon shall become like blood, and the stars of the heaven shall fall upon the earth like unripe figs that fall from the fig-tree, and the kings of the earth shall be afraid.

Herodias   Ah! ah! I should like to see that day of which he speaks, when the moon shall become like blood, and when the stars shall fall upon the earth like unripe figs. This prophet talks like a drunken man, . . . but I cannot suffer the sound of his voice. I hate his voice. Command him to be silent.

Herod   I will not. I cannot understand what it is that he saith, but it may be an omen.

Herodias   I do not believe in omens. He speaks like a drunken man.

Herod   It may be he is drunk with the wine of God.

Herodias   What wine is that, the wine of God? From what vineyards is it gathered? In what wine-press may one find it?

Herod (*from this point he looks all the while at* **Salome**)   Tigellinus, when you were at Rome of late, did the Emperor speak with you on the subject of . . . ?

Tigellinus   On what subject, my lord?

Herod   On what subject? Ah! I asked you a question, did I not? I have forgotten what I would have asked you.

Herodias   You are looking again at my daughter. You must not look at her. I have already said so.

Herod   You say nothing else.

Herodias   I say it again.

Herod   And that restoration of the Temple about which they have talked so much, will anything be done? They say the veil of the sanctuary has disappeared, do they not?

Herodias   It was thyself didst steal it. Thou speakest at random and without wit. I will not stay here. Let us go within.

Herod   Dance for me, Salome.

Herodias   I will not have her dance.

Salome   I have no desire to dance, Tetrarch.

Herod   Salome, daughter of Herodias, dance for me.

Herodias   Peace. Let her alone.

Herod   I command thee to dance, Salome.

Salome   I will not dance, Tetrarch.

Herodias (*laughing*)   You see how she obeys you.

Herod   What is it to me whether she dance or not? It is nought to me. Tonight I am happy, I am exceeding happy. Never have I been so happy.

First Soldier   The Tetrarch has a sombre look. Has he not a sombre look?

Second Soldier   Yes, he has a sombre look.

Herod   Wherefore should I not be happy? Caesar who is lord of the world, who is lord of all things, loves me well. He has just sent me most precious gifts. Also he has promised me to summon to Rome the King of Cappadocia, who is mine enemy. It may be that at Rome he will crucify him, for he is able to do all things that he has a mind to do. Verily, Caesar is lord. Therefore I do well to be happy. I am very happy, never have I been so happy. There is nothing in the world that can mar my happiness.

The Voice of Iokanaan   He shall be seated on this throne. He shall be clothed in scarlet and purple. In his hand he shall bear a golden cup full of his blasphemies. And the angel of the Lord shall smite him. He shall be eaten of worms.

Herodias   You hear what he says about you. He says that you shall be eaten of worms.

Herod   It is not of me that he speaks. He speaks never against me. It is of the King of Cappadocia that he speaks; the King of Cappadocia, who is mine enemy. It is he who shall be eaten of worms. It is not I. Never has he spoken a word against me, this prophet, save that I sinned in taking to wife the wife of my brother. It may be he is right. For, of a truth, you are sterile.

Herodias   I am sterile, I? You say that, you that are ever looking at my daughter, you that would have her dance for your pleasure? You speak as a fool. I have borne a child. You have gotten no child, no, not on one of your slaves. It is you who are sterile, not I.

Herod   Peace, woman! I say that you are sterile. You have borne me no child, and the prophet says that our marriage is not a true marriage. He says that it is a marriage of incest, a marriage that will bring evils . . . I fear he is right; I am sure that he is right. But it is not the hour to speak of these things. I would be happy at this moment. Of a truth, I am happy. There is nothing I lack.

Herodias   I am glad you are of so fair a humour tonight. It is not your custom. But it is late. Let us go within. Do not forget that we hunt at sunrise. All honours must be shown to Caesar's ambassadors, must they not?

Second Soldier   The Tetrarch has a sombre look.

First Soldier   Yes, he has a sombre look.

Herod   Salome, Salome, dance for me. I pray thee dance for me. I am sad tonight. Yes, I am passing sad tonight. When I came hither I slipped in blood, which is an ill omen; also I heard in the air a beating of wings, a beating of giant wings. I cannot tell what that may mean . . . I am sad tonight. Therefore dance for me. Dance for me, Salome, I beseech thee. If thou dancest for me thou mayest ask of me what thou will, and I will give it thee. Yes, dance for me, Salome, and whatsoever thou shalt ask of me I will give it thee, even unto the half of my kingdom.

Salome (*rising*)   Will you indeed give me whatsoever I shall ask of you, Tetrarch?

Herodias   Do not dance, my daughter.

Herod   Whatsoever thou shalt ask of me, even unto the half of my kingdom.

Salome   You swear it, Tetrarch?

Herod   I swear it, Salome.

Herodias   Do not dance, my daughter.

Salome   By what will you swear this thing, Tetrarch?

Herod   By my life, by my crown, by my gods. Whatsoever thou shalt desire I will give it thee, even to the half of my kingdom, if thou wilt but dance for me. O Salome, Salome, dance for me!

Salome   You have sworn an oath, Tetrarch.

Herod   I have sworn an oath.

Herodias   My daughter, do not dance.

Herod   Even to the half of my kingdom. Thou wilt be passing fair as a queen, Salome, if it please thee to ask for the half of my kingdom. Will she not be fair as a queen? Ah! it is cold here! There is an icy wind, and I hear . . . wherefore do I hear in the air this beating of wings? Ah! one might fancy a huge black bird that hovers over the terrace. Why can I not see it, this bird? The beat of its wings is terrible. The breath of the wind of its wings is terrible. It is a chill wind. Nay, but it is not cold, it is hot. I am choking. Pour water on my hands. Give me snow to eat. Loosen my mantle. Quick! quick! loosen my mantle. Nay, but leave it. It is my garland that hurts me, my garland of roses. The flowers are like fire. They have burned my forehead. (*He tears the wreath from his head, and throws it on the table.*) Ah! I can breathe now. How red those petals are! They are like stains of blood on the cloth. That does not matter. It is not wise to find symbols in everything that one sees. It makes life too full of terrors. It were better to say that stains of blood are as lovely as rose-petals. It were better far to say that . . . But we will not speak of this. Now I am happy. I am passing happy. Have I not the right to be happy? Your daughter is going to dance for me. Wilt thou not dance for me, Salome? Thou hast promised to dance for me.

Herodias   I will not have her dance.

Salome   I will dance for you, Tetrarch.

Herod   You hear what your daughter says. She is going to dance for me. Thou doest well to dance for me, Salome. And when thou hast danced for me, forget not to ask of me whatsoever thou hast a mind to ask. Whatsoever thou shalt desire I will give it thee, even to the half of my kingdom. I have sworn it, have I not?

Salome   Thou hast sworn it, Tetrarch.

Herod   And I have never failed of my word. I am not of those who break their oaths. I know not how to lie. I am the slave of my word, and my word is the word of a king. The King of Cappadocia had ever a lying tongue, but he is no true king. He is a coward. Also he owes me money that he will not repay. He has even insulted my ambassadors. He has spoken words that were wounding. But Caesar will crucify him when he comes to Rome. I know that Caesar will crucify him. And if he crucify him not, yet will he die, being eaten of worms. The prophet has prophesied it. Well! Wherefore dost thou tarry, Salome?

Salome   I am awaiting until my slaves bring perfumes to me and the seven veils, and take from off my feet my sandals.

Slaves *bring perfumes and the seven veils, and take off the sandals of* **Salome**.

Herod   Ah, thou art to dance with naked feet! 'Tis well! 'Tis well! Thy little feet will be like white doves. They will be like little white flowers that dance upon the trees . . . No, no, she is going to dance on blood! There is blood spilt on the ground. She must not dance on blood. It were an evil omen.

Herodias   What is it to thee if she dance on blood? Thou hast waded deep enough in it . . .

Herod   What is it to me? Ah! look at the moon! She has become red. She has become red as blood. Ah! the prophet prophesied truly. He prophesied that the moon would become as blood. Did he not prophesy it? All of ye heard him prophesying it. And now the moon has become as blood. Do ye not see it?

Herodias   Oh, yes, I see it well, and the stars are falling like unripe figs, are they not? and the sun is becoming black like sackcloth of hair, and the kings of the earth are afraid. That at least one can see. The prophet is justified in his words for that at least, for truly the kings of the earth are afraid . . . Let us go within. You are sick. They will say at Rome that you are mad. Let us go within, I tell you.

The Voice of Iokanaan   Who is this who cometh from Edom, who is this who cometh from Bozra,[16] whose raiment is dyed with purple, who shineth in the beauty of his garments, who walketh mighty in his greatness? Wherefore is thy raiment stained with scarlet?

Herodias   Let us go within. The voice of that man maddens me. I will not have my daughter dance while he is continually crying out. I will not have her dance while you look at her in this fashion. In a word, I will not have her dance.

Herod   Do not rise, my wife, my queen, it will avail thee nothing. I will not go within till she hath danced. Dance, Salome, dance for me.

Herodias   Do not dance, my daughter.

Salome   I am ready, Tetrarch.

Salome *dances the dance of the seven veils.*

Herod   Ah! wonderful! wonderful! You see that she has danced for me, your daughter. Come near, Salome, come near, that I may give thee thy fee. Ah! I pay a royal price to those who dance for my pleasure. I will pay thee royally. I will give thee whatsoever thy soul desireth. What wouldst thou have? Speak.

Salome (*kneeling*)   I would that they presently bring me in a silver charger . . .

Herod (*laughing*)   In a silver charger? Surely yes, in a silver charger. She is charming, is she not? What is it that thou wouldst have in a silver charger, O sweet and fair Salome, thou that art fairer than all the daughters of Judaea? What wouldst thou have them bring thee in a silver charger? Tell me. Whatsoever it may be, thou shalt receive it. My treasures belong to thee. What is it that thou wouldst have, Salome?

---

16 Bosra: a town in southern Syria.

Salome (*rising*)   The head of Iokanaan.

Herodias   Ah! that is well said, my daughter.

Herod   No, no!

Herodias   That is well said, my daughter.

Herod   No, no, Salome. It is not that thou desirest. Do not listen to thy mother's voice. She is ever giving thee evil counsel. Do not heed her.

Salome   It is not my mother's voice that I heed. It is for mine own pleasure that I ask the head of Iokanaan in a silver charger. You have sworn an oath, Herod. Forget not that you have sworn an oath.

Herod   I know it. I have sworn by my gods. I know it well. But I pray thee, Salome, ask of me something else. Ask of me the half of my kingdom, and I will give it thee. But ask not of me what thy lips have asked.

Salome   I ask of you the head of Iokanaan.

Herod   No, no, I will not give it thee.

Salome   You have sworn an oath, Herod.

Herodias   Yes, you have sworn an oath. Everybody heard you. You swore it before everybody.

Herod   Peace, woman! It is not to you I speak.

Herodias   My daughter has done well to ask the head of Iokanaan. He has covered me with insults. He has said unspeakable things against me. One can see that she loves her mother well. Do not yield, my daughter. He has sworn an oath, he has sworn an oath.

Herod   Peace! Speak not to me! . . . Salome, I pray thee be not stubborn. I have ever been kind toward thee . . . It may be that I have loved thee too much. Therefore ask not this thing of me. This is a terrible thing, an awful thing to ask of me. Surely, I think thou art jesting. The head of a man that is cut from his body is ill to look upon, is it not? It is not meet that the eyes of a virgin should look upon such a thing. What pleasure couldst thou have in it? There is no pleasure that thou couldst have in it. No, no, it is that thou desirest. Hearken to me. I have an emerald, a great emerald and round, that the minion of Caesar has sent unto me. When thou lookest through this emerald thou canst see that which passeth afar off. Caesar himself carries such an emerald when he goes to the circus. But my emerald is the larger. I know well that it is the larger. It is the largest emerald in the whole world. Thou wilt take that, wilt thou not? Ask it of me and I will give it thee.

Salome   I demand the head of Iokanaan.

Herod   Thou art not listening. Thou art not listening. Suffer me to speak, Salome.

Salome   The head of Iokanaan!

Herod   No, no, thou wouldst not have that. Thou sayest that but to trouble me, because that I have looked at thee and ceased not this night. It is true, I have looked at thee and ceased not this night. Thy beauty has troubled me. Thy beauty has grievously troubled me, and I have looked at thee overmuch. Nay, but I will look at thee no more. One should not look at anything. Neither at things, nor at people should one look. Only in mirrors is it well to look, for mirrors do but show us masks. Oh! oh! bring wine! I thirst . . . Salome, Salome, let us be as friends. Bethink thee . . . Ah! what would I say? What was't? Ah! I remember it! . . . Salome, – nay but come nearer to me; I fear thou wilt not hear my words, – Salome, thou knowest my white peacocks, my beautiful white peacocks, that walk in the garden between the myrtles and the tall cypress-trees. Their beaks are gilded with gold and the grains that they eat are smeared with gold, and their feet are stained with purple. When they cry out the rain comes, and the moon shows herself in the heavens when they spread their tails. Two by two they walk between the cypress-trees and the black myrtles, and each has a slave to tend it. Sometimes they fly across the trees, and anon they crouch in the grass, and round the pools of water. There are not in all the world birds so wonderful. There is no king in all the world who possesses such wonderful birds. I know that Caesar himself has no birds so fair as my birds. I will give thee fifty of my peacocks. They will follow you whithersoever thou goest, and in the midst of them thou wilt be like unto the moon in the midst of a great white cloud . . . I will give them to thee, all. I have but a hundred, and in the whole world there is no king who has peacocks like unto my peacocks. But I will give them all to thee. Only thou must loose me from my oath, and must not ask of me that which thy lips have asked of me.

He empties the cup of wine.

Salome   Give me the head of Iokanaan!

Herodias   Well said, my daughter! As for you, you are ridiculous with your peacocks.

Herod   Peace! you are always crying out. You cry out like a beast of prey. You must not cry in such fashion. Your voice wearies me. Peace, I tell you! . . . Salome, think on what thou art doing. It may be that this man comes from God. He is a holy man. The finger of God has touched him. God has put terrible words into his mouth. In the palace, as in the desert, God is ever with him . . . It may be that He is, at least. One cannot tell, but it is possible that God is with him and for him. If he die also, peradventure some evil might befall me. Verily, he has said that evil will befall someone on the day whereon he dies. On whom should it fall if it fall not on me? Remember, I slipped in blood when I came hither. Also, did I not hear a beating of wings in the air, a beating of vast wings? These are ill omens. And there were other things. I am sure there were other things, though I saw them not. Thou wouldst not that some evil should befall me, Salome? Listen to me again.

Salome   Give me the head of Iokanaan!

Herod   Ah! thou art not listening to me. Be calm. As for me, am I not calm? I am altogether calm. Listen. I have jewels hidden in this place – jewels that thy mother even has never seen; jewels that are marvellous to look at. I have a collar of pearls, set in four rows. They are like unto moons chained with rays of silver. They are even as half a hundred moons caught in a golden net. On the ivory breast of a queen they have rested. Thou shalt be as fair as a queen when thou wearest them. I have amethysts of two kinds; one that is black like wine, and one that is red like wine that one has coloured with water. I have topazes yellow as are the eyes of tigers, and topazes that are pink as the eyes of a wood-pigeon, and green topazes that are as the eyes of cats. I have opals that burn always, with a flame that is cold as ice, opals that make sad men's minds, and are afraid of the shadows. I have onyxes like the eyeballs of a dead woman. I have moonstones that change when the moon changes, and are wan when they see the sun. I have sapphires big like eggs, and as blue as blue flowers. The sea wanders within them, and the moon comes never to trouble the blue of their waves. I have chrysolites and beryls, and chrysoprases and rubies; I have sardonyx and hyacinth stones, and stones of chalcedony, and I will give them all unto thee, all, and other things I will add to them. The King of the Indies has but even now sent me four fans fashioned from the feathers of parrots, and the King of Numidia a garment of ostrich feathers. I have a crystal, into which it is not lawful for a woman to look, nor may young men behold it until they have been beaten with rods. In a coffer of nacre I have three wondrous turquoises. He who wears them on his forehead can imagine things which are not, and he who carries them in his hand can turn the fruitful woman into a woman that is barren. These are great treasures. They are treasures above all price. But this is not all. In an ebony coffer I have two cups of amber that are like apples of pure gold. If an enemy pour poison into these cups they become like apples of silver. In a coffer encrusted with amber I have sandals encrusted with glass. I have mantles that have been brought from the land of the Seres,[17] and bracelets decked about with carbuncles and with jade that come from the city of Euphrates . . . What desirest thou more than this, Salome? Tell me the thing that thou desirest, and I will give it thee. All that thou askest I will give thee, save one thing only. I will give thee all that is mine, save only the life of one man. I will give thee the mantle of the high priest. I will give thee the veil of the sanctuary.

The Jews   Oh! oh!

Salome   Give me the head of Iokanaan!

Herod (*sinking back in his seat*)   Let her be given what she asks! Of a truth she is her mother's child!

*The **First Soldier** approaches. **Herodias** draws from the hand of the **Tetrarch** the ring of death and gives it to the **Soldier**, who straightway bears it to the **Executioner**. The **Executioner** looks scared.*

Herod   Who has taken my ring? There was a ring on my right hand. Who has drunk my wine? There was wine in my cup. It was full of wine. Someone has drunk it! Oh! surely some evil will befall some one. (*The **Executioner** goes down into the cistern.*) Ah! wherefore did I give my oath? Hereafter let no king swear an oath. If he keep it not, it is terrible, and if he keep it, it is terrible also.

---

17 Land of the Seres: China.

Herodias   My daughter has done well.

Herod   I am sure that some misfortune will happen.

Salome (*she leans over the cistern and listens*)   There is no sound. I hear nothing. Why does he not cry out, this man? Ah! if any man sought to kill me, I would cry out, I would struggle, I would not suffer. . . . Strike, strike, Naaman, strike, I tell you . . . No, I hear nothing. There is a silence, a terrible silence. Ah! something has fallen upon the ground. I heard something fall. It is the sword of the executioner. He is afraid, this slave. He has dropped his sword. He dares not kill him. He is a coward, this slave! Let soldiers be sent. (*She sees the* **Page of Herodias** *and addresses him.*) Come hither, thou wert the friend of him who is dead, is it not so? Well, I tell thee, there are not dead men enough. Go to the soldiers and bid them go down and bring me the thing I ask, the thing the Tetrarch has promised me, the thing that is mine. (*The* **Page** *recoils. She turns to the* **Soldiers**.) Hither, ye soldiers. Get ye down into this cistern and bring me the head of this man. Tetrarch, Tetrarch, command your soldiers that they bring me the head of Iokanaan.

A huge black arm, the arm of the **Executioner**, *comes forth from the cistern, bearing on a silver shield the head of* **Iokanaan**. **Salome** *seizes it.* **Herod** *hides his face with his cloak.* **Herodias** *smiles and fans herself.* The **Nazarenes** *fall on their knees and begin to pray.*

Salome   Ah! thou wouldst not suffer me to kiss thy mouth, Iokanaan. Well! I will kiss it now. I will bite it with my teeth as one bites a ripe fruit. Yes, I will kiss thy mouth, Iokanaan. I said it; did I not say it? I said it. Ah! I will kiss it now . . . But wherefore dost thou not look at me, Iokanaan? Thine eyes that were so terrible, so full of rage and scorn, are shut now. Wherefore are they shut? Open thine eyes! Lift up thine eyelids, Iokanaan! Wherefore dost thou not look at me? Art thou afraid of me, Iokanaan, that thou wilt not look at me? . . . And thy tongue, that was like a red snake darting poison, it moves no more, it speaks no words, Iokanaan, that scarlet viper that spat its venom upon me. It is strange, is it not? How is it that the red viper stirs no longer? . . . Thou wouldst have none of me, Iokanaan. Thou rejectedst me. Thou didst speak evil words against me. Thou didst bear thyself toward me as to a harlot, as to a woman that is a wanton, to me, Salome, daughter of Herodias, Princess of Judaea! Well, Iokanaan, I still live, but thou art dead, and thy head belongs to me. I can do with it what I will. I can throw it to the dogs and to the birds of the air. That which the dogs leave, the birds of the air shall devour . . . Ah, Iokanaan, Iokanaan, thou wert the man that I loved alone among men! All other men were hateful to me. But thou wert beautiful! Thy body was a column of ivory set upon feet of silver. It was a garden full of doves and lilies of silver. It was a tower of silver decked with shields of ivory. There was nothing in the world so white as thy body. There was nothing in the world so black as thy hair. In the whole world there was nothing so red as thy mouth. Thy voice was a censer that scattered strange perfumes, and when I looked on thee I heard a strange music. Ah! wherefore didst thou not look at me, Iokanaan? With the cloak of thine hands, and with the cloak of thy blasphemies thou didst hide thy face. Thou didst put upon thine eyes the covering of him who would see his God. Well, thou hast seen thy God, Iokanaan, but me, me, thou didst never see. If thou hadst seen me thou hadst loved me. I saw thee, and I loved thee. Oh, how I loved thee! I love thee yet, Iokanaan. I love only thee . . . I am athirst for thy beauty; I am hungry for thy body; and neither wine nor apples can appease my desire. What shall I do now, Iokanaan? Neither the floods nor the great waters can quench my passion. I was a princess, and thou didst scorn me. I was a virgin, and thou didst take my virginity from me. I was chaste, and thou didst fill my veins with fire . . . Ah! ah! wherefore didst thou not look at me? If thou hadst looked at me thou hadst loved me. Well I know that thou wouldst have loved me, and the mystery of Love is greater than the mystery of Death.

Herod   She is monstrous, thy daughter; I tell thee she is monstrous. In truth, what she has done is a great crime. I am sure that it is a crime against some unknown God.

Herodias   I am well pleased with my daughter. She has done well. And I would stay here now.

Herod (*rising*)   Ah! There speaks my brother's wife! Come! I will not stay in this place. Come, I tell thee. Surely some terrible thing will befall. Manasseh, Issachar, Ozias, put out the torches. I will not look at things, I will not suffer things to look at me. Put out the torches! Hide the moon! Hide the stars! Let us hide ourselves in our palace, Herodias. I begin to be afraid.

The **Slaves** *put out the torches. The stars disappear. A great cloud crosses the moon and conceals it completely. The stage becomes quite dark. The* **Tetrarch** *begins to climb the staircase.*

The Voice of Salome   Ah! I have kissed thy mouth, Iokanaan. I have kissed thy mouth. There was a bitter taste on thy lips. Was it the taste of blood? . . . Nay; but perchance it was the taste of love . . . They say that love hath a bitter taste . . . but what matter? but what matter? I have kissed thy mouth, Iokanaan, I have kissed thy mouth.

A ray of moonlight falls on **Salome** *and illumines her.*

Herod (*turning round and seeing* **Salome**)   Kill that woman!

The **Soldiers** *rush forward and crush beneath their shields* **Salome**, *daughter of Herodias, Princess of Judaea.*

Curtain.

The Race of Leaves

Michael Field (1901)

Like Oscar Wilde, many other writers of the fin de siècle who were associated with decadence and aestheticism looked to ancient empires and lost worlds for inspiration. Some of the most interesting examples can be found in the work of **Michael Field**: a pseudonym for the collaborative work of Katharine Harris Bradley (1846–1914) and her niece and life partner Edith Emma Cooper (1862–1913). Today they are best known for their lyric poetry and diaries, although they did not establish themselves as 'Michael Field' until the publication of their plays *Callirrhoë* and *Fair Rosamund* in 1884 (Michael Field would later publish plays anonymously as 'the author of *Borgia*' after their real identities were revealed, referencing their 1905 verse drama *Borgia*). The bulk of their prolific creative output was also dramatic – they wrote more than thirty plays – dwelling on the ancient world as a way of engaging with social and cultural issues in late-Victorian England, including empire, industrial capitalism and the commodification of culture. As Ana Parejo Vadillo has persuasively argued, the crafted outmodedness of their plays can be alienating, but '[t]hrough this alienation, art could question the materialism of everyday reality and expose the illusion of [industrial] progress'.[1]

Bradley and Cooper dismissed popular interest in decadent literature and style as a modish fad of the late nineteenth century. They derided *The Yellow Book* and broke with the publisher Bodley Head, which were both key vehicles in proliferating decadent literature and illustration. Their dismissal as 'decadent' – where decadence is used as a synonym for being outmoded and obtuse – was linked more to nascent modernists wanting to distance themselves from Victorian literature of the Wildean period.[2] Nonetheless, more recent scholarship, at a time when decadence is again being celebrated in literary and scholarly circles, has also recognised the stylistically and thematically decadent qualities of their verse dramas.[3] Moreover, their plays thematise the waning of empires, including that most archetypal of epochs – the Latin decadence.

Only one of Michael Field's plays was performed in their lifetime. *A Question of Memory* was staged on 27 October 1893 at the Independent Theatre Society in London, although it was not well received. Nonetheless, they remained committed to dramatic form, and it was their drama that had the deepest impact on modernist dramatists in the twentieth century, even if scholarship at the turn of the twenty-first has tended to dwell on their poetry.[4] In this volume we include the second of three plays in their Roman Trilogy, *The Race of Leaves* (1901), which was preceded by *World at Auction* (1898) and followed by *Julia Domna* (1903). All three plays have an antiquated flavour, not

1   Ana Parejo Vadillo, 'Outmoded Dramas: History and Modernity in Michael Field's Aesthetic Plays', in *Michael Field and Their World,* ed. Margaret D. Stetz and Cheryl A. Wilson (High Wycombe: The Rivendale Press, 2007), 237–49 (241).

2   See also Marion Thain, *'Michael Field': Poetry, Aestheticism and the Fin de Siècle* (Cambridge: Cambridge University Press, 2007), 15.

3   For instance, Vadillo regards Michael Field's verse dramas 'as a key aesthetic genre, a decadent project'. Ana Parejo Vadillo, 'Another Renaissance: The Decadent Poetic Drama of A. C. Swinburne and Michael Field', in *Decadent Poetics: Literature and Form at the British Fin de Siècle,* ed. Jason David Hall and Alex Murray (Basingstoke and New York: Palgrave Macmillan, 2013), 116–40 (119). See also Sarah Parker and Ana Parejo Vadillo, 'Introduction', in *Michael Field: Decadent Moderns,* ed. Sarah Parker and Ana Parejo Vadillo (Athens: Ohio University Press, 2019), 1–24 (3).

4   See Parker and Vadillo, 'Introduction', 10.

just because they are set during the decline of the Roman Empire between 182 and 212 CE; the language, too, is archaic, and verse dramas were already regarded as outmoded in the 1890s. And yet their plays were also 'exceptionally experimental at the level of versification and radically theoretical at the level of content'.[5] The Roman Trilogy was part and parcel of a turn to Latin decadence in the late nineteenth century inspired by Walter Pater's *Marius the Epicurean* (1885), which furnishes *The Race of Leaves* with an epigraph. Michael Field frequently returned to this period, but the Roman Trilogy marks a culmination and perfection of their engagement with Latin decadence, which found the authors drawing parallels between the fall of the Roman Empire and the decline of the British Empire in their own day.[6]

The play is highly intertextual and builds on a number of different sources, including major Roman chroniclers (Cassius Dio and Herodian), Edward Gibbon's *The History of the Decline and Fall of the Roman Empire* (1776–89), and some more obscure works by Lucian, Ludwig Friedländer and Julius Sommerbrodt. However, Friedrich Nietzsche's writing on the Apollonian and the Dionysian in *The Birth of Tragedy* (1872) played just as important a role in its development, although they were fascinated by Dionysius long before engaging with his ideas.[7] Much more so than Commodus, it is Pylades who captures the Dionysian spirit most of all. Bradley and Cooper wanted to energise drama through depictions of rapturous passion and emotional intensity, making their engagement with antiquity about so much more than the romanticisation of an archaic age. Their frequent returns to antiquity were rooted in a desire to breathe new life into dramatic form – both antiquated, and ahead of their time – making clear how a work can explore decadent themes through decadent style, while remaining thoroughly modern.

---

5   Ana Parejo Vadillo, '"This hot-house of decadent chronicle": Michael Field, Nietzsche and the Dance of Modern Poetic Drama', *Women: A Cultural Review* 26, no. 3 (2015): 195–220 (196).
6   See Vadillo, 'This hot-house', 198.
7   See Vadillo, 'This hot-house', 204.

> *Like the race of leaves*
> *The race of man is:—*
> *The wind in autumn strows*
> *The earth with old leaves: then the spring the woods with new endows.*

Homer, *Il.* vi. 147. Rendered by Chapman.[8]

Leaves! little leaves! – thy children, thy flatterers, thine enemies! Leaves in the wind, those who would devote thee to darkness, who scorn or miscall thee here, even as they also whose great fame shall outlast them. For all these, and the like of them, are born indeed in the spring season – and soon a wind hath scattered them, and thereafter the wood peopleth itself again with another generation of leaves.

Marcus Aurelius. Rendered by Walter Pater.

Characters

Commodus, *Emperor of Rome, son to Marcus Aurelius and Faustina*
Cleander, *a Phrygian slave, Minister to Commodus*
Laetus, *Governor of Egypt, afterward Prefect of the Guard*
Quadratus, *a young Senator*
Eclectus, *an Egyptian freedman, Grand Chamberlain*
Pylades, *a Greek slave and pantomime-dancer*
Narcissus, *a wrestler*
Gabba, *a dwarf*
Glaphyrus, *a flute-player*
Fadilla *and* **Lucilla,** *sisters to Commodus*
Marcia, *his favourite mistress*
Sagana *and* **Folia,** *other mistresses*
Jallia, *a Christian slave, Marcia's servant*
Mneme *and* **Annia,** *singing-girls*
Slaves, pages, women, soldiers

Place

Rome: Acts One, Three and Four.
Laurentum: Act Two.

---

8 George Chapman (*c.* 1559–1634), dramatist, poet, best remembered for his translations of Homer's *Iliad* and *The Odyssey*.

Act One

Sunset: A garden of the Regia, full of almonds, peaches and judas-trees in flower. A fountain is playing; statues of Apollo and of Faustina are seen among the leaves. Afar, the noise of the games drawing to a close, is heard from the amphitheatre.

Enter **Fadilla** *and* **Lucilla**.

Fadilla   How blue a night to hold these blossoms.
Spring as full of summer as if dreams were real!
Why are you here, Lucilla?

Lucilla   Can you ask?
You too have watched with worshipping, faintheart
The love-star dawn on sunset, you have tasted
The breath of coverts.

Fadilla   Ah, how many times!
But now I do not court my happiness
Among the gem-like petals full of bloom,
And rich with twilight; no, my love requires
The fortunes of the world to be as branches
Platted for Eros' hiding-place; my lovers
Are generals or statesmen; and for pastime
I need the zest of politics.

Lucilla   I too.

Fadilla   No, no, unsay it. You must reach my age,
My forty years, before you own the right
To leave all bosom-loves for this hard joy
That the head takes in loving. Little sister,
You have our mother's childlike agelessness,
You are Faustina, save that you can frown;
And owe it to your face to live as she
For candid passion, impulse of an hour.
You who have been the wife of Lucius Verus,
Co-empress with your mother in her pride,
Though now the mere wife of a senator,
You have your honours still. Why should you strive?
Meddle no further with the dangerous world
Where Eros knits his brow, a politician,
And changes dart for axe.

Lucilla   Then you suspect . . . ?

Fadilla   Whom, what? Why are you restless? Turn your head!
It holds a plot.

Lucilla   To spring on such a one
When he is blind with heavenly cloud of flowers.
But in your politics, Fadilla, say,
Why do you favour Commodus?

Fadilla   I love
My brother; he and you and I are all
The children of Faustina – I alone
Have something of my father, and can pity
The lot that made us his. He forced our brother
To obstinate recoil. Philosophy,
That smiles on life, till life is made ashamed,
And sunders from each end for which it throbs,
Praise, glory, pleasure, how should it direct
Youth through its awful rapine? By the gods
Marcus is held as good and our fair mother
As evil . . . yet our father poisoned life
In each of us from childhood, for his voice
Withered illusion, and our urgent youth
To him was nothingness, to us a lie
That could not prove the truth it made us feel.
He spoke of us as leaves within a wind,
Leaves shaken diversely: and so we are,
Unhappy children! Be Faustina, sweet,
Be our fair mother with untroubled brow,
And a babe's faith in pleasure.

Lucilla   That is vain
I envy Commodus.

Fadilla   What snake is this
That strikes out from your eyes?

Lucilla   He has his bent
In everything, can ponder till he covets,
Then shape his own desire. I envy him
His crescent manhood, crescent majesty,
The entrancing terror of his yellow locks,
Emitting as he passes, sparks of light,
So quick, men deem them supernatural,
The settled beams of deity. Oh, look!

Enter **Commodus**.

Fadilla   Great Emperor, here is one who envies you.

Commodus   How charming!

Fadilla   Says that you enjoy and freely
All that men sigh for, all that pleases them.

Commodus   Philosophy, Lucilla! You forget
The lessons of our childhood, when, to mock him,
We stole upon our father with his books,
And then must listen; for he closed the scroll,
And spoke it out in homily, caressing
As if with phrases if he touched our cheeks.
He told us every joy was hollowness
That did not spring from reason, and besought us
To seek our praise from virtue. Ah, Lucilla,
My beauty, 'twas the mirror taught us truth!
We stroked the flashing thing, and then fell back,
And then approached it, till we understood
Our heavenly images. You courted love,
Won worship; while for me – how easily
The care of what an after age would say,
Buzzing about my name, slipped from my thoughts,
When I could hear a veritable shout
As every beast I aimed at took the arrow
Just in the mortal part and roared acclaim
To me as new Far-darter. I have made
My pleasures, never found them, never met them
Upon the highway, and what pleases there
For me has no concern. I am divine:
And when endowed with power unlimited,
As Emperor, I was met by multitudes
Poured forth, with boughs of laurel in their hands
And every kind of flower in bloom, I savoured
The spring-tide of a god.

Lucilla   When I was empress
I made my bliss myself; but now!

Commodus   I yield you
All honour, every ensign of the past,
The sacred fire, the purple, for my mother
Smiles through your beauty when I give it sway:
'Tis so I honour her. This rippled hair
Holds to the temples just as hers, this chin
Knows nothing but of homage. You are sore,
Lucilla, that you cannot keep your throne
Beside me as sole Empress; but consider,
Who is this wife, this rival? A mere form,
To ornament my empire, a blank shape,
To wear abundant tresses of pure gold,
And live unthought of. Do not envy her.

Lucilla   She has my throne.

Commodus   Not in my heart. This wife,
Crispina, holds no place and finds no honour
Where, with my kin, a single regnant woman
Triumphs above all strangers.

Enter **Marcia**.

Commodus   Love, the jewels
Flash round your brow; it is not framed for flowers.

Marcia   They fade. I never wear them.

Commodus   You will come
To the arena?

Marcia   Pardon me, my lord.
Spring lies too vast and sweet before my thoughts
For sight of carnage, and I bent my steps
To this soft, murmuring place to gather calm.
I will be ready to receive my lord,
Ah, exquisitely ready, in an hour.
Grant me but that. I do not need the mirror,
The unguent for renewal half so much
As the touches of the air.

Commodus   Then, if we part,
We, when we meet again, must lavish welcome
Inordinately full of joy. Lay on
Your breast all stones of azure and of green,
Meet me as Juno's bird. My Marcia, hear!
The amphitheatre's challenge! Te saluto,
Marcia!
          Slaves, heigh! Conduct me to the games.

Exit **Commodus**.

Fadilla   Fair lady, will you pace with me? I too
Would feel the stroking gentleness of eve,
When flowers and birds and winds are young together,
And Eros loves them all. Lucilla, listen,
My pious, star-ensnared conspirator,
To anything that love with Maia's voices
May whisper to you. Let the hour appeal,
And all the hour enjoins.

Marcia   Your servant, princess.

Exeunt **Fadilla** *and* **Marcia** *through an arcade.*

Lucilla   Venus, the nightingales begin to sing
Behind their footsteps; it is safe to call.
I die . . . The boughs are shaking. O Quadratus!

My throat is dry, he cannot hear my voice.
Quadratus!

Quadratus (*among the boughs*)   Love, your clasp! . . . The judas-tree . . .
Behind this branch! Give me your hand: a pulse
Is throbbing through the palm.

Lucilla   Speak of the deed,
Speak coldly.

Quadratus   Peer down through the blossoms, sweet.
You torture me.

Lucilla   Not now. I will not stay!
You shall not drag my arm.

Quadratus (*stooping forward*)   Down to our secret,
This bosomed dagger. Now, my waxen beauty,
You light, you glisten. I must have you swear,
Swear by the hilt . . .

Lucilla   You speak so noisily!
Be silent; oh, be swift! I suffer torments,
Stung by a need, a wish so obstinate,
While all beside revolts.

Quadratus   Your oath: but first,
Your brother will return – be certain, sweet –
By the dark, eastern passage?

Lucilla   I am sure.

Quadratus   He never will arrive. Swear by your eyes,
Your empire, that you love me and will love
And crown my love and when the days are safe
Make me at last your husband.

Lucilla   I have sworn.
My fate is yours. We cannot now draw back,
Can we, Quadratus, from the coiling deed
That holds us to it?

Quadratus   Are you false? Draw back!
Half of the senate holds to our attempt,
And you have sworn you will not rest until
I rule beside you. How you damp my heart!
Each moment of delay is risk of life
To me, to you, to all who follow us.

Lucilla   You mean that I am taken in a net,
That none of you will loose me.

Quadratus   None, my bird;

I least, your lover. By your oath, your cause,
By all the noble blood that glows for it
In youthful veins swayed by your loveliness,
We are committed to this night's attempt.

Lucilla   We are. Then loose me. Give me back my empire,
Give me my throne! We must not speak together
Till we are joined by . . . Oh, spur on the deed!
Its issue is our freedom: we shall laugh
And kiss and chide and trifle, when 'tis done.
Leave me and do my will.

*He lowers the dagger to her, hides it and goes out, while she watches him motionless
as in a trance. Turning suddenly, she starts at the sight of her mother's statue.*

Lucilla   What stable whiteness!
I would that I were human, she a ghost;
But I am marble too; all things are done
Round me as if round marble. Some events
Come thus, while we are stone. Fadilla thought
That I was here for pleasure, tender aim
Of grove and sky, I cannot share!

Pylades *enters through the flowering trees.*

Lucilla   The sounds
Of spring, each one a little, separate joy,
Self-gratulating, strike me envious.
The world is filling so with love.

Perceiving **Pylades**.

Lucilla   Ye gods,
A messenger? – with face like Ganymede's,[9]
Enticing kisses through the roseate pendants
And clusters of the branches.
One, a million,

She catches and kisses him.

For each is perfect, and the blossoms press
So softly to my forehead. Apparition
From Paphos, it may be I take farewell
Divine of love and happiness. You struggle,
Shame-faced and downcast, a mere mortal boy,
A slave, no matter if to me a god.
Nay, I will loose you. You have had the kisses

---

9   Trojan hero known for his beauty; desired and abducted by Zeus.

Of a sad, desperate woman. You may go.
There, take your liberty!

Exit.

Pylades   It was the Empress
Herself who kissed me; I am half afraid,
And the great wonder too! What did she mean?
She said I was slave, yet her embrace
Thrilled me as if with freedom. Oh, for that,
For freedom! And he sighed I was a god
To her . . . Apollo, make me god to all,
When on the Emperor's birthday I shall dance
The presence of thy deity 'mong men,
Thy servitude in Arcady, thy folding
Of flocks to music!
                    I will practise it:
For I can bring to mind the canticle,
So often having heard it to my steps.

He sings, moving in pantomime to the words. **Marcia**, *coming unseen by* **Pylades**
down an alley, watches him.

Pylades   Climb with me, Laomedon's[10] white fleeces,
Upward to the hill-tops, up to Ida,[11]
To unshaded dews and earliest dawning.
Young and lustrous, god and yet a servant,
As a star past rock and tree I climb.
Raise your heads erect, ye flocks, and listen
To the note I strike from off my lyre!
They have heard, they stand each head erected;
Thus they wait the Grazing-Tune that woos
Slowly to the ridges and the sky.
I have struck it: all submissive listen,
Till they feed in mystery, advancing,
Drawn to solemn paces by a spell;
Then to sharper strains one way they hurry,
Fleece by fleece around me, till I strike
Sweet, soft notes that lay them down to slumber,
I beside them, where the sun no more
Falls across us, but the chilling moonlight:
There we sleep, my flock and I together,
I, a god, though servant of a king.

*He dances the folding of the flock again, mutely, as if not satisfied with the gestures
and attitudes he had taken.*

---

10 Trojan king; nephew to Ganymede.
11 Ida is the highest mountain in Crete.

Marcia (*apart*)   He sees his god,
Ay, as he is and in his native land;
Can show him to the crowd. I envy him.
It is my vileness binds me to the Cross,
My bartered beauty, my disgrace. For outcasts
My awful outcast Deity, with birthright
Even to the throne of Zeus.

                              The song again.

Pylades   Climb with me, Laomedon's white fleeces,
Upward to the hill-top, up to Ida,
To unshaded dews and earliest dawning.
Young and lustrous . . .

His voice dies away and he again tries other gestures.

Marcia (*apart*)   Ah, the Nazarene
Will never draw the flower of men,
or breathe Warm on their flowering days. For innocence,
For the prayers that youth makes, speaking to itself
Or kindled by bright gales, He has no ear.

Pylades *suddenly approaches the statue of Apollo.*

Pylades   O Genius, O my Patron, thou that guardest
My tireless feet, the singers and the flutists
Who sing and play, while I am dancing thee,
Receive thy gifts of music and of verse:
Dower me with thine own life, breathe through my motions,
Act in me bodily, and fill all eyes
With presence of thy godhead; for thou can'st,
O Delphicus!

Enter **Eclectus** *with a scroll.*

Eclectus (*to* **Pylades**)   Begone! You dare intrude,
You, in this grove!

Marcia (*advancing*)   Why do you strike the boy?
I heard his voice afar, and he is fashioned
To stand unchidden 'neath the dangling purple
And knots of blossom. Do not banish him.
(*To* **Pylades**.) What is your name?

Pylades   They call me Pylades.

Eclectus   A pupil from the schools, a pantomime,
Named from his master Pylades, a Greek,
A slave . . .

Presenting a scroll, as **Pylades** *draws back among the trees.*

Eclectus   I bring you message from the mines
Where in Sardinian caverns by the sea
Your Christians suffer; you can ransom them,
Such is their faith . . .

Eclectus *pauses while she reads.*

Eclectus   But, Domina, the means
That they propose? You are my Empress; nothing
That you effect, touching the state, is foreign
To me, your chamberlain. I hate these Christians,
I fear their subtlety, their favouring wiles,
I fear lest they bring peril on your head.
Tell me, how would they draw you to their rescue?
The means?

Marcia   Myself, my place. O chamberlain,
You know how I am ranked.

Eclectus   You are an Empress,
My lord's Augusta. Keep your majesty.

Marcia   I am a Christian.

Eclectus   You have no religion;
You cannot have; you are yourself divine.
Think of your worshippers, establish them,
And set yourself deep in the stars. O lady,
Let me not see you fall, a meteor,
A fickle, broken light. You are a goddess
To my great lord, to me. Sway over us!

Marcia   I count among the slaves.

Eclectus   Is it as such
You hope to win your will? Base to my lord,
And, oh, most base to Rome, thus to betray her
To those who have no country and no king,
Who flatter and revolt.

Marcia   Even an Empress,
Eclectus, may beseech the life and freedom
Of chosen captives.

Eclectus   You speak truth, but these,
Your Christians . . . Will you read?

Marcia *is silent.*

Eclectus   Not from the scroll,
From lips of their own messenger I learnt
Their infamy; they bade me seek you out

In secret, praying you would use your beauty,
Your power, your arts, your place . . .

Marcia   Go! Say, Eclectus,
I am a servant well-equipped to serve.

Exit **Eclectus**.

Marcia   I have my power; I dare not cast it off;
For power discarded brings a great revenge:
But in myself my life is as a leaf
Wind-blown to utter ruin, carrying
Its death along with it. I wonder where
The truth is hid in me? With Commodus,
My golden athlete – for I love his strength,
The straightness of his aim, his open mimes
And the summer in his temper – or the Church,
That leads me through dark places to the stars?
Oh, I am unredeemed; I cannot pray!
But when I creep down to the Catacombs,
And see the faces there, and for lustration,
O God, Thy blood – Thou offering it, not slain –
Then I have craving for the utter white,
For Thee, O Spotless!

Pylades (*watching her at a distance*)   This is Niobe –
How perfect! – for she stands alone and weeps;
And yet one feels about her breast and feet
Her children clinging. Is she Niobe?
The supplication in her eyes, her tears!

Fascinated, he draws close up to her: at the sound of his footsteps she turns, smiling, toward him.

Marcia   So you desire your freedom?

Pylades   Past all hope.

Marcia   And on the Emperor's birthday you will dance
Apollo and the folding of the flocks.
I shall be there.

Pylades   You will!
Before I sleep
I always pray the gods to make of me
A perfect dancer, and then ask their blessing
Upon all beauteous things. Between my prayers,
I will make one for you.

Marcia   Sweet boy, my thanks.

Pylades   The Emperor's birthday!

He runs off among the trees.

Marcia (*seating herself, reads the scroll; then she looks up from it*)   I will liberate
Thy servants in the mines; and for Thy sake,
Thine too, the Greek, who dances to Apollo,
Shall dance in freedom. I am chosen thus:
Though my pure God can never dwell with me,
And all my days must pass in dust and shade.

Re-enter **Lucilla**.

Marcia   Empress!

Lucilla   My brother, will he come?

Marcia   Not yet; You hear the strife still clangs.

Lucilla   'Not yet, not yet!'
But one may clog impatience till it frenzies.
To tear up flowers be sacrifice to words
As cruel as 'Not yet!' Before their hour
Let these red hundreds perish.
                              What, you smile?

She strips a tree of blossoms.

Marcia   O lady, at this fury kindly urged
On senseless objects. So your royal brother
Shatters his murrhine vases at a blow
If one he loves offend.

Lucilla   You misconceive.
Fair courtesan, what can you know of fury,
The royal thing? Your veins have never brewed
The dancing ichor.[12] Can you know the play
Of Titans with the worlds, the punishment
That gods create for laggard destiny?
I rend these showering multitudes, with force
To dissipate the stars, the race of men.
Oh, I am hot with labour!

Marcia   Nay, take breath.

Re-enter **Commodus** *with* **Cleander** *and following.*

Marcia   Look up!

Lucilla (*the rent branches in her hand*)   Why, that's my brother Commodus . . .
How tossed his hair is! Commodus, I say . . .
I cannot. He is murdered . . . Commodus!

---

12 Blood of the gods.

She shrieks and falls senseless on the ground.

Marcia (*supporting her*)   What is her terror?

Commodus   That I am not dead,
That I have found her with her murderer's hands
Dangling my crown.

Marcia   O Emperor, she attempted . . .

Commodus   To slay me in the eastern passage, sweet,
To kill me in my heyday. 'From the Senate',
Her lover cried, 'and from Lucilla', failing
Just by that cry to triumph.
       Look at her,
Look at her, look! The likeness: why, it seems
As if my mother lay there on the ground
In a swoon of fast-clenched hatred. Nature, nature!
And I was disciplined to love her law,
And listen to her promptings as to truth.
Lies, lies, my philosophic father, lies!
Nature is false, or this is not my sister,
My mother in each trait. But where is truth?
Why, in this body that is safe from Mors,[13]
The archway-haunting spectre, safe for feasts
And love and glory and divine excess.
Crowns for the revel! In great cups of wine
Memory shall drown . . . but I must test the drink
Before I swallow: each imperial dish
Must wait its herald, the sure antidote.
Take up that woman; thrust her in a cell
Close as the grave. She is not yet unbrothered;
I will not have her slain before my eyes.
But shut her close.

Dragging **Marcia** *by the hand.*

Commodus   And we will come away.

Marcia   Emperor, you cannot mean that you will feast?

Commodus   All night and on to morning, on to noon,
On for three days. It is my gratitude
For having hoodwinked nature at her game.
Dish after dish!
    But ere the viands cool
There shall be search for stately senators,

---

13 Embodiment of Death in Roman mythology.

Dropped sudden from their place to the abyss –
Those aged foster-parents that conspired
Together for my ruin. I will break
Each precious natural bond, and piety,
That is but nature's grand-dam, shall be drawn
Along the streets and hooted. You agree?
Why, I could think you love me, such a flame
Is in the eyes you bend upon that traitor,
Marcia, my little whore.

Marcia   Lean on my faith.

Commodus   My pretty wanton, no.
I shall discover you some fatal day
Drugging my cup. But do not blink! I welcome
All monstrous circumstance, all passing riot
Of vanities, since all is vanity,
Nature and faith and pleasure, fame and love,
All indiscriminate deceptions, all
Hollows to fill with lamps and laugh beneath.

He totters toward **Lucilla**, *striking his breast and repeating the gestures and words of* **Quadratus**.

Commodus   'This from the Senate.' Nay, it is Lucilla
That strikes me to a spectre. How inane
The thought that I am living, how it gapes
Down to the darkness of a sepulchre.
My sister, ho!
     I would not have her slain,
Kept as she is in marble.
       Come away
From death, and pour libations.
         Flowers and statues,
Fountains and jets of foam, my mother's statue,
Lucilla's . . .

He comes back and stares vacantly at her, where she lies.

    Do you call this place my palace,
Or Pompey's Theatre?
       Soft, Cleander, write me
A secret list of all our senators.
Marcia, around us, vanity and spring!
Leaves, leaves, my father called us. Let us dance.

Act Two

The Central Court of the Imperial Villa at Laurentum. Marble seats among bushes of laurel; tripods smoking with healthful and precious substances. **Eclectus** *and* **Laetus** *are heard conversing behind the laurels.*

Eclectus   Welcome! And yet no audience, good Prefect,
If you have passed through Rome.

Laetus   Oh, fear me not;

They enter.

Laetus   I am scarce landed, full of healthful brine
Sick but for news.

Eclectus   Our exile tells the worst –
Rome is plague-stricken, Tiber in full flood.
Famine is in our streets, conspiracy
Has been among us and has failed, revenge
Is now among us and is doomed to fail;
Treason is with the crowd.

Laetus   But this must end.

Eclectus   Most surely it will end and of itself.

Laetus   How of itself?

Eclectus   The ancient deities
Are in their place; do not inquire of me.
Is Thebes disrooted?[14] You have seen the sphinxes,
The obelisks, the congregated kings
Huge on the painted sunshine. Power prevails;
But then how fed, how lighted! What is Power?
O Roman, did you catch the meeting lips
Of the Sun-God and Amenophis?[15]

Laetus   Nay, nay!
Religion holds me not.

Eclectus   I did but speak
Of Egypt and its clear, vibrating air.
Why leave a shore so healthful?

Laetus   Yet, I trust
There is no peril here.

---

14 Ancient Egyptian city.
15 The Greek name for Amenhotep, the ninth pharaoh of the Eighteenth Dynasty.

Eclectus   Where destiny
Fulfils itself as in the Roman streets,
That pour their starving hosts to threaten us.
Look well to the Pretorians;[16] they are sullen,
And if they fail we perish.

Laetus   I am warned.

Exit.

Eclectus   Sight of this fellow-mortal come ashore,
Safe from the waves, to close with deadly pest,
Renews the trepidation in my veins
For her, for Marcia. Blow, Hesperian breezes,
Blow steady through her lintel, give her health,
O my rose-lotus! Let the fatal barque
Sink with its thousands, if the flower of women
Is left on earth, unrent from us. The plague,
The terror – they have taught me how I love.

Enter **Commodus**.

Commodus   Where is the lady Marcia?

Eclectus   Still within.
No one has seen her stirring.

Commodus   You stand there
As if you feared to speak.

Eclectus (*bowing low*)   Lend me your[17] ear;
Be patient with my loyalty. You dream
That you are safe; and from the pestilence
You have security; but through these laurels
Your flattering nobles let no rumour pierce
Of deep-revolting Rome. Your minister,
The base Cleander, keeps, as private wealth
And fast-locked treasure, corn that should be flung
As bounty to the crowd. Food for the people
Is secret of all godlike sovereignty:
The famished multitudes are flocking to you
Behind these gates; and, when they come, prepare
The morsel to their appetite – Cleander.

Commodus   Another face to toss down to the void,
And turn from ruddy pleasantness to pale
And grinning horror! What is this you counsel?

---

16 Pretorians: imperial bodyguards.
17 'Your' appears as 'you' in the original text, probably a printer's error.

Famine is but the plague in leaner form,
A visitation from the gods. Cleander
Keeps these afflictions from me.

Eclectus   But prepare –

Commodus   O fool, this is Laurentum and not Rome.
Here I take rest from cares – no early visits
From formal nobles; the huge day to fill
With simple pastime and the solaces
Olympus smiles at!

Eclectus   Laetus is within;
Make sure of the Pretorians.

Commodus   Cease this folly.
Go, give command the Bestiarii[18]
Uncage that lion with the jutting tooth.
He shall affirm my prowess.

Exit **Eclectus**.

Commodus   I am here
A true divinity, among these odours,
Among these mounting flames. Let me conceive
That they burn up to me! And let Rome perish,
Or send her suppliants hither! Sweet to snuff
The heated fragrance. But how still it is!
No lizard threads his crevice: all the air
Pauses for some event.
                         Lucilla lives,
Yet while she lives my heart keeps dropping blood.

Drawing a parchment from his sleeve.

If I should do it,
A gulf would open at my very feet,
A dark abysm, with one staring face
To hold me to the bottom of the void.
She is a traitor . . . but that opes no gulf.
It is the refuse we throw in ourselves
Reeks from the fissure up to us, or gives
Its altered visage back. I am her brother.
See, if I look down in this fountain's bowl,
I see her brother's face, gold Commodus,
How handsome and how young!
                         If I should do it!

---

18 People (usually prisoners) who engaged in mortal combat with animals.

Her death is written: or is this the parchment
That grants her pardon and oblivion?
It is the parchment. Then I shall forget her,
And then . . .

            Ah, Zeus, thy eagles and their prey!
I must have idols, if I am a god!

Marcia *enters from without.*

Commodus   Bright apparition! What, my Morning! Health
Stepping to meet me! Were you always young
As now, this holy lustre on your face . . .

Marcia   And yet the secret of it! From the caves
I come and from the spices of the tomb.

Commodus   Marcia, you breathe it! . . . From the sepultures
Of your foul out-casts, from your buried god –
And this mock radiance on your face . . . You shall not!
The peril, gods!

Marcia   I shall not bring the plague.

Commodus   Your feet have trodden it. To lose you, dearest,
To lose you! You must never pass again,
Never desert me for a single hour.

Marcia   I will not. If I savour of the tomb
The secrets of my wondrous shadow-land
Are left behind, and I am sprung from Hades,
Eurydice, not praying to turn back,
Praying to walk with you, to share your griefs
And lighten them, if you will give me place beside you –

Commodus *laughs.*

Marcia   Not as Empress: as one sent,
A slave, a common hireling, but yet chosen
To guard you, O my Golden-haired, from death.

Commodus   What flowers are in your voice! If I could trust you,
If you could give me love!

Marcia   A faithful servant . . .
Oh, were you fashioned to believe! . . . has something
Created in his heart, something most real,
Something most sure; and it is thus I hold you
Amid the hollow gulfs.

Commodus   I loved my mother,
And when I think of her a gravity
Falls on my thoughts; then I am Commodus,

Solid and with ambition. But you cheat me.
Are you not cheated too at every turn?
You cannot love me though I give you all,
And you can pour no happiness: your heart
Is void and bitter.

A **Priest of Cybele** *enters and chants to his brazen rattle.*

Marcia (*drawing her hand across her forehead*)　Note the spectacle!

Priest　Cybele, Cybele, save us from death, Cybele, Cybele, strong to aid!
Fierce is the plague, fiercely it clears harvests of men from the light.
Cybele, Cybele, who now shall reap. Cybele, Cybele, who shall bind?
Save us from death, taming the plague as a forest lion is tamed,
Mother of all, Goddess most good, rolling in pomp through the lands.

The Courtyard fills to the **Priest**'s *chant:* **Pylades** *is among the pages.*

Commodus　I am arrested by this priest: he clangs,
And clangs and clangs, and so the earth is ruled
By one sole iteration.
　　　　　　　　　Corybant,[19]
I would speak with you of your mysteries.
This for your altars.

Gives a carcanet.

Priest　You would join the train?

Commodus　I cannot; I am secret to myself,
I cannot join a train. You draw processions . . .
So, I would draw them.

Priest　You have cast aside
Your carcanet: if you would lead the frenzy
I marshal, you must put away your nature,
Your manhood, pass a mutilated slave
Before the city. We, who are religious,
Are silent-lipped till we can speak with those
Who have put nature off.

Commodus　And then?

Priest　The frenzy,
The exaltation! We attain the god.
Then we can succour multitudes and bind them
Fast to our car, for then they grow confused
Between us and the power that ravishes.
You must not stay my cymbals. Rome is stricken,
I am her saviour. Give, and join the cry!

---

19 Attendant of the goddess Cybele.

He passes on clashing and begging; the crowd follows.

Commodus   A crowd is gathering round the Corybant,
And I am left in shade. Put nature off!
Ay, so I will, and then these mysteries
Will open to me. If indeed there were
A secret and a perfume at the flower
Of this wild ritual! But the priest assumes;
He is an actor merely.
                    Oh ye gods,
Ye gods, I am your equal; ye but dream
And dream, and dream your greatness and your blood.
That is reality. So you become
Or Zeus, or Hercules, or what you will;
All is as you have breath for in your sighs.
Marcia, you shall behold! I was about
To slay a grisly lion, as an archer
With mortal strength: now I am Hercules
Eager to rid Nemea of her pest.[20]

Marcia   Ah, could you succour Rome!

Commodus   That is no dream,
With that is no reality: the people
Are all illusion and their cries a painting
To rub off from the air . . .
We must put nature by, her cries, her qualms,
Leave her to perish as a wailing child
Far off behind us.
                    I shall lead a train;
You will be here to greet me. 'Tis not love
I ask for: be my echo through the hills,
Answer me back with softer voice, and I
Will ravish and undo you. Ecstasy!

He goes out.

Marcia (*wringing her hands*)   He is beside himself! To see him borne,
Swept on as by an eddy. Commodus!
It is as I were calling to the dead.

Pylades *creeps up to her and touches her.*

Marcia   Who is it plucks my sleeve? Ah, I remember!
(*To* **Pylades**.) I think I freed you; that should be enough.

Pylades   It is for freedom
To give you counsel. You must recollect

---

20 Home to the Nemean Lion, which was slayed by Hercules in the first of his twelve labours.

I am the substance of which kings are made,
Ajax, the vexed Atreidae:[21] all they suffer
I feel down to the quick, not from without,
As you are feeling.
              Think! Lucilla's knife
Is at his bosom still; and you are cold.
You wring your hands. Lady, it is a gesture
Of pity for yourself.

Marcia *remains silent.*

Pylades   He is a god;
Is – ah, we know the truth, he dreams it so;
And in a dream all must be of one piece,
All woven in one spell. Build him an altar,
Burn roses to him; then arrest his eye
In some great moulded action: if he change,
Change too, as, were he ocean-deity,
You would become Leucothea.[22]
                    You despise
This acting?

Marcia   It is very pitiful.

Pylades   You cannot choose: it is the parts we play
With most similitude! If Venus call
And we can answer lightly as her doves . . .

Marcia   The counsel of a pantomime. Go, seek
Eclectus, bring him hither.

Enter from without **Cleander** *and* **Slaves** *bearing arms and garments.*

Pylades (*shrugging his shoulders*)   Yonder pageant
Arrests the pantomime.

Marcia   Cleander, stay!
What dazzling beams you throw against our faces.
This panoply . . .

Cleander   Dear lady, a new gift
For your imperial lover. Gifts and gifts.

Marcia   Obsequious bounty, the mere residue
Of hoards beyond all count.

Cleander   An unkind thought,
The oyster must be nacreous in its mould
To offer you a pearl.

---

21 Atreidae: Agamemnon and Menelaus, sons of Atreus.
22 Theban princess who was transformed into a sea goddess.

Marcia   I do not need
Excuses for your private opulence:
I am not a Provincial you have robbed,
Nor a Patrician rendered poor to flush
Your coffers and provide gratuity
For Emperors. Spare me!

Arrested by the panoply.

But is this your gift?
The vizored helmet . . .

Cleander   Steel and beaten gold.

Marcia   A base secutor's outfit. And you take
These gladiatorial weapons, the short sword,
Even the apron . . .

Cleander   Silk!

Marcia   To Commodus!

Cleander   I meet his craving
By liberal fulfilment. Lady Marcia
Is less a neighbour to his aspirations
Than poor Cleander, though she lay her head
Against the subtle heart she fails to know
In every turn of fancy.

Marcia   Many years
The Emperor has been skilled in archery:
Such practice is not infamous; his gods
Have sped the dart with scarce diviner skill.
But such dishonour as your treachery
Would flatter in him is a crime that sullies
The universe he governs. If you love,
Cleander, if you love him, as you boast,
Spare him this fatal tribute, turn the slaves
Back with their servile burthen.
                          See, I breathe
As if he were in peril of his life.

Cleander   No, lady Marcia fears her perfect sway
Should suffer some abatement, her profession
Should lose heart-swelling virtue by the side
Of the gladiator's magic. I will stir
The strife and watch its issue.
                          Slaves, proceed.

Marcia   Most wicked demon!

Cleander (*to* **Pylades**)   You shall earn twelve pieces

Of gold to-night at supper, if you dance
Your Pyrrhic dance for one.
                                    And let your flutist
Be at your side in readiness, my sweet.

*He pulls the dancer's ear caressingly and goes out with his slaves in the opposite
direction.*

Pylades (*breaking into laughter*)   Secutor!

Marcia   Hush, you laugh! There is no evil
Not to be looked for, but if this befall
All things are overthrown. The darkness closes
Around me, and I feel that torrent powers,
As I defy and promise to arrest them,
Are eddying me away. Ah, Pylades,
What is your counsel now?

Pylades   You need no counsel:
Forget it all. Be but the thing you are,
Sightless, and full of ruin. Weep and weep,
But not for Rome.

Marcia   Secutor, oh!
I cannot weep for him.

Sound of voices and laughter.

And it may be even now –
I hear his voice, the honey in its tone
It breathes when soft in triumph. He is happy,
And yonder is Cleander.

Pylades   Shroud yourself.

Marcia   Is he accoutred?

Pylades   You must pass within;
I will observe in secret.

Marcia   A secutor!
But I will seek the Princess; she will feel
The ignominy slip into her blood.

Pylades   Pass quickly.

Exit **Marcia**, **Pylades** *hides in the laurels, while* **Commodus**, *dressed as Hercules in
a lion-skin,* **Cleander** *and a bevy of pages and women fill the enclosure.*

Pylades   A brave troop of revellers!
And now I catch the theme. 'Tis Hercules,
And all his little handmaids buzzing round
With kisses and with praise. A rich diversion,

To watch the Emperor playing pantomime.
And what a rose, that Sagana!

Commodus (*to* **Cleander**)   You fashion
My dreams to my own liking: that is greatly
And truly to be served. Before to-night
I shall be Paulus the secutor; now
Your Lucius Commodus is Hercules,
The slayer of a lion, such a beast,
An old and brindled sire, whose belly sent
Its hungered bay up that had been a roar
But that I cut it silent. From the conflict
I come to rest. How exquisite a dream!
I breathe Olympus, and, my labours done,
My burning sweat washed off, I am exalted,
As mortals ever must be to enjoy
Things perfectly celestial. Scatter flowers
To fill the air with coolness; fetch a cup
Crowned with dawn-fabling roses to the brim.
Be goddesses beside me, be as gods;
Let me create my creatures deities,
As I endue myself, my strength, my beauty,
With Herculean honours and the name
Of Jove's unconquered son.

Pylades *slips away among the laurels.*

Cleander   You need a goblet
Worthy divineness of so high a reach.

Commodus   And such you can present? Go, fetch your marvel,
My little, own Cleander.

Cleander   With six pounds
Of the best perfume of Niceros,[23] worthy
The nostrils of a god!

Commodus   Gifts, ever gifts!
And always gold to meet expenditure;
That is the one solidity of dreams.

Exit **Cleander**.

Commodus   And his last thought, the perfume! Sagana,
Soft as the spray, soft-bosomed as the rose,
Give me your hair for cushion. I am weary;
Fall round me and in concert hymn my toils.

---

23 A renowned perfume-maker.

(*Closing his eyes.*) How slumbrous in this land of cooler air,
Abounding with the laurel, in the smell
Of the sweet laurels, in the pleasant shadow
To hear each valiant act on women's voices,
As if it donned queen Omphale's attire.[24]

First Semi Chorus   Great Hercules in the Nemaean vale
Threw down his weapon on the sedgy grass,
And strangled the red lion with his hand.

Second Semi Chorus   And Lucius Commodus before the world
Struck dead a hundred lions, dart by dart;
Laid them in order on the drunken sod.[25]

First Semi Chorus   Great Hercules from fresh Arcadian woods
Bore the gold-antlered stag to Tiryns home,
The stag of Artemis with feet of brass.[26]

Second Semi Chorus   And Lucius Commodus struck down in death
Camelopardalis,[27] the stag with neck
Tall as a fir and spotted as the plane.

First Semi Chorus   Great Hercules through dazzling Psophian snows
Chased the tusked boar, and chasing mid the cold,
Caught him at last o'er-wearied in a net.[28]

Second Semi Chorus   But Lucius Commodus had rarer sport,
For with one aim he felled rhinoceros,
Of bulk gigantic, armed with hideous tusk.

First Semi Chorus   Great Hercules slew the Stymphalian birds
Beside the lake's swift-sliding waves; in vain
Were brazen claws and beaks and arrowed plumes.[29]

Second Semi Chorus   And Lucius Commodus with crescent darts
Struck Mauritanian ostriches, in flight,
That skim the ground on wings like swelling sails.

Commodus   Five of my dozen Labours! Oh, this chaunt
Rises an odour from those flowers – your lips!

---

24 Lydian queen who owned Hercules after he was forced into slavery.

25 The 'decadence' of Commodus is being mocked in these verses by comparing his killing of common
     animals with the labours of Hercules.

26 This deer is the Ceryneian Hind, which Hercules captured in the third of his twelve labours.

27 An astral constellation goes by this name, which is meant to represent a giraffe. Where Hercules
     captures the Ceryneian Hind, Commodus bears poor comparison in killing a giraffe (presumably while
     hunting).

28 The Erymanthian boar, captured by Hercules in the fourth of his twelve labours. The boar terrorised
     Erymanthus, which was later called Psophis and later again Phegeia.

29 The Stymphalian birds feasted on the flesh of men. They were slain by Hercules in the sixth of his
     twelve labours.

First Semi Chorus   Great Hercules . . .

Fadilla *and* **Marcia** *enter like mourners.*

All   See, see!

The women scream.

Commodus   'Tis rash to steal
Like ghosts upon my dream, 'tis a fresh murder.
To wound me now will draw the thunderbolt.
Away, or learn
That visions crush like mountains when they fall.
Vanish together! . . .
                    Marcia, you draw close;
Marcia, your eyes – the murdering, white light!
Leave me, fair boys; more room, a wider circle,
My wreath of coloured petals!
                       Marcia, speak,
Or die 'mid this god's feast!

Marcia   'Tis you must die,
My lord, unless –
(*To* **Fadilla**.) But tell him, Princess, all.
He will believe a lady of his blood.
Tell him of ruin, tell him he has lost
The Roman people, tell him he has lost
The moiety of his guard, that he must dread
From his own subjects what could never chance
By hand of barbarous nation.

Re-enter **Eclectus**.

Eclectus   All is lost;
Your Guard is broken; you are now defenceless,
And on the brink of slaughter.

Circle   Save us!

Fadilla   Save
Yourself, my dearest, for we speak but truth:
Outside these walls a fiery hatred marshals
The citizens. They have a single shout
Of hunger after justice, and one name
For all they hate – Cleander. Every voice
Demands his head.

Commodus   An execrable plot!
I cannot listen any more to words;
They are the language of conspirators.
(*To* **Marcia**.) But you have put your beauty quite away,

Made yourself hideous, distasteful. There,
Again I catch design; my sister too –
Cleander smote her lover. Envious, ha!
That was Lucilla's keynote. Agony!
I will not give him up.

Marcia   He is a traitor.
I say this in Truth's name.

Commodus   And through your eyes I look as to the bottom of the well.
Marcia, come nearer! You are deadly sure . . . ?

Marcia   Eclectus!

Commodus   No; swear to me by your eyes . . .

Marcia   Cleander is a traitor. He has brought
A host together, he has armed your people
To strike you dead unless you quell this strife:
He fraudulently bore the public grain
To private granaries, till famine raged,
And still it rages on. Although I tremble
To move you with the sorrow worst to man
Of finding falsehood in the services
That fashioned every day, I, who must die
So soon beside you, yet proclaim with Rome
Cleander is a traitor.

She gazes into his eyes.

Commodus   So you doom him,
So! Woman, how I hate you. From his youth,
When every office nearest to myself
Was his, and he familiar with my pleasures,
My needs, my health, my privacy, my sleep,
Even then he was a traitor? All must end
If such a hollow, such inanity
Gape round me as existence.

Re-enter **Cleander**.

Commodus   Let him die!

Cleander   The cup!

Commodus   He promised me
To bring it; it is brought. A poison-bowl!
Drink, drink, Cleander; pledge me!

Cleander*, startled, drops the cup and crouches at his feet.*

Cleander   I am lost,
Crushed by your sudden anger. Could I drink?

'Twas an oblation. Are you not a god,
And through my service? Dare you cast me off?
Dare you discard such deep fidelity?
Gods do not so desert.

Eclectus   You are condemned,
The crowd impatient.

Cleander   Master, by our youth,
By all my fond devotion . . . If I erred,
It was for you. I twisted circumstance
For you, I stole, I lied . . .

Marcia   Laetus!

Cleander   Her voice –
The harlot, my accuser!

Marcia   Laetus!

Laetus *enters with soldiers.*

Commodus   Take
Your victim, offer him!

Cleander *is dragged away.* **Commodus** *wraps his face in his mantle.*

Commodus   I shut my ears.
Truly I am a god; 'tis on this wise
The gods abandon, deaf to circumstance.

A long pause.

You cannot rate him. Why, he kept my rooms:
A little Phrygian slave, the cryer offered,
They bought him for me, and he jigged a dance
Of the mountain-loving Mother the first night
He placed my pillow.
Marcia, cling to me!

Marcia   My lord!

Commodus   Cling, cling as to a drowning man.
O Veritas, I loved him. Do not weep.

A distant cry and shouts are heard.

For me I must. A ghost cries after me;
And at the little bloodless Hades-moan
My heart grows soft.

Marcia   Oh, steel yourself. Cleander
Has fallen justly.

Commodus   So you will not weep!
He shall have justice in the Shadow-land.
Some parchment – quick!

Exit.

Fadilla   What moves him?

Marcia   Something moves,
Something! When men rise restless from their tears
One must not ask their errand.

Re-enter **Pylades**.

Marcia   Pylades!

Pylades   My master Pylades! Great lady, help!
Save him, O save my master!
He is called Cleander's friend, he is my most beloved.
You of the irresistible petition,
Who gave me freedom and Cleander death,
If what is terrible has terror for you,
The dreadful gulf, the joyless bark, deliver
My master from the teeming river-side.
Oh, he is hunted!

Eclectus   Marcia, do not listen.

Marcia   I speak for your dear master. You, Eclectus,
Take the poor boy away; see, I confide him
To your protection.

She pushes **Pylades** *behind* **Eclectus**, *on whom she leans for a moment, steadying herself.*

Eclectus   He imperils you.

Marcia   Hush, hush! Do you not hear the raving noise,
The loose, unguided step? Now if you love me,
You must not interpose. It is my hour,
And I alone can reckon with his mood.

Re-enter **Commodus**.

Commodus   This Justice is a dazzling wanton, heady,
Reckless and wild as Fortune's very self,
Who gives her favours to the meanest traitor,
Denies no man her bosom, fondles ghosts!
Ah, that is novel. Marcia you remain
The statue that I left.

Marcia   Your will, my lord?

Commodus   Most docile and most sweet, you will not blench.
I shall not see you weep! Call Laetus, call him,
As but a little while ago you called.

Marcia   Laetus!

Commodus   He tarries.

Eclectus *moves forward, discovering* **Pylades**.

Eclectus   Let me bear your will.

Commodus (*to* **Pylades**)   No – here is one. Come hither to my side,
Thou hyacinth – blossom, thou most sweet exchange
For bloodshed and a god's dull agony.
You weep, you weep.

Pylades   My master!

Commodus   Flower of Darkness,
Breathe me your sighs, and let me gaze on you,
Till grief is but a fragrance. And your sorrow,
Your suit?

Pylades   My master! Empress, speak for him.
You promised . . .

Marcia (*her hands on* **Pylades**' *shoulders*)   Nay, he best can plead, he begs
The life of Pylades, the pantomime,
His master in the dance, a fugitive;
But cannot speak for weeping.

Commodus (*to* **Pylades**)   Bear this sentence
Forth to the hall, to Laetus. It condemns,
One I found wholly guilty: she must die.

Fadilla   Gods, 'tis Lucilla!

Commodus   Bear the sentence, beauty;
And I will be your master. Dry your tears.
Ah, Marcia, this is well; you do not move.

Marcia   How could I?

Commodus   What a rigid ugliness
You stand. I hate you.

Marcia (*throwing off her black cloak and veil*)   But this bitter mourning
Is past, the mourning of my widowhood;
For you are safe.
(*Kneeling.*) And now, my lord, in token
You love this Marcia who has clung to you,
Who clings, will cling forever, grant this boon:

Forget Lucilla. Do not pardon her;
I cannot, but forget her.
                              And, to keep
Our names together, grave me on a medal
With you, your Amazon. So I am thanked
For this day's service that has guarded you,
Has kept you mine.

Commodus   Magnificent! O pride!
My Empress, my deliverer!

Marcia (*presenting* **Pylades**)   This freedman
Of mine shall be your servant. Yield protection
To his old master, he will straight forget him,
And dedicate to you the arts, the grace
Inclined you to him as a messenger.
Speed him with mercy.

Commodus (*to* **Pylades**)   What a sob! You promise
You will forget your master?

Pylades   Save him swiftly,
Or he will perish with Cleander's friends.
My most-beloved!

Commodus   For that he perishes.
My fleet, young god, but you shall see the shades
Grow pale with horror! I will people Hades
Thick as the Roman-streets. But first Lucilla!
Carry the sentence!

Marcia *presses back the parchment against his breast: he strikes her heavily.*

Marcia   Commodus, this touch
Is new to me . . .
Eclectus, quick, your hand!

Act Three

An Ante-room of the Regia: to the right the Imperial Bedchamber, to the left the Bathroom. Gladiatorial weapons lie about in confusion. A statue of Janus, wreathed, stands in the midst. It is the last day of the old year 192. **Eclectus**, **Sagana**, *and* **Folia**.

Sagana   We wait to arm the Emperor; it is dull
To wait so long, to wait so anxiously,
To shake one's bracelets or re-bind one's tresses
Hour after hour.

Folia   I tremble in each limb
At thought of his approach.

Sagana   And yet that fan
Of peacock-plumes, that loveliest veil of Cos,[30]
Like water round your bosom!

Folia   What are they?
If you had suffered ridicule and insult
Cruel as I have borne, your plumes and gauzes
Would hang as on a pyre.

Eclectus   This lady carries
Her hoops of pearl with spirit.

Sagana   I have learnt
My lesson from our queen of concubines,
The royal Marcia: for to daunt our lover,
Grown fatal since he shed his sister's blood,
She meets him in the kirtle[31] and the arms
Of a defying Amazon. He yields
On the instant to the freshness of her challenge;
He turns her slave, and her bold fancy masters
His thralled belief. She might have been a mime,
She acts with such free grace the part she chooses;
Not Pylades himself can rival her.
Some say he taught the new Hippolyta
The carriage of her shield, her doughty motions,
The port of her scant tunic.

Eclectus   It is false.
A most injurious falsehood! She herself
Dared all to cow the fiction-loving temper
Of Commodus, and gloriously prevailed.

---

30 Island of the Dodecanese.
31 Kirtle: unisex medieval garment, later more generally worn by women.

Sagana   Nude from the knee!

Eclectus   Her face – the floating hair
Soft round the helmet-cap; the face in arms.

Sagana   Then you admire her aspect, and the fiction
Gains on your faith.

Eclectus   We need some ancient stories
To help us to live on.

Folia   I cannot feign.
I can but pray 'O Janus, close the past.'[32]

Eclectus   And I would pray
'Make open vista for another year!'
Life passes like a ship, O Lord of Time,
Before thy twofold office.

Folia   Hark, at last
The Emperor quits the bath; I hear his feet
Splash on the marble. I am cold, so cold!
But Marcia comes.

Enter **Marcia** *as an Amazon and her servant* **Jallia**.

Marcia   The Emperor is within?

Eclectus, greeting! I have bought my gifts
Against to-morrow: and a flood of sun
Has filled the shops, has lighted up the coins
Of Janus, made the sweetmeats jewel-bright,
And purchasing a holiday employ
That wasted hours. I scarcely found a moment
To don my armour and disguise myself;
Yet Jallia would not help.

Eclectus   The child looks pale,
Your little servant.

Marcia   Winter-pallor, nothing
But discontent with one who is beloved.
Heigh-ho! The shops were gay, and as a bride
I trafficked everywhere and laughed, such gladness,
Strong as a panic, rocked my heart. This sun!
Your ancient god of light is god of change:
What would he do for me, even me? Remember
How I was born to these divinities,

---

32 A god usually depicted with two faces looking in opposite directions; associated with periods of
    transition.

And with my father and my mother worshipped
Our Janus, this dear symbol of a truth,
Time's image, that divine Eternity
Hath dispossessed of worship. Jallia shakes
Her solemn head, and you, Eclectus, fix
Your eyes on me as on the midnight stars.
I am a Christian, and to me at last
Old things are new; but Jallia hates the old.

Jallia (*in a sweet undertone*)   As false, abhorred, forbidden.

Marcia   Child, not so;
Their power is in them always, and the passage
Of old year into new for ever shows
The countenance of Janus, and for ever
Will stir the worship of our time-born race.

Eclectus   The Emperor!

Enter **Commodus** *from the Bathroom; he is dressed as an Amazon, exactly like* **Marcia**.

Commodus   What, my Amazon, fresh-travelled
From Thermodon![33] Before you could arrive
I hoped to meet you worthily. Ha, ha!
I can but laugh, the cymbals in me clash
To hail your gallant fairness.

Marcia   I am merry
This morning as if Caucasus had fed me
With gustful breezes. And how fares my lord?
Fetch me the wine-cup, Sagana.

Commodus   I slept
Unconscionably late, a dreadful sleep
Against my will, with none to waken me,
And faces round me on the walls of doom.
Wine, wine!

Marcia *fills the bowl* **Sagana** *presents.*

Commodus   Bold cup-bearer, my day begins,
My sun first rises with the flush of wine:
All other dawn is wan, improvident.
You usher-in existence!
(*He takes the bowl from her.*) To his love,
My Amazon, your Amazonius drinks.

---

33 River flowing through Cappadocia, now present-day Turkey and called the Terme River.

I am entirely yours. You see my shoulder
Is bare like this to which I press my mouth,
As Mavors[34] feeds his love on Venus' beauty.
Your moon-shaped shield between us! Ha, defence!
My queen, my queen, I must submit. Today
I front the world your representative
In war and conquest, bidden by a dream,
That crossed the mournful horrors of my slumber,
To wear your garment, swing your moon-shaped shield,
Lace on your buskins, press my shorter curls
With Amazonian casque, and let the world
See me become the woman I adore,
As Hercules became. I strive today
In the gladiators' school, equipped as you,
Hippolyta's giant image, sworn to prove
How men excel as Amazons the sweet,
Long-haired, pearl-tinctured fighters. You grow white?
Must a Gargarean[35] in your armour seem
So monstrous to your eyes? Hippolyta!
You swoon, faint-heart!

Marcia   No, loose me! By the girdle
Of Mars, I warn you from such insult: none
But women can display the moon-shaped shield.
Who was it, tell me, robbed Hippolyta
Of Mavors' belt? Great Hercules, my god,
My genius and my heavenly prototype.
You make a vain appeal, O warrior-love!
An insult: when the Emperor of the world
Wears in the world's eye everything that decks you
At your most perfect moments; when he vaunts
His singleness of worship by the choice
Of your attire for clothing; when he stands
Like some high peak in snow and steely ice,
A masquerading granite. Folia, there,
If you would 'scape a spear-prick for your sloth,
Search out the moon-shaped shield I bade you borrow
From the Lady Marcia's armoury.

Exit **Folia**.

Marcia   My lord,
You ever have been noble, and with honour,
All undeserved, have crowned me in the sight

---

34 Mars, god of war.
35 All-male tribe of warriors. Amazonian women met with them once a year to propagate bloodlines.

Of Rome and of the empire. See, 'tis I,
No Amazon, implores you to accord
Still that same honour to your handmaid, still
That deep-endearing courtesy. This garb
Is but disguise, an actor's make-belief
To give you private pleasure: such disguise
As Love for lovers puts on trustfully.
The Amazon is Amazon to you,
Not to the world, the gladiators' gaze,
Or the arena's laughter.

Commodus You are thankless,
Most dangerous to yourself in words like these;
A thing to be distrusted and abased.
Presumptuous woman, I have honoured you
By giving you the purple that I wear,
Hanging you with the jewels I have warmed
In triumphs and solemnities; no touch
Of royalty that gilds me but on you
It has been laid: and now when I assume
Your raiment, your short tunic, crescent-shield,
And manly cap of steel, you round your lips
On such a word as 'insult'. When by combats
Of valour with my compeers of the sword
I seek to make your dress invincible,
And in your guise receive the plaudits due
To mastery, you, whom I raise to heaven,
Cringe and implore retirement and neglect,
Or with indifference mock my love, allowing
The charm with which you sway it is a lie.
If you are not Hippolyta indeed,
As I am Hercules on current coin,
In everlasting marble; if your mind
Can make no truth of life's vacuity,
Basing its shadows on the strength of dream,
And filling them voluptuously with life-blood
Of riotous belief, then . . . .
                              But your face
Is dazzlingly an Amazon's.

Folia *brings him the armour.*

Commodus The shield,
The cap! I am the champion of this rage.
You fire me to exceed it. Arms, to arms!
That all may see you triumph. Amazon,
Your Amazonius!
                    Nay, you will not kiss!

A combat must be won, then lips shall clash;
You scorn unwarlike softness.

Eclectus   Sire, I ask,
As from an oracle, will Rome revere
An Emperor turned a woman?

Commodus   Hercules
Sits with the gods; he dressed as Omphale.

Eclectus   The theatres gibe him.

Marcia   Women laugh at him.

Commodus   They laugh – you say it! And to honour you
I took your male caparison, for love
Of your enchanting image, for the pastime
Of making it death-dealing. It is found
A feminine disguise, a harlot's prank,
Proud Marcia playing pantomime.
                                    You laugh,
You, from your womanhood; but I will drag
This dress of yours across such infamy
As you will recognise. What women dare
In secret, and their lovers hide shame-faced,
I will expose. My Amazon grows grave:
At least no laughter from these lips! Ho, girls,
Unmask your mistress, set her in your midst
In veils and scarves, a flaunting concubine.

Exit.

Marcia *fixes her eyes on* **Eclectus**, *meeting his. The women do not move.*

Marcia   Go, Folia, fetch me from the Emperor's chamber
His purple toga.

She sinks down on a couch.

Folia   Oh, I dare not, queen,
I dare not enter.

Jallia   I will fetch the cloak!

Exit.

Marcia (*as* **Sagana** *and* **Folia** *withdraw*)   The others slink away.
Eclectus!

Eclectus   Love!
You rise as to a call.

Marcia (*she comes to him*)   You can forgive
Even this disguise?

Eclectus   Even this.

Jallia *returns*.

Marcia   Brave Jallia, thanks.
Sweep it around me, sweep it round my knees,
Across my breast and shoulder. Let me kiss you,
That you refused even once to touch these weapons,
This fooling tunic.

Jallia   It was wickedness
To wear such garments, vile, idolatrous,
Displeasing to our God.

Enter **Pylades**.

Marcia   Oh, gently, child!
You should be gentle – happy, safe and tethered
In the green pasture.
Pylades!

Pylades   You start?
Empress, it is the hour you promised me
An hour ago; you said you needed practice
In the carriage of your spear; you would be ready,
Clad as Hippolyta. These trailing robes –

Marcia   I count my best possession. Come no more.

Pylades   In what have I offended?

Marcia   Go, my mood
Is bitter and unjust.

Pylades   You banish me!
But if you snatch from me each day's one hour,
If you will never come, nor lend a glow
To the story of my feet, nor sometimes laugh
As when you made me happy . . .

Marcia   Hush, you know
I love your dancing.

Pylades   But you shared it, queen;
It sprang from your white feet like flaming fire,
It wreathed your limbs, it made you in yourself
Free as the pliant stars and musical
As they in their continuance. One by one,
You were all highest goddesses that dance:
Hera the Queen, Demeter noble-browed,
Athena with severest cadence moving,

And heavenly Aphrodite, soft as ocean[36]
In step, with windy sweep of golden Loves
Round every measure.
                              All that I record
Is what you flashed or wove across my eyes.
I cannot dream a goddess or a nymph,
Or any woman; you have made a pyre
Of dim imaginations, you who are
The fearful, bright and whole reality.

Eclectus (*to* **Marcia**)   You scared your women; you are softness now
To the sly slave who drew you to his mimes:
You love his dancing – ay, and to Infernus
Would follow him, clear-hearted, jig on jig!
(*To* **Pylades**.) Begone!

Pylades   You know me of the Emperor's train,
Chosen to attend him.

Eclectus   Where? To the arena,
To bathe his wounds if he exceed his godhead,
And angry swordsmen mutiny! Begone.

Pylades   Then to the Emperor's rooms, where, chamberlain,
You know you cannot flout me. But not there,
Unless –
(*To* **Marcia**.) It is your pleasure.

Marcia   Bid farewell.

Pylades   Some mocking cloud is on me from the gods,
Not my true patroness. I never bid
Farewell to any shape of loveliness
In vision or on earth: there, I am free.

He takes up **Marcia**'*s spear and shield.*

Pylades   Your shield, your spear! Now you are left defenceless;
You will not conquer, woman with no arts,
And so no armour! Vale!

Exit into the imperial bedchamber.

Eclectus   Insolence!
How vile! He treats you – but it is no matter
For my concern,
Except that by that madman, that Secutor,
That Hercules to match your Amazon,

---

36 Hera, queen of the Olympian gods and goddess of marriage, women and family; Demeter, goddess of
    the harvest; Athena, goddess of war and wisdom; Aphrodite, goddess of amorous love and beauty.

I am (*with a laugh*) not trusted, but the single creature
He would not err in trusting; – chamberlain,
And guardian of his honour. Promise me
To court that wretched pantomime no more.
Burn up the clothes, take off that brutal casque.
No vestige of him!

Marcia   For the Emperor's sake
I put this armour on: some make-believe
Must be where women strive. I strive no more.
I am defenceless; I shall cast away
The tunic, all the legend.

She gives her helmet to **Jallia** *and dismisses her.*

Marcia   O Eclectus,
Put off your jealous anger, put it off,
For it may ruin, and it severs us.

Eclectus   Are we not severed?

Marcia   But if destiny
Grants us no further blessing, if the answer
To our dark prayers be this, I am content
To breathe with you, to share the mystery
Of fate, to part my thought with you as bread,
To lie in the dark of human ignorance,
Warm in the wraps of love. When souls are bound
In such inextricable unity
Death fumbles at the knot.

Eclectus   Oh, hush! My dumbness
Cannot break through at once. My love, my secret,
I think you have been with me in each barque
My soul has steered through Time; yet, agony!
I never may possess you.

Marcia   But the joy
Is mine of living to you as the grape
Lives to the sun, not to the gatherer.

Voices are heard.

Laetus (*within*)   The deed will cost your life.

Re-enter **Commodus** *with* **Laetus**.

Commodus   Eclectus, send
The furniture of the imperial bed,
The bed and all an emperor's state requires
To the gladiators' school: for I will seal

The year's commencement with a wondrous vision
To hold men's lids apart, while Rome herself
Shall quake from Capitol to Vale, beholding
Her lord ride forth from those forbidden portals,
As Hercules climbed up from Hell's own door.

Eclectus   You will be slain. If once the crowd admits
An insult it is unrelinquishing
Till the offender perish. Have you thought,
O Emperor, what your deed would violate
The omens of the year, the holiness,
The honour of your office, of the world,
Yea, of the gods.

Laetus   For you would show yourself
As if you lived in infamy among
The ever-infamous, the dregs and scum
Of serfdom and captivity.

Commodus   O fools,
What am I to my people? Magistrate?
The first Augustus laughs. Or general?
Vespasian, Hadrian and Titus wink
Across their armies.[37] If I claimed a crown
As poet, dancer, singer, I must stoop
To Nero's coronation. There and there
And there, I am not perfectly divine:
But each togated soul that claps the games,
And every swordsman from the fiercest stress
Of battle, every artist rich in lust
To feel the clang of metal start his brain,
Holds me supreme in the arena, perfect,
Miraculous, invincible.

Marcia   He raves
Dark-sighted, god-bedazzled! Commodus,
I do not doubt you; I would spur you on
To brave Hyrcanian tigers.[38] All you will
Is yours: in this the gods do not oppose you;
That is so terrible! In their contempt
The gods do not oppose. You will go down
And face the Senate; Janus will be there,
And tremble at his office to present
To Time this masking figure of a Power

---

37 Notable emperors of the ancient Roman world.

38 Extinct sub-species also known as the Caspian tiger, known for its ferocity. The chariot of Bacchus was drawn by tamed Hyrcanian tigers.

So awful. . . .
(*Turning to* **Eclectus**.) What were Egypt's mummied kings,
Their statues and their tombs to the quick Cæsar,
Who passes to Olympus' feasts as simply
As an invited guest. I see you fall,
And stoop and stain your majesty. You shall not.
I do not kneel, I do not flatter you;
I am your empress in my urgency,
I am your empress, for I love your honour
Far dearer than my life. You shall not go.

She guards the portal. **Commodus** *lays his hand on his Amazon spear;* **Laetus** *and*
Eclectus *range themselves by* **Marcia** *to protect her.*

Commodus   You shall not go! By heaven, I am no god
To you . . . You are no Amazon to me;
A servant tricked out in her master's robes,
A mere false-seeming, a deception, lost
To poetry and the truth persuasion rears
Among the blossoms of the rose to forge us
Belief as stout as mail. How women kill!
Cool things, damp airs! No banquetings of men,
No festivals of gods, no marriages
Of god and mortal but a woman's coldness
Can freeze blank-dead.
                    No Amazon to me!
All dreams are at an end; the world, that farce
Of dancing leaves, that fancied atellan[39]
Is breaking into nothing. Fertile Powers,
That picture forth the universe, I share
Your aim – to plant the void; but I alone
Of all the tribe of earth can neighbour you
In palpable ambition.
                    Triple band
Of enemies, Eclectus, Laetus, you,
My empress and my Omphale, my love,
The mistress of her master and the tyrant
Of the world's bosom . . . hence! You are as vain
As fraudulent as all things, and as worthy
Destruction at my hand. Ha, ha! Begone!
You disobey . . .
Fear to withstand my actual demon. Go!

Marcia (*moving from the portal*)   Nay, pass my lord, pass to your destiny:
I stand aside.

---

39 Atellan: an ancient masked farce originating in Italy.

Commodus   These are your apprehensions,
You hollow wanton! So you give your blood
To fortify my honour. Oh, the phrases
These shadows wear as garments! Now I see
From hill-top into valley of your fraud.
Traitress, conspirator with him and him,
The concubine of both for all I know,
For all I care. No protest!
(*To* **Eclectus**.) Take your serpent,
And hide her from the eagle of the world,
And the rushing of his feathers.

Eclectus   He is mad!
Marcia, this moment I command you, come!

Laetus *covers their exit.*

Laetus   Your will shall be accomplished in all points,
Your chamber furnished at the school, your horses
Led down, your fatal body-guard prepared.
All that your anxious ministers can do
To keep you sacred from the touch of harm
Shall zealously be done with many prayers.

Commodus   Ha, ha! With many prayers!

Laetus, *with a reverence, goes out.*

Commodus   Are you within,
My hyacinth-blossom, Philocommodus?
I hear your feet.

Re-enter **Pylades**.

Pylades   My Emperor.

Commodus   Fetch the tablet
I laid beside my couch.

Exit **Pylades** *within.*

Commodus   O treacherous spawn!
Marcia the chief, as she held foremost place
When I was mad, who now am mad no longer,
When I, who now can love no more, once loved:
Next, her protector, the rose-red Egyptian,
Who stood so ornamental in white robes,
I made him dear to me, and then that oily,
Most Roman Laetus . . .

Re-enter **Pylades**, *as he gives the scroll* **Commodus** *kisses him.*

Commodus   Ah, the linden-bark.

He writes, then turns suddenly to **Pylades**.

Commodus   Pigeon, you know the slave that yesterday
Heated my bath too hot?

Pylades   Diodotus.

Commodus (*writing again*)   But you are white and trembling. Pass within!
Yet first a word, my Philocommodus.
If your remembrance hold a thought of him
Who called you Pylades, I reckon you
My Anteros,[40] and on the wheel or cross,
Or by long, undeforming punishments,
Shall teach you love by hate. Go, smoothe my pillow.

Exit **Pylades** *within.*

Commodus   All old-year shadows, all should end like days,
Like hours, like moments that are stale and crumble
In urns or men's oblivion. Marcia, Marcia!
But, when my sister failed, I was a fool
To build myself upon a concubine.
A fool, I am a fool, a sight for gods
To thunder at with gross hilarity.
I am no son of heavenly Jupiter!
See, see! O mirror of myself!

He faces a gold mirror that reflects at the same time a head of Marcus Aurelius.

Heap up
The jest, ye Plautus-powers,[41] mirth-makers! See,
The statue of my father, our two faces,
Our bland and indistinguishable faces,
Set cheek by jowl – in marble one, in flesh
The other, yet self-same – our curls, our lids,
Smooth skin, caressing beards, and fatuous,
Tired smile at all that is not vanity.
O husband of Faustina and the father
Of Commodus! O good philosopher,
To whom the generations were as leaves,
And all that he begot and all his fame,
And all he loved and hated leaves of spring
Consigned in birth to autumn! Such is he.
Now rate his son, his double, from the womb
Of the famed harlot, whom in appetence
He set his eyes and heart on thirty years;

40 God of requited love.
41 Early Roman playwright (254–184 BC).

His son, the hated of the world, the hater
Of every vain allurement that his lust
Takes without relish, Commodus the sceptic
Of every faculty but sense alone,
Its truth of touch, sight, hearing, and their orgies
Of blood and lewdness! Judgment! Shouting Heavens,
The verdict of your laughter!
                                        Is there substance
In what we each call void – fame, propagation,
Toil, common joys? Is there in hollowness
Some jet of sap we heard not? No, today
Marcia has put suspicion of a virtue
In anything to shame. If I should die
She has so wrought I should be simply dead.
Tiber flows insignificant, yon fig-tree
Stands dark upon the cliff: all's outer show,
And there is nothing I can own or covet,
I who awakened, as the light, all life,
In this once copious universe. Ye twain
Athwart the gold, what desert in your eyes,
And ignorance how mortal! Worshippers
Of harlots, son and father, so disgust
Crashes farewell to both. A parricide,
Self-murderer too!

He dashes the gold mirror to the ground.
                                  And now for rest, for wine,
The blood of sleep, and Lethe, that is sleep's
White flesh, forgetfulness. My linden-scroll,
Companion of my pillow!

He lays his cheek on it.
                          Sleep, sleep, sleep!

He staggers into the bed-chamber.

Act Four

A Court of the Regia: wings of the royal palaces to right and left, surrounded by a portico that continues along a terrace at the back, commanding through the columns a view of the Capitol and part of the Roman Forum. It is a starry night. Bands of slaves with torches, crowns of flowers and instruments, followed by dancing-girls and beautiful cup-bearers enter the house on the left, but after a while return and hang about the portico.

Eclectus *enters from the house on the right.*

Eclectus   Shall I dismiss the troop, or let them tarry,
Vain garlands on the night? Our feast is made;
The Emperor lies oblivious.

Glaphyrus (*at a distance*)   Does he come,
Our Hercules?

Annia (*approaching*)   What news, grave chamberlain?
'Tis noised he will salute the Roman year
An outcast, such as we.

Eclectus   It needs your lips,
Wanton, to breathe such sacrilege.

Glaphyrus   Ah, ah!
As we!

Mneme and Others   As we!

Eclectus   But, silence! – or you go,
The bevy of you, to sharp punishment.

They shrink back; a shape joins them.

Who comes?

Glaphyrus   My lord, it is Aurelius Ilyx
To wrestle with Narcissus.

Enter **Narcissus**.

Narcissus   I believed
The banquet done, the violet-liquors tasted,
My match with Ilyx close.

Eclectus   So spectrelike
Grows the long preparation hour by hour
For one that does not come! Ilyx, Narcissus,
Go up into the Emperor's ante-room;
He is besotted and may need your help
To reach the feast, (*apart*) and she is there alone.
I send a guard.

Exit **Narcissus** *and* **Ilyx** *to the right; the revellers laugh together and sing low in the distance.* **Eclectus**, *left alone, turns to Orion.*

Eclectus   Star of Osiris,[42] hear!
Fix the great gulf of inability
Between my heart and hope. There is no peace
Like that when hope is exorcised, no guilt
Like that if hope be treason. Pure, white way
Of stars above my head, along such path
I would attain my happiness! Yet even
The stars involve me in disloyalty,
Seeming to promise what I most desire.

Enter **Marcia** *down the steps to the right, leading the dwarf* **Gabba**.

Eclectus   Marcia, I pace this threshold at your will.
Give me command.

Marcia   From Chaos I am come,
And in despair.

Eclectus   Shall I dismiss that troop?

Marcia   Oh, nothing may be done.

Eclectus   The Emperor sleeps?

Marcia   With brutal interlude. Take Gabba off;
He is a child and helpless.

Eclectus *leads the dwarf to the portico and returns.*

Eclectus   You look weary.

Marcia   The din of the arena in my ears.

Eclectus   Then he is mad?

Marcia   No, for his head is pillowed. He lies a victim,
Bewildered by the gods – So Pylades
Interprets, so it seems.

Eclectus   The pantomime
Is then your fellow-watcher?

Marcia   Tricked as Paris,
Waiting to dance. O gods, what do we wait?
What is the issue? Is that city Rome?
(*Rubbing her eyes.*) If I could sleep a little!

Eclectus   I will watch.

Marcia   Here, at the threshold.

---

42 Ancient Egyptian god of fertility and ruler of the dead.

Eclectus   I am chamberlain.

Marcia   And I . . . Oh, leave these titles!

Exit.

Eclectus   How forlorn
She passes from me; yet this faithfulness
To the great injured madness that we serve
Imprints me hers for ever.
                              Will he waken?
Will he go down to yonder prison-house?
The night is drawing closer.
(*With a gesture of imprecation toward the valley.*) O that spot!
I dread it as a tomb. My Emperor there,
Facing the light
Of time and in futurity's fresh dew!
Something will intercept. It is forbidden
That this law-guarded city, built so slow,
Encrusted with such dust, hoarding such treasure,
Should be so rifled of itself and by
Its inmate and its god.

Enter **Pylades** *from the right.*

Eclectus   What, Pylades!
Why comes this dizened pantomime to me?
Your business?

Pylades (*giving a scroll*)   Take this – read!

Eclectus   The Emperor's tablet!

Pylades   I found it lying open by his pillow,
Left in forgetful blindness.

Eclectus   And he calls you
His Philocommodus! Take back the scroll
You filched from him, the private commentary
He makes on each day's circumstance. Begone!

He tosses the scroll back.

Pylades   You will not read, you will not take this knowledge.
Fool, I would have you perish, ah, how gladly
Would see you caught in trammels of this gin.
But Marcia! – the swift loss of her! Oh, listen!
You will not read? Then hear! The letters flame
Scarlet before my eyes.
                              'Marcia' – attend!
Her name is first – 'then Laetus, then Eclectus

Shall die to-night, together with the slave
That yesterday heated my bath too hot'.

Eclectus   Give me the scroll.

Pylades   I bear it on to Laetus;
So she commanded. Will you still demur?
Within an hour . . . Do you not feel the peril?
My lord will wake with all this unfulfilled,
This desperate, lurking malice in his heart;
And cowering slaves beside him at his motion
Ready to draw caged tigers to his couch,
That emptying his fury he may sleep.
Will you . . . But listen! When she read her name
She covered up her face – thus! – while her tears
Brushed past the single ruby on her hand,
That from its burning dumbness sought to bring
Such passion to the birth as in her blood
Swooned and was secret. Suddenly she read
The tablet further: on the battlefield
Of her wan face peace fell like that the moon
Pours on the angry faces of the dead,
To reconcile them to their new estate
Of unabating quietness. She stretched
The tablet toward me. 'Bear it to Eclectus,
And afterward to Laetus.' Then she turned:
I left her brooding on the Emperor's face
With wide, undizzied eyes.

Eclectus   There, take my cloak;
You are half-naked, tremble.

Pylades   As I am
For swifter speeding.

Eclectus *runs up the steps to the right. The revellers from the portico surround*
Pylades *and hang on him.*

Annia   Philocommodus!
A lovely Paris, with his Phrygian breeches,
His jewelled ankles, naked, jewelled chest,
And shining mitre; eyes like precious stones,
And hair – Apollo's, when he hid his darts
In his own fleecy locks.

Glaphyrus   But mark Rome's dancer
A cheek like asphodel; a love-sick heart.
Which of our girls has struck the shepherd-boy
With such white pallor? Mneme, Annia?

Annia   Nay,
Only the fragrant wives of senators
Can win a glance from Philocommodus;
Or else the concubine of highest fortune;
Fame is so choice.

Pylades   Loose me! I bear a message.
The Emperor's mood is threatening.

Annia   Is he ill?

Mneme   Or angry? Will he give some dread command
Of massacre or torment?

Pylades   None can tell
What may be done to-night or who escape,
If thus you mob me and delay the fleetness
That is alone obedience to his will.

Mneme   A lie, a lie! The Emperor is asleep,
By yonder quietness over all the house.
You would escape us, proud, mendacious boy!

Annia   Well, if you will not give us smiles, nor words
Of kindness, nor a dance, nor rosy kiss,
You might remember that my throat is bare
Of ornament, my bosom has no gems,
Though white as yours – and softer.

Mneme   You are lavish:
And a few stones are nothing from your wealth.
'Tis such religion to adore you now
Your shrine is always loaded.

Pylades   Will you leave me,
At your own price, these jewels?

Mneme   Will we go?
Yes, Venus' body, if you give us these.

Pylades (*breaking the string of jewels hanging across his chest*)   There, take
them all.

Mneme   The torches to the ground!
What sapphires! O the blue stars of the sky,
I coveted – now won!

Annia   And this dew-diamond!
Not yours, 'tis mine.

Mneme   No, mine.

Exit **Pylades**.

Gabba   High Jove, 'tis mine.

Mneme   You bunch of roots, no human thing at all,
You claim a jewel, you who have no hands!

Gabba   I want it all the more, as you will want
A lover when your teeth and hair are gone.
Ha, ha! Your teeth and hair!

Annia   A canticle,
To drive the time along! And Glaphyrus
Shall blow his pipe.

Gabba   Then sing the famous hunt
Of Calydon,[43] sing how they tracked the boar,
One man and woman, dooming him to death,
One woman, Atalanta.[44]

Glaphyrus (*holding out a castanet to* **Mneme**)   Beat the time.

Canticum   Within Arcadia, green and lovely land
The Calydonian boar
Ravaged: he trod the grapes
Of summer into wine,
He shook the trees of leaves, he fouled the streams,
He spoiled the silver fields
Of harvest and the golden fields of corn,
Sprang on the quiet herd
And sleeping sheep, soothed by the rough-hewn pipe
Of shepherd from the thyme:
Arcadia, ruined by this only foe,
Was no more green and fair.
But Meleager came from Calydon,
A hero, doughty-armed,
And with him Atalanta, huntress white,
With quiver-parted breasts.
Among the woods they ran,
And found the boar stretched in terrific sleep.
Aroused, he headlong fled
In lurid panic through obstructing trees,
That stood as to avenge
Their savage usage on their flying foe:
Motionless hunters, they

---

43 Ancient Aetolian city. Home to the Calydonian boar – not to be confused with the Erymanthian boar
     (see n. 28) – that was hunted by several heroes in ancient Greek mythology, including Meleager.
44 Mythological heroine who won the hide of the Calydonian boar (see n. 43).

Helped in his death: the maiden's hurtling spear
Struck and her lover's slew.

Gabba   They struck, they slew . . . .

Enter **Marcia** *with* **Eclectus**.

Marcia   Go silently away,
All ye that wait the Emperor. He must sleep.
Disperse your watch, he will not come to-night.
I bid you hence.

Eclectus (*apart*)   Her voice as from the moon
Falls and enlarges solitude. The troop
Of feasters soon will fade.

Voices   We go, we go!

Annia (*in a whisper*)   My castanets!

Mneme   My garland!
(*With a smothered laugh.*) Ilyx, hush,
Be gentle! Glaphyrus no more descants
Breeze-murmurs on his flute.

Gabba   Good-night! No dreams.
Blest Emperor, no bad dreams!

They all disappear with their torches. **Marcia** *and* **Eclectus** *stand together in the night.*

Marcia   The fair-crowned train, the jugglers, the musicians,
His court of beauty, how it passes careless
From dread allegiance into night again.
His pleasures flow away and his life's fashion
Seeks its eclipse and quits him. Is my breath
Destruction? Ah, I grow too terrible
In judgment. God and Time alone should sweep
Existence to the void, a man's past days
And those he has provided for. The deed
We wait to do is tamer sacrilege
Than this we have accomplished – to enforce
That trooping off of strength and gaiety
And shame and all he loves: the rest is compassed
By undiverted purpose.

Eclectus   Cling to that.

Marcia   'Tis not from you, I must not learn from you
What shall sustain the hour. Be still, or speak
Of Laetus and his peril, of Narcissus
You won to stay and aid us. But be still.

I think it is enough to hear the sky:
Its darkness sounds and does not start the brain,
Nor set it wincing.
(*She gazes up, her hand against her lips.*) Ha, upon my finger
A touch of honey! I can taste it, clean,
Sweet honey from the cup I have just mixed.
Honey! You must not listen. Every word
You let me utter is a throe, a weakness.
Where's Laetus?
                    Are you weeping?

She pulls his robe from **Eclectus'** *face.*

Eclectus   No, the stars
Are gone, that's all; the pure, white way of stars.
Can you not let me be! Why should we trouble
To ask each other questions, while the heavens
Are baffling us with sorrow. Come within.

Marcia (*restraining him*)   Not there: You must not pass.

Eclectus *turns back into the shadow, remains motionless and again covers his face.*

Marcia   I am deserted,
Left with these murder-hands he cannot touch.
But yet, if I desist, we join the shadows
That flaunt across the void. Why should I fear
To take another name of infamy?
For him, for safety of that bowed, black head,
I will be bold, I will bear anything,
Even his eyes when afterward . . .

Enter **Laetus**, *followed by* **Pylades**.

Marcia   O Laetus!
Good Laetus comes, alert to save himself.
Here's courage, here's the aptitude!
(*Motioning to* **Laetus**.) To me!
I thank you for your promptness.

Laetus   What is done?
How would you meet this sudden treachery?

Marcia   We have command of the whole house. Go forward!
We must not linger. You shall hear our purpose;
It lies as clear before me as a vision
I have but to obey.

Eclectus (*suddenly turning to* **Laetus**)   The chamberlain
Must lead you to his bed.

Marcia   You keep your office,

You cling to duty as it were a chain:
You cannot know all things are in their season
Most holy, incorrupt.

Eclectus   Give me the torch.

Marcia, there is no haste; we could confer,
For if his sleep have changed him . . .

Marcia   Nothing changes
Nor sleep, nor death, nor passing of the years.

She beckons them to enter before her. Turning, she faces the night.

One breath of darkness, there! I have no need
Of the approving stars.
I drink the night's cool force, while life and death
Are moving far beneath me. Oh, this air!

She goes in.

Pylades   What is it she invokes? They pass within;
They are all there, and I am left without,
A pantomime before cloaked Thanatos.
O horrible!
And, oh, most false! Tricked in these gauds as Paris,
I am a pantomime. But there, to him,
Beneath his godlike breathing, I was simply
The lad, the flower. I did not dance to him;
Unmasked and moving up and down the room
I served him and he rested in my motions,
My patron and my god. What have I done?
I am not Hyacinthus any more,
Nor any more beloved. What have I done?
I have betrayed him, and it is my blow;
From me, his Philocommodus, he falls.
. . . Oh, I am winter-cold! It was not thus
I felt in acting, never thus. My patron!
I hate that they should lay him in the dust,
Choke the warm voice for ever. No more praise,
No godlike dances, no more make-believe
That there are heroes in our midst, no gods:
There, there – and all the garlands dropping off!

Exit within.

*The darkness has now become complete. For a long interval a soundless hush. Then a single slave with a horn-lantern comes out, followed by **Narcissus**, and slaves bearing furniture and rolls of carpet from the palace on the right. **Pylades** follows them. They disappear and the track of the lantern is lost. Again it is dark night. Gradually the burthen of the darkness is lifted, and through thinning obscurity voices are heard.*

First Voice   He has departed where he would. 'Tis time
To follow down the cliff. Come, chamberlain,
You must arouse our Emperor from his sleep,
True to your office – ha!

Laughter is heard.

A second fall!
Cling to the rock, and caution!

Voice (*within*)   Pylades!

Second Voice   I cannot thread this darkness, and beside,
You hear, she calls us.

First Voice   Leave the concubine; Rome calls.
You have the tablet in your bosom?
Coming at such an hour . . .

Voice (*within*)   Stay, Pylades,
I cannot be alone, you must not leave me.
Narcissus, Pylades!

First Voice   Ho, ho! I say,
Coming at such an hour, he well may think . . .
Where are you groping to?

Second Voice   The light has stirred
Behind that cloud. I would not look at it
Unless I have a patron I can serve
In the unknown wastes of Time.

First Voice   But dawn is come.
Hail the New Year.

Second Voice   No, straight to Pertinax.

*There is unbroken silence; gradually the greyness becomes lighter, the columns loom,
and through them the city appears softly wreathed by fillets of mist.* **Marcia** *comes
from the Palace and moves to the extreme verge of the terrace.*

Marcia   They should not all have left me in the darkness,
As though I had no purpose any more.
I grow a ghost and as a ghost most restless
To mingle with the living. In the room
They left me with his gladiator's masque,
And all his rich array. I tried to call them;
I could not, for there were so many names,
And one I must not utter. Pylades
Wept when he helped to muffle him. I think
That I was glad to see him weep; my heart
Was beating like a little shaken dust

Because he had no mourner. All the slaves
Shrank back, but one took up the poison-bowl,
And washed it clean and put it in its place . . .
It was his favourite bowl.
                              Come back to me,
Eclectus, come!
                    But I must recollect
That he will visit Pertinax, the palace
Must not be empty; all the little round
Of rule and riot must begin again.
So great is my accomplishing, almost
It seems as there were nothing more to do,
And I would journey very far away.
Ah, but my lover would not! Men so cling
To circumstance, when a great deed is wrought,
They creep about it and with gradual change
Add to it and destroy. But nothing matters
That may befall me now, if I may hear
My name set in his voice, no other word,
My name, and a great fondness.

Re-enter **Narcissus**.

Marcia   You return?
You shall not haunt the palace. And your hands.
It chokes my breath to see them.

Narcissus   He is laid
Among our own, among the athletes, proud
He should be of his burial.

Marcia   He strove:
You did not kill at once.

Narcissus   I struck him down
Before your eyes and in their lustre.

Marcia   Hence,
And hide your face!

Narcissus (*pointing down the valley*)   Why, do you stare so hard
Over our field, our portion? Hecate,
Would you dwell near the murdered blood!

Marcia   There, there,
Within that fort. . . . I must look down on it –
There, when they roll the heavy carpets out,
He will be found. His visage always faded
To half-obliteration when he slept.
He will be found, the golden curls pressed flat,

The gilded dust spilt in the weft and woof
Of the heavy wrappings. How he looked at me!
What glazed, disconsolate and patient eyes
He lifted as he drank the poison-cup! And then your hands. . . .

O Christ, be pitiful!

Narcissus   Do you invoke your God? He was the victim
Of Roman soldiers: step by step they slew.

Marcia   The darkness of that Majesty! Begone!

Exit **Narcissus**.

Marcia   O Christ, belovèd, if I might have taken
Thy body from the cross and washed it clean
And wrapped it in pure linen, I am made
For such low offices and so I love.
Jesu, I do not know Thee any more
After thy burial: but thy blood, thy shame,
Thou meek, unutterable God! I worship,
I never can forsake Thee. Was the valley
Like that, and then the little hill? How wide
The dawn of the New Year, how wide the light!

Re-enter **Eclectus**.

Eclectus   Marcia!

Marcia   Belovèd!

Eclectus   Oh, I thought you worshipped.
I would not come between.

Marcia   You beckoned me,
You called me and to hail with you the light.

Eclectus   O Erebus, I do not know your gods,
Or what you worship: they are men, are outcasts,
They never have been kings.

Marcia   I hail the light;
I turn to Janus and his dozen altars,
I turn to all his months, to all his years.
I do not tremble in this magnitude
Of sweetness: all I wrought was in the name
Of the great darkness that brings forth the sun.

Eclectus   I cannot argue. I have seen his body –
I have to tell you that; 'tis wrung from me
By torture. They had dragged him with a hook.
The Senators had kept him thus exposed
As carrion on the air, but Pertinax

Shed tears and bade that they should bury him
As the good Emperor's son. And after that
The streets grew quieter; a change was shed
Over men's faces. I was born to serve:
Marcia, and I will serve him to the end.

Marcia   Ay, the new Emperor?

Eclectus   Will you murder me –
As you have murdered. . . .

Marcia   Yes, my Emperor,
Mine on the coins for ever. He is gone.

Eclectus   He writ our fates together on one scroll,
And all his writing was a prophecy.
(*Seizing her hand.*) Where shall we go? When last you took my hand
You led me to his bed; but I have left him
Couched yonder in the valley.

Marcia   He is gone.

Eclectus   O Marcia, but you are a concubine:
You have seen many pass –
They pass before you as the leaves. My heart
Was fixed on him.

Marcia   Would I were in the valley!

Eclectus   With him? Ah, would we were! That is our place.
We have no season in the coming time,
And Janus close the past!

Marcia   Nay, we were lovers
In that old time.

Eclectus   Then Janus close the past.

He strikes his forehead on their clasped hands.

The End.

The Orgy: A Dramatic Poem

Lesya Ukrainka (1913)

Translated by Vera Rich

Lesya Ukrainka (pseudonym of Larysa Petrivna Kosach, 1871–1913) was a Ukrainian playwright, poet, prose writer, translator, publicist and political activist, who lived during the decline of Russian Empire. She witnessed the reign of the last Romanov emperor, Nicholas II (1894–1917) and the numerous strikes of the workers in Russia, as well as the Russian Revolution of 1905. Despite being a 'prisonnière russe' (Russian prisoner),[1] subjugated to Russia's colonial and oppressive politics, she continued to promote Ukrainian culture and write in Ukrainian. Her pseudonym, 'Ukrainka', the word for a Ukrainian woman, manifests her commitment to a gendered, artistic and national identity and throughout her life she was a staunch believer in her country's freedom, working with her brother Mykhaylo to promote Ukrainian literature and translate foreign classics into Ukrainian. Versed in several European languages (French, German, Italian, Polish), she translated the works of a number of European decadent writers, including Maurice Maeterlinck, Edmondo De Amicis, Gerhart Hauptmann, Stanisław Przybyszewski and Gabriele D'Annunzio, but as a feminist she was critical of the decadent patriarchy, particularly the depiction of women in French decadent literature who never seemed to rise above their stereotypes as either muses or whores: 'The decadents of the Baudelaire school continued the same old game: from the pedestal to the mud, from the mud to the pedestal . . .'.[2]

Like Michael Field, who used their verse dramas as vehicles for associating the past and the present, Ukrainka transformed Ukrainian literature by expanding its range to include a whole array of characters from classical mythology, scripture and world literature, both classical and contemporary, 'depict[ing] the acute social problems of contemporary life by means of familiar historical or legendary figures'.[3] Ukrainka's engagement with decadence, however, was as a writer working in an imperial-colonial context outside of the metropolitan centres of Paris and London. Reading her work in translation (we reprint Vera Rich's translation of *The Orgy* (*Orgiya*) for this volume), we come to understand that while the origins of decadence lie in late antiquity, the tradition was also shaped by modern colonial empires. Ukrainka's play is set in ancient Rome but it is principally concerned with late nineteenth-century Ukraine. As Constantine Bida attests, '[a]lthough her heroes have their origins in the ancient history of Babylon, Egypt, Greece and Rome, or in the medieval Roman world as well as in the period of American colonization and the French Revolution, she never wrote a genuine historical drama'.[4]

From 1901 until her death, and inspired by Alfred de Musset's use of the name *poème dramatique* for some of his dramatized poems, Ukrainka wrote ten dramatic poems, a genre that she introduced into Ukrainian literature. The play selected for this volume, *The Orgy*, is the last dramatic poem that she wrote, which she started in Kutaisi, Georgia in the summer of 1912 and completed while wintering in Egypt in 1912–13.

---

1   Lesya Ukrainka, 'La voix d'une prisonnière russe', in Lesya Ukrainka, *Povne akademichne zibrannia tvoriv u 14-ty tomakh,* vol. 7 (Literary-Critical and Publicist Articles) (Lutsk: Volynskyi natsionalnyi universytet Lesi Ukrainky, 2021), 397–9.

2   Lesya Ukrainka, 'New Perspectives and Old Shadows ('New Woman' of Western Europe Fiction)', in *Povne akademichne zibrannia tvoriv u 14-ty tomakh,* 120.

3   *Lesya Ukrainka: Life and Work by Constantine Bida. Selected Works, translated by Vera Rich* (Toronto: University of Toronto Press, 1968), 46.

4   *Lesya Ukrainka,* 46.

The play is set in the second century AD and is composed of two acts, the first set in the house of the Corinthian bard Anteus during the Roman domination over Hellas, and the second in Maecenas' mansion where he arranges a banquet at which is discussed the relationship of Greek and Latin languages and culture and the problem of Roman domination over the Greeks. As Bida comments, the play's principal preoccupation is with the decline of national culture, '[t]he problem of art in the life of an artist and of a nation and its significance for the nation'[5] and the distinction between the hero and true artist (Anteus) and the artist who surrenders everything for self-advancement and whose aesthetic ideals do not involve loyalty to his nation (Chilon). The play is an anti-colonial allegory for Ukraine's subjugation to Russia. Status-seekers like Chilon and Phaedon are rebuked by Anteus for committing treason against the national culture; they symbolise all those writers and artists who surrendered their national culture and rejected their native language as soon as Ukraine lost its independence.

The degeneration of Ukrainian culture never ceased to be an anxious concern for Ukrainka. In a letter to her brother, written in Berlin in 1891, she wrote:

> Never and nowhere did I feel so acutely how burdensome it is to be under the yoke. [. . .] I do not recall whether I ever experienced such difficult, unbearable and bitter desires as here in the free world. It affected me so often . . . that one can notice on my hands and neck the red traces of the yoke and the chains. Everybody sees these traces and I am ashamed before the free world.[6]

---

5   *Lesya Ukrainka*, 82
6   Yakubs'ky, 'Orgiya', *Tvory Les'I Ukrainky*, III, XI, quoted in Bida and Rich, *Lesya Ukrainka*, 84.

Characters

Anteus, *a singer*
Hermione, *his mother*
Euphrosyne, *his sister*
Nerissa, *his wife*
Chilon, *his pupil*
Phaedon, *a sculptor*
Maecenas, *a rich well-known Roman, a descendant of the famous Maecenas, the Prefect*
Atriensius, *a slave*
The Procurator
Guests at the orgy, slaves, slave girls, dancers, mimes, chorus of panegyrists

Place

The action takes place at Corinth under Roman rule.

Act One

The garden in the home of the poet and singer **Anteus**, *not very large, surrounded by walls with a gate in one wall; at the back of the garden a house with a portico in four columns and with two doors, one leading to the andronitis and the other to the gynaecium.* **Hermione**, *the mother of* **Anteus**, *sits on the threshold of the gynaecium, spinning. Knocking is heard at the gate.*

Hermione (*without getting up*)   Who's there?

Chilon (*outside the gate*)   It's Chilon Alcmeonides.

Hermione (*calls in the direction of the other door*)   Anteus, come out! A student's here to see you.

She remains sitting, but pulls her veil a little closer.

Anteus (*young, but of manly appearance, enters through the door and opens the gate to* **Chilon**)   Today, Chilon, you have come much too late. The students have all gone.

Chilon (*a very young lad, he speaks pantingly and with some embarrassment*)   Excuse me, but . . . But actually I have not come to study. . . .

Anteus (*pleasantly*)   Then be a guest.

He sits down on a bench under a tree and indicates to **Chilon** *the place beside him, but* **Chilon** *remains standing.*

Anteus   Why not sit down?

Chilon   I've business. . . .

Anteus   Is it so urgent that you can't sit down?

Chilon   It isn't that . . . but . . . please excuse me . . . I
Today must thank you for your teaching . . . I
Shall not come any more.

Anteus   Why? (**Chilon** *is silent.*)
It is true,
It's not for me to question you this way.
Evidently I did not satisfy
You with my teaching. So, no shame to you –
For it is I who ought to be ashamed.

Chilon (*earnestly*)   No, no, my master. Do not think this way.
Apollo be my judge, that I respect
This teaching like the Sacred Mystery!

Anteus   Then I don't understand.
(*He stops, then clasps his hand to his forehead.*) Ah, yes, of course.

(*He, too, is evidently embarrassed.*) Listen, Chilon . . . I'm prepared to wait
Until you've finished all my course of teaching.
Indeed I'd rather take no fees at all
From you, if that is causing difficulty.

Chilon   But, master, you are not a wealthy man.

Anteus   Chilon, I shall tell you all in truth –
Although you are still young to hear such things
But explanations otherwise come hard. . . .
Song, speech and music are my pay, you see,
And I place higher value on my art
Than on the money that it brings me in.
I have not taught talent to anyone,
Nor shall I – for the god alone can give it –
So, when instructing ordinary people,
Who never felt Apollo's sacred hand,
I teach them how to find a little pleasure,
How to pluck the strings in harmony
And to express their thoughts somewhat more clearly;
Then they pay to me a little money
And the account is settled. If the god
Sends to me a young man he has chosen,
For me to aid with my experience,
And I perceive that every lifeless form
Which I expound to him, once it becomes
Familiar to him sudden springs to life,
And the young genius in the ancient form
Resounds and sparkles with its own clear radiance
Like young wine in a goblet of old crystal,
Then I'm already paid in full, No, more –
I even feel some guilt, since I'm not able
To serve him as I'd like. You understand, now?

Chilon   Master . . .

He cannot speak for emotion, he hangs his head and covers his eyes with his hand.

Anteus   When your genius has surpassed
All of the forms and all the learning which
I possess and can impart, then, lad,
By all means leave me, I myself advise you,
But only, for the sake of Lord Apollo,
Still do not give up learning. Go to Athens,
There you will find teaching that's far, far better,
Than any we can offer here in Corinth.
And then when you have finished all the schools
Still go on studying, find yourself teaching
In books and people and in all the world,

But never, never tell yourself, 'Now I
Have finished all my learning.'

Chilon   This advice,
Master, gives me renewed courage. I
Assure you, I shall not be giving up
All learning, though now I am leaving you,
I'm going to study in the school . . . (*He is silent again.*)

Anteus   Which one?

Chilon   The one Maecenas has established here.

Anteus   Latin?

Chilon   Well, everything is Latin now.

Anteus   What's that? Have you and I, our native language
As well, all turned to Latin?

Chilon   Well, I meant
Roman, of course. I just mistook the word.

Anteus   If you've still not learned properly from me
How to avoid mistakes, in that new school
For certain there'll be still more such mistakes.
But I do not know what it is you'll gain there
Besides mistakes. In Latin poetry
I myself have taught you, probably
Everything that's really worth one's learning –
I do not think the rhetors in that school
Can give you anything that's new, for I
Know them too well. Indeed I think that you
Could teach them even now.

Chilon   I am quite certain
The teachers there can equal you in nothing
At all. But none the less, I am still forced
To go to them.

Anteus   What, then, is forcing you?

Chilon   Master, if I should stay with you, then I
Would become similar in fate to you.

Anteus   And for what reason does this fate alarm you?
Am I then the lowest among singers?

Chilon   Not among singers, no . . .

Anteus   But among people?

Chilon   I did not say so, but it still is true,
That in society you cannot find

The place that's truly fitting to your talent.

Anteus   But how will you prevent this happening
When you have finished at Maecenas' school?

Chilon   I may become a rhetor in this school,
And then in an academy somewhere.
Or I shall go to Rome. Conditions there
Are very favourable towards the pupils
Of this Maecenas. Still his family holds
The power they wielded in the Augustan age.
But in the meantime while I'm yet a student
I still can join the choir of panegyrists
Of Maecenas . . .

Anteus (*jumping up in rage*)   You? You're going to enter
The choir of panegyrists? Join that mob
Of traitors, wicked sinners against talent?
O, it were better to be dumb forever
Cut off your hands, grow deaf, than fall so low,
And this was once my best, my finest pupil.

A pause.

Chilon   Master, then receive my grateful thanks.

He takes some money from his pouch and gives it to **Anteus**.

Anteus (*waving him away*)   Go! I have taught you nothing! Get away
Out of my sight!

Exit **Chilon**, *hanging his head.*

Hermione   Anteus, and you didn't
Accept his money. Yet his father's richer,
A hundred times than we are. Willy-nilly
It's still your rightful earnings.

Anteus   Mother dear,
I have earned nothing but the bitterest shame.

Hermione   There is no cause that you should feel ashamed,
Except for throwing out to the four winds
Your hard-earned wages. In the end, my son
We'll come down to the bread of poverty.
Will it be right to you, when all your poor
Family must go and beg for alms
From these same Romans whom you hate so much?

Anteus   We have sufficient bread yet of our own,
Do not offend the gods.

Hermione   This is their will!

Certainly Aphrodite wished it thus
That I, not a rich daughter-in-law but
The daughter of a dancing girl, a slave
Was forced to welcome . . .

Anteus   Still no end of nagging?

Hermione   It isn't nagging, son, just the plain truth.
Didn't you pay, as price for your Nerissa,
All that your father left you, and a good
Slice of your salary?

Anteus   But do not blame
Just Aphrodite. All the gods of Hellas
Wished that I should buy out from slavery
A little child of the Hellenic race
It could have been your daughter, my dear sister
Who'd fallen into slavery.

Hermione   My son,
At least that isn't added to our troubles!
We have been able to buy out Nerissa.
But there's the dowry for Euphrosyne,
We can't provide one. Is it better
To be an old maid than to be a slave?

Anteus   My sister, without dowry is worth more
Than all the rich men's daughters.

Hermione   But who knows it?
At home with us she's not like Roman girls
Who wander everywhere. She's always in
The gynaeceum[7] and at work. And if
She goes out for a festival, the way
She dresses, nobody would notice her.

Euphrosyne *appears at the doorway of the gynaeceum, but* **Hermione** *does not notice her and goes on.*

Hermione   Nerissa always gets herself up well, Euphrosyne won't even wear one ribbon.

Euphrosyne (*young, but not girlish, wearing an everyday dress, she seems to be in the middle of her work. She bows, then embraces her mother*)   But mother dearest!
What's the good of ribbons
If one has beauty, what need to adorn it?
If one has not, a ribbon will not help.

Smiling she kisses her mother, then stands up straight.

---

7   Women's private quarters in a Roman household.

Mother, how am I to dress the pigeons?
I've finished boiling them.

Hermione (*standing up*)   No, leave them, leave them
I'd better do it, you don't know the way.

She hurries into the house.

Euphrosyne (*going to* **Anteus** *and putting her hand on his shoulder*)   Dearest
brother, why are you so gloomy?
Was mother going on at you again?
Don't pay attention – that's old people's way.

Anteus (*replying not immediately, as though he has not heard what she said.
After a pause his words come out as though involuntarily*)   Chilon has got ahead
of me.

Euphrosyne (*surprised*)   What way?

Anteus   He's going to join the choir of panegyrists.

Euphrosyne   What are you saying?

For a moment she is silent from surprise and anger. Then she collects herself.

Well, I'm not surprised,
His kind is always flighty.

Anteus   But in talent
Strangely enough, he far surpassed the others.

Euphrosyne   It seems to me, though, that Appollodorus
Who fled to you from the school of Maecenas
Surpassed that self-same Chilon in his talent,
Not only in intelligence. I've heard
How he can render the great speech of Haemon
From the *Antigone*[8] – indeed I could
Only just about hold back my tears.

Anteus (*with a gentle smile, putting his arm round his sister's shoulders*)   For you
yourself are my Antigone
It seems that I could even forgive Chilon,
If what he did he had done to relieve
A sister such as mine from bitter hardship.

Euphrosyne   But I would never forgive such a sister.

Anteus   Oh, you would not accept the sacrifice
Nor any other. But my dearest sister,
If I should wish for riches, it would be
For your sake, yours alone.

---

8   In Sophocles' play, Haemon implores Creon to forego his wrath by embracing change and rescinding
    his condemnation of Antigone.

Euphrosyne   And all in vain
Because I do not want it. (*Smiling.*) Mother'd quickly
Go and buy me a husband. That would be
Quite certainly a most disastrous purchase.

Anteus   All right, not wealth! But if I only could
Save you from miseries.

Euphrosyne   From miseries?
Where do you see such things?

Anteus   That I *don't* see them
Is due to you, my dear, and you alone . . .

Euphrosyne   And mother and Nerissa. . . .

Anteus   No, you know
That mother now has finished all her work
While our Nerissa . . .

Euphrosyne   Ought to start her work.
Is life in truth so sweet to you, that even
A honeymoon is something you find needless?

Anteus   I am ashamed, enjoying happiness,
When I remember that you pay for it
By your hard work. We have our happiness
But what, in the house of your birth, have you?

Euphrosyne   I have a brother. Even if forever
I live in spinsterhood, yet I shall never
Envy any wives or happy mothers
For their love serves only their families
But mine is for all Hellas. For in you
Anteus, is all our hope.

Anteus   Euphrosyne
How is it possible to place all hope
Upon one person?

Euphrosyne   Out of all the gods
Only Apollo has not ceased to love
Hellas, and in her there's still hope of life.
And while Apollo's reigning on Parnassus
The Muses will be there.

Anteus (*with a smile*)   Not without fame
Am I, with none but you to give me triumphs
For you are my true Nike![9]

---

9   Goddess, servant of Athena, and the embodiment of victory.

Euphrosyne   Nike must
Know how to do her duty. Wait a moment.

She breaks off two branches from a laurel bush, joins them into a wreath and steps on to the base of a column in the pose of the goddess of Victory, Nike stretching out her hand with the wreath.

And now, come over here! Bend your proud brow!

Anteus *approaches, smiling all the time, and bends his head in front of* **Euphrosyne**. *She smiling, and with tears of sincere emotion, puts the laurel wreath on her brother's head.*

Nerissa (*young, straight, very dainty, prettily dressed, stands on the threshold of the gynaeceum*)   What's all this?

Euphrosyne, *embarrassed, jumps down from the base of the column.*

Anteus   It is Nike who has crowned
Her poet. And when, also, Charis[10] will
Give him a pomegranate or a rose
Then he will be endowed with everything
That is right for mortal man to wish for.

Euphrosyne (*feeling somewhat ill at ease under* **Nerissa***'s cold looks*)   Roses are
flowering over there . . . (*To* **Anteus**.) But Nike
Has to go to the kitchen to help mother,
Because today we shall have a real orgy
We've bought some fish, and auntie's given us
Some good wine and a pair of pigeons, too.
And when I've baked some honey cakes, then even
Maecenas well might envy us our orgy.

With a somewhat forced smile she disappears through the doors of the gynaeceum.

Nerissa   Euphrosyne's a strange girl, always joking!

Anteus   Well, she is young. . . .

Takes off the laurels from his head, holding them in his hand. As he speaks he sits down and puts the laurels on the bench beside him.

Nerissa   But probably I'm younger
Although . . .

Anteus   Although 'moody from time to time'
You wanted to say that.

Smiling he embraces her. She receives his caresses with some reserve.

Anteus   Why what's the matter?
Are you not well, or has someone upset you?

---

10 One of the Graces and associated with kindness and benevolence.

Nerissa   But don't you really know? Why all the neighbours
Must long ago have learned by heart the speech
About my ransom and Euphrosyne's
Dowry, which mother trots out every day.

Anteus   What, every day?

Nerissa   Yes, it's the very truth.
I can no longer look Euphrosyne
Straight in the face.

Anteus   But dear Euphrosyne
Doesn't blame you for anything.

Nerissa   I know.
She isn't your Antigone in vain.

Anteus   Nerissa dearest. It is really naughty
To eavesdrop, and then put the blame on others.

Nerissa   Eavesdrop indeed! This isn't such a palace
That you can't hear all that goes on in it!

Anteus (*roused a little*)   Only the Romans now own palaces.
You'd have done better, then, to wed Maecenas.

Nerissa (*gentler than before*)   I am not blaming you for being poor
But doesn't every woman really wish
That wealth and riches may come to her husband?

Anteus   Yes, and to her as well!

Nerissa   To her as well.
Is that a crime? I certainly was not
Born to walk all day long beneath a yoke
Just as your sister does.

Anteus   Well, but you don't.

Nerissa   D'you think it's any easier for me?

Anteus   If it weren't easier, you'd work as well!

Nerissa   People have slaves to do the work.

Anteus   Nerissa,
It's somewhat strange to hear you speak this way.

Nerissa   Because I was a slave myself, you mean?
Well, I could earn my living, too, in freedom
If only you would give me your permission.
Since now there's nobody who wants me here,
I'm in the way, like a high, awkward threshold,
And you're to blame for that.

Anteus   Well, dear, enough . . .

Nerissa   Why not let me go to the theatre,
I shall adorn your sister with bright gold
And be a darling daughter to your mother
For certainly I can earn more by dancing
Than you by song and teaching ever can.

Anteus   Nerissa, stop! It is your grief that's speaking.
And, surely, I'm to blame for that. Forgive me

Kisses her. She bends toward him like a sulky child.

Anteus   My dearest one! My treasure! I'll not give,
I shall not give you to the shameless crowd.
You shall not go to them, to their false orgies
For the crowd does not know what's a true
Holy orgy, that divine creation.

Nerissa   Have you been to an orgy?

Anteus   Long ago,
When I was still a lad, there was still in Corinth
A bard's hetaireia, secret, of course
For any kind of guild must be a crime
To Roman minds.[11]

Nerissa   Well then? Were your orgies
Very luxurious?

Anteus   You just consider!
We would all meet together in a house
Like this of mine.

Nerissa (*surprised*)   Ah, so. . . .

Anteus   And in our goblets
The water always dominated wine.
We only could have Bowers in the seasons
When they are blossoming in field and garden,
But when Persephone to Tartarus
Returned, she robbed us of all decorations.[12]

Nerissa   Can orgies really happen without Bowers?

Anteus   We had them and they were exuberant.

---

11 Hetairoi: upper-class Grecian men, sometimes associated with the formation of guilds – though more
   usually with military, political or social functions. Hetaereia (or hetaireia) is therefore taken to refer to
   military bodyguards.
12 Tartarus is an abyssal place of judgement for the dead. Persephone was the queen of the underworld,
   and embodied springtide and the growth of vegetation.

Nerissa   But they took place quite secretly you say?
Then how were these exuberant orgies not
Heard in the street outside?

Anteus   Could people hear
From outside how our hearts were beating in us
Or could the light from fervent glances pierce
Through the stone walls and the thick draperies?

Nerissa   But what about your songs?

Anteus   Oh they were strong
In their inspiration, not in sound,
And in the muffled sobbing of quiet strings
We could hear the storms and tempests which
Were nurtured deep within the singer's breast.
We had wild curls, and they, like thyrsi,[13] called
Exclaiming to the sight 'Evoe, Bacche!'
And even if the goblets only held
Pure water, yet we still would go home drunk.
O how I've wished that you just once could be
At such an orgy. In the holy frenzy
You would dance, indeed, like a true maenad.

Nerissa   I have been to orgies many times.

Anteus   But not like these!

Nerissa   Maybe to better ones!

Anteus   That is not possible!

Nerissa   I do not know
What yours were like, but these to which I went
Often when I was still a little girl,
They were like carefree dreams.

Anteus   It's very wrong
To take a child along to such an orgy.

Nerissa   My mother *had* to take me there.

Anteus   I know.
Forgive me, I was speaking thoughtlessly.
I should have realised how heavily
The heart of a poor dancing girl must beat
When she is forced to take her only daughter,
A little girl still half in babyhood
To such a shameful spectacle.

---

13 Ornamental spear associated with Bacchus.

Nerissa   My mother
Never told me anything of this.
I always went off to the orgy gladly,
There I could eat my fill of dainty tit-bits,
And sometimes toys would come my way because
The guests would make a fuss of me.

Anteus   Don't think
Of it. I'm shivering at the idea. . . .
All this fussing was, for certain, dirty
And every word they spoke was soaked in filth.

Nerissa   I don't know. Then I didn't understand
Either dirty talk or shameless glances.
But even when still small I understood
Beauty, my heart beat faster from their praise,
As a lyre string does, touched by the plectrum.
On the high stage, the two of us appeared
Like two rainbows, one large and one small
On the bright highlands. The transparent veils
Brilliant with colours in the light-curved bow
Were spread across the cloudlets of the gold
And fragrant dust clouds. Then it seemed to me
That I was truly dancing in the clouds
Of heaven, and from the earth there came
Only bright blossoms winging up to me.
It was the guests who threw their flowers to us,
Carried away with passionate delight.

Anteus   But in these flowers, there hid, unseen, the cold
Serpent of debauchery and disgrace.

Nerissa   But I tell you that I did not know this!

Anteus   But still you do not know how Romans treat
The hapless dancing girls who are their slaves.
Do not forget what would become of you,
If you had grown up amid such orgies.
Remember what became of your
Poor mother who perished like a broken, cast-off toy,
In illness, in neglect and base contempt.

Nerissa   I recollect that I owe you my thanks.
Do not be afraid, I shan't forget!

Anteus   Nerissa, is this really necessary?

Nerissa   No, no, it is my duty to remember
That you have made into a human being
'The little monkey from Tanagra.'

Anteus   Stop!
I do not like it when you speak this way.
And I cannot stand the common nickname
That the vulgar Romans used to give
To a fair and dainty child of Hellas.
They were just jealous that their Roman women
Were heavy and ungraceful beside you
My fair Nerissa 'of the breeze-light foot'.

Nerissa (*thoughtfully*)   And what is that to me, now?

Anteus   What, my dear?

Nerissa   That 'breeze-light footedness' you speak about . . .
I'm not a dancer now.

Anteus   What's that, Nerissa?
Do you really not enjoy the praise,
Mine, and our friends' praise, modest but sincere.
Is it not enough to be at home
A hidden treasure, but a jewel so dear
That even Caesar cannot have a better.

Nerissa   'A hidden treasure' – I will tell you truly
That I am more sincere than you. You also
Are a hidden treasure, but I, Anteus,
Do not rejoice to know that your sweet lyre
Is not heard by the whole wide world, but only
By me and by a small group of your friends.
No! If I had the power, myself I would
Place you upon a lofty pedestal
Like the statue of Apollo-the-Cytharist,[14]
Then let the world be filled with the sweet songs
Which you would create up there on high.

Anteus   Do you think perhaps, that inspiration
Can raise me up more than a pedestal?

Nerissa   O yes, I'm certain of it!

Anteus   Still a child! . . .
But if you are so fond of pedestals
Then be content, for our friend Phaedon has
Carved in your image a Terpsichore,[15]
Set on a pedestal that's high enough.

Nerissa   And what is Phaedon doing with the statue?

---

14 Bronze statue of the god Apollo currently held at the Museo archeologico nazionale di Napoli in Italy.
15 Goddess of dance and chorus; one of the nine muses.

Anteus   Bringing it here.

Nerissa   And leaving it?

Anteus   Of course.
It's a friendly gift to us from Phaedon. (*A pause.*)
You're very quiet as if you're worrying.
What is it, my Nerissa?

Nerissa   I am thinking
How many 'hidden treasures' more will be
Hid in this house as in a mausoleum.

Anteus   I do not like to hear such words from you.

Nerissa   Well, when the stone Terpsichore arrives
Then I shall take from her the role of silence.

Anteus   Nerissa, you have freakish moods today.

Nerissa   In that case I shall go!

She gets up.

Anteus (*restraining her*)   No, no, my dearest!

Nerissa (*pulling away*)   Let me go!

Knocking is heard at the gate.

Look, someone has come to see you.

Nerissa *goes to the gynaeceum.* **Anteus** *opens the gate, and lets in* **Phaedon**, *a young sculptor.*

Anteus   Greetings, Phaedon!

They clasp hands.

Phaedon   I've just got a moment.
No time to stop.

Anteus   Why? Have you got some work?

Phaedon   No, I have finished work for the time being.
But now I have new worries. I am going
To a lord's orgy at Maecenas' mansion.

Anteus (*surprised*)   Were you invited?

Phaedon   Yes, and you as well.

Anteus   You're joking, or else fooling?

Phaedon   It's the truth
I tell you. I just dropped in to pass on
The invitation.

Anteus   Who gave it to you?

Phaedon   When I was with Maecenas I received it.

Anteus   You were with Maecenas? Why?

Phaedon   On business.
And d'you know, I never could have hoped
He was like that.

Anteus   Like what?

Phaedon   So cordial
And it's surprising that a great lord speaks
Like that. . . .

Anteus   And what is it that's so surprising?
That an all-powerful lord lets on his threshold
A lowly artist? Or that the fact,
Perhaps, that sometimes, too, a Roman knows
A little of fine art?

Phaedon   Oh, not 'a little'
He's a great connoisseur, a really true one.
He was the one that first valued your work.

Anteus   He was the first one? But I had a school
Long before Maecenas came to Corinth.

Phaedon   What is a school? The school is to your glory
Like a clay patera[16] is to a sculptor.

Anteus   It must have been something like to glory
Since this fine lord heard something about me.

Phaedon   To tell the truth it was blind chance that gave
Him news of you. One of your pupils came
Wanting to join the panegyrists' choir
And giving an example of his skill
He sang your epithalamy,[17] the same
One that you composed for your own wedding.

Anteus *makes a movement of disgust, but* **Phaedon**, *not noticing it, continues.*

Phaedon   I started a discussion with Maecenas
About the song, and then I told him who
The author was, and straightway he told me
To come and to invite you to his orgy.
And this indeed, means something, my dear friend!

---

16 A shallow ornamental bowl associated with libations.
17 Poem written for a bride anticipating the marital chamber.

Anteus (*restraining the annoyance caused by* **Phaedon**'s *last remark*)   Whatever
business could you have with him?

Phaedon   He bought a statue from me, not long back,
And I went to deliver it to him
Because the slaves might damage it in transit.

Anteus   What was the statue that you sold to him?

Phaedon   Forgive me . . . I ought really to have asked
For your consent. . . . But mighty lords don't like
To have to wait for things . . .

Anteus   You sold Nerissa?

Phaedon   A statue of Terpsichore, the goddess.

Anteus   If you knew how, you'd sell the goddess, too.
Into a Roman house of prostitution!

Phaedon (*getting up, offended*)   You have no right to speak to me like that!

Anteus   Certainly you will not like this insult
For you have sold your best work there, where all
That's holy to us is despised, derided.

Phaedon (*interrupting*)   Nobody there despises anything.
There genius is prized, there glory given,
Not only money. I did not betray
My dear Terpsichore, I only placed her
As in a temple, for men's admiration,
Is she, maybe, too holy for a temple
In your opinion?

Anteus   In my opinion, you
Blaspheme, to call that Roman's house a temple.
You sold yourself – for money or for glory
Together with your handiwork.

Phaedon   O Anteus!
You want to work me up so that I go
And buy the statue back again. For love
Or money it is quite impossible
Maecenas does not sell the things he buys.
But maybe that was not my final spark
Of inspiration. Maybe I'll be able
To create something better, and exchange it.

Anteus   You'll just exchange sin for a far worse sin.

Phaedon   I can't see what it is you want of me!
Am I, like you, to sit out all my years
With neither bread nor glory.

Anteus   It is right
Hellenes should suffer thus, if bread and glory
Can only be obtained from Roman hands.

Phaedon   No Hellene, he, who does not wish for glory.
Our fathers have bequeathed this yearning to us,
It is our grandsires' heritage.

Anteus   Our grandsires
From Mother Hellas' hands received their garlands,
Our fathers, though, allowed her hands to be
Fettered, and this deprived their sons of garlands.
So, Phaedon, since Hellas herself has no
Glory, Hellenes are obliged to bury
Deep in their hearts their yearning after glory.

Phaedon   And thus increase their country's lack of glory?
How may Hellas herself be glorified
When her children win no laurels for her?

Anteus   But not accept them from an enemy!

Phaedon   Why not? Homer himself said, 'Sweet the praise
Won from a foeman.'

Anteus   On the field of war
Not in captivity!

Phaedon   But glory's glory
Too, in captivity.

Anteus   Do not hope it!
They will allow us to bear our inglory
But Rome takes all the glory as her due,
And that Terpsichore which you have sold
Brings glory not to Hellas nor to you.
But to rich Rome that gathered all the treasures
From all lands, by the hands of that Maecenas.
Your work will give glory to his creation
But not to you, for you are but the slave
Whose skill adorns an orgy for the lords,
That orgy will always remain the lords'
Although it is the slaves' hands that prepare it.

Phaedon   For slaves there is no honour in an orgy.
But those who are invited there as guests
As you and I are . . .

Anteus   Do not hope for this
That I shall go with you to the orgy!
You seek the favours of the mighty ones,

But I'll remain 'with neither bread nor glory'
As you said, but maybe not without honour.

Phaedon   In all sincerity, I beg you: go.

Anteus   Indeed. For oxen bear the yoke far better
In pairs.

Phaedon   I plainly see you don't believe
That I can wish only what's best for you,
But yet although you've wounded me intensely
I still have not forgotten we are friends.

Anteus   What, I have wounded you and not you me?

Phaedon   See, Anteus, I'll buy back Terpsichore.
But you will not take back your wounding words.

Anteus   But you cannot buy back what you have done.
You put your art to shame, you made a goddess
Into a piece of mundane merchandise.
Even if out of slavery returns
Terpsichore – she'll be no more a goddess,
The marble not divine but a simple stone.

Phaedon   If it was once divine, then it will never
Turn back to simple stone, a work of art
Will be, no matter where, a work of art.
Your lovely epithalamy resounded
No worse there in the spacious Roman school
Than here at home in your poor narrow house,
If only you would sing it for yourself
There in the echoing palace of Maecenas
Accompanying it on a rich harp.

Anteus   Phaedon, please do not say such things to me,
For, if you do, forever I shall hate you.

Phaedon   Anteus, this is some strange obstinacy.
It's not the first time Hellenes have received
Foreigners' praise; what is disgraceful in it?

Anteus   Foreigners! Yes, but never conquerors,
For conquerors only have praise to give
When the conquered stoops and bends his brow,
Before him, and kisses the very dust
Beneath his feet

Phaedon   It was so with the Persians,
And the barbarians from the East. But never
Was it demanded of us by a Roman.

Anteus   Was not demanded of us? Who, then, stepped

Upon us, as upon a bridge to reach
The temple of the universal glory.
Whom did we, from barbarity's abyss
Bear to the height? Did we not lay ourselves
As cornerstone for our conquerors' mausoleum
And we have to rejoice that we can go
Into their vast and echoing palaces
And play a tune upon a plundered lyre?

Phaedon   Would it be better if the lyre were silent?

Anteus   Better, indeed.

Phaedon   I think it worse, however,
It is far better to build mausoleums
Even if not for us, rather than be
Like the wayside plants beneath the feet
Of conquerors. The conqueror, if he wishes,
With his armed foot can quickly trample down
All our pride with our headstrong dreams. . . .

Anteus   What? Better that we trample it ourselves
So as to save the conquerors some work?
Does the high priest of beauty think and speak so?
Only one thing is left, that he should act so.
You have not sold yourself – still worse! You gave
Yourself, like wet clay into foeman's hands.
And who will breathe in you the living fire
When you're no more creator, but created.
Go and serve your dear Maecenas, then,
Forget the mighty testaments of beauty,
Forget the deathless image of Prometheus,
Warrior against the gods, forget the torment
Of truth's great champion, Laocoön,
Do not recall Antigone the heroic,
Electra the avenger. From your thoughts,
Cast Hellas out, like chained Andromeda
Cast out to feed the monster, wearily
Awaiting Perseus who will rescue her.[18]
You are not Perseus, it is you who turned
To stone before the glance of Rome's Medusa.

---

18 These are all references to mythological heroes who defied the gods and rulers: Prometheus stole fire
(as a symbol of civilisation) from the gods for the benefit of humanity; Laocoön tried to convince the
Trojans to burn the wooden horse that sealed their fate, and was unjustly tormented by the gods as a
consequence; Antigone defied Creon's order for her brother's corpse to be desecrated; Electra helped to
avenge the murder of her father Agamemnon at the hands of her mother Clytemnestra and stepfather
Aegisthus; and Andromeda, chained to a rock as a sacrifice to Cetus, an oceanic embodiment of divine
wrath, whose will is defied by her saviour Perseus.

You do not recollect the higher beauty,
Beauty of contest, even without hope.

Phaedon   No beauty lives in powerless obstinacy,
But I see that I cannot speak to you
Of this. Goodbye. I'll go now.

Anteus   Farewell Phaedon.

Phaedon   Are we parting, then no longer friends?

Anteus   I fear that we may meet as enemies.

Exit **Phaedon** *shrugging his shoulders.*

Nerissa (*coming out of the gynaeceum as soon as* **Phaedon** *has gone*)   Anteus, I
simply cannot understand you,
Why were you so harsh to Phaedon, how
Is he so guilty?

Anteus   Eavesdropping again?
In that case you should have paid more attention.
You have realised, perhaps, your image
Will stand there as a spectacle of shame
Set in the mansion of a conqueror.

Nerissa   What spectacle of shame? What conqueror?
Is this Maecenas guilty that his grandsire,
Or maybe his great-grandsire fought the Hellenes?
Now, too, Maecenas does not take away
Our treasures or our works of art by force.
He purchases them, for a good price, too.

Anteus   He pays in gold that's gathered in for Rome
From the conquered, namely, we ourselves.

Nerissa   Maecenas does not gather it himself,
Your father, after all, left you some money
You didn't ask who got it nor what way.

Anteus   I know it was acquired quite honourably.

Nerissa   Maecenas certainly must think the same
About his patrimony. He returns
A certain part of it to us, to Hellas,
And yet for this he's your worst enemy.
In your opinion, it would be the best
If all our works of art were lost in corners,
If artists lost their skill and power through hunger,
If moss grew on the marble, rust on harp strings,
If Hellenes would become barbarians
Lest they should serve the Romans in some way.

Anteus   There are enough to serve them, I shall not.

Nerissa   But no one is demanding service from you.
Has Maecenas hurt you by inviting
You to his reception through a friend?

Anteus   Reception? Do you still think that Maecenas
Would invite a singer to his orgy
Just to have a friendly conversation,
And not to sing to entertain the guests.

Nerissa   And what if you did sing a little there,
Your songs have been heard in that house already.

Anteus   Well, that's no fault of mine.

Nerissa   Yes, it's your 'fault'
You gave your pupils songs to copy out.
That means that you yourself have sent them out
Into the world. And that a Roman valued
These songs more highly than your countrymen
Is normal. Blame Maecenas, if you like!
In Hellas, now, he, only he, is famous
Who has been praised by Rome, and Corinth values
Her singer only when she's losing him.
If you went to Rome, though, with Maecenas,
And gained the triumph you deserve so well –
Because Rome knows how talents should be crowned –
When you came back to Corinth afterwards
Your native laurels would be spread before you
Like primroses in spring, beneath your feet.

Anteus   I do not wish to trample native laurels.
Triumphs in Rome would seem disgrace to me.

Nerissa   What are you waiting for?

Anteus   For recognition
In my own land, unhelped by conqueror's grace.

Nerissa   When will that happen? When your life is over?
Posthumous glory is the usual gift
For singers like yourself. But while they live
There is none to hear them, none to see them.
As if they are deep buried in a grave.
Plunging themselves deep in their thoughts and dreams
Such singers stay, unmoving in one place,
While over them rushes, impetuous,
The coloured Bacchanalia of life
And throws its flowers and laurel leaves to him
Who best knows how to catch them in their flight,

For such as you only the faded leaves
Are left, only the funeral wreaths remain.
Do you think that you will vanquish Rome
By such a tomb-like immobility.
If I were you I would shine forth resplendent
With your bright genius and that of Hellas,
I would rule triumphant on all stages,
Would take by storm forums and porticos
Until my name had quite blocked out the sound
Of Caesar's name. Ah, that indeed would be
True victory.

Anteus   And everyone would say:
'What splendid bards our Rome is buying now!
Hellas has quite declined into her dotage.'

He takes **Euphrosyne**'s *laurel wreath into his hand.*

Anteus   See, Nerissa, this one wreath alone
I gained in all my life, but it is dearer
Than all the triumphs which you praise so much.
If wreaths like this are called funereal
Then let death come as quickly as he will.

He puts the wreath on his head with a proud quiet smile.

Nerissa   Anteus, listen for I can no longer
Bear this. One may choke and suffocate
In the tomb-like air of this close house.
You or I must go out in the world.
I love you so much that I can agree
To live upon your glory, but I cannot
Live without glory of any kind
I am a Hellene.

Anteus   And you want to win
This glory among Romans.

Nerissa   Among Romans
Or others, it is all the same. I need
Glory, like bread, water or air. If you
Cannot provide me this necessity, then I shall go
To win it for myself, I do not want
To die for lack of it. I am still young.

Anteus   And by what method will you gain this glory?

Nerissa   The same as you, by practising my art.

Anteus   You still want to go back upon the stage?
(*After a pause.*) Well, Nerissa, I shall tell you truly

If you are not called by a vain whim
But by the muse Terpsichore, I shall not
Dare to argue with the goddess. Maybe
You can in truth bring back to life for Corinth
The holy mystery of Dionysus.

Nerissa   O, not for Corinth, no, do not think that!
I am not tempted by Corinthian praise.
Maybe Nerissa living will outweigh
The stone Terpsichore Maecenas has,
When she today will dance for him in person
The dances of Tanagra.[19]

Anteus   Are you raving?

Nerissa   No, I am not in frenzy yet.

Anteus   You cannot
Go to the orgy.

Nerissa   And why can't I go?
The Roman women can go everywhere,
Why can we not follow their example?
I'll go and say 'My husband is unwell,
But so as not to disappoint Maecenas
He sent me, being his wife, to the reception!'

Anteus   You shall not go there!

Nerissa   Will you lock me in?
Then I indeed shall know with certainty,
That you have bought me into slavery.
Yet sometimes even slave women escape.
Put not your trust in your strong locks.

Anteus   Nerissa!

Nerissa   What is your will, my lord? (*A pause.*)
Decide it now.
Either it's you or I.

Anteus   O, if I had
The power to tear you clear out of my heart
And cast you, like a venomous reptile under
The Roman's feet!

Nerissa (*with a short petulant laugh*)   You cannot do it, then?
Well, then, you must give in. Maybe one day
You yourself will thank me for it. I

---

19 Grecian town, also called Poemandria. Its principal temple honoured Dionysus.

Shall not go back on what I said. If not
You, then I shall go and gain some glory,
Yes, and today; I've waited long enough.

Anteus (*after a heavy silence*)   Yes, I shall go. I shall be better off
Among the Romans than home here with you.

Nerissa   Go then. But first take off those silly twigs
From off your head – you're not going like that?

Anteus *puts his hand to his head, takes off the laurels, looks at them sadly, and puts them where* **Euphrosyne** *stood when she crowned him.*

Euphrosyne (*from the depths of the house*)   Nerissa! Call to Anteus! Come and dine!
The lavish orgy is all ready now!

Anteus *quickly runs to the gate.*

Nerissa (*catching him up*)   Where are you off to, then? You must get changed.

Anteus   Let me go. Euphrosyne will come
And I'll not dare to look her in the eyes.

He runs out of the gate.

Euphrosyne (*coming through the door*)   Where's Anteus, then?

Nerissa   He's gone off to the orgy.
He had an invitation from Maecenas.

Euphrosyne   Your sense of humour's odd!

Nerissa   I am not joking
See, there the faded household laurels lie,
Today he will bring fresh ones home to us
Received from connoisseurs.

Holding her head high, she goes into the house.

Euphrosyne (*clasping her head*)   Can this be true?

Act Two

In the house of **Maecenas**, *a descendant of the famous* **Maecenas** *who lived in the time of Augustus. A large, sumptuous reception room decorated for the orgy, divided by an arch into two unequal parts. In the first, smaller part (in the foreground) is arranged a triclinium[20] for the host* **Maecenas** *and his two guests of honour – the* **Procurator** *and the* **Prefect**. *A low dais has been set up, covered with carpets, for the performances of singers, mimes, and other artists; in the other larger part, at the back, there are many tables surrounded either by couches in the Turkish fashion or benches in the Roman fashion, where guests of different types and ages, both Greeks and Romans, are sitting and reclining. The banquet has only just started and is going very dully, apparently because the guests hardly know each other, and feel ill at ease under the gaze of the triclinium of honour in the front part of the room. On the dais, a* **Choir of Panegyrists**, *among them* **Chilon**, *is ending its song.*

Choir (*singing*)   Light out of Light
    Nascent forever,
    So the illustrious
    House of Maecenas,
    From ray to ray shining
    Flows forth its ever
    Radiant light.

When the choir finishes singing, **Maecenas** *inclines his head to the coryphaeus[21] and makes a movement with his hand neither exactly directing nor inviting the members of the* **Choir** *to take their places at the banquet in the back part of the reception room. The* **Choir** *take their places at the furthest tables at the very back. Slaves are serving drinks and dainties. Slave girls distribute flowers.*

Maecenas (*beckoning to a slave major-domo*)   Let the mimes perform here for the moment, And afterwards, the Egyptian 'boneless maidens'
Who do the acrobatic tricks with swords,
Only be sure it doesn't last too long!
Each must perform only for a few minutes
And nobody must come on more than once.
(*To the* **Prefect** *and the* **Procurator**.) For, you can guess, these monkeys are not deaf
To praise, clap once, and you'll be sure to have
A mighty task to get them off the stage.

Meanwhile the major-domo goes out and there start to appear on the stage mimes who perform short farces in dumb show, Egyptian tumbler girls, with swords, jugglers and juggler girls with bright balls, etc. The guests clap for them from time to time, sometimes throwing them flowers and sweets. Very little attention is paid to them by

---

20 Dining room or area.
21 Leader of a chorus.

Maecenas *and the guests of honour who talk together.* **Maecenas** *in a somewhat soft voice, the* **Prefect** *with an even, monotonous, somewhat drawling tone, the* **Procurator** *loudly and effortlessly.*

Maecenas   I must admit this orgy I've prepared
Is somewhat reminiscent of the Kingdom
Of Shades before Pluto's triumvirate.[22]
You won't believe how hard I've had to work,
Somehow to overcome this cautious shyness
And mutual distrust, to join together
Into one kin, the two-fold branches of the
Corinthian people – Greeks and Romans.

Prefect   Friend,
Already you've achieved a mighty work,
You have a panegyrist's choir worth hearing.
Even in Rome such aren't heard every day.

Maecenas (*waving his hand*)   Eh! What's this choir. The place, to speak sincerely,
For poetry like this is in the kitchen.
For truly they would rather have leftovers
Than laurels . . . I crave your forgiveness, that
I entertain you with such paltry shows.
(*Even quieter.*) For such are suited only to the crowd
But I hope I can make it up to you
With something else. For I have found a singer,
A true one. He is not, so far, well known,
But that's shame to the Greeks, not to the singer.
I shall show Corinth it is necessary
To have a Roman to assess the worth
Of art, for otherwise art goes to waste –

Procurator   This singer will come soon?

Maecenas   I do not know.
I sent an invitation, but the answer
He sent to me was not quite clear!

Procurator   Well, really!
Inviting them! You ought just to command them!

Maecenas   Commanding is not fitting here. This Anteus
Is not a slave but a free citizen.

Procurator   Is he a Roman citizen?

Maecenas   Well, no,
But still he is of noble birth. In Corinth

---

22 Pluto ruled the underworld. The same god was referred to as Hades in earlier times, a name that became synonymous with the underworld itself. Commonly associated with the Eleusinian Mysteries.

His family was renowned from ages past,
In olden times some heroes came from them.

Procurator   In the eyes of Greeks, all men are heroes,
If someone in a squabble flings a platter
And hits his neighbour's head – at once he's famous.
A discus-thrower! . . . (*He laughs.*)
So, too, are their poets;
One botches Horace up in the Greek style
And straightway he is crowned, a laureate!
In the Athenian Academy.
You can buy laureates at two-an-obol,[23]
One will be poet, one philosopher!
But watch out that you get your obol's worth.

Maecenas   Do not forget, my friend, the gods above
Have no love for ingratitude. Remember,
In days of old Rome went to school in Greece.

Prefect   Certainly it is a lazy scholar
Who does not finally surpass the teacher.

Maecenas   Indeed, yet still the scholar must be grateful.

Prefect   Rome has paid for tuition lavishly,
She gave to Greece peace and law, which Greece
Had never had, not since the dawn of time.

Procurator   But Greece in the most famous of her schools
Has only taught to Rome some old wives' tales,
Which are a disgrace to our religion
And are an insult to intelligence,
Like a dog's tail, wagging without purpose.
That's all their learning. Never have the Greeks
Made or created more than that. They didn't
Even have a language of their own.

Maecenas   What's that you're saying? Didn't have a language?
Friend, now you're telling us something unheard of.

Procurator   Well, there was the Ionian dialect,[24]
The Attic and I know not what besides,
Each writer had a jargon of his own.
But a strongly tempered speech like ours,
Single and universal, the Greeks never
Had, from the beginning.

---

23 Obol: ancient coinage.
24 Attic and Ionic were related dialects in ancient Greece.

Maecenas   This is so.

Procurator   As for their poetry, to tell the truth,
It cannot stand comparison with ours
That elegance of language, such as Horace,
No Greek has ever reached, nor ever shall.

Maecenas   Nevertheless, it was a Greek who taught us
To honour our native tongue. A Hellene captive
Founded Latin poetry, not a Roman.

Procurator   Because he had to take his master's language,
The master surely's better things to do
Than chop his native language up in trochees.[25]

Prefect (*to* **Maecenas**)   My friend, you are not going to insist
These stanzas were not botched and badly bungled
And the language not in clumsy style.

Maecenas   Who knows, my friend, from whence the spark was born
Out of which first came fire upon the earth.
Maybe it was but a trivial ember,
Yet all the same we ought to pay it honour,
And to respect father Prometheus, though
He may be nothing but a common thief.

Procurator (*to* **Prefect**, *indicating* **Maecenas**)   Here, indeed, is a fruit of the Greek
learning

Prefect   Maecenas is a well known 'Phil-Hellene' –
He's almost ready to split off from Rome
A Republic of Corinth. (*He laughs.*)

Procurator   Jokes are jokes,
But still, from such Phil-Hellenism might
Come some loss to Rome.

Maecenas   Don't be alarmed.
For the old governess remembers well
How much she needs support in her old age.
If Rome should grow angry with Greece and cast
Her off, then Greece would cry, 'Behold, I perish!'

Prefect   Our friend, indeed, is right; it is a pity
That our liking for foreigners has led us
Into a situation where we too
Ourselves have turned into barbarians.
We have now learned 'Latin of Africa'
From our black-faced 'Roman citizens.'

---

25 Trochee: a metrical foot consisting of a stressed syllable followed by an unstressed one.

Maecenas   Still, we can't do without barbarians,
We are obliged now to renew the blood
Worn out from labour, toil and dissipation.
Would you rather wish that all our peoples
Should employ barbarian tongues forever,
Would that really be for Rome a glory?

Procurator   Let them hold their tongues till they have learned
Latin correctly!

Maecenas   That's a bit too hard!
To learn a language properly in silence –
Even Demosthenes[26] could not achieve it.

Procurator   Then what is one to do?

Maecenas   What I am doing.
To teach by favours, even gifts, all leading
Foreigners to love and honour Rome.
For her who truly loves will soon resemble
The one beloved in body and in soul.

Procurator   Phil-Hellenism made you soft. It would be
Interesting to know how, for instance
You'd get taxes in 'by gifts and favours'
You'd get a lot in!

Maecenas (*smiling*)   On this point I must
Lay down my arms. In this you are the expert.

Anteus (*entering*)   The singer Anteus has arrived.

Maecenas   Ah, call him
Here. No, wait! When Anteus starts to sing,
I'll give a sign, then let the dancing girls
Come in. But not before then, understand.
Watch me, Now go!

Exit **Atriensius**.

Maecenas   These accursed slaves
Time after time have spoiled all my arrangements.
In their opinion, orgies are just farces.

Anteus (*on the threshold*)   Greetings to you, illustrious lords.

Maecenas   Hello there!
But come up closer. Standing on the threshold
Does not befit the darling of the muses.

---

26 Greek statesman revered for his oratory.

Anteus *comes nearer but there is no place for him at the table, and he remains standing in front of the reclining guests.*

Maecenas (*to the guests*)   This, my friends, is the most costly pearl
In all the Gulf of Corinth.

Anteus   You, Illustrious,
Have placed excessive favours upon me,
To Corinth, though, you gave too little honour.

Maecenas   Why too little honour?

Anteus   For you cannot
Count up all the pearls found in our gulf
And estimate which one is the most costly.

Prefect   To love one's native town is right and proper,
But one must not forget the honest truth
And gratitude. If, indeed, in Corinth
There are so many pearls of art and learning
Then this is the achievement of Maecenas.

Maecenas   It is a rooster-style achievement, friend.

Procurator   Whatever do you mean by this, Maecenas?

Maecenas   Because I go searching in all the dunghills
And there I scratch up all my costly pearls.

Prefect   But still, you don't gobble them like a rooster
But put them in a setting.

Anteus *silently moves away.*

Maecenas   Anteus, stop!
Where are you going?

Anteus   Back where I belong.

Maecenas   I see you are offended.

Procurator   It is strange
How sensitive these Greeks are!

Anteus   Yes, indeed,
Strange that we have still not grown accustomed
To letting conquerors freely call our country
A dunghill, and call us ourselves, when we
Are not put in a 'setting', simply refuse.

Maecenas   You, it is, puts thorns into my words,
And not I. All my guilt must lie in this
That somehow my tongue slipped, but it was made
That way, created slippery by the gods.

Blame Jupiter, then, or Prometheus – you
Must know far more than I which one to blame.

Prefect   And I, bypassing all the guilt and blame
Will turn to the achievement. My Maecenas,
This time I truly have a case to bring
Against you.

Maecenas   How?

Prefect   It was not you, but I
That first discovered this fine pearl.

Maecenas   Indeed?

Prefect   Moreover, my achievement is still greater,
Because I didn't gobble up the pearl,
Though gobble it I ought to, when I found it.

Maecenas   I'd like to know better what you mean.

Prefect   Oh, this is no great mystery. Once I
Uncovered, rather, covered up for good,
A secret bard's hetaereia in Corinth.
The youngest member of this guild, it chanced,
Was this same singer. When I had observed
His tender youth, I spared him. He alone
Is left now out of all that brotherhood,
Because there are no more hetaereias,
You know, left anywhere in all the world.

Anteus   You are mistaken, there is still one left.

Prefect   Where?

Anteus   Up on Mount Parnassus.[27] Nine and One
Take part up there in a most secret orgy
And hide themselves with thick and heavy clouds
From the eyes of the law!

Maecenas   Ha, ha! Precisely!

Prefect (*changing his drawling tone to a different, sharper one*)   It is not now
'precisely' so, Maecenas
The 'Nine and One' – that's Phoebus and the Muses[28] –
Are not at all a secret hetaereia,
But a panegyrist's choir. They have to

---

27 Mountain sacred to Dionysus and Apollo, home to the muses, and with Delphi on its southern slopes.
28 Phoebus was another name for the god Apollo. There were nine Olympian muses (Calliope, Clio, Erato, Euterpe, Melpomene, Polyhymnia, Terpsichore, Thalia and Urania), who were the goddesses of science, art and literature.

Earn their nectar and ambrosia, too,
And so they have to sing their panegyrics.

Anteus   To whom?

Prefect   Why, to Rome's genius, of course!
Parnassus and Olympus, all the holy
Mountains have now come beneath her power's
Imperium, only those gods can prosper
Who have the rank of Roman citizen,
Or, at the least, the favour of Maecenas
The universal, *he's* Rome's genius.
Whatever gods would not submit to him
Were driven out, or even crucified.

Anteus   And then what happened? Did they die of it?

Maecenas (*quietly, leaning towards the* **Prefect**)   My friend, excuse me, but the vulgar crowd
Maybe could find this jesting sacrilegious.

Prefect (*drawling again*)   May the gods forgive! But still a Roman
Could not let a Greek have the last word.

Maecenas (*loudly, to* **Anteus**)   We have had quite enough of human speech.
Now it is time, Anteus, for you to use
The speech of gods.

Anteus   Illustrious, forgive me,
But the muse has no wish to help me. Maybe
Today she is not feeling very hungry,
And without her I'm like a stringless lyre.

Maecenas   Has my friend really spoiled her appetite?

Prefect   I shan't apologize for what is true,
As for the muse, who *today* is not hungry,
She must remember, even for the gods
Tomorrow only comes to those who earn it.

Anteus   Quite often he who cares not for tomorrow
Will have eternal fame.

Voices are heard in the atrium.[29]

Maecenas   What's all that noise?

Atriensius (*on the threshold*)   Illustrious master, it is some Greek woman
Who came and asks permission to come in,
That she may stand upon the threshold here
And listen while the singer Anteus sings.

---

29 'Atrium' is spelled 'antrium' in the original, which is most likely a printer's error.

Maecenas   Who is she? And of what estate.

Atriensius   She says,
That's she's the singer Anteus' wife.

Maecenas   Let her in, then.

Exit **Atriensius**. **Nerissa** *appears on the threshold and bows without speaking.*

Anteus   Well, what's all this, Nerissa?

Nerissa *remains silent and shyly covers herself with her veil.*

Anteus   Go back home at once!

Maecenas   Excuse me, Anteus!
I am the master here, I'll not allow
Anyone to drive away my guests
You are free to stay here or to go
But likewise is your wife free, while she still
Remains a guest beneath Maecenas' roof.

Anteus (*to* **Nerissa**)   Do you wish to stay here?

Nerissa (*quietly but firmly*)   I am staying.

Procurator (*quietly to* **Maecenas**)   You're no fool about this – she is lovely.
Wherever did he find himself this nymph?

Maecenas   Such women are found only in Tanagra,
Believe me, I'm an expert in such matters.
(*To* **Nerissa**.) Have you been married long?

Nerissa   Less than a month.

Maecenas   Oh, Anteus, do you really need the muses
To help you, while it's still your honeymoon,
You should be able to sing like a god
When this fair Grace is standing there before you.
But why is she hidden beneath a veil?

Anteus   Such is the custom among Hellene women.

Maecenas   But in my home we hold by Roman custom,
And it has its own laws. You must permit
Your wife, therefore, to unveil herself.

Nerissa *without waiting for* **Anteus** *to answer, unveils her face and shyly looks at*
Maecenas.

Maecenas   By all the gods! Just look at her, my friends,
She's the Terpsichore of marble which
I purchased only yesterday from Phaedon.
Can this be chance? No, chances such as this
Cannot occur. (*To* **Nerissa**.) Were you the model for it?

Nerissa   Yes, my lord.

Maecenas   Well, can you also dance?

Nerissa   I don't know. . . .

Maecenas   You don't know? Terpsichore
Doesn't know, though she's the goddess of the dance.

Anteus   She means that she is not a dancing girl
And therefore cannot dance outside her home.

Maecenas   Then I shall visit you some day at home.

Anteus   I shall be honoured. But I do not know
If you will chance to see Nerissa there,
For in my home, mother and wife and sister
Live all the time in the gynaeceum,
And I daren't venture to invite you there.

Maecenas   Your custom is not good.

Anteus   But it is hallowed
By age. I did not set it up, Illustrious.

Procurator   But still you keep it up quite willingly.

Maecenas   Well, this is nothing strange. I understand
Anteus, jealousy. I placed the stone
Terpsichore not in the atrium but
My own tablinum,[30] lest she be profaned.

Anteus   For this, indeed, I owe you heartfelt thanks.

Maecenas   Then show this gratitude in deeds,
Namely in song. (*To a slave.*) Euthymus, go and bring
To us the lyre which I have bought today.

Euthymus *brings a large, richly inlaid lyre.*

Maecenas   Anteus, this lyre's the gift of the whole world
Its horns from bison of the German forests,
The Africa elephant gave ivory
For inlay and Arabia's land sent gold,
The wood from the mysterious Indian jungle,
And the mosaic from the land of Sinai,
The strings, the finest in the world – Italian,
And mounted in bright silver brought from Britain.

Anteus   Only it seems there's nothing Greek in it?

Maecenas   All will be Greek when it belongs to you.
For I shall give it to you as a gift
If you would like to have it. Touch its strings.

---

30 Room situated to the side of an atrium in Roman houses, often used for storing tablets.

Anteus (*he touches the strings casually, not taking it from the hands of the slave. The strings give quiet but strangely beautiful and clear notes.* **Anteus** *gives a start of admiration*)   What a strange and lovely tone it has.
Give me the lyre, boy!

He takes the lyre in his hands.

Oh, how very heavy!

Maecenas   You do not need to hold it for yourself.
There is a slave for that. Euthymus, kneel
And hold the lyre the way the singer tells you.

Euthymus *kneels and supports the lyre for* **Anteus**.

Anteus   No, we must not permit it to get used
To this; at home I have no slaves at all.
And it will have to hang up in the air
Upon the strap.

Maecenas   The way of old-time rhapsodes!
That's very pleasant! Hang it up, Euthymus.
Up there where the big lamp is hanging now.

Euthymus *hangs the lyre on the large candelabrum, taking down the big lamp from the candelabrum.* **Anteus** *steps on to the dais and touches the strings more strongly than before. . . . Hearing the melody,* **Chilon** *and* **Phaedon** *jump to their feet.*

Chilon (*to his fellow choir members who are sitting at the back tables, busily eating and talking*)   My friends, be quiet! Anteus is going to play!

Phaedon   Anteus! Sing us the epithalamy.

Anteus *stops, lets his hands fall, and bows his head. A pause.*

Maecenas   Anteus, what's the matter? Are you ill?
Or can't you, maybe, manage such a lyre?

Nerissa (*to* **Maecenas**, *calling from the threshold*)   My husband is not long up from
an illness.
(*To* **Anteus**, *pleading and quietly.*) Anteus, you mustn't overtax your strength
Completely. Better if you would permit
Me to express your gratitude for you
To the Illustrious lord. Though not a dancer
I shall dance, as is Tanagran custom
As my mother taught me. They'll excuse us.

Maecenas   I am quite willing, though it would be better
If you in your two persons would unite
Music and dance into a wedded pair.

Anteus   My wife is not aware of what she's saying
At all. I feel quite well and strong, and I

Shall play and sing to you – but without dancing,
For this I was invited and agreed,
But your dances, Nerissa, are not for orgies.
I hesitated as I had to seek
Suitable songs within my memory.

Phaedon   Sing the epithalamy! That's fitting.

Anteus   No, it's not fitting. We're not at a wedding.

Maecenas   Why not? Imagine in this house takes place
The nuptial feast of Hellas and of Rome.

Anteus   I see an orgy here before my eyes
And so the songs I think of are not bridal
But Bacchic, rather.

Procurator   Well, that's even better.

Anteus *approaches the lyre again.* **Maecenas** *signs to the guests to be quiet, the voices die away, only the clink of goblets can be heard as the guests go on drinking.* **Anteus** *recites the first line solemnly, without music, then suddenly without a prelude, begins to sing, accompanying himself loudly and confidently in the rhythm of the Bacchic dance.*

Anteus   Do thou, O universal gift, assist me now!
O chime! O chime! Play! Play!
Wake the spirit of orgy for us!
Give a voice to dumbness of slaves!
Do thou stir sluggish blood for us,
Grant a strong thrust to our hidden forces!

Maecenas *gives a sign to the atriensius, dancing girls and corybantes[31] run in and begin the Bacchic dance.*

Anteus   We begin the Bacchic dance
Frenzied spring will transform the orgy
Cold and fear disappear from souls,
Like the mountain snow in the sun,
Dionysus! Reveal thy wonders.

He goes on playing in the same rhythm without words and does not notice that **Nerissa** *has unostentatiously joined the group of dancers.* **Anteus** *then changes the rhythm to a slower, different one in another key.*

Anteus   Quietly dancing, Order harmonious
Peacefully summer comes shining
After the tumult of noisy spring
And in solemnity the feast is prevailing.

---

31 Armed dancers who honoured the goddess Cybele with their dancing.

*With the change of rhythm, the dancers stop, only **Nerissa** goes on dancing always keeping behind **Anteus**. She dances quietly, gently, smoothly, slowly. **Anteus** does not see her at all, and, carried away by the music, takes up his former rhythm only with still more force.*

Anteus   O chime! O chime! Play! Play!
Let us feel in ourselves young strength,
Make us drunk with trans-human force.

*The dancing girls and corybantes once more encircle **Nerissa** with the Bacchic circle, but **Maecenas** stops them with a sudden movement and a shout.*

Maecenas   Stop, all of you and let Nerissa dance!

*At the shout, **Anteus** stops, turns and cannot control himself from surprise and shock at seeing **Nerissa** in the forefront of the dancers. **Maecenas**, noticing this, clasps his hands.*

Maecenas   Musicians! Come and play the Bacchic dance!

*Enter musicians with double flutes, cymbals and drums. They play the Bacchic dance. **Nerissa**, after an instant of confusion, blinking her eyes begins a rapid dance with the uncontrolled but beautiful movements of a maenad. Some of the guests clap to the rhythm of the music, others snap their fingers. **Maecenas** beckons to **Euthymus** and whispers something to him. The latter brings an ornate box and hands it to **Maecenas**.*

Anteus   Nerissa, that's enough!

Maecenas   No! dance on, goddess!
Dance on, most lovely muse Terpsichore!

*He takes from the box a diamond necklace, and holds it high with both hands, enticing **Nerissa** to him. **Nerissa**, without ceasing to dance, approaches **Maecenas**, her eyes are burning, her movements are lithe and sinuous like a wild beast. The guests get up from their seats and crane forward, trying to get a better view of **Nerissa**. They throw flowers at her and there is thunderous applause.*

Voice from Panegyrists' Choir   It is our muse!

Procurator (*leering*)   The pretty little thing!

Prefect   This muse most certainly won't die of hunger.

*Nerissa approaches **Maecenas** and kneels before him on one knee, leaning back as if ready to collapse with weariness but a delightful and coquettish smile plays on her lips. The **Procurator** rushes to support her, but **Maecenas** forestalls him, putting the necklace on her neck and supporting her in the same movement.*

Nerissa   Thank you, my lord!

She tries to kiss his hand.

Maecenas   Not so, immortal one.

He kisses her on the lips. **Nerissa** *rises.*

Procurator (*moving up a little on the couch, and offering her a goblet of wine*)   Come here, Bacchante, rest beside the tiger!

Nerissa *goes to him. There is strained laughter in the crowd.* **Anteus** *suddenly tears down the lyre from the candelabrum and hurls it at* **Nerissa** *with all his might.* **Nerissa** *staggers and falls to the ground.*

Nerissa   Help me! He has killed me!

Anteus *bends down to her and sees that she is dying.*

Anteus (*quietly and almost peacefully*)   Yes, I've killed her.

Prefect (*calling the slaves*)   Fetch the vigiles![32]

Anteus   Stay, let me finish.

He takes a string from the lyre and turns to **Chilon** *and* **Phaedon** *who are standing in the front of the crowd.*

Anteus   Friends, I am setting you a good example!

He strangles himself with the string, and falls dead beside **Nerissa**.

Curtain.

---

32 Civil force of the state.

OBLIVION AND THE OCCULT

Madame La Mort

Rachilde (1891)

Translated by Kiki Gounaridou and Frazer Lively

The French novelist and playwright **Rachilde** (née Marguerite Vallette-Eymery, 1860–1953) stands as a rare example of a woman being welcomed into the circles of the symbolists and decadents of the Parisian fin de siècle. This was due in no small part, as Jennifer Birkett acknowledges, to 'her willingness to play and play up to the decadent stereotypes [. . .]; animal and goddess, ingenious infant and perverse adult'.[1] She wore her hair short, and she wore men's suits after applying to the police for permission to do so, which pertained as much to class and station as gender at the time.[2] At the same time, her take on a nascent feminist movement was at best condescending in the 1890s, and she later positioned herself against feminism following the publication of her pamphlet, *Pourquoi je ne suis pas féministe (Why I am not a feminist)*, in 1928. Her novels and plays can also be seen to be shaped around queer male fantasy, but she nonetheless opens space for her female protagonists to derive pleasure from power. Equally, her anti-feminism needs to be read alongside what Diana Holmes describes as a 'passionate revolt against the role and identity ascribed to women'.[3] It is also important not to lose sight of the broader historical context of a career forged in the thick of male-dominated artistic and literary circles.

Rachilde was a prolific writer, penning forty-six novels between 1880 and 1946, which gained her notoriety almost from the outset with the publication of *Monsieur Vénus*. Her career as a playwright was more compact, being largely (although not exclusively) confined to the 1890s. She not only wrote for the theatre in this period, but actively supported the emergence of a theatre scene traversing various genres and styles, but especially decadence and symbolism. She played a crucial role in enabling Paul Fort to establish his short lived and itinerant Théâtre d'Art (1890–93) by actively contributing to the commissioning of new plays, making good use of her contacts as a member of the editorial committee for the influential journal the *Mercure de France* (revived as a symbolist journal in 1890). Two of Rachilde's own plays were staged with Fort's Théâtre d'Art, including *La Voix du sang* (*The Voice of Blood*, 1890), which was performed on its opening night. Her best-known play, *L'Araignée de Cristal* (*The Crystal Spider*, 1892), was also performed at its successor, Lugné-Poe's Théâtre de l'Œuvre (1893–7). It is also worth noting that Rachilde helped to launch the career of her friend Alfred Jarry, supporting him 'financially and emotionally', and persuading Lugné-Poe to produce *Ubu Roi*, 'the play that made Jarry famous', after its premiere at the Théâtre de l'Œuvre in December 1896.[4] In short, Rachilde played an important role in stimulating modernist theatre in Europe.

Madame La Mort was written for Fort's second programme with the Théâtre d'Art in March 1891. What is most striking about *Madame La Mort* is its stark juxtaposition

---

1   Jennifer Birkett, *The Sins of the Fathers: Decadence in France 1870–1914* (London and New York: Quartet Books, 1986), 159.

2   For a nuanced overview of Rachilde's 'sartorial non-conformity', see Melanie C. Hawthorne, 'Writing as Cross-Dressing', *Rachilde and French Women's Authorship: From Decadence to Modernism* (Lincoln and London: University of Nebraska Press, 2001), 101–13.

3   Diana Holmes, *Rachilde: Decadence, Gender and the Woman Writer* (Oxford and New York: Berg, 2001), 1.

4   Frazer Lively, 'Introduction', (102–4) in Rachilde, *Madame La Mort and Other Plays*, trans. and ed. by Kiki Gounaridou and Frazer Lively (Baltimore and London: Johns Hopkins University Press, 1998), 3–53 (4).

of realism in Acts One and Three – which take place in a domestic setting – and a bizarre central act in which the eponymous 'Madame Death' appears in an ethereal, liminal world that is more in line with a symbolist sensibility in representing the inside of the dying protagonist's mind, Paul Dartigny. Decadence slides across both styles. It is there to be found in the neuroses and languor of Paul as he converses with the rational Jacques Durand in the opening act, and it is there in the hallucinatory occultism in Act Two, after Paul smokes a poisoned cigar and wrestles with powerful drives luring him either to the material world, or to an erotically-charged embrace of transcendence – and death. It is also notable that Fort and Rachilde both worked on Anatole Baju's review *Le Décadent* (1886–9) in the years just preceding the establishment of a symbolist theatre and the inaugural programme of the Théâtre d'Art.[5] *Madame La Mort* therefore encapsulates framings of decadence that understand it as an art of border crossing: in this case both stylistic border crossing, and the staging of a liminal space between the world of the living and oblivion.[6] It condenses into a single entity both the stylistic promiscuity of decadence, along with several thematic preoccupations: neurosis, ennui, inverted gender dynamics, eroticism, idolatry and – as per this section's theme – oblivion and the occult.

---

5 Hawthorne, *Rachilde*, 161.
6 For more on decadence as an art of border crossing, see Liz Constable, Matthew Potolsky, and Dennis Denisoff, 'Introduction', in *Perennial Decay: On the Aesthetics & Politics of Decadence*, ed. by Constable, Denisoff and Potolsky (Philadelphia: University of Pennsylvania Press, 1999), 1–32 (11 and 25).

Characters

Paul Dartigny
Jacques Durand
Doctor Godin
Jean
The Veiled Woman
Lucie

Notes on the Characters

Paul Dartigny is a young man between twenty-five and thirty, pale, tall, thin, with a delicate, weary face. His feverish eyes never look directly at the person to whom he speaks. Casual black suit, very close fitting, like a glove. At his neck, a woman's scarf. Paul is a cold man, easily exasperated.

Jacques Durand is a pleasant young man, the same age as Paul, a high school friend. Glowing pink face, alternately radiant or sullen, with no middle ground. He is dressed in style, with a hat, monocle, and cane. Affectation of great geniality.

Lucie, the well-behaved 'call girl' type. In company, respectable manners resembling those of a society woman. Elegant attire, cumbersome parasol. She speaks loudly, in a decided voice, and sometimes falls into a sort of forced sentimentality, which she fakes on purpose. A girl who likes wellbred gentlemen.

Doctor Godin: Young, proper, well acquainted with death, which hardly bothers him. He speaks rapidly, with a dipped voice.

Jean: Modern servant, *without a trace of the comic*. The dignified bearing of an office employee and not the foolish look of a flunkey who is there to make the audience laugh. He speaks carefully and properly.

The Veiled Woman: Young, lithe woman, completely covered by a dust-grey veil over a long dress of the same grey.
    Mournful voice, but clear and sharp. She never shows her feet, nor her hands, nor her face: she is an apparition. She walks, turns, moves, without a sound, like a shadow, but gracefully. She does not look like a ghost: she is not returning from the dead, she has never existed. She is an image, not a living being.

In the second act the symbolic character **Life** is played by **Lucie** in a pink evening gown, with flowers, diamonds, and a fan. Her hair is loose.

The Setting

The play takes place in Paris in the present.

Act One

Scene One

A very dark smoking room, draped in black. At left, in the back, a black sofa facing the audience. At right, a desk covered with papers, books, a cigar box, matches. At centre, a small table covered with a black cloth, a small box on top of it. At the back, a double door. An enormous vase of mimosas on the mantel, at left, in front of a mirror. Armchairs and carpet, black with yellow brocade.

Paul Dartigny (*stands near the table, holding a little key in his hand. He puts the key into the lock of the box. He is alone. He speaks feverishly*)   Will it be today? My nerves are terribly on edge from this cruel game . . . Oh, Madame, you always keep me waiting! This pointless flirtation makes you seem like a real woman . . . Madame, please have pity on me . . .

He plunges his hand into the box, turning his head away, as if afraid to see what he has touched. He pulls out a cigar which he examines carefully, then, deep in thought, he lets the lid fall back. An argument is heard behind the door at the back. The servant appears.

Jean   Monsieur, I could not keep him from coming in . . .

Paul Dartigny (*impatiently*)   Who is it? I have already told you that I wish to receive no one, no one! . . .

The servant leaves. **Jacques Durand** *appears at the doorway.*

Scene Two

Jacques Durand   I see! You have shut yourself in now! You let me argue with your servant for an hour, and you are here all alone! (*He walks around the room.*) And all the little black ornaments! How cheerful! (*He stops in front of* **Paul** *who has hidden the cigar in his hand.*) But here I am, and I'm staying! (*He sits, puts his hat down, and taps his leg with an air of self-importance.*) Go ahead, make a face. I have made up my mind to take root in this chair until you take me by the shoulders and throw me out. I am very patient, you know . . .

Paul Dartigny (*smiling and sliding his cigar into his vest pocket, next to his chest*)   I know.

Jacques Durand   Look! What's the matter? Aren't you ashamed to hide from the light like an owl? Oh, my friend, it's a beautiful afternoon! Springtime! Sun! All you see out in the streets are flowers on little carts and women in big hats . . . We are going out, the two of us . . . You're not expecting anyone, are you? Besides, I have something to say to you . . .

Paul Dartigny   Go ahead.

Jacques Durand   Give me a cigar first.

Paul Dartigny (*goes to get a cigar box from his desk and offers it to* **Jacques**)   Choose one.

Jacques Durand (*looking at them and making a face*)   Can't I taste the others then? . . . Yours . . . you know, those you reserve for your personal use, you egomaniac . . . over there (*he points to the box at the table*) in that box which is always locked, your servant says . . .

Paul Dartigny (*notices that he has left the key in the box, and rushes over to it. He takes the key out and puts it in his pocket*)   No! . . .

Jacques Durand   We have no manners anymore!

He sits back down.

Paul Dartigny (*dreamily*)   Send you in my place and risk running into you again? That would finish me.

Jacques Durand (*astonished*)   You're going out? You have a date? (*Joyfully.*) What will Lucie say? . . . I'll go with you wherever you plan to go, I really will . . .

He gets up.

Paul Dartigny (*coldly*)   It's a long way.

Jacques Durand (*grumbling*)   Another hoax, of course! (*He sits back down.*) You're not smoking anymore?

He lights his cigar.

Paul Dartigny   Yes, when I am alone . . . my special cigars . . . not all men relish the same smoke. (*He sits across from* **Jacques**.) You wanted to say something to me, Jacques?

Jacques Durand   Oh! . . . Nothing that will inconvenience you, I'm sure. I forced my way in here because I need five hundred francs: a trifle. I'll pay you back along with the rest, in a month or two.

Paul Dartigny (*gets up to go to his desk*)   No trouble. (*He opens the drawer.*) Why didn't you say so, my friend? Giving occupies the mind. It is good to feel generous at certain times. I thank you for furnishing me with this final illusion . . . You want? . . . How much? . . . I have forgotten the amount.

Jacques Durand (*offended*)   You are lucky, not to have to count your money! Seven hundred francs . . . But I'll pay you back: I give you my word. It's just . . . (*he counts on his fingers*) the tailor, the club, Nini, and a big watch the size of a hazelnut, which I gave my dear little sister Angèle for her birthday . . . The little darling wanted it so much! . . . Don't sneer! I still have some family spirit, and I think everything can be taken care of: diamonds for Nini, so be it! . . . but a watch for that innocent young girl, my sister!

He taps the ash off his cigar with a self-satisfied smile.

Paul Dartigny (*handing him the money*)   Here are your seven hundred francs, my friend. You have beautiful feelings which are a pleasure to witness, and for that I congratulate you.

Jacques Durand (*putting the money in his wallet with satisfaction*)   Thank you. Don't laugh. You and your ironic remarks are unbearable.

Paul Dartigny (*gravely*)   I wouldn't know how to laugh. There is no reason!

Jacques Durand   I believe you, but you look like a man in a dream . . .

Paul Dartigny   Forgive me. (*Smiling.*) A dream is a stairway to the sky: I am very high, very far away . . . I no longer know where I am.

He sits down again, his head turned away.

Jacques Durand   Spring fever. As for me, all my beautiful feelings, as you call them, are bursting up in my chest all at once, and I would like to find a chance to put them on display.

Paul Dartigny (*softly*)   The boutique on the thirteenth floor.

Jacques Durand (*letting out great puffs of smoke*)   Just now I gave a coin to a beggar: ridiculous, eh? . . . I am going to pay off my debts . . . probably.

*He approaches **Paul**'s chair.*

Jacques Durand   And I would like to cure you of your neuroses, take you out into the sunshine, to women, to the world . . . Help you, do you hear me! . . . You have had a dreadful winter: you must shake it off this summer, my dear Paul.

*He slaps **Paul**'s shoulder.*

Paul Dartigny (*lowering his head and looking at him, surprised*)   I don't like the sun.

Jacques Durand (*crossing his arms*)   You don't like the sun! (*Forcefully.*) You are an absolute monster!

Paul Dartigny   Ah! This theory is spread by devotees of the sun, since creatures of the moon are in the minority.

Jacques Durand (*furious*)   You don't like the sun . . . Why, if you please?

Paul Dartigny (*calmly*)   The sun makes unpleasant creatures visible and I can't stand its arrogant attitude in the face of ghastly situations. It seems to me that the sun is like those drunks who come out of a wedding and force you to drink to the health of a bride . . . (*a pause*) whom you don't know.

Jacques Durand (*laughing*)   All you have to do is pull the curtain, and it's gone! (*He shrugs his shoulders.*) Not to like the beauties of nature! I swear, he must be corrupted, completely corrupted.

Paul Dartigny (*containing himself*)   Oh, Jacques, Jacques. Let's not argue anymore! It is so trivial, these endless conversations about the tastes which you have and those which I have not. It would be better for each of us to stay home alone, I assure you.

Jacques Durand (*sitting back down*)   You are most unpleasant! . . . After lending me money, it's not very polite, my dear friend.

Paul Dartigny (*looking at the ceiling*)   It's true . . . Pardon me, because I would like to believe that you are more and more inflated with beautiful sentiments. Nevertheless . . . I would prefer you . . . deflated.

Jacques Durand   Are you still on morphine these days?

Paul Dartigny   No. I don't take drugs anymore. I am not such a coward as to keep using artificial means: I will go straight to the point.

Jacques Durand   And the point is?

Paul Dartigny   You are very curious, my friend.

Jacques Durand (*playing with his cane*)   Yesterday I ran into Doctor Godin, who expressly told me that you had taken a turn for the worse.

Paul Dartigny (*with interest*)   Is that why you came here, Jacques?

Jacques Durand   For that and also for . . . the other thing . . . which I needed. I confess that your state of mind is more annoying than upsetting. Oh, if you were sick, with typhoid fever for instance, I could bring myself to sleep on this sofa and take care of you all night . . . But just between us, your case is more comical than dangerous: it's an imaginary illness.

Paul Dartigny   Why would typhoid fever be more dangerous than an illness of my imagination, my dear friend?

Jacques Durand   You would be in danger of dying, for heaven's sake!

Paul Dartigny (*with a mocking laugh*)   You all fear death almost as if you worship it.

Jacques Durand   But my dear, dear friend, personally, that's all I fear!

He stands up.

What else should we all fear if not that?

Paul Dartigny (*in a calm voice*)   Death is a woman. I see no reason not to enjoy her company. It's that simple.

Jacques Durand   You are talking gibberish. (*Getting excited.*) Either you have some love story on your brain, or you're just arrogant, and a good catastrophe, a real illness will cure you better than all our sermons would. Listen, my dear Paul, at bottom you are an egotist: you give because you don't need anything, you don't like women anymore because you had a lot of women, you don't like society anymore because you were part of it whenever you wanted . . . Yes, an egotist! And the proof, your cigars locked up for the past two weeks. Even your servant is disgusted by that behaviour: you act as if you don't trust him . . . You're putting up a big smokescreen. Bored with life? Come on! At your age? . . . I am an old friend: I am going to drag the whole truth out of you. (*A pause.*) The truth is your pride is hurt. You have tried every social circle, one after another, and they have all turned you down. (*He counts on his fingers.*) You frequented artists: you failed. You frequented salons: you don't even know English. You frequented women: they don't like you . . . Aside from Lucie, you haven't got a hope. My friend, your misfortune is that you squandered your wealth to gain knowledge instead of living an honest life. Your famous pessimism only serves to throw powder in our eyes and it's nothing but a bad education: not to live like the rest of the world is sheer impoliteness, everyone tells you so . . . You, the *blasés*, the hypochondriacs, you simply have bad manners . . . Personally, when I eat beef, I resent watching my neighbour ask for veal. . . . After all, what are you complaining about? You're rich, an orphan, free, without a wife . . . and without a mother-in-law.

Paul Dartigny (*looking at the ceiling, no longer listening*)   What's the matter with him? What mother-in-law? His words ring in my ears like a death knell . . . But unfortunately, now it strikes me that even a death knell can be ridiculous.

Jacques Durand (*grasping his arm*)   I insist that you be happy to be alive, do you hear me! . . . Godin says that you must have stolen poison from him and this will lead to trouble. The doctor really said so, believe me. You're not going to play a bad trick like suicide, are you? And Lucie, that pretty girl, that treasure of grace and beauty, who, I am sure, doesn't cost you as much as a society woman, how do you know what she does when you are away from her, when you shut yourself up for a whole week with your daydreams? . . . Oh, those horrible daydreams, if I could catch them! . . . (*Menacing gesture.*)

Paul Dartigny (*coldly*)   What she does? . . . I have no idea. Try to restrain yourself from telling me, please . . . Oh, the sound of your voice gets on my nerves, like a needle, Jacques. My syringe of Pravaz[7] is preferable.

Jacques Durand (*solemnly*)   There is one thing, Paul.

Paul Dartigny   What, my friend?

Jacques Durand (*pointing his finger sententiously*)   In depravity, there is Pravaz! (*Happily.*) That joke is good enough for the Club.

Paul Dartigny (*he rubs his forehead and stands*)   And in the bourgeois soul, there always sleeps . . . an old gossip columnist.

Jacques Durand (*exasperated*)   Come on! . . . Bourgeois, we are all bourgeois: you, me, Lucie, Godin, and the grocer across the street!

Paul Dartigny   I am afraid you will even have children.

Jacques Durand   . . . Who, let's hope, won't be like you – deranged!

Paul Dartigny (*philosophically*)   Especially if they are Lucie's.

---

7   Charles Gabriel Pravaz (1791–1853): French surgeon famous for innovating an effective hypodermic syringe.

Jacques Durand   No, I assure you, Lucie is very attached to you. She is a nice girl, quite without malice.

Paul Dartigny   Like you: you were made for each other! (*Dry laugh.*)

Jacques Durand (*uneasily*)   You're not suspicious of me, I hope . . . Look, we're alone: how much do you pay her?

Paul Dartigny (*gesture of suppressed rage*)   Oh! I don't know! I pay her?

Jacques Durand   She is elegant! . . . Oh! Style . . . purity of lines . . .

Paul Dartigny   She is like the lily from the Bible . . . She spins sometimes and saves up a lot . . . a very common flower, all in all.

Jacques Durand   So, what do you expect? . . . You would deserve it if I flirted with her right in front of you, my friend, in revenge for your stupid contempt. Luckily, I still have respect for my friendships.

Paul Dartigny (*in a heavy voice*)   All I ask of you is not to flirt . . . or make love to her in front of my eyes . . . while I watch.

Jacques Durand (*in an outburst*)   You are becoming coarse . . . Just now you were blasphemous!

Paul Dartigny (*surprised*)   Blasphemous?

Jacques Durand (*serious*)   You spoke about the bourgeois a moment ago . . . Well, the bourgeois, and I am one of them, we have one virtue: we believe in God . . . from time to time.

Paul Dartigny   Which separates you from the beasts, I know! My compliments!

Jacques Durand (*going back and forth, very excited*)   Bourgeois! It's a mouthful, that word! . . . What do you mean by this sort of insult anyway?

Paul Dartigny   You said it yourself: you, me, Lucie, Godin, the grocer across the street . . . Or even (*stressing his words*) a man whose feet are on the ground, a man who seems better balanced than the others . . . But when he stumbles he crushes everything, and when he falls he never gets back up. Are you happy?

Jacques Durand (*sadly*)   My name is Jacques Durand: it's bourgeois, I feel it, all right! A label like that classifies you forever. One of my aunts wanted to baptize me Gaëtano! I'm sorry no one listened: Gaëtano is even better than Carolus . . .

Paul Dartigny (*smiling*)   You miss Gaëtano.

Jacques Durand   Don't laugh, Paul! Your mother must have had aspirations like that, too. All our mothers were romantics.

Paul Dartigny (*gloomy*)   My mother . . . (*musing*) She was a gentle soul who suffered everything . . . (*A pause.*) and understood nothing! . . . As a child when I leaned my head against her heart, I felt the sound of her sighs the way one can hear, behind a curtain of crumpled silk, a wind that moans, blindly, in the night . . .

Jacques Durand (*laughing*)   The poor soul evidently liked silk dresses, since her blouse rustled in such a pleasant manner . . . And your father?

He relights his cigar.

He was a bon vivant, it seems to me?

Paul Dartigny (*coldly*)   A very distinguished gentleman: he used to seduce our maids.

Jacques Durand   Shut up, my dear friend. All our fathers did the same thing, and we owe them our respect!

Jean *comes in.*

Scene Three

Jean   Sir, Doctor Godin is here. He is in a hurry.

Paul Dartigny (*shrugging his shoulders*)   Another one! . . . Let him in, if he is in a hurry . . . Perhaps I am at the point of death.

Doctor Godin *comes in from the door at the back at a brisk pace. He gives a rapid handshake to* **Jacques Durand** *and speaks in his ear.*

Jacques Durand (*out loud*)   So, you still hold to your opinion? . . . I examined him from every angle . . . I think he's fooling us. He doesn't have any poison, I assure you, my dear doctor.

Doctor Godin (*quite calm, he puts his hat on the table and stands facing* Paul)   My dear friend, no arguments, since I have a patient waiting. From shelf number 5 of my consulting room, someone has taken a vial with the number 9,698 and a green stopper, containing a brown liquid. Now, firstly, you are obsessed with suicide. Secondly, I have no confidence in the integrity of madmen of your type, at least as far as dangerous drugs are concerned. Thirdly, you will return my vial, because *nerium oleander* is a costly poison. Conclusion: if I had an hour to waste today, I would insult you, and end by exchanging the customary pair of seconds . . . Do not lie, my friend, I am certain of it: you have a wrinkle in the middle of your forehead . . .

Jacques Durand (*carried away*)   The medical examination didn't take long at all! Godin, you are priceless.

Paul Dartigny   I wouldn't lie about anything so petty . . . Yes, it's the truth, I did steal the poison from you.

He goes to his desk.

How much do I owe you?

Doctor Godin (*angry*)   Damn it! What did you do with it?

Jacques Durand (*jumping back*)   Oh! This is not possible! . . . What did you do with it, you idiot?

A moment of silence.

Paul Dartigny (*in a very gentle voice*)   So . . . you absolutely refuse to leave me alone, both of you?

Doctor Godin (*tapping his hat*)   My dear friend, are you making fun of me? I am in a hurry, and I cannot sell you the poison because of the police . . . They are amazing, these neurotics! You would put me in a fine pickle . . . if you were dead! . . . Now, hurry up and return it to me . . . I give you ten minutes.

Paul Dartigny (*with dignity*)   One minute will suffice, my dear Godin. (*He points to the box on the table.*) I threw one poisoned cigar in there along with thirty harmless Havanas. Look for it. As for me, I have been expecting it for two weeks now. I wanted to achieve the supreme climax of a rendezvous with Death . . . But Lady Death, my Lady, has not appeared yet . . . To make herself desirable is part of her role as a woman, after all.

Godin *seizes the box and puts it under his arm, while* **Jacques** *lets out a cry and immediately throws down his cigar.*

Doctor Godin   Splendid! . . . Only demented poets commit suicide with poisoned cigars! . . . How the fin de siècle mocks us with this business! . . . In the morning, Monsieur Lover-of-Death, you would have paid the price! . . . Between us, I advise you to hang yourself, it is more amusing, because *nerium oleander* makes one go a little insane and it has a rather bitter taste . . . My dear Dartigny, I have the honour of wishing you good day. Monsieur Durand . . .

He shakes **Durand**'s *hand.*

Jacques Durand (*seizing his cane*)   I'm going with you, doctor!

Paul Dartigny (*with an ironic wave of farewell*)   Bon voyage!

He moves away from them, then pulls the cigar from his vest pocket and lights it.

I, too, want to depart. With this cigar, they leave me a last chance for escape . . . and the opportunity to prove my egotism . . . if I am an egotist. (*He smokes.*)

Godin *and* **Jacques**, *already in the doorway, move back to allow* **Lucie** *to pass through. The doctor steps aside;* **Jacques** *bows ceremoniously.*

Jacques Durand   It is a pleasure to see you, Mademoiselle. You look lovely . . .

Doctor Godin   Let's hurry, please. Good day, Madame.

The two men exit. Then **Jacques Durand** *comes back in and, from the threshold, calls out to* **Paul**, *who is still standing with his back turned.*

Jacques Durand   I am going with the doctor and bringing back a carriage. We'll drive to the park together: this will take our minds off the problem. Until later, Mademoiselle.

Scene Four

Lucie (*lifting her veil*)   What problem?

The door closes again.

Paul Dartigny (*smoking dreamily*)   Will she come?

Lucie (*astonished*)   You were waiting for me, my little Paul? (*She puts her arms around his neck.*) Were you really waiting for me? . . . (*Exaggerated caresses.*) Answer me, come on.

Paul Dartigny   Perhaps . . . I am waiting for a veiled woman. Why do you take off your veil?

Lucie (*irritated*)   Don't tease. You never wait for me!

Paul Dartigny (*smiling*)   Lord, no more than the spring, and you always return.

Lucie (*offering him her lips*)   You are really annoying with your jokes . . . Come on, try to act nice.

Paul Dartigny   This smoke doesn't bother you?

Lucie (*shrugging her shoulders*)   As if I'm not used to it, with all of you!

She kisses him.

Paul Dartigny (*letting out a cry and jumping back. Expression of joy mixed with terror*)   Oh! Don't kiss me anymore . . . My lips are bitter . . . At last! You are here, Madame! . . . (*He draws further back.*) Oh, Lucie, didn't you see a grey shawl floating . . . in this smoke . . . around us? The unknowable woman is passing by! . . . I saw her as clearly as I see you . . . (*He hides his face in his hands.*) Oh, it's terrifying and divine! . . . Lucie! I swear to you that I saw her as I see you . . . there, behind you . . . just the way I have dreamed her . . .

Lucie (*losing her temper*)   You have taken drugs, haven't you? You took morphine, and you will fall asleep or say crazy things to me . . . (*She throws herself into an armchair.*) Life with you is so delightful!

Paul Dartigny (*goes toward her with a bewildered look*)   Can you smell the fragrance of withered roses? (*Animated.*) Where are the roses? Where are the roses? . . . In your corsage or in my heart?

He looks carefully at **Lucie**.

Lucie (*tapping her foot and twisting the handle of her parasol*)   Me? . . . I have perfume on my handkerchief, that's all.

Paul Dartigny (*straightens up and begins smoking again*)   No doubt: a perfumed handkerchief is a very vulgar luxury . . . (*He struggles against a slight dizziness.*) Forgive me, Lucie, I am a little ill and I am treating you badly. My nerves are on edge. First, the sound of Jacques' voice . . . Then yours . . . which grates on me like your diamonds shining in bathroom mirrors . . . (*He staggers and crosses his hands over his chest.*) You have clawed at my soul with all your nails . . . (*He falls into an armchair.*) Do you think about death sometimes, Lucie?

Lucie (*in a hissing voice*)   Always joking! . . . Oh, do I ever want to walk out on you!

Paul Dartigny (*standing back up, distraught*)   Go get me a glass of water, Lucie. There is a horrible bitterness in my mouth . . .

Lucie   I am not your maid! . . .

She stands and goes to fix her hair in front of the mirror.

Paul Dartigny (*kneeling on a chair near her*)   You are cruel, my dear . . . (*Very softly.*) You are charming . . . fresh and painted like Life . . . I took care of you in my will, you know . . . (**Lucie** *turns and smiles.*) You deign to smile, your eyes light up . . . We are all mortal, my darling . . . Beautiful eyes! . . . Yes, your eyes are a crystal over an abyss, and I who have leaned over them, I have glimpsed truth . . . I thought I loved you more than Death, and you brought me to nothingness and repose . . . You threw me into her arms. I bless you.

He kisses her hands.

Lucie (*laughing*)   What great style you have, telling yourself stories! . . . A first class burial, huh!

Paul Dartigny (*smoking and speaking slowly*)   I am afraid, Lucie . . . I am very ill and I wouldn't want to seem insistent, but . . . you have come at the same time as She. It is not my fault . . . Do you need me, Lucie?

Lucie (*tidying her clothes and speaking very quickly*)   Darling, I want to move to Monceau Park. The total will be three thousand francs.

Paul Dartigny (*delirious*)   I will fill my tomb with gold and precious stones . . . Come with me, if you dare.

Lucie (*scornfully*)   Where do you want to make me go? . . . The country, like last fall? . . . Not before the Grand Prix, you understand! . . . I know them, your tombs full of gold and precious stones . . . An empty house, huge beds that make you cold down to your bones, and it rains all day long . . . Thanks. No one's going to catch me at that game again!

Paul Dartigny (*sinking down on his knees*)   Oh! I saw red flames . . . The terror! . . . (*He hides his face in* **Lucie**'s *dress for a moment.*) I feel like a little sick child, and every woman should be a mother to a man in pain . . . Lucie, I saw sparks burning on this carpet! Have pity . . . (*He lies at her feet.*) I would love you so much if you only kept quiet!

Lucie (*giggling*)   But you're drunk! . . . That stuff must be good! . . . What did you have to drink? . . . You are drunk, Paul!

Paul Dartigny (*gets back up, exasperated*)   What did I have to drink? . . . You idiot, I have drained the whole chalice! . . . I am satiated with life! . . . Get out of here! . . . Let me sleep . . .

Lucie (*she shakes her head as she looks at him*)   Being alone with him, it's not very safe. He's going crazy . . . Look, Paul, let's talk more seriously . . . Those three thousand francs, I need them . . . It's not funny, I mean it . . . Paul! . . . (*shouting*) Paul! . . .

Paul Dartigny (*moves across the room, holding onto the furniture. When he gets to the sofa at the back, he speaks wildly*)   Who is calling me? . . . Is it my beloved? . . .

He sinks down on the sofa.

Lucie   Oh! I've had enough of your stories about strange women!

Noise behind the door. The servant comes in.

Scene Five

Jean   It's Monsieur Jacques Durand again.

He leaves.

Jacques Durand *comes in.*

Jacques Durand (*bows*)   I am not disturbing you?

Lucie (*enraged*)   Disturbing us! . . . Come on, look at him: he is falling asleep in front of me. He is asleep on his feet! . . . Oh! He ought to be slapped! . . .

Jacques Durand (*smiling*)   Morphine, his consolation! . . . You can't always get what you want . . . Godin agrees with you, Mademoiselle, we must give him a talking to . . . and it's more urgent than you can imagine . . . (*irritated*) And I was just bringing a carriage! . . .

Lucie (*furious, she goes to the sofa where* **Dartigny** *lies*)   One . . . Two . . . You are not coming? . . . You don't want to come? . . . (*Pause.*) Fine, I am going to the park with him! . . . Are you coming? . . . (*She takes* **Jacques**' *arm.*) Good night!

Jacques Durand (*bowing*)   We won't be back until dinner.

They exit.

Paul Dartigny (*trying to sit up*)   Don't make a sound . . . Oh, don't make a sound . . . I can smell the fragrance of withered roses.

Act Two

Scene One

A garden on a spring day in soft, hazy light. Banks of light-coloured shrubs and rose bushes. Dominating the stage in the back, a cypress shrouded in mist. At centre, a stone bench that looks like a tomb.

Paul Dartigny (*stretched out on the ground in a rigid pose, his head leaning against the stone bench. He is very pale and seems to be asleep. Then he wakes and murmurs in a faint voice*)   ... Withered roses ... (*He sits up.*) What country is this? ... Why am I in this strange garden? ... (*He stands up, his hand on his forehead.*) My head is light and cold like a snowflake, and yet my body feels very heavy ... (*He takes several wavering steps, looks around, then smiles.*) It is absurd ... and charming ...

Lucie's Voice (*far away*)   Paul! ... Paul! ...

Paul Dartigny (*listening*)   That tearful voice makes my blood run cold ... Yes, I inhabit the country of the ultimate fantasy ... Here, every dark illusion will attack me ... Am I only sleeping, or am I already dead? ... The scent of these flowers has a disturbing subtlety: they try to dissuade me, they offer me their pious lies, and yet ... I sense in them ... a terrifying smell of earth ...

Lucie's Voice (*nearer*)   Paul! ... Paul! ...

Paul Dartigny   Lord! She again! Always she! ... (*He clasps his hands above his head.*) Ah, Madame, you my great beloved, you the comforter, you the Absolute, come to my aid! ... A terrible thing is about to happen, I foresee it: I must witness the hour of my death ... (*Recoiling.*) If I could see your face! ... If I could only touch you! ... (*Moment of silence.*) No more ... She no longer calls my name ... I am dead already ... Forgotten ... (*He falls back on the stone bench and looks at the garden.*) Oh, what a ravishing country! ... The air here is as sweet as honey ... I want to stay here, to get drunk from the sweetness all around ... then sleep, I am very tired ... I have walked for thirty years! ...

Lucie's Voice (*very close*)   Paul! ...

Lucie *comes out from the grove. She wears a pink evening gown, loosely draped, and a diamond necklace. Her hair is loose and she holds a fan.*

Lucie   Paul! ...

Paul Dartigny *shudders and stands up, his eyes blank.*

Scene Two

Lucie (*runs to **Paul** and throws herself at his feet*)   You want to leave me, but you said I was your life!

Paul Dartigny (*with difficulty, turning his head away*)   It is true, I did say you were my life . . . I cursed you too, do you remember that? In those days, you were my lover. But now step back and let the supreme ecstasy appear: you are nothing to me anymore . . . *She* is here, I know it, near us . . . Don't argue with her over my body, since you did not know how to hold on to my soul . . . (*He tries to push her away.*) What demon wants to show me life in the face of a lover . . . (*angrily*) who abandons me?

Lucie (*still on her knees; hanging on to* **Paul***'s hands*)   No. You belong to me! (*Fiercely.*) I'll cling to your body the way ivy still clings to a tree cut at the root . . . I won't let you fall into the abyss . . . I feasted for so long on your flesh and blood that now I am the stronger. I love you! . . .

Paul Dartigny (*sadly*)   Oh, vain words! . . . This is a part you must have played for so many other men! . . . Enough, get out of here! (*Harshly.*) You make me sick . . .

Lucie   What can I do to prove my love to you?

Paul Dartigny   Stop it! . . .

He turns away toward the back of the stage, then recoils with a hollow cry: he has just seen, standing against the cypress, a grey form shrouded in mist.

Scene Three

Lucie (*still on her knees, reaching out to him*)   Come back, Paul! . . . I am mistress, I am wife, I am mother . . . You have no right to run from me . . . I order you to stay.

Noticing the grey silhouette, she stands up and rushes to him.

Oh! That hideous woman! . . . My rival, Paul! . . .

Paul Dartigny (*curtly*)   Yes!

Lucie (*enraged*)   He is insane!

She holds him in her arms.

Paul Dartigny (*continuing to look at the* **Veiled Woman***, who comes forward slowly, slowly, but not as if walking: she is gliding. He pleads*)   Save me, Madame, if you are She whom I await! . . . Save me, I implore you! . . .

The Veiled Woman (*closer and closer, moving out of the mist*)   Soon!

Lucie (*beside herself*)   Miserable phantom who subverts the healthiest minds and turns the most noble hearts to ice, where have you come from? . . . Oh! I will protect him from your black magic! . . . I have the power of desire, and the flesh I have kissed so often will surely rebel at your touch . . .

The Veiled Woman (*gliding a step forward, while* **Paul** *shrinks back, still in* **Lucie***'s grip*)   The flesh you have kissed for so long will rot more quickly.

Paul Dartigny (*trying to break free*)   I am in agony . . . Madame, have pity on my suffering . . . It is only a courtesan drunk on her own words . . .

Lucie (*tightening her grip*)   Don't worry, I won't let you go now! I hold you, we are one . . . (*She turns to the* **Veiled Woman**.) Between your ugliness and my beauty, what do you think he will choose, you rambling old princess?

The Veiled Woman (*gliding a step forward*)   It is not for him to choose: you are his body, but I am his soul.

Lucie (*speaking passionately to* **Paul**)   You thought I was pretty once . . . (*She shows herself off.*) Look at me, I have all my diamonds . . .

The Veiled Woman (*gliding a step forward*)   Indeed all the tears he shed since he was born sparkle at your throat.

Lucie (*pleading*)   My dress is pink: it was spun from the dawn . . .

The Veiled Woman   You made your dress by tearing off his skin . . .

Lucie (*fanning herself*)   I fan myself with April breezes . . .

The Veiled Woman (*still advancing toward* **Paul**)   Your fan is fever's wing.

Lucie (*leaning on* **Paul**, *who sobs*)   I break open the shells of birds' eggs with my delicate nails.

The Veiled Woman   She bloodies forests when she is in heat.

Lucie (*more insistent*)   Remember my expert ways of pleasure. One night, the stars left the sky because they didn't dare look at us anymore.

The Veiled Woman (*still advancing*)   And, defeated by fatigue, he fell into a sleep as heavy . . . as my arm.

She lifts her right arm.

Lucie   You make me laugh.

The Veiled Woman (*now quite close to* **Paul**)   You may well laugh now . . .

Lucie (*covering* **Paul** *with kisses*)   You loved me so much!

The Veiled Woman (*coming between* **Paul** *and* **Lucie**)   You deceived him so much!

Paul Dartigny (*writhing in pain*)   Have pity, Madame, end my suffering! . . . (*He sobs.*) Her hair was so long! . . .

He looks at **Lucie**.

The Veiled Woman (*wraps* **Paul** *in her veil*)   My veil is even longer.

Lucie (*shrinks back, struck with fear*)   Paul, I would have given you beautiful children.

The Veiled Woman (*with a scornful gesture, leaning on the young man's shoulder*)   Wretched woman! You kill love with this idea of procreation, because love is the only god who cannot multiply without vanishing. Ridiculous whore, you trade your kisses for the base coin of pain! You are an animal who drowns pleasure in dung. And your children are pledged to me from their cradle. Unnatural mother, without logic and without purpose, living in daylight and denying the night. Go! For him you were a useless servant whom he paid too dearly!

Lucie (*shrinks back to the stone bench and calls in despair*)   Paul! . . . Paul! . . . (*with a weaker voice*) Paul! . . . Paul! . . . (*faintly*) Paul! . . .

She disappears behind the roses.

Paul! . . .

Scene Four

Paul Dartigny (*one knee on the ground, in front of the* **Veiled Woman**)   Thank you, oh my sovereign and only love! Allow me to bow before you. I was nothing but dust. I return to dust. (*He kisses the hem of her veil.*) You are finally here, mysterious woman. I waited for you at every nightfall . . . I have dreamed of your beauty: will I never see you?

The Veiled Woman (*softly*)   No!

Paul Dartigny (*timidly and with love*)   The breeze here caresses . . . It sways the flowers, Madame, and your veil is very light . . .

The Veiled Woman   I do not stop the breeze: it passes through me.

Paul Dartigny (*horrified*)   Do not say that, my queen, you will freeze my blood.

The Veiled Woman   It is already frozen.

Paul Dartigny (*stands, and, led by her, reaches the bench, where he sits. She remains standing at his side. He takes her hands*)   My love! . . . Forgive me, my mouth is still bitter with Life's kisses . . . I am impure. You will purify me.

The Veiled Woman   By burning your bones.

Paul Dartigny   What will become of my soul, this soul which belongs to you? . . . Is there a God?

The Veiled Woman (*pointing towards the sky*)   Watch the turtle doves glide: what do they need except sweet air and sunny weather?

Paul Dartigny (*tenderly*)   You are a woman, because you speak in riddles, my cruel fiancée! . . . But is there eternal love?

The Veiled Woman (*pointing to a rose bush*)   See how these roses shed their petals: they take longer to dry . . . than a woman's tears.

Paul Dartigny (*stands*)   Where you live, is it at least permitted to know pride?

The Veiled Woman   There is no greater pride than silence.

Paul Dartigny   Must I be quiet?

The Veiled Woman   You only imagine you speak.

Paul Dartigny (*with despair*)   Oh, horrible dream! . . . To hear her, to touch her, and not to know if it is She! . . . (*A moment of silence.*) Into what exquisite turmoil this creature of darkness throws me! Will I die or live? Will I find emptiness beneath this veil, or royal beauty? . . . (*He approaches her.*) Tell me, might I sometimes, sleepless in our shadowy bed, press your form against my chest, like the body of a woman . . . who would resist? . . .

The Veiled Woman   I represent the end of these vanities. You will sleep.

Paul Dartigny   I will sleep deeply! (*Joyfully.*) For how many centuries?

The Veiled Woman   Do you know the number of centuries since you met me? . . . Action has ended and time is no more.

Paul Dartigny   At last, can you tell me who you are, you, Death?

The Veiled Woman (*in a very hollow voice*)   I do not know.

Paul Dartigny (*transported*)   I adore you, and you are ravishing, my beloved! . . .

He puts his head on the **Veiled Woman**'s *chest and falls back on the bench, half asleep.*

The Veiled Woman (*sweetly*)   Come, the hour is here, the nuptial bed is ready. Sleep, my unhappy lover.

She wraps him in her arms and in her veil.

Paul Dartigny (*faintly*)   Let us sleep . . . together, is it not . . . together . . .

The Veiled Woman (*softly, spreading out once and for all the folds of her veil*)   Forever.

Act Three

Scene One

Same scene as Act One. **Paul Dartigny**, *dead, lying on the sofa at the back. Half-darkness at the rise of the curtain.*

Jean (*enters through the door at the back*)   Monsieur! . . . Monsieur! . . .

He goes up to the sofa.

Very good, here he is, fast asleep! . . . And the other two are over there in the living room, in the midst of . . . kissing each other probably . . . What a dog's life! . . . With this maniac here, you never know which end is up . . . (*Louder.*) Monsieur . . . (*He leans over the sofa.*) He is sleeping with his eyes open now . . . (*Uneasy.*) Drugs these days will do this to you . . . But what's the difference, his eyes look funny anyway! . . . Monsieur! . . . (*He lifts* **Paul**'s *arm, which falls back down limp.*) What! . . . (*He is confused.*)

Jacques Durand (*behind the door at the back, knocking with his cane*)   We are here, my friend, and Mademoiselle Lucie (*burst of suppressed laughter*) is very hungry, I assure you . . . (*Raising his voice.*) If you make us wait, you are just a coward! . . . (*More laughter.*)

Jean (*raising his arms*)   Lord! It's too much! (*Shocked.*) I think he must be . . . dead! . . . I have no job, and the police will interrogate me! . . .

Scene Two

Jacques Durand (*enters with* **Lucie**, *who carries a bunch of flowers*)   Well? . . . Are we still sleeping off the morphine? . . .

The servant stops him and puts a finger over his mouth, looking toward **Lucie**.

Jacques Durand   What? . . . What's the matter? . . . Is he still asleep?

Jean (*nodding his head*)   I think so, Monsieur. (*He goes towards the door.*) I am going now . . . If you need my services . . .

He leaves.

Jacques Durand (*surprised*)   That Jean is strange! . . .

Lucie (*putting the flowers in a vase*)   Now you see, my dear Durand, it's unbearable! Even his servant is crazy!

Jacques Durand (*biting the handle of his cane*)   My poor dear! Well, we won't get to eat dinner together?

Lucie   No. I don't want to make a scene. (*She takes off her hat.*) Must be sensible . . . (*She goes up to the sofa and leans over the corpse.*) Come on, Paul, you are making fun of us, aren't you? . . . I am hungry, it's dinner time!

Jacques Durand (*grumbling*)   It must be even more pleasant when they are alone! . . . (*He lowers his voice.*) Lucie! . . . Lucie! . . . Remember our walk in the park, when . . . you wanted . . . to acquire . . . a new . . . (*he hesitates*) friend.

Lucie (*smiles at* **Jacques**)   Jean! . . . Bring us a lamp.

Jean (*coming in almost immediately, with a large candelabrum filled with lighted candles*)   Here, Madame.

He puts the candelabrum on the table.

Lucie (*irritated*)   I asked for a lamp, not this altar piece!

Jean *leaves the room very quickly, while watching* **Lucie** *return to the sofa. She looks at* **Paul Dartigny***, then lets out a horrible scream, and runs to the other end of the room.*

Jacques Durand (*frightened*)   What's the matter, Lucie? . . . Paul, what have you done to her? . . . (*In turn, he goes and leans over the sofa.*) Oh! Lord, these staring eyes . . . this pallor . . . But . . . (*He recoils.*) But he is dead! . . .

A moment of silence. **Lucie** *falls on her knees and buries her face in her dress.*

Jacques Durand   Help! . . . Oh! It's not possible! . . . (*He runs to the door.*) Jean! . . . A doctor! . . . Jean . . .

The servant comes in right away.

Jean (*in a respectful tone of voice*)   Is something wrong, Monsieur Durand?

Jacques Durand (*showing him the corpse*)   He is dead! . . . He was killed!

Lucie (*she rolls on the carpet, in hysterics*)   Help! . . . Help! . . .

Jean (*running to the sofa*)   It's the drugs! . . . He must have taken too much . . . Poor Monsieur! I really think you are right. He doesn't look well.

Jacques Durand (*dazed, he walks around the room while* **Lucie** *drags herself along holding onto the furniture*)   It's horrible . . . horrible! . . . My poor friend! Like that, all alone, and we thought we had saved him today! . . . Jean, keep it quiet: we don't want the neighbours on our hands . . . Lord! Lucie, calm down. (*He helps her up and places her in an armchair.*) Quiet! . . . Don't scream, I beg you . . . Jean, go get Doctor Godin. He will know what to do! . . . Paul must have committed suicide . . . In any case, I don't know any more than anybody else! . . . Try and do something, Jean . . . Get vinegar . . . Rub his hands . . .

Jean goes out.

Jacques Durand   So that our conscience is clear at least! . . . Come on, Lucie, come on now! . . .

A moment of silence. Only **Lucie***'s sobs can be heard.*

Jacques Durand   You loved him that much! . . .

Jean *comes back bringing a decanter and a cloth. He goes over to the corpse.*

Lucie (*wringing her hands*)   Lord! I am so afraid! . . . (*She tries to breathe.*) Monsieur Durand, don't leave! . . . Oh, those eyes, that mouth . . . Poor Paul! . . . That it should end like this! I knew it would! . . . (*She cries.*) I am so unfortunate . . .

Jacques Durand   Yes, we are truly to be pitied.

Jean (*composes himself and speaks in a restrained voice*)   Monsieur Jacques, there is nothing to be done: he is cold . . . But we could search the drawers: a suicide always leaves some sort of explanation.

Jacques Durand (*no longer daring to look in the direction of the sofa*)   My knees are shaking, Jean. Search if you dare. As for me, I can do no more . . . (*He leans against* **Lucie***'s armchair.*) A dead man in a room, it's like a punch in the stomach . . . (*He shivers*) No, I can do no more . . . I was his best friend . . .

Lucie (*in a panic, clutching* **Jacques***'jacket*)   You must not leave me! I would be terrified . . . Don't you think they could accuse us of killing him?

Jacques Durand (*trying to breathe*)   You are losing your mind! . . . Why would we have killed him? (*Tenderly.*) We all loved him, you, me, his servant.

Jean (*covering the dead man's face with the cloth*)   I should go get Doctor Godin then?

Jacques Durand   Go quickly, my friend. Bring him right away: we cannot stay here, Madame and I . . . We may be accountable . . . A suicide is a serious matter, very serious . . . (*A pause.*). Because usually the police get involved.

Jean *leaves.*

Lucie (*wiping her eyes*)   What will become of me?

Jacques Durand   Poor little girl! . . . (*He clasps her hands.*) Be brave. You won't be without friends . . . (*He lowers his voice.*) Did Dartigny ever used to talk about a . . . will, in the middle of his fits of melancholy?

Lucie (*with her hand on her forehead*)   Yes, I think he made one . . . Wait a moment, he was talking to me about it this afternoon . . . (*She gets up.*) There, in the desk . . . the right hand drawer. (*She turns towards the sofa.*) His face is covered. I like it better that way. (*She tries to walk a few steps.*) Oh! I was so terrified! . . . I thought he was laughing in my face . . . (*frightened*) and he was dead! . . .

She leans on **Jacques***' shoulder and walks to the desk.*

Jacques Durand   Be careful . . . You never know what they can accuse us of . . . This is a terrible situation.

Lucie (*rummaging through the drawer*)   Look, here is a letter for me . . . Ah, never mind, I am opening it . . . It's not the will, but maybe it talks about it. Anyway, it is addressed to me. (*She reads.*) 'My dear child, I cost you many smiles, and in leaving you the rest of my fortune, I remain your debtor. I hope my suicide will cause you no pain. I beg you to write nothing on my tombstone: if this does not seem too preposterous, my dear child, in six months, you will share my opinion. Your humble servant, Paul Dartigny. Postscript: My will is at Monsieur Varin's, notary, 23, Bethune Street.' (*She breaks into sobs.*) The poor man! . . . He was crazy!

Jacques Durand (*pensive*)   Yes, crazy indeed . . . When life is so beautiful!

Lucie (*sitting at the desk, her head in her hands*)   No one can accuse me of ruining him. I never asked him for anything.

Jacques Durand (*whispering*)   Well, is he leaving you his little piece of property near Fécamp? . . . Because it seems, that's all he had left . . .

Lucie (*sadly*)   How should I know? That place is just a ruin, with an ordinary ocean view, and dark, cold rooms . . . Anyway, I am going to leave . . . (*She begins to cry again.*) Who could have told me that I would be leaving before the Grand Prix, and without poor Paul!

Jacques Durand   That's beyond our control! . . . (*Mechanically, he caresses her hair.*) Listen, my darling, you must compose yourself, be a lady. Doctor Godin is on his way, and perhaps the police . . . And then, their questions could upset you in the midst of your grief . . . Those kinds of people have no respect for great sadness . . . The hell of it is, they have to have the facts! Even if you were his widow . . . (*She makes a gesture of protest.*) No doubt, you are going to tell me that illicit love, just like the other kind, has its rights . . . (*preoccupied*) Let's hope this madman made a proper will . . .

Lucie (*quickly*)   I'll find out right away. I can take care of myself, I've got a lawyer!

Jacques Durand   Ah! . . .

A moment of silence. Frightened, they turn toward the corpse.

Lucie   His mouth was so stiff! . . . Tomorrow morning, he will be really ugly, the poor man . . . He took poison, is that it?

Jacques Durand   Lucie, I assure you, it would be better for you to leave, before Godin gets here.

Lucie (*with dignity*)   It's my duty. He believed that I loved him, I shall stay.

Jacques Durand   Have I offended you, my sweet? . . . Forgive me, I am not in my right mind, such a disaster . . . And the doctor is late . . . This silence around us . . . Come on, let's just talk, it will be better . . . (*He goes near her.*) Lucie, will you allow me to be your companion?

Lucie (*sitting up straight*)   Just like that, right away, before he is even buried? . . . Oh, Monsieur Durand, you are completely wrong about me. We could simply talk, I am a respectable girl.

Jacques Durand (*quickly*)   Lucie, I meant nothing indecent. It is not a protector or a guardian I am offering you: it's a friend . . . (*A pause.*) And it is Paul's friend, more than anyone else, who has the right to help you through this ordeal . . . In any event, as I told you today, I love you like my little sister . . . (*he hesitates*) And if I held you a little too close when I said this to you, here, in front of this corpse (*he holds out his arms*), I offer you my apology.

Lucie (*taking his hand*)   You are so good . . . (*They both look at the corpse over their shoulders.*) His eyes were so bright! . . .

Jacques Durand (*making a face*)   Glassy, you mean . . .

Lucie   This doctor will never come!

Jacques Durand (*hurried*)   I'd like to go look for another one.

Lucie (*stands up and puts her arms around his neck*)   And leave me alone, with this dead man? . . . Oh, Jacques, Jacques! . . .

Jacques Durand (*pressing her to him*)   Thank you. Now I know that you care for me. And if something could console me for the loss of a dear friend . . .

They look at the corpse again.

Lucie   We'll never laugh together again! . . . Dear Paul! He was really demented. There is no reason to lie about it anymore, it was almost ridiculous . . . He saw everything in black! . . . And the manias, the egotism . . .

Jacques Durand (*quickly*)   As for that, I agree. To go so far as killing himself without leaving me a word, me who loved him and felt sorry for him . . .

Lucie   It is true. He did forget you . . . But . . . (*She hesitates.*) he must have lent you money: he lent some to everyone, as a sort of a joke.

Jacques Durand (*hesitating*)   No . . . What he lent me before, I already paid back . . .

There is noise behind the door. **Lucie** *jumps up in a panic*, **Jacques** *lets out a sigh, obviously relieved.*

Jacques Durand   It's the doctor.

Jean *enters, followed by* **Doctor Godin**, *who puts his hat on the table then goes to the corpse.*

Scene Three

Doctor Godin (*removing his gloves*)   He kept one cigar: the good one. We could not have predicted this contingency . . . In any case, I did not have the time to interrogate him . . . In sum, a very unpleasant affair . . . (*He notices* **Lucie** *and bows slightly.*) Madame . . . believe me, I understand your distress . . . I didn't see you at first . . . (*He lifts the cloth which covers the dead man's face.*) Poor boy, but what a malicious thing to do! . . .

Lucie *leans her head on* **Jacques'** *shoulder, and* **Jacques** *puts his arm around her waist.*

Doctor Godin   He is still holding the end of his cigar between the index and the middle finger of his right hand . . . (*He examines the cigar and smells it.*) Of course! . . .

Jean (*pointing to* **Jacques** *and* **Lucie**)   Monsieur and Madame will be able to testify because they were the ones who found him dead . . . I thought he was sleeping . . . (*Sadly.*) Oh, he was a strange master . . .

Doctor Godin (*examining the corpse*)   This man was built to live a hundred years, word of honour . . . They are obstinate, these neurotics . . . (*He stands up.*) Dartigny proceeded according to the following formula: my *nerium oleander* was inserted, with the help of a syringe, into the tip of the cigar . . . The alcohol evaporated, and the poison, well-spread in the tobacco leaves, retained all of its efficacy . . . The smoker's saliva dissolved it . . . (*Officiously.*) A toxic dose is ten drops, twenty drops would be lethal . . . No screams, no pain, no vomiting, no great struggle . . . At first, a short period of excitation characterized by agitation, disquiet, constrictions of the thorax, anguish, then hallucinations of sight and hearing . . . Next the senses fail, the eyesight grows dim, the ears ring, the limbs weaken, the sick man collapses, several spasms occur, and a fainting fit ends the scene . . . A clean death. He chose a very distinguished mode of suicide . . . (*To* **Jacques Durand**.) No family, eh?

Jacques Durand (*respectful and a little stunned*)   An orphan, doctor. He didn't even have a distant cousin.

Doctor Godin   That will simplify the situation . . . Then good causes and hospitals will inherit his estate? . . . Since you were intimate with him, you must know his intentions on this matter . . .

Jacques Durand   No, it is Mademoiselle.

Lucie *puts on her hat.*

Doctor Godin (*bowing*)   Naturally.

Lucie (*in a trembling voice*)   May I leave now?

Jacques Durand   You understand, doctor, she needs to pull herself together . . . And I insist on going with her, because I am dying of hunger. We will return after the usual preparations . . . (*Emphatically.*) Mademoiselle should not watch over this body. A justifiable sense of decorum obliges her to leave . . . (*More loudly.*) And I agree.

Doctor Godin (*indifferent*)   A servant will suffice for the formalities. In any case . . . (*philosophically*) since there is no one else . . .

He bows to Jacques *and* **Lucie**, *who go out rapidly.*

Scene Four

Jean (*very anxious*)   Does the doctor think that I will be interrogated?

Doctor Godin (*carefully placing the tip of the cigar in his briefcase*)   I do not think so, my friend . . . (*After a moment's reflection.*) Now give me something to wash my hands.

Curtain.

Lilith

Remy de Gourmont (1892)

Translated by Dan Rebellato

Remy de Gourmont (1858–1915) was among the most important writers and critics associated with symbolism and decadence of the fin de siècle. As well as being a prolific writer, he worked on the editorial committee for the *Mercure de France* alongside Rachilde, and both writers fostered the careers of some of the best-known playwrights of the period, including Alfred Jarry. Gourmont began experimenting with symbolist and decadent tropes and themes around the time that he was writing his play *Théodat* in 1888 (although it was not published until 1893). This was also a time when his interests in the occult began to take shape, particularly through his amorous relationship with the influential *demi-mondaine* Berthe de Courrière. As the literature Robert Pruett points out, Courrière was not only 'an eccentric *grande dame* among Parisian occult circles by the time she met de Gourmont in 1887'; she was also an eccentric whose reputation was legendary, epitomized in a series of theatrical and blasphemous acts like 'feeding consecrated wafers to stray dogs, and seducing priests (possibly inspiring the plot of *Théodat*)'.[1] As Pruett argues, it is really only after meeting Courrière that Catholicism and the occult rose to prominence in Gourmont's creative output toward the end of the 1880s and into the 1890s, not least in the eroticism and the 'anticlericalism evident in the blasphemously polemical tropes' that pepper the pages of *Lilith.*[2]

Lilith was first published in the French decadent/symbolist journal *Essais d'Art Libre* in September-October, 1892, and then immediately afterwards in a nearly identical stand-alone edition by the journal, whose editors perhaps saw in a prominent figure like Gourmont a chance to raise the profile and income of their fledgling journal. A few years later, the play was republished with some revisions by the *Mercure de France*, with his near-contemporary play *Théodat*, in an edition that was reprinted several times. As it seems probable that this latter edition represents Gourmont's final preferred version of the play, we have used the *Mercure de France* edition as the basis for his translation.[3]

Lilith is a heretical iteration of the story of Creation and Fall of Man – and Woman – that merges Genesis with the Hebraic legend of Lilith: Adam's first wife who was made by Jehovah from the same clay as Adam, and hence his equal, only to be damned to Hell because of her sexual awakening. The play situates sin as an existential characteristic of humanity, and as a site for the indulgence of pleasure in Hell as Lilith and Satan gratify erotic desires otherwise denied to humankind. This is especially noteworthy given that possession narratives were explicitly gendered in discourse surrounding the medicalisation and institutionalisation of women at the turn of the century, be it with regard to the advent and treatment of hysteria, or an assumed sensitivity toward the ill-effects of modernity. Hence, as Pruett observes, the centrality of the demonic archetype 'to the fin-de-siècle debate over sexuality allowed Gourmont to engage with the complex tensions between factions of science, spirituality, and moral politics in his own way'.[4]

1 Robert Pruett, 'Remy de Gourmont and the Crisis of Erotic Idealism', PhD thesis, St Cross College, University of Oxford (2021), 9.
2 Pruett, 'Remy de Gourmont', 13.
3 The three versions of the play are Remy de Gourmont, *Lilith. Essais d'art libre* 2 (1892): 49–147; *Lilith*. Paris: Essais d'Art Libre, 1892; and *Lilith Suivi de Théodat* (Paris: Mercure de France, 1906).
4 Pruett, 'Remy de Gourmont', 114.

The version of *Lilith* that appears in this volume was translated by Dan Rebellato, who underscores the significance of Catholicism on the development of decadent literature in the late nineteenth century. 'Catholicism', he writes, 'with its purple and its incense, was always fertile ground for the sensuous intensities of decadence, and [Gourmont's] work moved in that direction, his poetry filled with the suffocatingly perfumed flowers, richly coloured jewels, and sonorous medieval incantations'.[5] It is the bringing together of Catholicism and eroticism that makes Gourmont's play so subversive, as well as the disruptive power and potential of female dissident sexuality. Gourmont's play is not 'feminist', but it does incorporate a feminist archetype as well as feminist themes, at one point overwhelming Satan with an irrepressible, uncontainable lust. This scene is also very comic – the play is steeped in satirical, blasphemous humour – and the dialogue, especially, is suggestive of Gourmont's desire for the play to be treated as a stageable entity, however unstageable some of its stage directions may seem.

---

5   Higgins and Rebellato, 'Decadent Plays'.

male and female created he them

 Genesis 1.27

Characters

Jehovah, *Creator and Lord Almighty*
Satan, *Angel, Prince of Evil*
   Also as a beetle
   Also as a serpent
Adam, *first man*
Lilith, *first woman*
Eve, *second woman*
Raziel, *Adam's teacher*
Gabriel, *Prince of the Angels, Lord of Rise and Fall*
Michael, *Prince of the Virtues, Guardian of Beauty*
Azrael, *Angel of Death*
Raphael, *Prince of the Archangels, Lord of the Animal Kingdom*
Ridwan, *Archangel, Guardian of Earthly Paradise*
The Earth
The Figure
The Night
The Sun
The Shadows
The Silence
The Peach Tree, *tree of Good and Evil*
The Sycamore, *tree of Life*
The Lion
The Serpent
Oriphel, *Prince of the Thrones, Companion of Souls*
Zachariel, *Prince of the Dominions, Lord of Forms*
Samael, *Prince of the Powers, Lord of Punishment*
Anael, *Prince of the Principalities, Lord of the Plant Kingdom*
The Seraphim
The Cherubim
The Thrones
The Dominions
The Powers
The Virtues
The Principalities
The Archangels
The Angels
The Nephilim, *Or The Evil Ones*
The Animals Of The Second Creation

Little Sodom
Little Gomorrah
The Lusts
An Angel

Place

The play is set in the Valley of Hebron; in Earthly Paradise; in Hell; on the banks of the Euphrates; in a forest.

Scene One:[6] The Valley of Hebron

*The **Earth** glows with primordial joy. It is cool and mild; the **Sun** ripples delicately through glimmers of love.*

In the new trees, the sparrows play hide-and-seek with the sparrowhawks; the tigers roll in the fresh grass with deer; and in the clear water of the azure rivers mischievous minnows nip the tales of the great lizards asleep on the rosy sands.

Jehovah *is out walking to enjoy the world's first pleasures, and glorious contentment shines from his great brow.*

He appears borne upon a cloud floating as high as the sun: **Gabriel** *behind him, fanning him with his scented wings;* **Michael**, *his diamond sword burning lines into the air that spell out God's holy name;[7]* **Azrael**, *with dark eyes, looking, thinking;* **Satan**, *his secret heart longing for dominion over all things.[8] This is **Jehovah**'s modest procession:* **Michael** *drifts ahead;* **Azrael** *on his left and* **Satan** *on his right, as the Lord's confidant.*

As the cloud passes by, the trees incline their tops, a worshipful shiver ripples through the grass, the great lizards dip their tails in the blue water, the tigers and deer kneel, the sparrows and sparrowhawks' games fall quiet, and everywhere voices arise to sing Hosanna.

Jehovah (*stroking his flaxen beard with divine fingers*)   My works are good.

We hear mysterious distant hymns.[9]

The Seraphim   Hosanna! Your works are good, Lord. Even in the outer world, beyond this sphere, where we soar as symbol of your Lordship, the fragrance of the new world gladdens our spirits. Be fruitful, be fruitful yet. Hosanna! Lord, your works are good! Hosanna!

Satan   Yes, but will it remain good? That's the problem. What do you say, Lord: does this world not need a king?

Jehovah   The world will have its king.

---

6   To make the play easier to work with and refer to, I have editorially added scene numbers (there is more than one scene in 'Hell' or 'Earthly Paradise' which could be confusing when discussing the play).

7   The French refers to the Tetragrammaton, the four-letter Hebrew word יהוה usually transliterated as YHWH, or Yahweh when spoken, if it is spoken at all (certain observant Jews in the Talmudic tradition will not pronounce the name of God); YHWH also gives the derivative form Jehovah. Spelled out using the Hebrew letters it is YOD-HE-VAV-HE.

8   Jehovah is accompanied by four celestial figures drawn from somewhat different theological traditions, with Michael and Gabriel featuring in most Abrahamic traditions, Raphael more associated with Catholicism and Azrael more with Islam.

9   We are now introduced to various orders of heavenly beings whose names and ranks derive from Christian angelology such as the fifth-century *On the Celestial Hierarchy* by Pseudo-Dionysius the Areopagite, which determined that there are nine kinds of angels ranked in three levels: the top comprising the Seraphim, Cherubim and Thrones; the second rank comprising the Powers, Dominions and Virtues; the third rank comprising the Principalities, Archangels and Angels.

The Cherubim   Hosanna! Your works are good, Lord. The wisdom of the fixed stars have seen them and they worship. Hosanna! Lord, your works are good. Hosanna!

Satan   And who is this king, Lord? Has your Lordship already made a choice?

Jehovah   You will see. Have patience!

Satan   Excellent Lord. He wants to surprise me.

The Thrones   Hosanna! Your works are good, Lord. Wisdom, which is our law, gives praise to your Absolute Wisdom. Amen. Hosanna! Lord, your works are good! Hosanna!

Jehovah   . . . Yes, I will shape him like so, with my own hands . . .

Satan   Lord, you're not thinking of creating something new! You work too hard, Almighty. You don't want to tire yourself out.

The Dominions   Hosanna! Your works are good, Lord. We send love to this last-born of your Grace. The clouds of our hearts will rain upon its life. It will enter the loving circle of our eternal gaze. Hosanna! Lord, your works are good! Hosanna!

Jehovah   . . . made from the very same stuff as the Earth . . . this king will be a true Earthly king.

Satan   But, my Lord, what about us, your angels?

The Powers   Hosanna! Your works are good, Lord. They are righteous. Hosanna! Lord, your works are good! Hosanna!

Satan   My Lord?

The Virtues   Hosanna! Your works are good, Lord. Absolute Beauty looks and finds a sister. Hosanna! Lord, your works are good! Hosanna!

Satan   These choirs do go on a bit! With all this adoration, I can't get my hooks into him. My Lord?

The Principalities   Hosanna! Your works are good, Lord. Your creation embodies the highest of all principles. Hosanna! Lord, your works are good! Hosanna!

Satan   Lord? Dear Lord?

The Archangels   Hosanna! Your works are good, Lord. They share their being with eternity. Eternity alone has existence and as you have stamped your works with the mark of Eternity, so have they existence. Hosanna! Lord, your works are good! Hosanna!

Satan   My Lord? My beloved Lord?

Jehovah   Leave me be. My word must be fulfilled.

Satan   I genuflect before my creator's word. (*Murmuring to himself.*) Am I to be usurped before I even take the throne?

The Angels   Hosanna! Hosanna! Hosanna!

Jehovah   The time has come and this place suits me well.

The procession instantly obeys **Jehovah***'s word. The Master thinks and centuries go by. All voices fall silent. The angels worship, but* **Satan** *does not join in the universal prayer. Centuries go by, and the dark world beams in primordial joy.*

Jehovah (*awakening and stroking his flaxen beard*)   My works are good. (*He adds*)[10] Let us now make Man.

Satan   'Man'? What kind of animal is that?

Jehovah   Gabriel, hear me. With my own hands, I will make a being who will be the king of this world. Go to the Earth and fetch handfuls of white, black, red, yellow and blue clay. With these I shall create the Earthly Prince, Man: the Earth's true son – and its master.

Gabriel (*he goes and returns*)   My Lord, I did as you asked, but the Earth replied: 'You may not take clay, nor dust, nor stone. I would not let my own substance be used to make creatures who will one day drench me in blood.'

Jehovah   Since when did the Earth have the gift of prophecy? I do what I must. You go, Michael. My word must be fulfilled.

Michael (*he goes and returns*)   My Lord, I did as you asked, but the Earth said the same to me as to Gabriel.

Satan (*to himself*)   Maybe he won't get his clay!

Jehovah   Let's hear it, Satan. Do you have some advice for me?

Satan   My thoughts are but a shadow of your thoughts. I humbly beg leave to keep my counsel. Please continue, My Lord.

Jehovah   Well then, you go. Talk to the Earth.

Satan   My Lord, alas, my eloquence is hardly the most persuasive . . .

Jehovah   Azrael then, you go.

Azrael (*he goes and returns*)   My Lord, I did as you asked. The Earth said the same to me as it said to Gabriel and Michael, but I insisted and here is the clay. The white, the black, the red, the yellow, and the blue. To fulfil the word of my creator, I have brought you forty cubits.

Jehovah   This is good. Now servants of my will, leave me.

The **Angels** *vanish high into the heavens; the clouds disperse and, inclining towards the sun,* **Jehovah** *begins to handle the clay. Absorbed in his task, the divine craftsman works joyfully, and when the clay becomes too dry, he rises and fills his hands with pure water from the river and anoints the rough and ready form. As he continues, the work takes shape. As shadows lengthen his work gains in intensity, and by nightfall,*

---

10 It is worth noting the unusually novelistic device here, which is part of Gourmont's challenge to theatrical convention.

the figure is complete; **Jehovah***'s actions take centuries to decide but mere hours to perform.*

Jehovah   I am pleased. But it is not quite finished. Sun, make this figure strong and I will return to give him Life.

At the Lord's command, the **Sun** *illuminates the dark horizon with a shower of sparks before sinking behind the far Qaf mountains,*[11] *hurrying in his nocturnal course towards tomorrow. Meanwhile,* **Jehovah** *gathers the fine scraps of leftover clay that will serve him well another day. He hides them by a fig tree under fallen branches and in the strange form of a luminous vapour dissolves into the cool evening air, dispersing throughout peaceful nature.*

The Night   Oh you sweet shadows, and you blessed silence, watch over this figure that stands in the valley below. He is in your care till tomorrow. Brush the dew from the morning roses from his bed and let not the dawn's song harm his delicate fateful ears.

The veils of shadow gather over Man, but now they fade. Silence walks slow and thoughtful around the sleeping figure, but now it stops.

The Night   Come, Sun. I give you my power.

The **Sun** *flashes in the dark sky and one of its rays pierces the thick primordial gloom, falling on the figure.*

The Sun   See me rise from the abyss. Receive my fiery embrace, still-sleeping Man. Make yourself strong in the radiance of my light, you wet clay; let my warmth be the Sacrament that makes you worthy of Life.

The Angels   Hosanna!

Gabriel   What a strange creature. He's not like any of us.

Michael   He is beautiful.

Azrael   Jehovah's boundless fertility is astonishing.

Satan   Hm. Doesn't look very sturdy to me.

Azrael   Hush now.

Gabriel   Let us pray.

Michael   This new form makes even the first creation humble. I tremble with joy before a thing of such perfection.

The Angels   Hosanna!

In the distance, we hear the great thunder of **Jehovah***. The* **Angels** *disappear, but after a moment* **Satan** *reappears by the figure of Man, armed with a huge rock. He throws the rock at the figure's head: the rock bounces away leaving the Man unharmed.*

---

11 In early Islamic cosmology Mount Qaf is a mythical mountain range that forms a ring around the earth and marks the boundary between this world and the spiritual world beyond.

The Sun   Too late, Satan. I have turned the soft clay into unbreakable diamond.

Satan   Don't be so sure. Clay is clay.

He disappears. **Jehovah**, *emerging from a silver cloud, draws himself up, a band of jewels adorning his brow, the four letters of his name*[12] *burning in the air above his head. Over his long blue robe his flaxen beard cascades in majestic coils.*

Jehovah   The ordeal is over. Sun, I give you eternal life. You will endure like the king who breathes your sun-warmed air. And on that Day when all return to live in Me, when Creation itself, now Word again, returns to the comfort of my eternal breast, as birds return to the nest, on that day, Sun, you will be saved to adorn in glory my Congregation of the Chosen.

He leans over the figure and from his divine mouth breathes Life into the mouth of clay. The soul finds its dwelling place, and gradually the sleeping flesh awakens; blood fills the veins, the heart begins to beat, the arteries swell, the skin floods with colour, the chest heaves with a gigantic act of respiration; the arms and legs adjust to resemble those of a living sleeper; like a wave, the figure's insides begin to animate, its masculinity asserting itself. Then, from the extremities and depths of the body, the Breath of God rises to the head: the lips redden, the nose quivers, the eyelids flutter and there are movements in the astonished eyes, blue as the sky reflected in them. There the Breath pauses for a moment to imprint on the pupils the first insatiable desire for the beauty of the infinite, then it rises again, and this living hive begins to hum with activity.

Jehovah   Behold the king of the Earth, as I am king of the Heavens. Behold the Conscience of Life, as I am the Conscience of Being. He sleeps; come Angels, and before he wakes, worship him.

The Seraphim   Hosanna! We worship Man. He shares in our power. Hosanna!

The Cherubim   Hosanna! We worship Man. He shares in our wisdom. Hosanna!

The **Thrones** *worship Man, finding wisdom in him, and all the Legions follow Jehovah's commandment, finding in his new work the Symbol of their own virtue.*

Michael, Gabriel, Azrael   Hosanna! We worship Man, God's anointed representative, the viceroy to the Highest of the High; we worship him, for such is Jehovah's will. Hosanna!

Jehovah   And you, Satan, why do you not bow before Man?

Satan   He's not bad to look at, don't get me wrong, but there's a distinct air of mud about him.

Jehovah   Be silent, pride does not become you. Where are your great works? I and I alone may glory in my achievements. Get out of my sight; your name will be among the damned.

---

12 See n. 7.

Satan   Very well, but I take my Nephilim with me.

Jehovah   Do not drag your brothers into damnation with you.

The Nephilim   Satan is our prince and we follow him.

Jehovan   Ha! Then you shall all be damned.

Satan   My Lord, these careless words free us from our vow of obedience. To disobey you, My Lord, will be our pleasure. We will be your eternal enemies. You will have to answer to us, My Lord. As you are the day, beloved Lord, I will be the night. Strength against strength. I will regain the kingdom you have stripped from me through means of which you cannot dream, dear Jehovah. My hour will come. Throne against throne. You want me to worship Man? It will be he who worships me. Altar against altar. I salivate for my prey; I will lie in wait for him on the straight roads, leap on his back, beat him to the ground and through your creature you shall be disgraced.

Jehovah   Be gone, be gone. I will fill hell with you and your followers.

Satan (*gesturing to the sleeping man*)   I name him also among them.

Satan *exits, followed by his loyal followers to the consternation of the* **Angels**. **Jehovah**, *frowning, is distressed at* **Satan**'s *threats. But he inspects his troops: they are innumerable, their shining wings filling the vaults of heaven. Who cares about a few deserters?*

Raphael[13]   What should we do, Lord?

Jehovah   Nothing. My word will be fulfilled. All is foreseen. Come, Raphael, take that wretch's place by my side. And you Raziel, I put Man in your care. Watch over him, teach him the names and purposes of everything, teach him about life, taking care not to unsettle his freedom. Now, my Angels, leave me.

The **Angels** *disappear into the vast heavens and* **Jehovah**, *left alone, plants a garden. It is like the world in miniature. From cedar to hyssop, from mouse to lion, a Second Creation quickly takes shape, for this gardener has all the elements to hand and with a motion of his staff transports each of them to their assigned place. At his command, a babbling fountain begins to spurt water at the centre of the lawn, ready for afternoon amusements. The stream divides into four delightful rivulets, which spread out to all points of the compass, festooned with irises and laughter and fish and song. All he has left to do is raise up the two magical trees, the Tree of Knowledge and the Tree of Life. After a moment's hesitation, he settles on a peach tree and a sycamore, and he sanctifies them with a touch of his staff.*

Jehovah   In your fruit, Peach Tree, I place all knowledge. In your leaves, Sycamore, I place Life.

All is complete but to enclose the garden. He surrounds it with a girdle of cactus plants, better than stone, safer than cement. All is complete.

---

13 Gourmont has not indicated when Raphael appears.

Jehovah   Adam, arise. Come, enter the Paradise I have made to delight your eyes and satisfy your soul. Walk and eat, drink and dream, be happy. All this belongs to you, all but the peach and the sycamore. Those trees are mine and mine alone. The peaches strengthen my mercy and in the shade of the sycamore my eternity is renewed. Go, Raziel will tell you the rest.

Scene Two: Earthly Paradise

Adam   What voice was this that spoke within me but not from my lips? Am I blessed with a body as well as a will? The sound of those words was sweet to me but I can not make those sounds myself. The sounds I make now seem in quite another key . . . But how fine I am and how vast. The enormity of my being extends unto infinity: all this I am and I am all. Within me are the sky and the sun, the animals that crawl and birds that fly. How I long to discover myself, explore myself . . . well, the sun appeals first of all . . . but not unless I want to burn my fingers . . . do I have the power to hurt myself?

His hands raise to the sweet and pale sun, trying to seize it, before staring in bewilderment.

That's annoying! I wanted the sun . . . How vast I am! Truly I extend unto infinity. Yet some parts of my own self elude me . . . I'm going to play with the birds.

He reaches out to grab a bird swooping by but his hand comes back empty.

What? Not even the birds? What about these blossoms? They'll surely feel soft against my skin.

Desperately, he stretches out his arms towards the blossom trees, but the movement tugs the rest of his body and he starts to walk. His muscles work together beautifully, flexing with such grace that his legs carry him to the trees without conscious effort. It is a cherry tree in bloom with fruit in abundance: the red cherries and the pink flowers captivate him for a moment and he touches them but is disappointed by the ordinary sensation. **Raziel** *comes to help him, offering him a flowered branch for him to smell, then gathering a handful of cherries and placing them, one by one, in his mouth.*

Adam *begins to understand.* **Raziel***, then, as* **Jehovah** *has commanded, begins the education of the first man. Within a few hours, his remarkable intelligence has grasped the fundamental mysteries of the universe. Nothing surprises* **Adam** *now; he knows all he needs to carry himself easily in this world. The distinction between self and other has been a little upsetting, but because he is obedient and* **Raziel** *is very skilled, he eventually accepts this disconcerting distinction.*

Raziel   These are for walking. These are for holding. These are for listening. These are for seeing. This is for eating. And this is for . . . this is for . . .

Adam   Do . . . you not know?

Raziel   Let's ignore that for now. I'll check with Jehovah.

Adam   Please do find out. I'd like to know what every part of my body is for.

Raziel   I promise. Farewell. I will return. On high, a full-blown war is raging, and Michael has trusted me with an important role . . . but don't worry, we will win the day. Relax now. Sleep.

Adam *obeys* **Raziel***'s command. His eyelids close; he stretches out on the grass and goes to sleep, soothed by the babbling fountain. When he wakes, he is no longer the innocent* **Adam** *of his first day, but a lord and master with plans and dreams, who walks with confidence, taking pleasure in his estate. But he is sometimes uneasy: whether sleeping or waking or contemplating his lush, sweet lawns, a vague sense of boredom spreads through him. He ponders the mystery that the Angel could not explain, but can find no answer.* **Raziel** *has returned almost every day; they have spoken easily but he still is no better informed:* **Jehovah** *only replied with an enigmatic smile. And anyway he's usually busy in conversation with* **Michael**. *But as soon as the war is over, as soon as* **Satan** *is vanquished, says* **Raziel**, *he will find out.*

Adam (*melancholy, lying on his front, trailing his fingers in the water*)   I'm bored.

Raziel (*suddenly appearing, then disappearing immediately after speaking*)   Have patience. Jehovah is thinking of you. But Michael is about to launch the final attack.

Adam   Thank you! But I'm just so bored.

He plucks a few blades of grass and casts them into the water which carries them away on the current. When he has picked all the grass around him he says again:

I'm bored.

Eventually he sleeps, but in the first semi-conscious state between waking and sleep, he feels as though a higher will is overwhelming his brain and dragging him down into his primal darkness.

Scene Three: The Valley of Hebron

Jehovah   My sceptre is in my hand, my crown firm on my head. So why am I afraid? All my angels are loyal and the Nephilim are buried beneath an avalanche. Angels they were, just like the others; but now they are Demons, lost in damnation. Now I need no longer fear them, I pity them. Why did I bring them into being? And when I did so, why did I place in them the seed of their future disobedience? If they criticised me for that, what would I say? Simply this: all creatures are imperfect, because they are the product of another; if they were perfect they would be the equal of their creator. No thank you very much! Once I had resigned myself to my own creative powers, I could not have created a better world than this. Yes, 'resigned myself' because otherwise my divinity could never have fully shown itself: the world was born from my mind and in the world's mind I will live, a righteous exchange. When my handiwork is completed, I will rest until that day I return to destroy the fleeting creation of my infinite powers.

And where am I now? With Man, the source of the rebellion . . . Man, Oh Man, you creature of sorrow. So let us complete this now. Raziel[14] said Man was bored, which I knew and had foreseen. I endowed him with a strong will but no means to satisfy it . . . but I was thinking: did I not have a little more clay put aside?

Beneath the branches by the fig tree he finds the clay he used to make man and starts to work on them, quickly fashioning a second figure.

I have been thinking: it is not good for a man to be alone.

The new creation quickly takes on the required form. With the palms of his hands he forms curved breasts and hips; he shapes and fills them, building the figure up so much that at the moment he goes to complete the head he finds he doesn't have enough clay. So he grabs a handful from her womb leaving a deep hole and with it supplies the woman with her missing brain.

Finally, he breathes into her nostrils, saying.

Arise. Your name is Lilith.

Lilith (*standing up and twisting her hips gracefully, running her hands over her beautiful breasts*)   Give me Man, my Lord.

Jehovah   Already?

Lilith   Give me Man, my Lord, the man for whom I was made.

Jehovah   Do you have not a thought for me?

Lilith   Give me Man, my Lord. Give me my master.

Jehovah   I am your master.

Lilith   Man is man as I am woman and he is my master.

Jehovah   Oh no! Oh no!

Lilith   I am his woman and his mistress.

Jehovah   Oh no! Oh no!

Lilith   Give me Man, good Lord.

Jehovah   Oh no! Oh no!

Lilith   Give me Man, mighty Lord.

Jehovah   Oh no! Oh no!

Lilith   Give me Man, great Lord.

Jehovah (*striking her with his staff*)   Enough!

---

14 In all editions of the play, this name is given as Azraël, but in the play Adam's teacher and intermediary with God is the anagrammatic Razael, so I suspect this is an error and have changed it.

Lilith *is ashamed and starts pleading. She cries, she falls to her knees, wails, begs forgiveness, but* **Jehovah** *is unmoved.*

Jehovah   You will not have Man. You exist and I cannot destroy you, but I damn you. You are not the first. Go find Satan. I give you to him and him to you. You are the two misfortunes of my creation; mate and breed demons. You will not have Man.

Lilith   Lord, have pity on your creature, have pity on this woman . . .

Jehovah   You are no woman. You are a monster.

Lilith (*she looks herself up and down and says*)   A monster? A monster? Could I be?

Jehovah   Azrael!

Azrael (*descending as commanded*)   Lord?

Jehovah   Take this creature to Satan. Let them have each other.

Lilith   Is he a man?

Jehovah   He'll do.

Lilith   Then I accept – until I can have the other! Farewell, my Lord!

Azrael *takes* **Lilith** *off. As they go:*

Jehovah (*thinking, dismayed*)   What have I made? A foul creature and a bad omen. I must have been distracted. I will start again. But since natural means have failed me, I will use magic. Poor Adam.

Scene Four: Hell

Azrael *hands* **Lilith** *to* **Satan** *and delivers* **Jehovah**'s *message.*

Satan   Welcome. It seems Jehovah's foolishness has provided me with company. Welcome, fortunate refugee from his withered fingers. Welcome, beautiful daughter of pleasure. Welcome, Lust. I have been missing that vice. Well, this is more enticing pleasure than pride. Pride is hollow.

Lilith *permits him, her eyes closed, to caress her breasts with both hands.*

Satan   So firm, so soft, so warm . . .

These physical attentions delight **Lilith**, *who convulses, writhes and squirms. But* **Satan**, *not knowing this woman, dumbly begins to grope at her like a thick dough. He drools, his eyes bloodshot, his efforts becoming frenzied, as he growls, barks and bites.*

Then, with a skilful move, **Lilith** *calms him; she sinks to her knees, grave, submissive and kisses him as a man is kissed. Then she lies down, bringing with her* *the cowed demon, who now understands at last the deeds and depravities for which she hungers.*

Satan   Yes, these had to be our first kisses. We have broken love for eternity. We have turned it inside-out. I worship you, woman.

Lilith   I worship you, male.

Satan   Female, I give you the seed of my night.

Lilith   Male, I give you the prayers of my morning.

Satan   I shall inhale the smell of your sex as if it were a bouquet of lilacs.

Lilith   I shall feed your sex as a mother feeds a young bird.

Satan   My universe fills your darkness.

Lilith   Your ecstasy fills my senses.

Satan   We have achieved communion between our species, do you understand that? In four or five thousand years, this will still provoke bitter laughter. You appreciate the blasphemy of it.

Lilith   Oh my daily bread.

Satan   Oh my chalice of new wine.

Lilith   I hunger for your flesh, my he-goat.

Satan   I am thirsty for your blood, my she-wolf.

They launch at one other as if mounting an attack, twisting themselves into violent shapes. Finally they collapse, crushed, mouths open, fingers hooked inwards like claws.

Lilith (*speaking first, in a voice filled with lust, each invocation leading to a caress*)   Yod,[15] male, God and Phallus, centre of the Earth and Spirit, I worship you, י, male.

Satan   *He*, female, Beauty and Womb, spirit of lust and lethargy, I worship you, ה, female.

Lilith   *Vav*, copulation, female and male, proboscis and calyx, tomorrow's darkness, I worship you, ו, copulation.

Satan   ה, female!

Lilith   Call me not *He*, call me Sterility. Am I not The Infertile?

Satan   No, you shall have a son called Sodom and a daughter called Gomorrah.

Lilith   Bless them and be they the only ones I would be the happiest mother of all mothers. Amen. Oh Father of all vices hereafter, come to my joyful lips.

---

15 The two of them are spelling out the name of God (see n. 7), presenting an interesting challenge for performance.

Scene Five: Earthly Paradise

Adam *is asleep.* **Jehovah**, *who has just placed him in this state of unaccustomed oblivion, watches over his creation with an indulgent eye, lost in thought, his fingers running through his flaxen beard.*

A gentle perfumed breeze plays with **Adam**'*s hair and* **Jehovah**'*s cloak of deep purple flutters like a battle standard around his uncreated limbs.*[16]

Jehovah *continuously runs his holy fingers through his flaxen beard, keeping* **Adam** *asleep, as he prepares to scale the mysterious heights of his supernatural power.*

Jehovah   The woman I created for you has defied my will, Adam, almost as though my creative powers were exhausted. Maybe my destiny ends there, with you, my masterpiece and nothing perfect will come from these hands again. But you, who are perfect, you who are beautiful, you who are holy, you whom the Seraphim themselves, the distant guardians of Infinity, greeted as a brother, you will provide me with the seed for the companion you seek. Where should I take this seed from? Which scrap of your body shall I choose?

Jehovah *contemplates the sleeping man.*

The ear? Then she would be curious.
The brow? Then she would be proud.
The eyes? Then she would be flirtatious.
The nose? Then she would be a sensualist.
The mouth? Then she would be a gossip.
The tongue? Then she would be a liar.
The palate? Then she would be a glutton.
The hand? Then she would be a thief.
The foot? Then she would be faithless.
The heart? Then she would be jealous.
The belly? Then she would be lustful.
I need to make a body that is steadfast and loyal.

And **Jehovah** *reaches into Man's body and pulls out one of his ribs, sealing up the flesh around the gaping wound, staunching the blood with his crimson cloak.*

There. Man will bleed and love the wound. Ah but those faults that I wanted to shield from Man's helpmeet, will she have them? I feel old, my hands shake, I'm fearful, as if I'm consigning Adam to damnation. But onward, the die is cast. This piece of flesh wants life.

He touches it with his staff, saying:

Be woman.

---

16 This obscure phrase ('ses membres incréés') refers to the idea that God created the world but is Himself not created. The Athanasian Creed refers to God as *pater uncreatus.*

The woman rises, her body veiled by her long hair. Her first movement is to the fountain, to admire herself.

Jehovah   Well, Adam will have nothing to complain about: they are made of the same substance. If one falls, so will the other and they can find consolation together on their way down. Arise Adam, and see the one born of you.

Adam (*gets up and seeing the woman, says:*)   Yes, this is my flesh, she is flesh of my flesh, bone of my bone, blood of my blood. While I slept, Raziel came to tell me of Lilith's wickedness. Save me from her, Lord, and give this one to me.

Jehovah   I give her to you, but remember that you must be at once father, brother, and husband to her. She is the last exertion of my powers, a mere sketch; your love will complete her. Let her name be Eve. Farewell my children. Be happy.

He goes, troubled by a vague premonition that disturbs his universal soul.

Eve *has divided her hair into two silky blonde tresses, wearing her hair like a cloak. She contemplates her appearance in the fountain.*

She leans forward, then straightens and looks round, her young eyes full of pure and innocent pleasure.

Adam (*approaches her, arms outstretched*)   I had everything yet nothing like myself. I have feelings I can't put into words. To see you there, you whom I always desired without knowing it, fresh as the morning and sweet as the evening. I am two and I am one. What a sacrament we have to perform. I love you.

Eve   I love you.

They approach, tentatively, but as soon as they touch, they entwine easily. They are united and at the height of their passion they soar together as one in a glorious flight that expands into their consciousness and then throughout the span of each human life. It feels to them as though days and night have passed, that the seasons have rolled by, and that their lives are conjoined, taking pleasure in the constant plenitude of inexhaustible love. Untroubled in their dreams, their minds at night are as joyfully entwined as their bodies by day, extending in sleep the pleasures of their flesh. When they open their eyes toward morning, it is with a smile of desire as they feel their aching limbs restored.

Eve *admires* **Adam***'s lithe muscles and* **Adam** *the graceful ease of the woman.*

The two are glowing and magnificent. Their skin is like creamy mother of pearl, tossed by the sea, shimmering with the pink of dawn and the blue of the sky.

However, the woman's spirit and her senses have been awoken and her curiosity drives her relentlessly to question **Adam***. She is like a young child making a first trip away from home.*

Eve   Tell me, what was the world like before you?

Adam   Before me there was nothing but the Word of God.

Eve   Do you look like God?

Adam   Yes, Raziel told me that God made me in his image.

Eve   Is he as beautiful as you, as strong, as lovable?

Adam   He is infinite.

Eve   I love you more than him.

Adam   You must love him above all, certainly above me.

Eve   But I don't know him. You are my God. Anyway, tell me: why is the Sun brighter than the Moon?

Adam   In the beginning, they shone equally on the Earth. God created them together to provide light as he worked, but then he blew out the moon to create a difference between night and day.

Eve   How does the Sun move?

Adam   On a chariot pulled by three hundred and sixty angels. When he has finished his day's journey, he returns to sleep beneath the throne of God.

Eve   And how is the night made?

Adam   Every evening, an angel takes a handful of shadows, then relaxes their grip and scatters the night across the sky.

Eve   Who taught you all these extraordinary things?

Adam   Raziel.

Eve   Raziel? Can I meet him? Please say yes. Tell me: why is the sky blue?

Adam   It reflects the great blue mountain, Mount Qaf, which is as blue as your eyes.

Eve   Why are my eyes blue?

Adam   Ah, that I don't know.

Eve   You must know. Who will teach me if you won't? I don't have my own Raziel.

Adam   But even if I don't know . . . so what? They are lovely.

Eve   I want to know.

*A **Lion** approaches, mild and magnificent. He stops before **Eve**, twitching his tail, begging to be stroked.*

Oh what a beautiful lion! Come, brother lion, and play with me!

*She strokes him, scratches his belly, runs her rosy fingers through his thick mane. The **Lion** sits up and begs, roars softly, and rubs himself against her hip.*

My beautiful lion!

*She runs off, the **Lion** chasing her, and as soon as he catches her the game begins again.*

Adam (*watching them with an amused smile*)   She's quite mad! She's a child!

Raziel (*watching, unnoticed by* **Adam**)   How are you, Adam. Happy?

Adam (*jumps with surprise*)   Oh! Yes . . .

Raziel   Do you now know all the secrets of your body?

Adam   Yes.

Raziel   You are so happy that jealous people are planning to destroy you.

Adam   Is God not beside me?

Raziel   God is beside you, but do not forget his commandments. Remember what he bade you do, remember what he forbade you do. Keep an eye on your wife.

During these words, **Eve** *has returned, riding on the obliging* **Lion***. With a branch from the cedar tree she laughingly thwacks him on the rump; the* **Lion** *jumps up and leaps back gently to the ground before* **Raziel***, with* **Eve** *clinging to his mane. The* **Lion** *lies down at his feet, closing his eyes in happiness.*

Eve   Were you talking about me? Are you Raziel?

Raziel   I am Raziel. You are welcomed among all creatures, radiant beauty.

Eve   Why are my eyes blue? Adam doesn't know.

Raziel   To make them, God took two fragments of the heavens and in each one was a star.

Eve   Thank you, that makes me happy. Tell me another thing: Adam says before him there was nothing but the Word of God.

Raziel   Why are you asking me? What a man does not know his wife should not be told.

Adam   It is no shame not to know what happened in the world before I was made. Did Life and Consciousness not exist before me?

Raziel   Life, yes: plant and animal. Consciousness, no. And you were right, Adam: before your creation, the Earth was a mere phantom. But the heavens existed with all their ethereal tribes and before the heavens, Jehovah and the Law, that is now and evermore. The first thing God created was a Reed and anything he wished to create he told the Reed to write down. The Reed wrote and God created everything the Reed wrote. He made the Earth, the sun and moon, the stars. Then he turned the heavenly spheres on his wheel. At the fifth hour of the sixth day, Friday, Jehovah started to make Man: and that is all that I may tell you.

Adam   We thank God for having made us.

Eve   Life is lovely. Truly, I am having such fun . . . isn't that right, beautiful lion? Farewell, Raziel.

Raziel   Her love is so innocent! She's sending me away. Well then, be beloved you two. I must go.

As soon as **Raziel** *disappears,* **Eve***'s eyes gleam divinely, her arms part to embrace* **Adam***, and the work of the flesh is completed once more.*

These renewed pleasures are no lesser than the first and each day produces new heights of ecstasy.

They eat the fruits and the bitter herbs, they drink water from the fountain from their cupped hands or lying on their bellies. Often, **Eve** *is tempted by the jewelled peaches of the forbidden tree, but* **Adam** *reminds her of* **Jehovah***'s words, and she has no wish to displease he who created love.*

Scene Six: Hell

Lilith   They look happy.

Satan   They can't get enough of each other.

Lilith   It's not fair.

Satan   We'll have our revenge, don't worry.

Lilith   Your kisses are cold, why? And nothing, not your touch, nor your bites, nor the wicked ideas of our diabolical minds, nothing inflames my dulled desire.

My ecstasies are flowing out like water through a puncture, my senses are dead like old leaves, my soul as numb as the clay from which Jehovah made me . . . rip me open till the blood pours down my thighs, let's make a bloody feast of love . . . Where is that Satan, firm from the first, who rose like a God before my enraptured eyes, you who for whom I thought I would always hunger, where are you? An unripe fruit falls from my famished mouth . . . ah now if I had only had Man . . . he used to be mine . . . it's him I want . . .

Satan   Take him then.

Lilith   Are you joking?

Satan   No, I'll let you have him, and I'll take the woman.

Lilith   What?

Satan   I've been thinking about it for a while. Yes, I'll let you have him . . . Poor God! If you had only heard him going on and on: 'My works are good. Truly my works are good . . .' Poor God! You've done my work for me . . . Yes, Lilith, I will let you have Man, I'll place him in your power for you to degrade: laugh at his tears, turn his pleasure to shame, his home to a madhouse and his bed into a brothel. As for the woman, I will remake her in your image . . . she will cry in ecstasy like a mother whose child is abducted by a wolf . . . *In vulva infernum.*[17] And the Euphrates could flow through it without putting out the fire.

---

17 Latin: 'In the hell-womb'.

Scene Seven: Beyond the Cactus

Satan (*who has transformed himself into a dung beetle, enjoying himself by rolling dungballs*)   Hah! I certainly have the look and habits of a future God. This is no step down. Listen, Serpent!

The **Serpent** *approaches. His eyes are emeralds, his tongue an arrow of diamond, his body a silver necklace encrusted with amethysts, with a tapering ruby at the end of his tail. As he unwinds his coils, deep fiery sparks ripple through him. He looks disdainfully at the beetle.*

The Serpent   And what do you want with me?

Satan   To see you up close. You are so beautiful.

The **Serpent** *rises up to his full height, balanced on his tail, smugly showing off his sparkling jewellery.*

Satan   And I have some advice to ask of you. You are so wise.

The **Serpent** *puffs himself up, nodding.*

Satan   Why don't we enter Paradise? It seems so peaceful in there.

The Serpent   That is forbidden and the Angel Ridwan who guards the gate would cut me clean in two! So no thank you!

Satan   Oh, but you are so cunning, you could pass through a wormhole. Slide between a couple of cactus plants, you'd be through in a flash. You're so clever.

The Serpent   And what about you?

Satan   Open your mouth and you can hide me in your stomach. Nothing is impossible for a clever snake like you.

Flattered, the **Serpent** *agrees to the ruse, slithering beneath the cactus hedge, alert for sounds, seeking out the dark paths. Soon he emerges into the sunshine of Paradise and frees* **Satan**.

Satan   And now give me your skin, your shape, and your soul.

This wheeze appeals to the **Serpent** *who begins divesting himself of these things.*

Dressed as a serpent, but still with that angelic face that neither pride nor lust has disfigured, he glides off in search of his victims.

Scene Eight: Earthly Paradise

Adam *and* **Eve** *are sitting on the grass in the shade of the flowering willows. They play and talk as they eat the fruit they have picked.*

Eve   Life is truly good. To think that I shall be young and beautiful and queen of all things, always and for ever.

Adam   Yes, we were made for eternal pleasures and if we exhaust these, if our spirits lead us elsewhere, Jehovah will give us all the new experiences and ecstasies we need.

Eve   What else could you wish for? For me, I love you and that's enough.

Adam   I have you and that is all I want.

And desire once again joins and conjoins the two holy lovers.

Sensuality, like a high sea that rages through the night, sends powerful waves of eternal love swelling and churning through their fated hearts.

Afterwards, as they wake, they return from the infinite. With deep mutual regard for the other's ability to give them pleasure, they exchange sacred kisses and go wandering hand in hand down several paths, eyes half-closed, trembling at having touched heaven but happy to be returned to Earth – already imagining the next delight.

As they walk and recover their senses, tenderness shines in their eyes.

They are silent.

They drink water from the springs, pet the animals that come to lick their feet, wave to the birds, smile at the flowers that give so generously of their perfume.

Eve   Oh what a beautiful creature! Look, Adam! His head is the colour of the Sun, like Raziel. Goodness, he is winding himself around Jehovah's peach tree!

Adam   Who are you?

Satan   A friend. A true friend.

Adam   Did Jehovah send you?

Satan (*chuckles*)   Let's just say I'm a fan. You're so happy and why wouldn't you be; all this is yours, animals and objects, plants and fruits – well (*chuckles*) not all the fruits.

Eve   Yes, all of them, we are masters of this garden.

Adam   No, he's right, Eve, remember that this peach tree is off limits and this sycamore too.

Satan   Oh, so things are not as happy as I thought. I came here expecting perfect happiness, absolute freedom, and instead what have I found? Prisoners! With chains on your wrists and fetters on your ankles.

Adam   We are happy and free.

Satan   Free to obey on pain of death.

Adam   But I never even think of this peach tree. It's nice to look at but I'm sure the fruit is sour.

Eve   I admit that I often fancy one but it's no hardship to go without. And remember, sweet creature: the fruit is poisonous.

Satan   Who told you that?

Adam   Jehovah. He said, 'if you eat these fruits, you will die'.

Satan   My little ones! You can make people believe anything you want. I think Jehovah's playing a trick on you, my friends. Despite his pompous manner of speaking, he has a great sense of humour. Use your common sense. This is called the Tree of Knowledge – the Knowledge of good and evil. Good and evil: an interesting distinction but not one that means much to you – in fact it only means something to Jehovah. That distinction is the essence of his divinity – so if some creature were to really understand it, it would make them equal with their creator. In other words, eat and you shall know; eat and your ignorance will fall away; eat and you shall be Gods. Do you understand? It's your ignorance that will die, not you.

Eve   What if we were to try it, Adam?

Adam   No, that's a terrible idea. In fact, no, I don't even want to look at it. It scares me this tree. I feel my hand reaching out against my will towards the delicious fruit . . . No!

He turns away and walks a few steps away, stopping by a cherry tree, and starts eating the cherries.

Eve, come here, and you – deceiver! – be gone.

Satan   Bit of a coward, your husband, isn't he? Be honest, do you never get bored with him?

Eve   Never, I worship him.

Satan   Yes but to be blunt, someone as slender as you, as fair, as intelligent, as lively, as beautiful, such a creature surely deserves to sit alongside God. And she could, if she just said the word. Wouldn't it be a fine thing to know everything, to be able to explain everything. Is there anything worse than an unsatisfied curiosity?

Eve   It's true, I am always so curious, you have no idea how curious. What are these fruit like? Very sweet would you say?

Satan   Find out for yourself.

Eve   Tell me.

Satan   They look like it. So refreshing!

Eve   Just looking at them feels good.

Satan   Well then, collect your husband and stop worrying. They're lovely, a gift from the Gods.

Eve   Oh but I want them so much.

Satan   A young woman must be smart and obedient and resist temptation . . . No touching the delicious fruit, pretty girl . . . ! It's forbidden! Tut tut!

Eve   I want one.

*She picks a peach, her beautiful teeth sinking into its sweet flesh – and **Satan**'s eyes shine with hellish fire.*

Eve   Oh it tastes so good! It tastes like love. Try it, Adam. I feel like I'm drinking life itself. Divinity is running through me. The juice! Adam, come, take one of these. And you, thank you, thank you, what's your name?

Satan   Satan.

Eve   Oh my sweet Satan, thank you. I love you.

Adam   She's eating the forbidden fruit but she's not dead. Give it to me.

Eve   Bite in my bitemarks.

Adam (*after taking a bite*)   Now I feel strong, I feel tall, like I could touch the sky.

*The Heavens tear open. The veil of the Universe is torn away. The **Sun** rains burning fire down on Nature; the grass shrivels; the animals run frantically for the cover of trees – but the trees grow pale and, for the first time, the leaves fall. The **Sun** laughs.*

The Sun   Once I used to smile at the simple pleasure of ordinary things and Innocence, like a myrtle bush, gave off a fragrance that soothed my restless heart. That still shade wherein the world once dreamed. Sin has conquered you so now I laugh. I burst with laughter.

*Suddenly, **Adam** falls to the ground, overwhelmed.*

Adam   The light, the light! It's burning my eyes!

Eve   Adam, what is this storm blowing through me? It's hot and cold and I'm scared, I'm scared.

Satan (*concealed in the leaves of the defiled tree, he sings out in triumph*)   Oh Almighty Lord, your reign is at an end. The Earth is mine, their bodies are mine, their souls are mine. I am king and I rise up to crush all lesser kings: the female, ashamed but wild with desire, will foreswear her lover's bed and kiss my sweet arse.

And my seed will enter her pregnant womb to baptise the fruit of every human union in my name.

The empty arrogance that is their weakness will pollute their soul like mine is polluted by that hyena with red fangs, desire.

They will sleepwalk through their life under the dusty veil of indolence, paralysed by fear, cloaked in cowardice – their conscience floating like shit in their bloated bowels.

Deadly anger rising in their pure-white cheeks will twist like a bindweed around their parched tongues and down into their chests, scratched at by their bloody nails, a misshapen purse will beat as if it were once a heart.

Eventually – and this will be particularly enjoyable – I will watch over their befouled children, and once the descendants of Lilith have emasculated the males, I will give them virgins who only open their legs to them in dreams.

Eat, my little ones, eat. Good yes? Do you feel yourself becoming godlike? How *do* you feel? Tell me . . . Not too much though! Leave some for later or you'll give yourself a tummy ache, my sweet young gods.

Adam   I don't know what you're talking about, but I do feel extremely agitated: Knowledge is suffocating me. Ignorance has gone and left in its place a deep abyss. I know . . . but what do I know? . . . I know that I know nothing. Give me back my animal self, you tempter. What are we to become? Sun, please, enough. My skin is burning.

Satan   Gluttony and Cowardice: two sins down, five to go. Let's carry on.

Eve   I don't feel well, but these sweet fruit are soothing me. From now on, this is all I shall eat.

Satan   Oh but what's this? Look, you're both completely naked!

Adam   You're right. Oh I feel so ashamed!

Eve   Completely naked . . . I feel cold.

He watches them as they blush, because with the woman's eyes on him, the man has found himself seized by new feelings – or at least ones neither he nor **Eve** *had previously encountered.*

Adam   Let's cover ourselves. Let's put some leaves around our waists.

Eve   Let me look at you. Let me touch you.

Adam   Remember we're not alone.

Eve   Come to me, I want you.

Panting she arches her back, her breasts heaving, her chest rising and falling, delighted for the first time by her own feminine beauty, whose attractions have until now been veiled by ignorance.

Adam   Cover yourself!

Eve   Why? Aren't I nice to look at?

Satan   Gluttony, sloth, cowardice, and lust – if we can get that list up to seven, I'll be happy.

Adam   Look, put these leaves on.

While **Adam** *creates a girdle of leaves and tries his best to hide his awkward nakedness, she fashions a crown of greenery, trailing vines around her like a necklace.*

Eve   Look.

Satan   You are quite delightful with your pretty adornments, though Adam and his girdle . . . oh dear . . .

Adam   Keep out of this, you foul creature.

Satan   Gluttony, sloth, lust, anger.

Adam   Eve, take those trinkets off and put on a girdle like mine.

Eve   You're just jealous, aren't you? You know how ugly you look . . .

Adam   Jealous, me? Hardly! I'm just as beautiful as you are.

Satan   Gluttony, sloth, lust, anger, jealousy and pride.

Eve   Look, take my crown, and give me the girdle. I like the pretty flowers you've used . . .

Adam   No, make another one. This one's mine.

Eve   Please!

Adam   No, it's mine, do you hear me? Mine! Mine!

Satan   And greed, thank you. The last bead in the rosary. Farewell! We'll see each other again.

Satan *disappears.*

Adam   So he's gone – the monster!

Eve   Oh he's not so bad.

Adam   Be quiet! You will look at no other creature but me.

Eve   Oh really!

Adam   You want to watch yourself.

Eve   You're no fun.

Enraged, **Adam** *raises his hand to his impudent wife, but something unusual interrupts this first marital quarrel.*

The branches of the holy peach tree suddenly lengthen becoming canes which then are brought down violently on the guilty pair's backs. They run, the cruel scourge following them, driving them to the gates of Paradise. There, flanked by angels with swords of fire and thunder, stands **Ridwan**. *At that moment,* **Jehovah** *descends on a cloud, with* **Raphael** *beside him where* **Satan** *used to sit.*

Jehovah (*stroking his flaxen beard*)   What have you done?

Adam   Nothing.

Eve   Nothing.

Jehovah   Why these leaves?

Eve   We were cold.

Jehovah   You are lying. You must be the guilty one.

Eve   My lord, my lord!

Jehovah   Tell me everything.

Eve   We barely took a bite, if that, and it was only to please a dear creature called Satan.

Jehovah   Enough. We know all.

He points to the **Sun**.

Jehovah   You have sinned. Here is proof and punishment . . . That star that enumerated your pleasures will now count your woes. Every day, the sun will rise on your boredom and set on your despair. Your skin will not be bronzed but burned. The sun will expose your evil deeds and reveal your bestial natures: you are nothing more than animals. You were ignorant; now you are fools. You were the masters of all the perfection you could bear; now you are slaves of Knowledge whose truths are fleeting. You wanted to know but what do you know? The one thing I kept from you: that the world is evil.

What shall I do with you? You deserve death, but to destroy the consciousness of life . . . you were the dust that I crowned in eternal glory and now you are but beasts of sorrow. Thanks to you, alas, the Earth is cursed never to bring forth anything but rocks and thorns, unless you water it with your own sweat. Eve, you will remember me, when you give birth; man too will tremble to his very depths, when flesh painfully parts from flesh. A bond shall exist between you; you will suffer less by sharing in your suffering, though suffer you shall. Why did you disobey me? Come, my word must be fulfilled. Leave this paradise and take possession of the Earth. The world is wide. Fill it with your misery.

Adam *and* **Eve** *obey, leaving but casting frequent glances at paradise lost. Already when they speak, the inevitable words 'in the old days' scatters through their conversation. Thus is born in the hearts of the exiles the legend of a Golden Age. They repeat it so that they may one day tell it to their children and their children's children. They go, sad and proud of the fabled bliss whose dawn colours glow in their memories.*

Jehovah   Fly, my birds. What will become of them, under the cruel gaze of the watchful sparrowhawk? My sweet birds in whom I took such joy and what have they left me? A broken cage.

He enters the Garden and his terrible gaze withers the grass and the bushes, the trees and the beasts, every living thing. On his word, the angels set about destroying this masterpiece of all gardens.

May the Tree of Knowledge burn like firewood.

Lightning strikes the Tree of Knowledge and burns it to the ground.

May the Tree of Life meet the same end.

And **Jehovah**'*s command is obeyed.*

So do I make wilderness. Above all the Sycamore had to be destroyed, because if with the Tree of Knowledge it had conquered Life, what would I be then? A God among gods, but not the God of gods. I was afraid when Raziel came to me in tears to speak of the disobedience of my creatures. But now, all is well, my reign endures. But maybe I should abdicate and give my Son authority over the Earth. The Heavens are enough to occupy me in my old age. Everything I do now turns bad: the last of my angels defy me; Man has walked the same road into prideful disobedience; and Woman, that damnable design . . . But no, I will have the final word, until the end, down through the centuries, I will continue to declare: My works are good.

The Lords of Heaven   Hosanna! Your works are good, Lord! Hosanna!

Jehovah   Sycophants . . . ! Listen, Oriphiel. Lord of the Order of Thrones, your duties are changed by a new commandment. Listen, all of you. I have made several changes which you must know. Sin has sired Death and the harvest will be through the generations – each will feel their mortal agonies in their own time – and then, when each is freed from physical torment, bring them to me that they might receive judgement. Those that Satan the Damned won to his cause, I will give to him; the others, I shall give to my Eternal Son. This is your new duty, Oriphiel.

Oriphiel   I will pass between heaven and Earth, as you command, and I will gather the dying breaths of humanity in these hands. *In manus.*[18]

Jehovah   Zachariel, Lord of the Order of Dominions, you shall govern the forms of all creation and ensure nothing born shall deviate from the form of its makers.[19] You will preserve the species and see that none encroach on another, that the tiger not lie with the lion, nor the ass mate with the mare; that Woman not sleep with a demon, nor Man with a goat; that the pollen of a dog rose not trouble the pistil of the periwinkle, and if the minnow try to fertilise the eggs of a trout, his seed be sterile. Watch over these kingdoms: destroy the primordial soup in which all that lives and moves or does not move was made. Let not the plant eat nor the animal produce flowers, and let nothing grow among the fearsome gemstones and unfathomable creatures in the sea's depths. Let all eyes be given sight, let each organ have its distinct role, let antennae that hear be not those that feel and if minute creatures build forests beneath the ocean waves, let their works be destroyed, because I am the Creator and nothing may have essence or form that comes not from my hands. This is your duty, Zachariel.

Zachariel   This will test my angelic powers but with your help I will succeed.

Jehovah   Samael, Lord of the Order of Powers, take the punishment lash, ensure its knots are made of thorns, so the flesh spurts blood and even the least of the wounds infect and putrefy. You will spare the strong, so they stay strong enough to crush the weak. For the sickly, show no mercy, give no respite, be their unceasing tormenter: let

---

18 Latin: 'In hands'. Perhaps what is unheard here is 'tuas' (*Your* hands), a common formulation in the Latin Psalms; Oriphiel is acknowledging that his own hands are God's hands.

19 Gourmont's Jehovah denies the theory of evolution here.

their breathless hearts forever batter at their feeble chests. Let them crawl on their scrawny knees and may sharp stones poison their joints. Let a frozen rain fall on their bare heads as they pray. Let them cry acid tears that burn the pupils from their eyes. Let them lament and the lamentation choke in their throats. Let them raise their fearful trembling hands to me and let those hands be withered by palsy. Let them pilgrimage to worship at my altar, and let their journey be blighted by mortification of their rotten bones and wasted muscles. Let them beg for bread and water and have their heads washed in their own shit. Let them still beg for their lives, and let them live on. Let all that be done in the name of Justice, for I am the Just God. These are my commands beyond understanding: I have my reasons. That is your duty, Samael.

Samael   It is cruel, My Lord, but if it is your wish, I shall be your executioner.

Jehovah   Michael, Lord of the Order of Virtues, be the keeper of beauty. To you I entrust every colour and shade, the pallor of a lily and the whiteness of a breast. Zachariel shall watch over the essence of form in the mystery of creation; you shall take care of outward show. Your mission is more particular and more delicate. From time to time, you will make appear in all species supreme examples, resembling the ideal, and you will require everyone else to venerate this aristocracy whom they will hate from the depths of their hearts. You will place my mark on the bellies of women, certain chosen mothers, and the child that emerges will have a sign on their foreheads and flames in their eyes. Of these paragons, the females will be endowed with outward beauty, the males with inward beauty. These men, held in special contempt, will live on through their intellectual and spiritual works, which are the highest forms of beauty. But their flesh will be barren, their semen spilled in vain, like the double-flowered rose whose seeds cannot germinate.[20] They will live alone, but I will encircle their solitude in clouds more magnificent than those that accompany the rising sun and by night they will be visited by wonderous visions. You will permit them pride so that in the midst of their despair at living in a wicked world, they will not be denied all pleasures. This is your duty, Michael.

Michael   You honour me, my lord, and your will shall be done.

Jehovah   Anael, Lord of the Order of Principalities, I give you the kingdom of vegetation and to you Raphael, Lord of the Archangels, I give carnal generation.[21] Share between you this singular and double task: may you be the prodigies of pollen and sperm. Keep watch over kisses and blossoms. Observe the soft touch of breath from the wind and the soft touch of breath from a mouth. Stimulate the sensuality of contact, whether stamen brushing the delicate carpel or the panting male entwined with a woman aroused to the depths of her sex. And when those fruitful wombs cradle a new life within them, come Gabriel, first among the Angels, and oversee its first growing and, after its entry into the world, its second. Then when he is big and strong,

---

20 In several double-flowered plants the reproductive organs have become petals, making them lush and beautiful but unable to reproduce in the ordinary way.

21 'Carnal generation' is a theological concept that goes back at least to St Augustine and refers to the purely physical creation of children, to be contrasted with spiritual generation in which the child is baptised in Christ and remade in the love of God.

you will make him bend, weaken his muscles, crease his brow, dim his eyes, and if Samael[22] spares him, you will make him an old man. Finally you will drop a death rattle into his throat. Then Azrael, your brother and your lieutenant, shall rise up like a thief and murderer, to crush the old man's chest between his knees and squeeze that restless soul from his body. These are your duties. Go all of you, Lords of my will, and let the new world begin.

The Lords of Heaven   My lord, we are your obedient servants.

They go and in their uplifted voices we hear the words which now seem to **Jehovah** *empty words.*

The Lords of Heaven   Hosanna! Lord, your works are good! Hosanna!

Jehovah   Now that I have dealt with the eternal order of life, I'll withdraw. I need a rest – for good.

He runs his hand several times through his flaxen beard – then climbs onto his cloud and, rising slantwise, vanishes into the burning noon-day sky.

Scene Nine: On the Banks of the Euphrates

Naked and desolate, those fateful leaves still draped around **Adam**'*s waist and* **Eve**'*s neck, the two lean against the trunk of a cedar tree that is their shelter and home, lamenting their lot.*

They live, barely, by eating the sparse grasses around them.

Adam *has grown thin,* **Eve** *pale. They are restless and nervous about the future.*

Eve   We could throw ourselves on the Lord's mercy.

Adam   He has no mercy.

Eve   We could pray. Perhaps our anguish will stir something in him.

Adam   Pray? All I can do is curse. Why did you give us everything, Lord, only to take it all back? Why did you allow an Angel to be more powerful than you? Did you plan this together? You created the tempter. These contradictions are too complex for my young understanding: the master hands his power to the slave and the slave uses this power to cut the roots of the master's tree. You gave us freedom without guidance, set us on a path with our eyes closed: was it not inevitable that we would stumble at the first impediment? and who placed the stones in our path but you? You who sees what is to come? You have damned me. I am full of hatred for you. I will not worship you.

---

22 Given that no Samuel appears in the play, this appears to be a printer's error and I have reverted to an earlier version of the text.

Sun – you whose light our sin ignited and inflamed – Sun: be my God. You have been gentler than Jehovah: you are harsh but strong. You comforted us during our exodus, you kept us warm in our nakedness, you brightened our eyes. Sun, I worship you and, even as you dazzle my eyes, I worship you still.

And river – you whose blue waters washed our bloody feet and slaked our parched throats – I worship you too.

And green world – you whose lush vegetation transforms within us to blood and life – I worship you too.

And may you all be our protectors, verdant stars that populate our own sky.

And deceitful Moon, Woman will kneel as you show yourself on the horizon, dedicating her own blood to you as an offering to appease your bloodlust.

Raziel (*appearing among the exiles*)   Jehovah is God and there is no other God but Jehovah.

Eve   Oh Raziel, why did you abandon us in our hour of danger?

Raziel   I was with you. I spoke to your hearts but your hearts did not listen.

Adam   You should have shown yourself and spoken to us face to face.

Raziel   God forbade me do so.

Adam   Ah God. I will never understand this God.

Raziel   He does not ask to be understood but obeyed. Why did you disobey his orders? But let us not dwell on what cannot be undone. I am here to give you consolation. All that happened was written in the Book of the Word of the Almighty so you are less to blame than it appears. Jehovah himself has seen this and sent me to you. His fundamental goodness would not let him abandon you entirely. Though his Word must be fulfilled.

Look, I have two leafy branches that I tore from the Tree of Life before God, in his anger, had it destroyed. Plant this one, it is a cutting from the tree from which will come Salvation. This other is endowed with creative power and will never wither so long as you believe in it. If you strike it on the ground the first things you form in your mind will appear.

And finally, your embraces, which have until now been barren, will start to produce the consolation of children, generations of children, and one of the children of your children will be born who will one day make the world new again and plant a new eternal Paradise.

Eve   God told me before that I would have children, but how? Explain this mystery, Raziel. Will it hurt?

Raziel   Your belly will swell like a river in summer rain and, when you are swollen fit to burst, you will lie down and your burden will be lifted. The more tears in the birth, the greater the rejoicing after.

Eve   And my beauty?

Raziel   It may be affected a little, but the fruit of your womb will console you with its laughter.

Eve   I don't want to have a child.

Raziel   More than your beauty, more than your own life, you will love the flesh of your flesh.

Adam   She will fall in love with the fruit of her womb and she will leave me.

Raziel   Things were so much better once but all is not lost; the joys have not faded entirely. You will still have moments of delight. Now come with me, we are to work and I will teach you how to live.

Scene Ten: A Hillside Overlooking the Euphrates

With **Raziel***'s gentle help, a wooded area of earth has been burned away ready for use. With the wood that survived the fire,* **Adam** *has built a hut: logs, vines, saplings, branches are his raw materials. Our first ancestors lived in the Age of Wood (a material much neglected by our science).*

Eve (*keeping an eye on the roots she has cooking in hot ash*)   This midway state between myth and history that Raziel calls 'prehistoric' is no fun. Apparently we're only now starting to exist and before, in the Perfect Garden, we were mere phantoms of God's imagination.

The earthly Paradise was just a sketch, a model for what we must make ourselves, with our imperfect hands, with back-breaking work and the sweat of our brows. Only after a few thousand years will life become bearable again, will the intelligence lurking within us blossom in our descendants' heads and a higher and fruitful ease will be the fruit of ceaseless work by prayerful generations.

Oh how I miss my perfect Garden, the clear water of my fountain, my lilies, my peonies, my shimmering azaleas, pink as my young fingernails, white as my virgin breasts.

And my obedient birds, the gracious butterflies like great wide eyes, those big beautiful beasts who would play with innocent Eve. Where are you my sweet lion, my favourite one, my friend?

She cries but all of a sudden, the **Lion** *slinks in catlike across the ash and through the burnt trees. A few steps away from* **Eve***, he stops, sniffing the air, scratching at the earth, lashing his flanks with his magnificent, plumed tail.*

Eve   Is it you, is it really you? You've come to play with me? Yes, there you are and just seeing you I become a child again.

She runs towards the watchful **Lion***.*

My sweet lion!

The **Lion** *lets out a terrifying roar, tenses in a crouch and then leaps.* **Eve** *faints and the wild beast's claws sink into a fallen tree. Surprised to have missed its prey, the* **Lion** *tries to find her by smell, but* **Raziel** *appears and the animal slinks away growling.*

Raziel   No more playing with lions.

Scene Eleven: Inside a Palisade

Raziel *has just said farewell to his charges and returned to the duties awaiting on high in* **Jehovah***'s court.*

Sitting on the doorstep of this primitive hut, **Eve** *is sewing together some delicate figleaves to make clothing.* **Adam** *is fire-hardening a pick that he'll use to clear the earth.*

Eve   Why am I spending so much time on this? It'll only fall to pieces after a day. This is miserable. And I'm cold.

Adam   I was thinking though, with the mystic staff that Raziel gave me, I could summon up animals with fleece to clothe us. If I make a sheep appear, I'll shear it, you spin it, I'll weave it, you sew it and we'll be warm again.

Adam *strikes the ground and a ewe appears which immediately gives birth to two lambs, one male, one female.*

Eve   My go! Give me the staff!

Eve *strikes the ground and a she-wolf appears which immediately gives birth to pups – and the she-wolf, spying the lambs, bares its teeth, eager to eat them and enrich her milk.*

Disturbed, **Adam** *strikes the ground once more and this time a pair of dogs appear and chase the wolves away. The mother wolf escapes with one male pup in her jaws. The dogs set upon the others, breaking their necks.*

Eve   Give me the staff. I'd like a sweet little creature. And I know exactly which one to choose.

Adam *hands it over and* **Eve** *strikes the ground, producing a nest of mice which immediately run towards the grain supply and wreak their tiny devastation.*

Adam   You are terrible at this.

He strikes the ground once more and a litter of Angora cats comes into being.

They should sort that lot out!

Eve   And now some pretty blue and red feathers to put in my hair.

Adam *strikes the ground and a crowd of hens appear, gathered around a radiant and preening cockerel.*

Eve   Ah that's more like it. My farmyard is looking a bit less deserted. More! More! Let me do one!

Eve *strikes the ground and scarcely has the new form taken shape than the cockerel lets out a cry of alarm and the hens flutter about in agitation, shaken by the new arrival.*

Good morning, Mr Fox. How lovely you are. We're so alike. We have the same smell. We have the same spirit.

Scene Twelve: Evening in the Hut

They have created a fairly comfortable living room: thick warm woollen carpets on the floor, durable clothing by day and warm blankets by night. The hearth glows with a roaring fire and on the table, set on four rough-hewn legs, are laid a lovely roast chicken, milk, eggs, and wooden bowls of spiced mead.

When they have eaten and drunk their fill, their cheeks are pink, their eyes shining, their blood hot, their gestures lively. Passionate sparks shoot up and down their limbs, and begin to concentrate in certain parts of the body.

Since they were expelled from the Garden, their weakened bodies have experienced nothing like this. Once, in their days of heavenly freedom, they had known nothing but long, slow, profound ecstasies, no sooner wished than gratified – but they had never known desire.

Adam *looks at* **Eve***, with wide hungry eyes;* **Eve***, her eyes cast down, shoots restless flashing glances at* **Adam***.*

Their hands meet, then their lips. With small, graceful movements they make their way down onto the fleeces they have piled up to make a bed.

The first time their bodies make full contact, they shudder with a pleasure that is almost painful. Then the pleasure, dimmed for a moment as they try to find a shared rhythm and movement, starts to build again to new frenzied heights, rising in great leaps that hurl them into ecstasy, leaving them more shocked than happy.

Eve   Not yet, not yet! Please, stay with me!

But **Adam***, a deep sadness inside him, pulls away and rolls onto his side.*

Scene Thirteen: The Hut by Day

Adam *cuts a reed, dips it in a reddish liquid and writes hieroglyphs on a wide sheepskin:*

Sefer Yetzirah:[23] Chapter One.

By thirty-two Paths of Wisdom, יהוה,[24] God of Israel, God of Now and Always, God of Mercy and Grace, Almighty God of the Highest, God Everlasting, by these magnificent and occult paths did Holy God engrave his name in three ways: Sepher, Sephar and Sipur – that is The Number, The Numberless, and The Numbered – contained in the ten Sefiroth, which are ten properties, excluding the unnameable, and twenty-two letters . . .

Adam   Yes, my views of Jehovah have become more reasonable. Raziel has instructed me in the catechism. Why fight against Strength itself? Better to serve him that he might protect me and glorify him in the mystery of his endless depths . . . Who is better qualified than I to offer a few clear words on the First Days? I know a great deal and my instincts are very strong . . . I now know the difference between *Void* and *Without Form* . . . *Void* is a line that snakes around the earth. *Formless* are the secret stones in the Depths from which the Waters came. I have been given the power to see between YHV and YVH, between HYV and VHY, and between VYH and HVY.[25] I do not know how came to be the 231 gates,[26] I will make the eighteen mothers walk three by three. To א [Aleph] I will give the Reign of Air. To מ [Mem] I shall give the Reign of Water. To ש [Shin] I shall give the Reign of Fire.[27] In exchange for my submission, Jehovah made an agreement with me, the covenant of the fingers and the covenant of the toes,[28] and the 22 letters were revealed to me: this is why I comprehend all mysteries.

---

23 The *Sefer Yetzirah* [The Book of Creation] is a work of Jewish mysticism, whose origins are obscure (probably dating from the third or fourth centuries), which sets out the fundamental principles of the universe encoded in the numbers from one to ten and the twenty-two letters of the Hebrew alphabet. The passage included here is a version of the opening section of the text. For a translation and commentary, see Aryeh Kaplan, *Sefer Yetzirah – the Book of Creation: In Theory and Practice*, trans. Aryeh Kaplan, 2nd edn (Boston MA: Weiser, 1997).

24 See n. 7.

25 This refers to a passage in the *Sefer Yetzirah* in which the three different letters (Yod-He-Vav) that make up the name of God (see n. 7) can be permutated to produce six combinations, which become all the opposing directions on each of the three axes of three-dimensional space. See Kaplan, *Sefer Yetzirah*, 80–2.

26 231 is the number of possible pairs of different letters in the twenty-two-letter Hebrew alphabet. The *Sefer Yetzirah* describes this through the image of a circular wall with each letter representing a door through which there are twenty-one paths to the other letters, creating 231 possible connections between two doors. See Kaplan, *Sefer Yetzirah*, 108–24. It is thought that meditating on each of these permutations will begin to connect us with God's own principles of creation.

27 According to Kabbalistic traditions, the three 'Mother' letters – Aleph, Men, Shin – parallel the three letters in the Tetragrammaton and are sometimes thought to be their source. They also correspond to air, water and fire. See Kaplan, *Sefer Yetzirah*, 40–2 and 145–6. 18 does not appear to have a particular privileged place in the Kabbalah, though it is a lucky number in some Jewish traditions, because it is associated numerologically with the word [חי] Chai meaning 'Life'.

28 The *Sefer Yetzirah*'s mystical numerology sees the ten decimal digits as linked to ten more fundamental metaphysical forces, the Sefirot, each of which embodies a different quality (Wisdom, Love, Beauty, etc.). God's creation of the world (by his own hands) is mirrored in humanity's ten fingers and ten toes. The twenty-two letters of the Hebrew alphabet are also supplemented by ten vowels, the Sefirot thus endowing Hebrew itself with mystical authority, which may explain Gourmont's insistence on printing the Hebrew letters; there is, then, a complex chain of associations that link numbers to fingers to language. See Kaplan, *Sefer Yetzirah*, 23 and 32–3.

Eve (*sneaking up behind* **Adam** *and placing both hands over his eyes*)   If you comprehend all mysteries, tell me: whose fingers are these?

Adam   Oh what a theological puzzle! Given that there's only one woman on the whole of the earth, I *wonder* which woman's these fingers could be . . .

Eve   That's a nice way of reminding me that I had a daughter and I lost her . . .

She breaks away in tears, throwing herself to the ground a little way away.

Adam   It's impossible to do any proper work round here.

He picks up his reed pen and thinks.

When I've finished this, I will make a start on the *Sefer Raziel*: a few modest proposals for the use of children.

Eve   Oh yes? What children? Where are these children of yours? I had a girl and she died and I had a boy and he died.

Adam   And then, if my inspiration sustains itself, I will establish a series of treatises: the first on Creation; the second on Relations of God and Man; the third of the Essence of Divinity; the fourth on Love . . .

Eve   What do you know about love? You don't know how to do it, how can you talk about it? Put your pen and parchment down and pay attention to me . . . tell you what, stick this in your treatise: 'If you want to be happy, pay attention to your wife: this is the Aleph and the Shin of all practical wisdom. The rest is vanity, for if you don't pay a woman any attention, she will be bored and if she is bored, she will be in a bad mood, and if she is in a bad mood, life for you both will be hell.'

Adam   I think God's truth will do me.

Eve   Watch out for temptation.

Adam   Where would that come from?

Eve   Where did it come from first time?

Adam   You – Corruption herself – dare give me lessons?

Eve   Come on, don't be mean. You've no idea – I'm so bored!

Adam *who had prided himself on having only spiritual hunger, yields to the woman's insinuations – but their ecstasies are muted, each of them, in their heart, yearning for new loves.*

Scene Fourteen: Hell

Satan   We need to set little Sodom and Gomorrah a good example.[29] Be the instrument of perverted lust . . . I will break open a new and secret door . . . I will be the conqueror of a virginity both singular and plural.

---

29 Although Gourmont does not make this clear until the end of the scene, their children are Sodom and
   Gomorrah and they are present in the scene.

Lilith   May my skin be dissolved, may a demon cut me new holes to let out all the diabolical cravings that consume me.

Satan   You are the archangel of depravity, the angel of pleasure and damnation, the queen of twisted sensuality, a true animal of lust.

Lilith *gives herself anew to her demon's sensual passions.*

Satan   I am broken!

Lilith   I want more.

Satan   My orgasm was like my guts spilling out of me. I am a hollow tree, my softwood, my sap eaten away by black ants.

Lilith   I want more.

Satan   You've had everything.

Lilith   That was nothing.

Satan   Pitiful though humans are, they find a kind of joy in simple things that is unavailable to me. My pleasures are like the cries of a prisoner being flogged and Lilith is my torturer. I envy their humanity . . . Oh I will darken the last lights on their blue waters and Evil shall reign again.

Lilith   Is the hour of my revenge at hand?

Satan   It is.

Lilith   I will bear Man's child?

Satan   You will.

Lilith   The man who was my destiny and was denied me, will I finally feel his body against mine?

Satan   You will and it will be a double adultery for us. You will give birth to Lust in all its forms and without stopping until finally you are mother to Sterility . . . Can you hear that? Lusts throng around your hips, clamouring to be born.

The Lusts   We will have large, dark, shining, flashing eyes. We will have cruel mouths, redder than the lips of a vampire. Our breasts will be as firm as the beaten muscles of a young wrestler. Our legs will be as slender as the branches of an ash. Our androgynous soul will be double like our loins and its seat will be the hell between them. Open up, Lilith's womb and let us in!

Lilith   Enter me and let your blood feed my desire.

Satan   Adam will be their carnal father and I will console ill-matched Eve for her sorrowful motherhood. I will give her a son that lives. He will be tall, strong and tough. He will fight his brother-to-come and as she foresaw, the fearful Earth will shiver at the hot red caresses of fine fresh blood. Oh Earth, Cain and his brother will water you well. Your colour will change: your ploughed fields will turn to crimson mud and your rivers to veins and arteries.

Lilith   Come!

Satan   We can be yet more evil. Our kisses must transmit all filth and diseases. We must dream up more supreme corruption.

Lilith (*eyes burning with an emerald flame*)   The wildest lusts will be ours in all their horror.

Satan   You burning dew of my hell. You brimstone flower of my infernal garden. I love you with all my hatred.

He transforms into a goat, but **Lilith** *remains a woman.*

Lilith   Oh, my sweet-swelling buck.

Young Gomorrah   Oh how handsome he is!

He resumes his devilish form and **Lilith** *becomes a goat.*

Satan   Ah my fine-smelling she-goat.

Little Sodom   Oh how beautiful she is!

Lilith   These are just illusions!

Satan   All is illusion but the suffering of others.

Scene Fifteen: An Enclosure in a Woodland Clearing

Adam *is glumly dissecting a flower in a pointless search for the meaning of life.*

Eve *passes by and kisses him on the forehead, goes back into the hut and closes the door.*

Satan *and* **Lilith** *enter, looking ravishing, swathed in layers of diaphanous cloud.*

Satan   Go, unsettle his mind.

Satan *hides behind a tree.* **Lilith** *walks past, kicking up the dead leaves with a bare foot, showing herself off, blowing on her cloak of mist that ripples and exposes a breast, a flash of shoulder, a glimpse of her stomach, a knee. Eventually:*

Adam (*looking up, mutters in alarm*)   A woman! Another woman!

Lilith *blows him kisses, and runs off into the shadow of the trees.*

Adam *puts his flower down and climbs over the fence, hurrying towards the apparition whose tinkling girlish laughter guides the confused man to her.*

Eve (*coming out of the hut*)   A man! Another man!

Satan *greets her with great charm and* **Eve**, *choosing to avoid this danger, runs from the enclosure. She glances at this strange young man cleverly and swiftly taking in his whole appearance. But now we hear her cries of fear and* **Satan** *finds her easily, because she has tripped and fallen on a mossy bank.*

Adam *and* **Eve** *come back in from opposite sides, he pretending to collect plants,* **Eve** *making a show of enjoying the smell of a posy of flowers she has hastily picked.*

Adam   You been for a walk? Hello, are you crying?

Eve   I'm so bored.

Adam   Oh so am I.

Scene Sixteen: The Forest

As the pitiful adulterers return to their hut and quarrel, contrite before the cold hearth, eternally chastened that to sin again has been so clearly pointless, a small and lowly angel, a wandering cherub, kisses the ground below the cutting of the Sycamore that **Adam** *planted the year before, and has just flowered for the first time.*

Jehovah (*crying with joy, sobs:*)   Salve, lignum crucis.[30]

The voice of **Satan** *blows between the trees, seeming to respond ironically:*

Satan   Amen.

---

30 Latin: 'Hail, wood of the cross!'

Ennoïa: A Triptych

Jean Lorrain (1906)

Translated by Jennifer Higgins

As Robert Ziegler writes, along with being a 'perennial object of gossip and scandal, terror of Parisian journalism, accomplished *conteur*, poet, and novelist', the author and playwright **Jean Lorrain** was also 'a fervent practitioner in the cult of Sarah Bernhardt', whom he met in 1886; the problem was that he was '[u]nable to persuade the actress to arrange for his works to be staged', despite writing roles that were 'tailor-made for Sarah', prompting him to pen his posthumously published novel *Le Tréteau* (1906).[1] (In the book, Bernhardt's equivalent, Linda Monti, refashions a playwright's play in ways that induct him into the dangerous superficiality and licentiousness of the theatre). But Lorrain did more than come to terms with rejection through his writing. He was a dandy who embraced theatricality, jewels gilding fingers and a carnation crowning his lapel. To speak of Lorrain's relationship to theatre, then, is to speak of more than the stage, although no fulsome account of his writing would be complete without recognising the time he invested in the writing of plays like *Ennoïa*.

Ennoïa is depicted in early Gnosticism as a matriarchal figure who embodies suffering whenever she takes on corporeal form, but she also exerts a powerful influence in the material world. However, it is likely that Lorrain was drawing inspiration more directly from various titans of nineteenth-century art and literature than the sources they were working with. He was a long-time admirer of Gustave Moreau, particularly his depictions of 'a gorgeous symbolically-transfigured vision of a world dominated by lust and luxury [. . .] where eroticism is inextricably linked with cruelty and death'.[2] The atmosphere that Lorrain conjures in this play captures such a vision, and hearing the language spoken aloud in Jennifer Higgins's translation for the present volume, which is rich and resonant, emphasises the extent to which this is the case.[3] The second influence was probably Gustave Flaubert's *La Tentation de Saint Antoine* (*The Temptation of St Anthony*, 1874), which inspired Odilon Redon's lithograph and homage to the book, *Hélène (Ennoia)* (1896). Such weighted intertextuality is likely to have appealed to Lorrain, especially the obscurity of Ennoïa relative to her more notorious *femme fatale* kin, like Salome.

Ennoïa was first published in 1906, the year of the author's death from a botched enema aged fifty-one. It is presented in three acts, all of which are very different from one another save for the presence of a new embodiment of Ennoïa, who dies and is reincarnated in an endless cycle of decay and renewal. She is always reborn as a beautiful woman who threatens men with their downfall, just as she, in Lorrain's play, falls foul of the men who persecute her. Unlike the men, though, she is effectively immortal. In Act One she appears as a wayfarer in rural France who appears to be at the mercy of an old man who uses her to lure men to their doom. The act then transitions into a tableau that finds her metamorphosed as Frédégonde: the wife of the Frankish

---

1   Robert Ziegler, 'Narcissism as Theater in Jean Lorrain's *Le Tréteau*', *Dalhousie French Studies* 72 (Fall 2005): 63–9 (63); Francis Amery, 'Introduction: The Life and Career of Jean Lorrain', in Jean Lorrain, *Monsieur de Phocas*, trans. Francis Amery (Sawtry: Dedalus, 1994), 5–20 (13).

2   Amery, 'Introduction', 10.

3   A rehearsed reading of Lorrain's *Ennoïa* was staged at the Albany Theatre in London on 10 November 2021. It was presented alongside several other plays in this volume, including excerpts from Kyōka's *Kerria Japonica*, Barnes' *The Dove*, and Rebellato's translation of Remy de Gourmont's *Lilith*. The programme was curated and produced by Adam Alston and Jane Desmarais, and was directed by Jonathan Meth.

sixth-century ruler King Hilpérig. In Act Two, she is reincarnated as Genèvre: better known as Guinevere in Arthurian legend, here both eulogised for her unparalleled beauty and condemned for having an affair with King Arthur's groom. In Act Three, Ennoïa appears as Lore (Lorelei in German folklore): a courtesan exiled from her homeland after a Governor's son dies in a brawl over her love. The play ends with Lore throwing herself into the Rhine – 'her face ecstatic', as the narrator tells us – although the structure of the play suggests that she will be reincarnated again, endlessly.

Ennoïa embodies bewitchment and oblivion, and her beauty corrupts the social world. She is both siren and victim, and as such she is a quintessential decadent type. However, she also transcends the capacity of the writer to condemn her, finally, to the grave. This play therefore reflects the double-edged representation of women that tends to characterise decadent drama written by male playwrights of the period: at once at the mercy of the men who imagine her, and yet capable of surpassing her tormentors, even beyond death itself.

Characters

Act One
Narrator
The Old Man
Hilpérig
Hildebert
Mérowig
Luitprand
Ennoïa[4]
Frankish vassals and soldiers

Act Two
Genèvre, *Queen of Brittany.*
Morold, *nephew of Arthus, King of Brittany and husband of Genèvre.*
Geryn
A Captain
Onfroy, *Genèvre's equerry.*
A female attendant
Knight of the royal guard, barons, men of the people, soldiers.

Act Three
Loreley
The Governor
The Bishop
The Man in Green
A Soldier
First Bourgeois
Second Bourgeois
A Captain of the Reiters[5]
A Reiter
A Man of the People
An Artisan
A Woman of the People
An Old Woman
A Herald of Arms
A Decon
First Lansquenet[6]
Second Lansquenet
Third Lansquenet
Men of the people, merchants, Bourgeois, women of the people, deacons and **clerics.**

---

4 The translation maintains the French spelling for all character names, even when there is an English equivalent, in order to maintain the French context of Lorrain's perspective on the mythical and historical figures in the play.
5 Reiter: a cavalry soldier, usually serving in Central Europe and Germanic-speaking areas.
6 Lansquenet, or 'Landsknechte': a mercenary foot soldier.

Act One

Tableau One[7]

A gothic room with thick pillars supporting its high, vaulted ceiling. The **Narrator** *is sitting at the foot of a pillar, an ancient missal open on his knee.*

Narrator (*reading*)   Hilpérig, King of the Franks of Metz and Neustria[8]
Was riding one evening with his train, loaded with gold and silver,
And with amber chalices, enamelled and glittering.
He was returning, at the doleful, slow pace of the horses,
From pillaging some rich abbey far away,
When he caught sight of a woman, crouching by the side of the road,
Barefoot, resting her face on her knees,
Pale, with tawny hair,
Sleeping.
Nearby an old man, nearly bald,
Stood watching over her.

Scene One

The stage lights up, revealing a dusty road running through huge fields of corn. Yellow crops stretch to the horizon, and in the distance black smoke rises from the burning abbey. At the side of the road, on the right, a woman is crouching by the ditch. She is very pale, poorly dressed in greyish rags, and her yellow hair hangs messily over her face. She seems to be sleeping. An **Old Man** *wearing a tattered robe stands next to her; between them there is a large bronze vase, above which a blue flame flickers.*

On the other side of the road, opposite the woman, stand **Hilpérig** *and his vassals,* **Mérowig, Hildebert** *and* **Luitprand***; Frankish soldiers hold their horses' reins.*

Hilpérig (*in a low voice, to* **Mérowig**)   Never did a tawny mane
Shine so brilliantly under the pure sky . . .
Who can she be?

Mérowig   She seems plunged deep in an unfathomable dream,
And makes no sound.

Hilpérig (*worried*)   Who is that man standing near her?

Mérowig (*to* **Ennoïa**)   Now, girl, come closer.
The king wants to speak to you.

---

7   The numbering and placing of scenes and tableaux in Lorrain's original text are inconsistent. In our version, where both scenes and tableaux are present in an Act, each tableau is linked to the narrator's monologues.

8   Metz is a city in the north of France. Neustria formed the western part of the Frankish Kingdom.

Ennoïa *doesn't move.*

Mérowig   Hey! Can't you hear?
(*He shrugs his shoulders.*) These beggars!

Hilpérig (*his eyes fixed on* **Ennoïa**)   How pale she is!

Mérowig (*to the* **Old Man**)   You, over there. You're not asleep, I suppose, or deaf?

Hildebert (*putting his hand to his sword*)   Is your grey head tired of living, then? Do you want us to break it?

Hilpérig   Peace, Hildebert, enough! And you, old man,
Answer me . . . Who is that woman?
(*In a low voice, to himself.*) Oh! That mournful, dreaming look!

The Old Man (*immobile*)   She is blind and can't hear. Her soul
Has left her.

Silence. He takes a step towards the king and points to the bronze vase.

A strange spirit lives in the flame
That you see wandering, fine and blueish
Under her ragged dress, and the night of the tomb
Has possessed her for more than a thousand years.

Hilpérig (*impatient*)   The girl?
The flame? Your words are like a puff of smoke, they flicker
Like a will-o'-the-wisp over a pond.
(*Pointing to* **Ennoïa**.) Who is she? What is her name?

The Old Man   She is a child
I brought along with me, Sire, because she has no family.
She has followed me everywhere since then, poor girl.
She and I wander together now.

Hilpérig   So she is blind and never speaks!

The Old Man   Never? No. Sometimes for a whole year
She stays completely taken up in her dream,
Absent, elsewhere, far away, without words or voice:
Then she wakes up, and for months together
She pours out speeches about marvellous things
And the people follow her along dusty roads.

Hilpérig   Make her speak.

Hildebert (*in a low voice to* **Hilpérig**)   My Lord, this man mumbles
A strange language, and underneath her fiery hair
This motionless, blind-eyed woman,
Is very strange.

Hilpérig (*thoughtful*)   Strange and solemn
It is true, but she has an air of

Caressing charm, and sweetness
Envelops her.

Hildebert (*pointing to* **Ennoïa**)   My Lord, her arms are grey with mud,
Her eyes bruised where she has been struck.

Hilpérig (*to himself*)   But she has a strange charm . . .
(*Addressing the* **Old Man**.) Make her speak.

The Old Man   I must warn you that
Evils endured in times past still sob in her voice,
And its childish tone, lamenting and painful,
Distant and weak, seems the echo of some
Human pain. One evening, hearing her moan,
Some soldiers took fright . . .

Hilpérig   That's enough! . . . Make her speak,
I said!

The Old Man (*resigned*)   Speak, Ennoïa, speak. Tell us your dreams.

He takes her hand, helps her up, and brings her slowly over to the king; with his other hand he has taken the flaming vase and holds it upright behind her.

Ennoïa   My dreams! . . . Dear Eden, oh land of Lies!
The tree there is monstrous, immense, with marvellous fruits
Whose brilliance illuminates
The tigers and wolves nestled around its roots at night.
The slender branches are full of divine souls
Fluttering and taking flight, criss-crossing the blue;
My eyes are enchanted, and I listen to the golden voice
Of the gentle, invisible archangel advising me.
His powerful harmony bewitches my ear;
And in the scented shade, deep in the great soundless woods,
I drink his strong, delightful words,
My heart too full, beating with love . . .

Hilpérig   But she is Eve,[9]
Eva the sinner.

The Old Man   Don't disturb her dream
Or the spirit will fall silent.

Hilpérig   Make her speak again,
Old man, make her speak.

The **Old Man** *touches* **Ennoïa***'s shoulder.*

Ennoïa   The oars moved
Effortlessly, the sail swelled in the wind, the galley

---

9   Eve appears variously in the play as Eve, Ève, and Éva.

Sliced the foam, and I, afraid of displeasing him,
Listened and smiled, gazing into his eyes.
'Who cares if I sow endless trouble in my country?'
He said, 'And in my city, and in lovely Hellas?[10]
You will be mine, in my beautiful house!'
How sweet your room was, my friend, with its rich panther furs
From Asia and Egypt, high in your palace . . .
He would come, his arms cool and
Amber-scented, and sit meekly at my feet
On the thick carpets, and there, for days on end,
Far away from the battlefields and shouts of victory,
He told me stories, stroking my hair,
And in the evenings we climbed the towers together.
There, along the battlements, both pale with love,
We gazed at the two camps in the hazy distance,
Where lights and beacons were appearing;
Ulysses with his captains assembled
By their tents, or Achilles with his golden helmet
Driving an armoured chariot through the sands.

Hilpérig   Luitprand, do you remember that evening around the table
When two wandering poets, Romans, they were,
Musicians and jugglers, came to sing old verses
That conjured up these things?

Luitprand   I remember, Sire, you had them sit among the boxes of sweetmeats
Scented with sage and roses,
And eat until dawn.

Ennoïa   One evening they rubbed ointments
And rose oil into my skin, and then sold me
To amuse the people . . . So I was lost
Forever, and there for the taking, on the road.
One night I was standing playing on the cittern
For sailors dancing at the back of a tavern,
When a storm began to pound the roof; the only lantern
In the shack went out and I, amid blows,
Curses, and the shouts of all those drunken men,
Was crying, when a man came through the fray
And took me by the hand.

The Old Man   That was me. I found her
Drinking with the human dregs of the ports.
I took her with me out of pity;
She has followed me ever since, this poor thing plucked from the abyss.

---

10 Hellas: the lands of ancient Greece. Hellas might also refer to the legendary city of Phthiotis, and to a
   Byzantine province of southern Greece.

Adulteress, innocent and victim by turns,
She was Ennoïa, Barbelo, and Prunikos.[11]
She is of all times; the ancient Greek god Eros,
Astarte of Sidon, still sometimes embraces her.[12]
Helen of Troy, Homer, and Stesichorus[13]
Cursed her memory, and the pagan hero
Had her for a concubine . . . In Rome a common man
Who loved her, took her, all dishevelled, and cut her throat;
And the kings under Tarquinius[14] seized her and raped her
In the body of Lucretia[15] . . . She was Delilah
Cutting Samson's hair[16] . . . She slit
Attila's throat in their wedding chamber.[17]
Under the leather tents, where guard dogs watched,
Her shadow wandered through Israel with Judith's,[18]
And many throats have met her cruel arm and
Bled.
False, idolatrous, prostituted to all,
She's been everywhere, pleasure-weary;
She sang in every dive, stood on the corner in every town,
Kissed anyone who passed, used all sorts of love.
Thieves have known her bewitching grace.
In Sidon, in Syria, she was their mistress,
And drank the bitter gains of her night with them.
By day she hid a priest in her bed,
Still warm from the men passed through the night before.
So I, seeing her still plump and resplendent,
Bought her from the thieves for a fortune
And restored her to what she had been, dressing her in such splendour
That handsome young lads and greedy old men
Whose arms bore rings of precious jewels,
Followed us through the town with red eyes

---

11 Barbelo: Gnostic reference to the divine embodiment of femininity, and to an androgynous Creator. Likewise, Prunikos represents a feminine aspect of God – specifically that which pertains to divine knowledge.
12 Astarte: Goddess associated with sexual love, fertility and war. Lorrain made frequent reference to Astarte across his literary works.
13 Stesichorus: Greek poet, revered in his time but now his works are largely lost.
14 Sextus Tarquinius: son of the semi-legendary, tyrannical and final king of Rome, Lucius Tarquinius Superbus.
15 Lucretia: Roman heroine. Her rape by Sextus Tarquinius is said to have sparked a rebellion that led to the overthrow of Lucius Tarquinius Superbus.
16 The Book of Judges and Hebrew Bible depict Delilah as a treacherous figure who discovered the source of Samson's incredible strength – his hair – before ordering a servant to cut it, enabling him to be captured and handed over to the Philistines.
17 Attila: fearsome ruler of the Huns between 434 and 453 BC; scourge of the Roman Empire.
18 Judith: Hebraic heroine depicted in the deuterocanonical Book of Judith. Her legend today is most closely associated with her decapitation of the Assyrian general Holofernes, who was tasked by Nebuchadnezzar with exacting vengeance on Israel after refusing to aid his warmongering.

When we passed by their houses together,
Their hands full of gold.
Nero[19] was captivated by her
And put her to death. He found her too beautiful
And was afraid of loving her; Gaius Caligula[20]
Poisoned her; Titus exiled her.[21]
And the stricken crowd took her for the moon,
So pale was her forehead.
And that is my fortune.
I take her with me, to kings and powerful men,
And filthy crimes and bloody crimes,
All the treachery of a deranged past,
Overflow onto the throne and the debased purple.
That is my triumph and all I want;
To dissolve everything.

Mérowig   Sire . . .

Hilpérig (*to himself*)   Oh, to awaken the eyes
Under that heavy hair, to seize the secret, supreme enigma
From that sad, pale forehead,
To possess the mystery!
(*He beckons to the* **Old Man** *and whispers in his ear.*) Bring her to the palace
This evening. A valet will receive her
At the door.

He gives him a purse.

Narrator   And the horses, who were eating silently,
Took up their lazy, dreamy pace again,
And the Frankish king's exhausted cortège disappeared
Along the path through the corn.

The stage goes dark again, everything fades out.

Tableau Two

The gothic hall, the **Narrator** *sitting in the same place as in Scene One. This second scene must be silent. As the* **Narrator** *reads, the stage will light up and one by one the characters will act out the lines supposedly being read from the book in the scenery described.*

---

19 Nero: ancient Roman emperor, reigning from AD 54 until AD 68. Nero was regularly referenced by decadent writers in Europe in the late nineteenth century.

20 Caligula: ancient Roman emperor, reigning from AD 37 until AD 41. Like Nero, Caligula was also a favoured reference among the late nineteenth-century decadent *literati* in Europe.

21 Titus: ancient Roman emperor, reigning from AD 79 to 81. Unlike Nero and Caligula, Titus was largely well-regarded by ancient Roman chroniclers, including Suetonius.

Narrator   Towards evening, having drunk
Three jugs of mead and two of Rhône wine,
The Frankish king summoned Hildebert to his throne
And gave him an order. A pleasant one, surely,
Because the valet smiled in the shadows.
Just then,
A man, leading a strange veiled
Figure, stamped his shoe three times
On the threshold, and the heavy, iron-panelled door
Opened silently. With a bitter laugh, the man
Pushed the woman ahead of him into the room.
The widow Frédégonde, pale and sinister,
Entered the Merovingian[22] king's chamber;
And war, hatred between slaughtered Christian kings
Poison, murder and adultery,
All came in with her. Under the austere arches
Frédégonde listened to the steps of the Frankish kings.
She crossed her bare arms over her white breasts,
And heard, gathering and rising in the still-shadowy distance,
Future disasters and innumerable crimes,
All evils born of woman and bequeathed to the descendants
By the ancestor, and joy flashed in her eyes.

Curtain.

---

22 The Merovingian dynasty emerged as Kings of the Franks in the fifth century, before expanding into the
   largest realm of western Europe in the sixth century.

Act Two

Tableau One

The gothic hall, the **Narrator** *seated with the book on his knee.*

Narrator Page twenty, third volume of the book of legends,
How it was, when Arthus reigned over the Norman races,
From the forests of Carléon[23] to the mountains of Pen Armor,[24]
That Ennoïa, the golden-haired eternal wanderer,
Reappeared, filling kings' hearts
With guilty passion.
                    They called her Genèvre; she was pale,
Slim and supple with pure, wide eyes,
A beautiful lily from a far-off century
Opening in goodness, calm and light,
As if she were a saint blooming in a glasshouse.
She lived in the souls of adoring knights,
Weary mercenaries and soldiers, their feet bleeding,
Trudged the dusty roads quavering 'Genèvre!'
Hers was the sweet name invoked by the lips
Of frightened captives and wounded, despairing men,
And it was like a cool kiss on their foreheads,
For she was whiteness, and had a dream within her.
A joyful sound of bright gold and birds on the shore
Rang out in the palace where her beauty lived;
And the royal castle blazed day and night,
Like a summer evening, lit by torches.
A never-ending feast laughed under its arches,
With dwarves sounding trumpets on the towers.
Happy Brittany, its storerooms filled with
Wheat, rye and barley, its barrels brimming with rare gold
Plundered at dagger point from barbarian peoples,
Blessed Genèvre and her handsome warlike king
Until, preferring the equerry to the crowned knight,
The azure-eyed queen with the flaxen hair
Heeded the advice of the Evil one, and,
Making a criminal of the loyal friend,
Installed Adultery with Betrayal

---

23 'Caérleon' is probably Caerleon, the Welsh town where Arthur is said to have had a court.

24 'Pen Armor' is a mysterious reference, although it probably designates a headland or peak (Pen) in Armorica (Arvorig in Breton). This is the ancient name of a region in Gaul between the river Loire and the river Seine in Brittany. Archaeological discoveries in Southwest England (more famously Arthurian territory) suggest links between Armorica and the Britons – particularly Cornwall – between the fifth and seventh centuries (like Welsh and Cornish, Breton also derives from Celtic British).

On the throne; then, Murder, Fear, and Malady
Kept watch over Genèvre's bed;
And Shame made men's hearts burn with anger.

Scene One

The stage lights up to reveal a bedroom in the royal castle at Carléon: a huge hanging tapestry takes up the whole backdrop, giving onto a moonlit gallery. On the left is a state bed covered with precious cloths and a mound of cushions. **Geryn** *is reclining on the bed, almost lying down, in court dress . . .* **Genèvre** *is at his feet, her elbows resting on his knees. It is night . . . oil lamps are burning.*

Genèvre   Why do you unwind my arms from your knees?
With your great, proud eyes and your face bright as dawn
Aren't you the adored man, desired, possessed, loved
By a queen who is half mad and, in truth, tired
Of lies. I love you!

Geryn   Yes, we struggled
For many months, my beautiful commander,
But you wanted it!

Genèvre (*kneeling upright*)   I want to stoop to you again,
Not caring for useless honourable renown.
Are you not the most beautiful? Are you not the true king
Because chosen by me, the Lady and the Queen?
Look, I place sovereign greatness at your feet,
The sceptre and the history of triumphant ancestors . . .
And this kiss, forbidden and prohibited by every law,
Has a savour of snow and fruit on your lips.

She embraces him and kisses him on the mouth.

I love you and I want you; do you love me?

Geryn   Genèvre!

Genèvre (*threateningly*)   Yes, you say *Genèvre*, and I see your eyes
Gazing at a different image. They are distraught, and avoid
The two eyes full of prayer and love that implore you.
Well then, I know only too well what grief devours you.
(*Chanting the words.*) There is a loyal, noble heart, a proud
And good spirit, who has faith in us and loved us only yesterday . . .

Geryn   Be quiet.

Genèvre   You as a brother and I as his Lady . . .

Geryn   Genèvre!

Genèvre   Our two names alone lived in that soul:

How can we ever dare appear before him again!
Ha! Weakling! Do I, and the mysterious gift
Of my pure young body and soul
Subjugated to your every desire, mean nothing to you?
(*Sneering.*) You betrayed him, though, this saint, this knight, this king.
So then, the sin is committed, and if it was a crime,
It is irreparable, and the intoxicating abyss
Where we both lie makes you my prisoner.

Geryn   Arthus entrusted you to me.

Genèvre   That butcher king.
Arthus, that brutish pillager, that hero of bloodshed
Always off making war in the wild western
Marches, coarse and ruddy like a pagan from the North.
Has he ever deigned to weigh the silk and gold
Of my hair, to admire the solemn grace
Of my movements or my soft blue eyes?
I've taken back the oaf's treasure. He did not value it.
My body is an altar wanting to be adored,
And I love you, Oh Geryn, enough to make you its high priest!

Geryn   Your pride is immense, Genèvre!

Genèvre (*she gets up*)   Perhaps;
But look hard at me. Have I not every right?

Geryn   Does your beauty free you from your vows?

Genèvre   The servile
Cowardice of kings has taught my soul
Complete disdain for all except love.

Geryn   Oh woman!

Genèvre   The woman in me revolts at the animal
Love of this soldier in a crown. The brutal
Embrace of a man still warm from killing
Horrifies me. He comes home thinking that a piece of gold
Taken from some barbarian or a wounded, captive
Prince, buys my bed and my kisses.
A Dane greased with tallow treats his slave like this;
And I am proud, yes proud, of having broken the shackles.
Am I an inert prey, the sad spoils
Of a night plunderer who leaves in the morning,
Like an elk hunter running back into the scrub?
And I love you, I love you and that is everything.

Geryn   Witch!

Genèvre (*tenderly*)   A witch bewitched, then! The spell

Is in your voice, your mouth and your lovely eyes;
And remember, Geryn, everything pointed towards our downfall.
We rode our horses slowly down
Through the full-grown rye and past the green hill
Through the marches of Brittany. Armor and its castles
Opened up at our feet in perfumed finery,
And the towns hailed me, the beloved
Newly-wed, the king's wife.
You, a gallant knight in a fine gold helmet riding a white palfrey,[25]
You watched over my progress and directed the escort.
Arthus had summoned you to bring me to him . . . What did it matter
If my heart had gone to you like a child,
Finding in you its master and true king?
You possessed me the instant you saw me.
Your voice, your eyes, your hands brought me naked to you
And I didn't dream of resisting, Geryn.
It was a sin, then. I had just begun to exist;
My dream was starting, I was starting to live.
Above our heads the sky seemed drunk.
For three days, in the towns of our fathers
There were tournaments for the Seigneurs and solemn games,
And at every halt they sang songs for my engagement.
The courtiers took me all the way to Cornwall,
And there my mother, in tears, put me into your arms.
Then I left my family, and I didn't cry;
A time began of wild horseback rides,
Side by side with you along roads carpeted
With sage, through celebrations in warring villages.
Children scattered us with flowers as we passed.
The queen would sometimes sleep at an inn,
And dawn would find her still in love and still a virgin.

Geryn   That time of love without remorse was sweet, Genèvre!

Genèvre   Ours is a philtre in which everything sinks and sleeps.
Let me intoxicate you with the old fervour
Of those ten days lived in the melancholy
Of dewy mornings and evening splendour.
Oh! Those huge skies, green-gold, filled with streaks of shining cloud.
And those daytime halts in the green hollows of clearings . . .
Then setting off again through the pink heather,
Leaping up to adventure, strong against the wind,
And we were always moving towards the rising sun!
That wedding journey was a few short days,
At the slow, charmed pace of our two ambling mares,
But it is all my life and it is all my love!

---

25 Palfrey: a costly horse esteemed among the nobility in the medieval period.

Scene Two

A Voice   Help!

Another Voice   Stop them!

Voices   Guards!

A Woman's Voice   Help!

Genèvre (*getting up*)   What is it?

Female Attendant   Oh! Madame!

Genèvre   Well?

Female Attendant   The people
Have broken into the palace courtyard and are shouting threats.
They smashed the door, and the steps
Of the keep are already strewn with murdered guards.

Geryn (*putting his hand to his sword*)   I'll go.

Genèvre   No, you stay.
(*To the* **Attendant**.) And who are they looking for,
This torrent of people?

Female Attendant   You, My Lady, listen to their cries of anger
Proclaiming your name.

Voices   Down with Genèvre, down with her!

Other Voices   Bring the adulteress onto the balcony!

Genèvre   What are they saying . . .?

Voices   And Geryn with her, the traitor!

Genèvre   Our two names?

A frightened **Captain** *enters, running. Sounds of the crowd.*

The Captain   Oh! My Lady, there might still be time,
Run away, quickly, take some secret staircase.
The crowd is on my heels, following close behind;
They're deranged, dogs, a horde . . .
And Morold, the king's nephew, is driving the riot.

Genèvre   Ah, Morold! That name explains everything!
Morold, the face of a traitor and the heart of a disloyal dog!
He's the one stirring up this trouble, is he? And leading
The rebellious masses.

The Captain   Yes, my Lady.

Genèvre   Have the hundred royal vassals of the guard fled, then?

The Captain   Vassals, guards, seigneurs, the whole court is with him.

Voices (*getting closer*)   Bring the adulteress to the balcony!

Genèvre   Can you hear roars of the
Beast, the crowd?

The Captain   Oh, save your head!
Flee!

Genèvre   I, run away? I will wait for my people and my nephew.

Guards enter suddenly and fall to the ground, murdered; tumult, shouts. The tapestry at the back opens wide, revealing a crowd armed with pikes and scythes, carrying torches; in the first row are horsemen and armed barons; **Morold** *is at the front. Behind, we see the gallery lit by the moon.*

Scene Three

Morold (*showing* **Genèvre** *and* **Geryn** *to the people*)   There, what did I tell you?
Look, all of you. The sin
Is clear and flagrant, and the adulterous bed
Is there before your eyes! The mystery
Is pierced like a wineskin, and I did not lie to you:
(*Pointing to* **Geryn**.) She had this perjurer for a lover.

Geryn (*putting his hand to his sword*)   What did he say?

Genèvre (*to* **Geryn**)   Leave this toad to drool out his bile.
Morold is a bastard. His mother was a slave.
The sufferings of his past excite his emotions.

Morold (*to* **Genèvre**)   My old, sickened anger towards you
Is what drives these scoundrels, these knights, this crowd, this rabble.
You mock and offend them with your stupid woman's anger.
But we will break you, woman, like a reed!
Where is your distaff[26] now, where are your spindles?
These purple cloths and silk cushions
Are the insolent luxury of a harlot.
And while my king, my master and your husband,
Defends our borders, you, amid jewels
And vases of agate and translucent amber,
Receive a lover and act the courtesan.

Geryn (*rushing over to him, sword held high*)   You've said too much.

Morold *breaks* **Geryn**'s *sword with a blow of his iron mace. Horsemen surround* **Morold** *with their shields.*

---

26 A distaff is a tool used in spinning, to hold the fibres before they are wound around the spindle.

Morold (*to* **Geryn**)   Stop there, handsome groom.
Who would consent to cross swords with you
Without blushing, now that you betray your vows?
The insult of being a carpet knight, a pretty favourite,
Fits you like a glove! The husband did indeed
Believe you a faithful friend and entrusted her to you,
For then people still praised your radiant, untainted glory,
And your honour and your loyalty;
Geryn the proud and chaste knight was held up as an example.
Fickle honour, loyalty whose steel is fragile
And poorly tempered,
Three months with the lady's beautiful eyes and now
A look and a smile have destroyed all that!
Vows to your king, honour, reserve,
All these melted like snow at a breath from her lips,
And now, wandering in shame, despised by all,
Your poor soul caught up in the burnished hair
Of an unfaithful and false woman, with adultery
Like a living remorse in your solitary heart,
You will live bound in the shroud
Woven by your own hands, your eyes, and your mouth . . .
And women will flee from the shame of your bed,
For you will be a turncoat traitor in everyone's eyes!
Go now, I pity your sad, weary look;
Somebody else will punish your crime and your weakness.
Go now, your presence accuses your mistress.
Take pity, in your turn, on this body
Overcome with pain, and don't proclaim your fault and hers any longer
Before this assembled crowd.
Go, the way is free . . . and the ancient house
Where your old servants won't know you any more
Awaits your regrets and your useless tears.

The crowd parts silently before **Geryn**, *who hesitates.*

Genèvre   Go. I will follow you.

Geryn *exits.*

Scene Four

Morold (*mockingly*)   Not just yet.
Your royal highness will surely wait for dawn
And the king's expected return.

Genèvre   What,
Have you told him already?

Morold   No. Ratbert here,
The palace messenger, is about to set off for Scyone.

Genèvre   Let him go.

Morold   You smile, and roar like a lioness
As you hear prison bars and the chill of a coffin
Closing around your conceit;
Because these angry people, whom your eyes
Barely see, will demand the death of the
Adulterous queen. In betraying her king,
The queen betrays the dynasty, and the people
Will not abandon their right, fired as they are with the bitterness
Of so many past wrongs . . . And your fortune
Is entirely in the hands of this bastard whom you hate,
Poor woman finally caught in the mesh of our nets.
It was I alone, do you hear me, who tore the veil
Hiding all your ignominy, and the misery
In which you flounder here is all for my pleasure.

Genèvre   Your voice seems to tremble with desire!

Morold   What?

Genèvre   What a fierce lava lust can be!
Watch out, Morold . . . what do I care about you,
Slave, and these people thronging at my door?
The future is nothing to me, because I have the past.
I have known the kisses of the man I adore.
His memory still embraces and possesses me
And my trembling body is still with him.
Since he left, everything is dead, everything has fled
And my bewitched dream is no longer bound to earth.

Morold (*showing her to the people*)   All of you, listen to her proclaiming
the adultery,
Glorifying her sin and shamelessly
Sullying Arthus yet again with this public affront.

Genèvre (*addressing the people*)   Yes, then, freely and with my head high I admit it,
And no blush will tinge my cheek.
A man appeared and I loved him madly,
I took him before God as my master and lover.
For me the crime lies in subjection to the love
Of a man I abhor, but the one I adore
Has a right over me in life and in death.
I cheated your king, but I didn't love him.
Only one man has filled my life and made it blossom!
The obsequious guile and spiteful envy
Of a coward have set betrayal in my path:

(*Indicating* **Morold**.) Were it not for that man I would be free of suspicion
And Arthur's glory would shine untainted.
The people will choose the lover or the coward!

Morold (*walking towards her*)   Ha!

A Voice (*in the crowd*)   Let her speak!

Another Voice   Put her to death!

Voices   She's right.

A Voice   This Morold is a cheat.

Morold (*threateningly, to* **Genèvre**)   Ha! Poison tongue!
(*Shrugging his shoulders.*) And these idiot people who acclaim her now! . . .
(*Turning to the crowd.*) Get out of here, all of you, except you four.

*He gestures to four men to stay. Murmurs from the people who withdraw. The tapestry
falls back into place.* **Genèvre** *and* **Morold** *remain alone with the four men.*

Scene Five

Genèvre   Heavens,
Are you afraid they'll take my part now?

Morold   Ha! The people's anger has barely descended
Upon your head, and your lips already utter threats?
I recognise you too well, miserable Genèvre,
Impure animal, proud, eternal Herodias![27]
In another time, with Herod Antipas,[28] it was you,
Drunk with blood, who made your daughter Salome dance
In the midst of a celebration, to get the head
Of a sage, and your fingers made two holes in his eyes!
Then, among the Franks, you had the tall, red-headed vassals
Tie a queen of Burgundy to a horse
And kill a prelate on the altar: Frédégonde
Was your name. And then, now here now there,
You repeated all the treacheries of other dismal Delilahs
In those far-off times.
But now I have caught your winged hands in my iron hands,
The ghoul's mask is torn away at last
And the insulted husband will punish your sin.

---

27 Lorrain was familiar with Oscar Wilde's *Salome* (1891), included in this volume, and hence also
Wilde's particular take on Herodias as a mother who takes pleasure in her daughter Salome's demand
that she be served the head of Iokanaan (John the Baptist) on a silver charger.

28 Herod Antipas (20 BC–AD 39): ruler of Galilee. Associated with the murder of John the Baptist and the
crucifixion of Jesus after sending him to the court of Pontius Pilate.

This exquisite grace and this blonde beauty
Will be annihilated with one movement, one word,
By me, the hideous bastard, the dwarf, the vile animal! . . .

Genèvre (*mocking*)   Be quick then, Morold. What if the king forgave me?

Morold   What is she saying?

Genèvre   I'm saying that I have quivered naked
In his arms and I await his coming without fear,
I have the strong perfumes of memory on my side.

Morold   He might forgive?

Genèvre   Just as he might punish.

Morold   No. He will have pity, I'm certain: the coward!

Genèvre   As would you, if I were to put you to the test,
Poor cripple who has never known a kiss, sad lover!
Why the trembling hands, the faltering voice?
Why this agony in your dull eyes
When I come close to you? Ah, wretch, you love me!
Lust has you tight! But another fear
Torments you, Morold; I know that one too:
If I am the wandering phantom of adultery,
You contain all the rancour of the lonely vanquished.
You hate nature and all that is human.
Massacres yesterday and murders tomorrow:
That is your dream. With the old world reduced to dust, you want to
Break everything, drown everything in blood and dissolve it!
Evil for the pleasure of evil, sombre and naïve,
Makes you chaste and cruel. I recognised you straight away
In the tumult and disorder. You wander
Like a ghost trying to destroy a kingdom.
But where would your plans be if the loathed prince
Whom you want to depose, were to pardon?

Morold   He will pardon you.

Genèvre   Let me get to the door, then,
Quick, and give me an escort to the fields.
Your hatred binds you but I go towards love!
But be quick, Morold, before dawn comes;
(*Looking into his eyes.*) Beautiful as I am, danger follows me about.

Morold   And misfortune.
(*To the four guards.*) You, accompany her
Out into the countryside, take her outside the walls.

The four men surround **Genèvre**. **Morold** *gives her his coat.* **Genèvre** *wraps it around her and takes a step towards the left.*

Genèvre (*to* **Morold**)   I leave you here, Morold, to your murky plans;
May you succeed!

Morold (*to* **Genèvre**)   Run to your infamy,
Go, shameless dog, eternal enemy!
Go, my hatred follows you: we will meet again.

Genèvre *exits left, escorted by the armed men.* **Morold** *goes back towards the tapestry, his back to the audience. The stage goes dark again.*

Narrator   And amid the roar of the people and the barons,
They followed the hordes, each with their desires:
Genèvre towards love, Morold towards chaos.

Tableau Two

Narrator   Brittany is soaked in blood. The husband, the insulted prince,
Cornered the lover in his village. He avenged
The affront to the throne by hunting the boudoir knight
Through the fields and woods.
To defend himself, Geryn assembled his followers
And vassals, and called on the heathens for help,
And, for six long months, war and famine
Have devastated the ruined country, which is lit
By the glow of fires that never go out.
The queen is said to be deep within a closed convent.
The bitter, dogged hatred between Arthus and Geryn
Has finally seen its last day.
Panic reigns in Geryn's camp. They have all fled
And on the battleground, where night is falling slowly,
Not a tear or a groan, not a shadow moves.
A red sky bleeds far off on the sorrowful horizon.

The theatre lights up to reveal a plain strewn with bodies. On the right, a little heap of bodies piled up; a tragic red sky ignites the darkened horizon; high in the sky, a light like blood bathes the battlefield.

The stage is empty.

Scene One

A Voice (*faintly*)   Water!

Enter **Two Stragglers**, *one supporting the other.*

First Straggler   Another step, take courage!

Second Straggler   Is there far to go?

First Straggler   Keep walking, come on.

Second Straggler   Oh! I'm dying; my doublet
Is soaked with blood. Leave me.

He stops.

First Straggler   A little further! . . .

Second Straggler (*sinking to the ground*)   Leave me to die here!

First Straggler   Poor friend!

He exits. Silence.

A Wounded Man (*raising himself up with his hands*)   Dawn . . .
The sky is pink.

He falls down and dies, groaning.

A Voice   Water!

Enter **Genèvre**, *wrapped in a large man's coat, followed by* **Onfroy**.

Genèvre (*she stops on the left*)   Oh! Don't leave me.
Dear Onfroy, I'm afraid. My feet
Slip in blood at every step!

Pause.

Such a ferocious silence!
What awful astonishment can have stifled
The cry that still opens their mouths, their eyes? It's horrible!
These dead; there are so many of them! My shame and terror
Grow when I think that a kiss from my lips
Scattered this carnage and that an hour of passion . . .

A voice   I'm thirsty.

Genèvre (*terrified*)   Somebody spoke.

Onfroy   Somebody dying.

Genèvre   Where?

Onfroy   Stop, there are too many of them!

Genèvre   Blood, so much blood!

She steps on bodies as she retreats.

It sprays over me, splatters all over.

A Voice (*faint, singing*)   The girl, tra la, that I love, tra la, with her beautiful auburn
hair . . .

Genèvre   Is someone calling?

Onfroy   Oh no, just a memory of love

In a dying moan, a poor dying creature who . . .

Genèvre   Always
Love. Sinister scourge, it is blind but it devours!
These men remember it even as they are dying!
Does he, at least, remember? In that obscure cloister
Love still haunted the pure, austere hearts
Of the nuns, and I learned . . . But Onfroy, your hand is trembling;
Are you afraid now? Come, and we will search together.

Onfroy   Someone . . . stop talking.

He points out three men passing along back of the stage, leaning over the corpses.

Genèvre   They have gold necklaces
In their hands. Who are they?

Onfroy   They're plundering the dead.
Corpse robbers.

Genèvre (*watching them*)   Oh! Look, they're lifting up
A wounded man. What are they doing?

Onfroy   They're finishing him off.

Genèvre (*hanging on to* **Onfroy**)   Let's go, Onfroy, let's go! I'm afraid, it's too horrible.

Onfroy (*pointing to the dead*)   Madam, what if my kind Master is among them?

Genèvre *stops. The men have disappeared.*

Genèvre   Geryn among these dead and wounded men; your master
Dying in the shadows and calling me, perhaps,
Who knows? Cursing me?

Onfroy   You!

Genèvre   Me. A stench of crime
Rises from these dead, an odour of remorse,
And contemplating this red sky and this vast charnel house,
I feel a shroud thickening around me.
My soul will never love again,
A tomb gapes inside me.

Morold, *who entered a few moments ago on the right and is watching her, suddenly moves to stand in front of her.*

Scene Two

Morold (*mocking*)   A revenant
Might find bed and board there, if he tried
Hard enough. A man is always master of

A woman.

Genèvre (*recoiling*)   Morold!

Morold   You weren't expecting me?
I did say to you: we'll meet again. Step by step
I've been following you since dawn . . . Oh! In the shadows, at a distance.
I knew I'd find you this evening in the silence
Of this battlefield. Is it crowded enough?
You can be proud, and survey it well,
It is your masterpiece. All of them fell
For love of Genèvre, their swords in their hands and your name on their lips!
You can take pride in this red scene of butchery.
The groans of the dying that you have just heard
Must charm your heart and invigorate your soul.
A great triumph for the queen and for the woman.

Genèvre (*not moving, her eyes lowered*)   Go on, engulf me in a useless stream
Of insults, mockery and laughter: I won't listen any more.
You can no longer disturb the infinite sadness
Of my soul, Morold. Something immense and proud
Has descended upon my disgrace;
All arrogance is dead in this desperate heart.
The haughty, adulterous Genèvre, despised
By her people, is no more. It is her death throes
That you have come to insult, and you cannot know
How deep my despair descends!

Morold   That is true. Well now, here you are, buried alive
In fruitless regret and melancholy,
Having lost both your lover
And your crown . . . And those charming eyes
Will be dulled forever by mourning and tears.
The future seems heavy with trouble.
Here you are, wandering now and homeless,
With nowhere to rest your bruised head,
Alone with your distress, defenceless,
Poor abandoned thing, between the bitter resentment
Of your people, who hate you, and the rage of a king;
Betrayal, anguish and terror.
Compared to you the dead are happy, wretched woman!
They no longer live and suffer.

Genèvre (*immobile, her jaw set*)   Vile beast!

Morold (*slyly*)   But why should you always treat me as an enemy?
Look at me, Genèvre. A dormant love
Can sometimes rave and seem like hate.
Oh, the cruel torment for a proud soul

To know that it is crippled, vile and scorned
By the woman it adores . . . When just one kiss . . .
But, wretched woman, wandering and with no kingdom,
What if I could bring salvation?

Genèvre   The spectre,
The vampire from the tomb would save
The dying woman?

Morold   Genèvre, listen. A dreadful decree of
Destiny draws us to one another;
If I am indeed the shadowy prophet of evil for evil's sake,
Then your divine beauty, the bitter and cruel torment
Of men, is a trusty tool in my hands.
I have always loved you, yes, I admit it now.
I may have turned the wheel of fortune to my own ends,
But only because your cold disdain, oh golden queen,
Had humiliated me, broken me, filled me with rage,
And my sickened heart thought itself enraged.
The throne made you so high, so distant! . . .
But I, son of a slave, a cripple, cheerless and alone,
Said to myself: 'My own hands will weave the shroud
Where I will bury this face and this snow-white breast,
And I will dig a trap beneath her royal feet
Into which everything will fall, her throne and her pride;
Then, when the tomb is ready, I will open her coffin,
Seize her hands by the tomb's edge
And say to her: live again, be my queen or succumb!'
If I horrify you, blame nothing but love!
Woman, I can restore your kingdom, your sceptre
And your tarnished glory, all before dawn;
And you, so recently scorned and mocked
By your mutinous people, will, by tomorrow,
Crush them under your heel, those disloyal imbeciles.
I hold the fate of your lands in my hands.
Geryn is vanquished, you know; the twelve princes
Who revolted with him are dead, captive or wounded.
Thirty thousand of their men cut down today
Lie dying here. It was the whole army.
As for Arthus' army, it is bloodied and decimated
By six months of battle, fever, and hunger,
And drags itself through the fields; its path
Is strewn with dying men never to be lifted up
Again by their comrades. The peasants are finishing them off,
For the whole countryside is prey to bandits,
Rebellious peasants who are the sons of these cursed times,
And bands of robbers lay waste to the land.
These terrible troops, these angry souls,

Pillaging countryfolk and craven mercenaries,
Are all my army. I can summon them
From the dark roads with one movement,
An innumerable crowd roaring and swelling
Like water flooding across the plains.
One word from you, Genèvre, one word and I obey.
Arthus and his flock of exhausted shadows
Are slowly returning, amid the jeers
Of the starving people, to the walls of Pen Armor.
We can easily surround them.
Do you want us to bring the victor's army to you
Bound hand and foot? Say something! To you in your alarm
I can bring a whole throng of ardent defenders,
Of conquerors too. But you are crying,
And you stand still and mute. Does a ghost
Possess you? Reply. Think. I offer you a kingdom:
Brittany, Ireland, and all the old splendour!
(*With a cry.*) Oh! You still hold Geryn's love dear?

Genèvre   I've already told you, leave my agony in peace,
The pain of a being whose eyes are finally open. The infinite
Sadness of my soul is indifferent to everything.
I have no more heart or desire, no more disgust.
What do a sceptre and a worthless kingdom mean, in my distress?
What does Geryn matter to me? The past is a faint aroma,
Already dissipating, a scent of incense.
The abyss of pain into which I descend, grieving,
Envelops me forever in a sea of shadows
And I can see nothing but a flock of mournful birds:
The remorse that has settled on my mind for always.

Morold   Oh, I see it only too clearly in your wild eyes:
Does Morold the man disgust you, and do your lips
Refuse the bastard, the lame wreck? Ah Genèvre,
Necessity will get the better of these sad refusals.

Genèvre   Me, disgusted by someone! My God! Sweet Jesus!
(*Pointing to the battlefield.*) But if I could bring these eyes white as sheets back to life,
I would drink and kiss their wounds;
Genèvre is dead in me, I told you.
Another soul has been born, and this cursed place
That was once my heart, haunted by pride and lust,
Bleeds, a great wound open for ever more.
All I want is to resuscitate these dead, give life to the wounded,
Open these lifeless eyes with pious kisses,
Return these sons to their anguished mothers
And husbands to widows, to be loved, oh chimeras!

To share the pain of these poor suffering ones,
Be the comfort and hope of unhappy people,
To raise all those who grovel and suffer far from the sky they beseech
Up from the chasm, with one gesture!
That is the only love that enflames my senses.
(*Making to leave.*) Morold, leave me to the wounded.

Morold   Oh, poor madwoman, that's enough! I've listened to you too much.
Your heart has gone over to pity, you are lost!
While you were deaf to everything, walled up in your royal pride,
You disdained the cries of the ranting, scrambling people
On your doorstep, the mud, murder and filth.
You prospered, superb, amid the agony
Of people and kings, and triumphed over destiny
Because your power was underpinned by death,
Death that protected your role as the supplier
Of battlefield fodder, oh deadly lover!
But today your heart, your heart that you believe
Purified, bleeds and weeps and opens itself to pity
And your flesh is troubled by the cries of the wretched:
The poor, the suffering, vile mobs
Of ungrateful cowards who, if helped, will have nothing for you
But base insults, tricks and angry affront!
Pity, in your heart? Pity, the terrible sponge
That drinks the strength in us and eats away
At our old humanity like a hideous cancer?
Pity, that lie, that inanity?
Once a man had a blind, mad, girlish love
For rags and wounds, just as you have,
A man took pity on suffering, as you do!
The suffering people struck him, sold him, crucified him.
Those poor, good people for whom your heart trembles and cries.
Go on, tend to their wounds, poor woman; they will
Torture you, laugh at your terror,
And, when, on a whim, they have put you on a cross,
Nailed to a gallows, astonished and indignant,
You will call to me for help, poor visionary,
But it will be too late when you call me!
Good deeds from the dying are not gratefully received.
You don't move, and refuse to hear me,
But you will hear them shouting, even if I have to split
That hardened heart and smash it to pieces!

Turning to the dead and raising his hand over the battlefield, in a loud voice.

Now, wake up, stand up,
All of you sleeping over there, stand up, open your ears!
The queen with the azure eyes, with the bright hair,

Wants your opinion; she wants to consult Death.

Genèvre (*horrified*)   What are you doing?

Morold (*still facing the battlefield*)   Tell Genèvre about her fate.

Genèvre (*clutching* **Morold**)   The mass moved . . . Oh God, what is this awful
dream?
One corpse smiled, another is getting up! . . .

*The battlefield comes slowly to life. The dead and wounded raise themselves up with
their hands and, still lying down with their heads raised, look towards* **Morold**.

Morold (*to the* **Corpses**)   The queen is here, soldiers; she adored you,
She still loves you, dear deceased. She wishes . . .

A Reanimated Corpse   Genèvre the adulteress?

Morold   Did you hear that?

Another Corpse   That ignoble woman
For whose sake I'm already being devoured by worms?

Another Corpse   And I by flames?

A Wounded Man (*to* **Genèvre**)   Why have you come here? To caress a dead man,
Or to bite him? Vampire!

A Corpse (*lifting himself up and addressing the others*)   Aha, who still wants
To have a good time? A prostitute
Is among us.

All the Corpses on the Battlefield   Genèvre!

Morold (*to* **Genèvre**)   Can you hear their jeers
Rising under the red sky, hailing you in the distance?
Those men love you, this evening is proof.

Genèvre (*clinging to* **Morold**)   Oh Morold! . . . Oh Morold!

A Wounded Man (*to* **Genèvre**)   Oh, is it you, little hussy? . . .
Let the dead sleep in peace . . . Go back to your den!
Back to your palace.

The Cheerful Corpse (*who has already called the others*)   Aha, the queen is here,
Looking for a man, my friends!

A Corpse   She wants it!

A Corpse (*standing up*)   Here I am.

Genèvre *staggers, her eyes closed, and leans against* **Morold**.

Morold (*to* **Genèvre**)   Genèvre, are you still so fierce and determined
To follow pity?

Genèvre (*her eyes closed*)   My soul is a suicide

And prefers this charnel house and its immense affront
To my old sin.

Morold (*drawing back, his arms folded*)   They will kill you.
They will make you suffer.

Genèvre   Suffering is deliverance.

Morold (*suddenly moving away*)   Oh, she is mad.
(*Addressing the* **Corpses** *and pointing to the queen.*) Love her well, good corpses, I
entrust her to you.

Morold *exits, leaving* **Genèvre** *in the middle of the battlefield.*

Voices   Genèvre the adulteress! . . .

A Great Babble of Voices   Oh, oh, over there?
The queen is among us! Wake up, lads!

Curtain.

---

29 She is sometimes referred to as Lore, sometimes as Loreley.

Act Three

Tableau One

Narrator (*reading*)   Lore[29] was gentle and blonde, with eyes like honey.
Her consoling beauty made heaven seem possible,
And her gaze was tantalising, like an emerald
Glimpsed on the seabed. Her burnished hair
Ran over her bosom in a golden stream,
And such was the splendour of her beautiful white breasts
That she seemed like the dawn passing by:
Everyone, even the beggars, loved and desired Lore.
She was the night-time obsession of sons and husbands.
Her image haunted the sleep of outlaws,
And beneath her long brocade and silk robes
She was the scandal and the pride and the joy
Of a whole besotted people, mad with love,
Bewitched by her skin and her eyes, worshipping her beauty
As a priest worships the Virgin Mary.
Lore was a courtesan, and her flowered robe
Opened each night for a happy lover:
By day she poured the intoxication of her blonde beauty
Over the dazzled empire;
Lore was the spring and the smile of the world.

The stage lights up; a market square in an old town on the banks of the Rhine is revealed, crowded with people: a mass of human heads and raised arms fills the stage. On the left, downstage, are the steps and pillars of the town hall; there are pointed roofs and gabled turrets on the horizon.

Voices   Put her to death! Kill the harlot!

A Reiter (*on horseback*)   Hey, Brabanters,[30]
Disperse these scum; get rid of these troublemakers!

A Man of the People   Down with the lansquenet, death to the beautiful harlot
Whose door is golden and whose threshold is red!

Voices   Put the witch on the scaffold! Kill her!

A Bourgeois   They're going to charge.
Shall we go home, neighbour?

Second Bourgeois   I, go home? I love danger.
I like seeing these scoundrels beaten.

First Bourgeois   It excites you, does it?

---

30 Brabanter: a mercenary soldier.

Second Bourgeois   Oh!

First Bourgeois   This braying crowd
Chills me with horror. A mob of executioners! . . .

An Artisan   Down with soldiers, my friends!

Throws a stone at **Lore***'s windows.*

An Artisan   Take that through your windows,
Whore!

Voices   Won't you come out of your lair, witch?
Death to her!

The Reiter   Go home, or you'll get a beating; get back!

First Bourgeois   There's going to be trouble. I'm going home. Did you see the
bodies
From last night?

Second Bourgeois   No.

First Bourgeois   One of them has a good twenty black holes
In his jerkin, bleeding black like mulberries;
Another's got seventeen. I counted the wounds.
But here they come, carried on stretchers.

The crowd parts, murmuring; stretchers carrying bodies pass by.

Second Bourgeois   Oh, all their eyes are drowned in grief and pity:
Those ten fine young men, full of pride and passion
Yesterday, cold today.

An Old Woman   All dead, and the hussy
Still living . . .
(*Shakes her fist at the soldiers.*) And these scum too!

She throws herself at a stretcher and clutches the corpse.

My son! Oh, my child! Ludwig!

The Reiter   Take her away.

Reiters *take the woman away.*

Second Bourgeois   It makes me shudder.

The Old Woman's Voice (*in the distance*)   My child!

First Bourgeois   She's the mother!

Voices   Death to the troops! Down with them!

Sounds of windows breaking.

First Bourgeois   They're breaking
Another window with their stones.

An Artisan   The bourgeois
Are protecting Loreley. Death to the toffs!

First Bourgeois   I think
We really must go home now.

A Man of the People   The law
Is on the wench's side, and the soldiers are complicit . . .
To arms! Down with the soldiers!

Second Bourgeois   A mass of cavalry
Is gathering under the market hall, and they're pulling
Down the youngsters who climbed up the pillars:
There's going to be terrible slaughter.

First Bourgeois   Would you hand her over
To this frenzied crowd?

Second Bourgeois   Ha! If you want peace,
The end justifies the means.

First Bourgeois   You admire cowardice!

Voices   There she is! There she is!

Second Bourgeois   What? Are the people cheering her now? Listen.

First Bourgeois   The crowd is like a woman:
It spins like a weathercock, and Lore and her golden eyes
Have changed the wind.

Second Bourgeois   True, there isn't a sound now.

First Bourgeois   Massacre and debauchery
Are all forgotten, before the pearly skin
Of this adorable body and the innocent pink
Of her breasts. Beauty is the mysterious,
All-powerful, vanquishing philtre that corrupts the world.

Second Bourgeois   The fact is, the harlot is divinely blonde.

First Bourgeois   Then look at these men, rioters and soldiers!
Aren't they walking slowly, their foreheads bowed,
Behind the captive with the blonde locks?
Don't they look as though they're leading a witch to be judged?

Second Bourgeois   A . . .

First Bourgeois   A guilty woman, at least. Think, ten men are dead!
Her case is serious. And the council has come out;

He points to the provosts[31] of the merchants and magistrates who have just assembled on the steps of the town hall.

---

31 Provosts served as magistrates and administrators in France in the Middle Ages.

And the huge doorway is covered with drapes
Of mourning.

A Herald (*coming up onto the steps*)   The governor.

There is a movement in the crowd: an old man dressed in mourning, his hair and beard white, appears on the steps. The judges make way for him.

The court.

The judges form a circle around the **Governor**.

A Woman of the People   These creatures!
Do they need provosts wearing fur to judge them?
Haven't we got the Rhine for rabid dogs?
Throw the harlot in the river! Into the water with her!

Another Woman of the People   Why not strangle her
With her yellow tresses, her and all those like her?
Then we'd be done with her. Death to her!

The Crowd   Death to the harlot!

Second Bourgeois   The unrest is rising up again . . .

First Bourgeois   And boiling more fiercely.
Alas, she has the women of the town against her.

The Crowd   Justice! Hang her! To the gibbet with her!

First Bourgeois   It's the base mob,
Grim-faced, drunk from all the hard times.

The Crowd   Justice! Kill her! Kill her!

Second Bourgeois   The judges seem deaf.

First Bourgeois   And the procession is still far away, and moves
With slow steps. There's going to be a struggle.

A Man   How pale the governor is!

First Bourgeois   Ah, friends,
You would turn pale for less. He only had one son,
Who, for love of Lore, died in the brawl.

Second Bourgeois   She is lost, then.

First Bourgeois   Alas! I fear
Some terrible infamy is brewing here.

The Crowd (*drawing back*)   Here she is, here she is!

The **Crowd** *parts, pushed by the* **Reiters**. **Lore** *appears, surrounded by an escort. She is wearing a formal robe in pale brocade decorated with irises and anemones in*

green gold: her bare arms and bosom are covered with jewels, and her blonde hair
falls down over her shoulders from underneath a pearl-embroidered escoffion.[32]

First Bourgeois   Oh! Those enchanting eyes!

A Reiter (*pushing* **Lore** *ahead of him, addressing the* **Governor**)   Seigneur, here's
the girl. We found her
Half mad with terror and barricaded
Into her home, besieged by the crowd.
She was hardly moving, and looked almost dead.
(*Leaning over* **Lore** *and shaking her.*) Come, speak, defend yourself. Tell your story.
Your life depends on it.

Voices   Take her to the stake, the witch!

The Reiter   Can't you hear them shouting! Smother your fear!

Lore, *fallen to her knees, remains still, stunned.*

The Reiter   She is dead, or dying.

The **Reiter** *moves away.*

Lore (*she crawls to the* **Governor**'*s feet and tries to grasp his hands*)   Seigneur,
punish me,
Punish me, be just and severe. An abyss
Has opened beneath my feet, and I am lost inside it, a victim
Dragging down into censure and disgrace
All those who have loved me . . . and who will love me!
Those bleeding corpses are still at my door . . .
Like my dead friends. Put me to death.
I know that my passing . . . cannot bring them back;
But at least they will see that I wanted to die
To follow them . . . My lord, remember though
That I am a woman, and I am young, and weak in the face of suffering!
My kind Lord and Seigneur, may I be put to death . . .
But, in the name of Love, do not make me suffer!

The Governor (*frees himself from her grasp and pushes her away*)   Now, have you
finished scuffling your pale hands
Under the feet of these officers of the peace, and using the paving stones
Like a bed of corruption? . . . She thinks she will move me
With this golden hair . . .

Leaning with one hand on one of the judges, he addresses the people.

Listen! Did any one of you,
Bourgeois, nobleman or peasant, witness the crime?

---

32 An escoffion was an ornate headpiece worn in the Middle Ages.

May he come forward bravely and identify the victim,
The time, and the place. I'm waiting.

A long silence.

Nobody will reply? I have nothing more to say.

He sits down on his seat, his face pale.

The Bourgeois   What? Not one witness?

The Governor (*seated, through clenched teeth*)   Idiot, accursed people,
Whose brutality is softened at the sight
Of a pearly escoffion and a white bosom!
(*To a* **Herald**.) Sound the three calls.

The **Herald** *plays three notes; the crowd is silent.*

The Governor   Will none of them speak?

A Soldier (*an old man, comes forward*)   Yes, I will!

The Governor (*turns towards him aggressively*)   Who are you, then?

The Soldier (*proudly*)   I was at Montferrat,[33]
Your Grace. Oh, the heat that day,
The city had been taken three times and abandoned.
But my forehead has the gash to show for it.

He removes his helmet to reveal a scar on his forehead.

The Governor   All right!
(*Pointing to* **Lore**, *slumped on the steps.*) Do you recognise the girl sprawled there?

The Soldier   Poor cornered deer, with the hounds set upon her.
I believe you. I witnessed their skirmish
From the pantry, where I had dined well with
Monsieur d'Alençon's men, for the French Conte d'Evreux,[34]
Your son, if you will pardon my naming him,
Had brought ten with him, gentlemen like him

---

33 Montferrat: region in Northwest Italy. The region was established as a march (borderland) of the
Kingdom of Italy and Holy Roman Empire in the tenth century, and its marquesses were related to the
Frankish Kings. The marquesses regularly participated in the Crusades of the Middle Ages. Lorrain
might be referencing the Crusades or warring factions between the Pope and Holy Roman Emperor
(Guelphs and Ghibellines) in Montferrat in the thirteenth century, but it is more likely that he is
referring to the Italian Wars (1494–1559) given the Soldier's speech that follows.

34 Count of Évreux: noble title of the Norman dynasty, as well as subsequent dynastic houses. Monsieur
d'Alençon could refer to various counts and dukes of France from the tenth to the nineteenth centuries.
It is tempting to think that Lorrain might have been referencing William IX, Marquis of Montferrat
(1486–1518), who was married to Anne of Alençon (1492–1562), daughter of Margaret of Lorraine,
Duchess of Alençon (1463–1521) – a namesake that Lorrain might have found it difficult to resist.
William forwarded pro-French policies, and played a role in the Italian Wars that came to a head in the
1510s when protecting Montferrat from invasion by the Duke of Milan.

To dine at the child's house . . . The pitchers were emptied
And they were about to leave . . . A cursed throw of the dice,
To decide the night of the lovely girl
And who would stay, caused the fight,
For she makes men jealous.
One remark led to another and they came to blows,
My Lord will understand . . . Now, since the terrible murderess
Was becoming frightened, they went outside to argue in the dark.
All ten came to the foot of the stairs
And charged . . . Good God! Such a clashing of steel!
My heart was pounding . . . The girl, half dead,
Was crying out for help, crying murder, calling for me, for aid . . .
Useless cries . . . the pages and valets were upstairs licking the plates,
And didn't care to run down to see the killing!
And there you are . . . That the poor child now accuses herself
Is beyond me: her suitors kept her safely locked away.
She lived in the shadows and only went out
On feast days . . . People think her brokenhearted,
Or that's what the bourgeois said about her.
For myself I think her mad, and her ways uncivil,
But incapable, alas, of causing pain to others;
On the contrary . . . Well, she may stand accused today,
But I always pitied her and I still pity her.

Voices (*in the crowd*)   Oh, Governor! Give us the beautiful Lore!
Give us back the beautiful girl!

Other Voices   Bravo, soldier,
You talk without trembling and speak the truth!

The Governor (*through clenched teeth*)   Turncoat.
Some contented lover has paid for this invented
Story.
(*Bending over* **Lore**.) You heard, disgraced girl.
This ghastly crowd absolves you. The dazzling blasphemy
Of your beauty pleases them. Go back to where you're expected.
But not where you think, hussy, not to the den
Where freshly spilt blood makes your lips even redder,
Your eyes brighter, your bosom firmer and more white!
Leave the massacred troops to their parents,
Their brothers and sons; leave our beloved dead
To our bitter tears: these mothers' despair
Forbids you to stay a minute longer in this town.
Your crimes cannot be judged
By an honest man; leave here, witch! You must go
Barefoot to Rome, and in some forgotten cell,
Or at a consecrated stake, you must serve your wretched sentence!
Go away, don't crouch on these stones any longer.

Lore (*on her knees*)   Seigneur, have pity, I am afraid . . .

The Governor   The pale faces
Of the dead frighten you.
(*Addressing the* **Reiters**.) Move on now, go on.

The **Reiters** *leave, and* **Lore** *is left alone.*

The **Governor** *addresses the people, pointing to* **Lore**.

The Governor   People, I abandon her to your just anger.

He goes back into the courtroom, followed by all the judges. **Lore**, *who has got to her feet quickly, her eyes wild, very frightened, is suddenly surrounded and seized by the crowd.*

Voices (*one after another*)   We've got her at last! Take the witch to the scaffold!

Lore   Have mercy . . .

A Voice   Mercy? And will you give me back my brother?

Another Voice   I only had one son: handsome, young, loving, happy;
What did you do with him?

Lore (*trembling*)   Have pity!

First Bourgeois (*to the other*)   Let's go. This is too awful.

Voices   To the stake!

Other Voices   To the scaffold!

A Voice (*louder than the others*)   No, to the cathedral!

A Voice   To see the bishop.

The Bourgeois   Listen.

Distant Voices   *Dies irai, dies illa.*
    Solvet saeclum in favilla
    Teste David cum sybilla.[35]

The Bourgeois   Silence. Something like a groan
Weeps and moans in the distance.

A Man of the People   Death to the witch!

The Bourgeois   Are you deaf?
It's the Office for the dead, and, in his velvet mantle,
His mitre, beaded with silver, his shot silk chasuble,[36]
Here is my Lord the bishop with the holy host,
Come to give absolution . . .

---

35 Day of wrath, Day of anger / Will dissolve the world in ashes / As foretold by David and the Sybil.
36 A vestment worn by clergy for celebrating the Eucharist.

A Woman   To our slaughtered sons?
Hand the harlot over to him, and . . .

Another Woman   No, not to the clergy,
She is beautiful, and would set the priests' hearts on fire!

A Bourgeois   His lordship the bishop is upright and honest . . .

The Woman   Let the reiters
Hang her from the thieves' scaffold!

Lore   Have mercy!

Group of People   No, hand the guilty woman over to the curates.

Other People   Yes, justice, justice.

A Man of the People   And let her be judged and condemned
Without cowardly indulgence.

Men and Women of the People   Yes, justice.

A Woman   And vengeance!

A Man of the People (*he takes* **Lore** *by the arm and forces her to kneel*)   And you,
feeble-hearted, fear-stricken slut,
On your knees, murderess, and beg for mercy!

*During this scene, the sounds of religious chants have drawn closer, alternating
women's and men's voices.*

> *Quantus tremor est futurus*
> *Quando judex est venturus*
> *Cuncta stricte discussurus.*
>
> *Tuba mirum spargens sonum*
> *Per sepulcra regionum,*
> *Coget omnes ante thronum.*[37]

*Penitents, women in mourning, and a whole funeral cortège process slowly, carrying
banners, candles and a large crucifix; they take over the stage and the crowd makes
way for them:* **Lore** *is alone in the midst of the deacons and penitents. She is kneeling,
dishevelled and distraught.*

Women's Voices   *Mors stupebit et natura,*
Cum resurget creatura,
Judicanti responsura.[38]

Lore   Why these holy chants and funeral candles?
I'm afraid! I am always afraid now. Oh adored Christ,

---

37 How much trembling there will be / When the judge comes / And strictly examines all things. / The
tuba will send its wondrous sound / Throughout earth's sepulchres / And gather all before the throne.
38 Death and nature will be / Astounded / When all creation rises again.

I begged you for shadows, where I could bathe
My sickened heart and soul.
Here they are at last, and burning with fever,
My body is frightened and trembles like a hare.

Voices   *Judex ergo cum sedebit,*
  Quidquid latet apparebit
  Nil inultum remanebit.[39]

Lore (*still without moving*)   What are all these figures in mourning around me?
(*She gets up and looks over the shoulders of the priests and the women at the cortège.*) They are following a body . . . a body in its coffin!
(*She counts the coffins, between the shoulders of the penitents.*) One coffin, two, another, and another! . . .
(*Crying out and rushing to the front of the stage.*) Oh, I understand at last . . . Cruel Lore,
It's their blood that clings to you and makes you stumble.

The **Bishop** *appears at that moment underneath a canopy of black velvet carried by four clerics; he is wearing a black mitre and a mourning mantle. Choirboys hold his cape, and others wave censers, the rest of the cortège follows.*

Men's Voices   *Quid sum miser tunc dicturus?*
  Quem patronum rogaturus?
  Cum vix justus sit securus?[40]

Voice (*from the riot, in the distance*)   Let the bishop decide and command: to the stake!

Other Voices   The scaffold of the Rhine!

The Bishop (*stops*)   Does the people's anger
Dare dictate God's will to him? Stand back!
On your knees, impious people!
(*Addressing the priests.*) And you, my priests,
Cast the shadow of the crucifix over this body.

The cortège stops. Women kneel, the man carrying the crucifix holds it over **Lore** *and the priests group themselves around her.*

Voices (*from the crowd*)   Do not have pity, Bishop!

Other Voices   Pronounce the sentence:
The noose or the stake.

Other Voices   The Rhine or the gallows.

Lore (*still kneeling*)   Their hatred pursues me and my hideous past
Suffocates me.

---

39 When the judge takes his place / What is hidden will be revealed / Nothing will remain unavenged.
40 What shall a wretch like me say? / Who shall intercede for me? / When the just ones need mercy?

A Woman's Voice   No, send the leper to jail! Throw her in a cell!
Let her be cold and hungry, let her body expiate!

Lore (*falling face-down on the ground with a loud cry*)   Oh!

The Bishop (*bending over* **Lore**)   What do you want, poor soul lying at my feet?

Lore (*who has heard him, raises herself up slightly*)   What do I want? Death.
(*Crawling to the* **Bishop**'*s feet.*) Punish me. I have sinned.
My life's crime, that was hidden from sight,
Is laid bare, my doings are criminal, dreadful:
(*Turning to the faithful.*) Your sons all bled under my ferocious kiss,
Good people.
(*With a sweeping gesture.*) I filled these coffins;
Punish me, but please, take me away from here!
I am suffocating . . .
(*Moving on her knees.*) These slow steps, these hoods, these coffins,
These flickering candles, these praying women
Terrify me. I am afraid . . . these sacred hymns
Hurt me: I open my desperate arms in vain
And still want to pray; but no, I am a witch,
And am cursed, alas! . . . the sky and its light
Madden me, and I horrify myself
Just as I horrify these angry people who drive me to you.
Bishop, listen to me, save the human race!
Punish me but, I beg you, have them take me away:
The blood rises to my eyes, I am ashamed to speak . . .

The **Bishop** *is frightened and curious, and bends over* **Lore**.

A Decon   She is in her death throes.

A Cleric   Oh, that strangled breath!
Hell is already reaching out for her.

The Bishop (*leaning over* **Lore**)   She is a visionary.
Has she any parents?

The Cleric   My Lord, she has no mother.

The Bishop   And no brother?

The Cleric   She is alone and lives abandoned.
She is Lore.

The Bishop (*shuddering*)   Loreley . . .
(*As though praying, looking upwards.*) A sad and painful name . . .
So she is eternal, alas! The courtesan
Crying at Christ's feet?

He walks towards **Loreley** *and stretches out his hand over her.*

The Bishop   Go away from here. I could not pronounce your death sentence.

Go into a convent, shave that golden hair,
Hide that snowy face and those bright eyes
That cast a spell . . . hide them forever.
For despite myself I feel the sweetness of a kiss in your gaze.
This is the only punishment I can inflict on you:
That silence and night should fall on your famous beauty,
And that scandal should be forgotten . . .

The **Bishop** *crosses the stage slowly; the backdrop becomes shadowy and fades away.*

Narrator   And in the smoky shadows
Of the candle, towards the weeping Christ at the altar,
The bishop disappeared, pensive and solemn.

Tableau Two

Narrator (*reading*)   At the foot of the old, sun-bleached ramparts,
A woman with a pale, sad face walks
Silently, a pauper's coat half open
Over a dress covered with green-gold swirls.
Who would recognise her without the glowing hair
Spread over her bloodstained arms? It is Lore,
Lore, the blonde girl with the pure, gentle eyes,
Who takes the rough path along the ramparts,
Escorted by armed men,
Into exile.

The stage lights up: we see a path through fields of wheat and crops, and, on the horizon, the green of the banks of the Rhine. A huge rock divides the stage in two, dominating both the path and the river; in the distance, on the other bank of the river, are towers and the hazy silhouette of a town. The sky is stormy, with strangely shaped clouds. It is dusk.

Enter **Lore**, *walking very slowly with her head lowered and a coat of rough cloth thrown over her shoulders. Her hair hangs loose.*

Three tall Lansquenets in red follow her at a distance, their shoulders hunched under the weight of their pikes.

Lore (*to herself*)   The abbess saw my tears,
And divine exile was closed to me.
She turned me away to face scorn and terror;
And this chaste, harsh rejection from her, a woman,
Made me doubly prey to these mercenaries.
(*After a pause.*) Oh, only the abyss is open to the unfortunate.

At that moment a handsome, clean-shaven man wearing green armour and a helmet, appears in a glow of light behind the girl.

Lore (*not seeing him*)   The world shows no pity to innocents. It loses them
And for the fallen it has

The Man in Green   Neither pardon nor justice.
Everybody, the governor and the bishop included,
All of them threw you from their midst like a rotten fruit,
Into the dark cloister that opens even to murderers.
So, crushed beneath your ignominy,
You who were pardoned by a bishop and renounced by a people,
Where are you going, poor wandering being, sick of everything?
Your heart heavy with ancient rancour and disgust,
Where are you going now, in your flowered dress,
Loreley? A leper colony,
That is the unspeakable, painful future that awaits
Your twenty years: growing old among lepers,
Bandaging bleeding bodies and cleaning wounds!

Lore (*she has stopped, her eyes staring*)   And yet the nests chirp in the hedges.

The Man in Green   And the poppies blaze in the ripe wheat.
There is a delicate scent of carnations floating in the sky,
The sky that quivers with a faint sound of bells.
Do you know which old wall covered in flowers
Spreads this scent, and why the red eyes
Of those soldiers in the shadows shine more brightly because of it?
That perfume, which makes the hearts of your escorts
Tremble as they breathe it, is carried on the wind
From a little old town dear in their memory.
When the past flees from us, what does the future matter?
Their childhood was there, among those turrets
And distant bell towers. The turtledoves
Of their first loves coo there in the evenings.
The town where we were born is our last hope,
Supporting and reviving us on our deathbed!
And your people, Lore, have been pitiless, and banished you.

Lore   Alas!

The Man in Green   There are no more bright tomorrows for the outcast.
Your eyes will never again see the town, with its tower
Watched over by a flight of stone dragons, light up and glow
As it appears at a turn in the road, in a copper sunset,
Its roofs, tiled in pink and green, its crumbling
Walls, your scattering of childhood memories
Still hanging from the fleurs de lis of the spires!
The sad cortège of lost happy days envelops you
Like a whining swarm of pale dried flowers.
Standing in the path through the wheat,
You try in vain to find, in your endless dreams,

The cool, shady home
Lost in the noisy, crowded streets
Where you grew up; your grandfather, trembling as he moves,
Still sitting by the hearth between two Medusas
On the fireplace, and the bedroom's hexagonal window panes,
Shot through with purple iris, warm lights
That brightened the winter dawn and your awakening.

Lore   Stop, your voice casts a spell on me and tears me apart;
It is a cunning poison poured drop by drop
Into my soul, and my strength dies hearing it.

The Man in Green   Lore, do you remember the return of spring,
The flowering basil in the window
Of your first lover, that proud young reiter
Who took you along the lanes on moonlit nights?
He loved you, Lore. Another lover
Followed him, though, a slender captain
Of the lansquenets, red hair, black eyes, a haughty look;
Then, after the solder, so many rich, handsome Seigneurs.
Where are the lilies of your honour now,
Unhappy girl, cursed and rejected by everybody?
Have they tortured you enough with love?
For you gave way to them, but only through terror,
And their terrible kisses always revolted you.
But it was you who were banished as a drunk would be turned out!
Too beautiful to die and too beautiful to live!

He disappears. **Lore**, *with a loud cry, walks downstage.*

Lore   I have heard too much.
(*Looking fearfully around her.*) Nobody but my three guards,
Complaining, and tired of my lingering.
(*Taking her necklaces in her hands.*) You, my heavy gold necklaces, you, poor aquamarine,
With your green eye I loved to see glowing on my chest,
And you, jewels of love forgotten on my fingers,
Wake up, shine with the brilliance of the past,
Make me beautiful again! Lore begs you.

She turns and walks slowly towards the three guards. As she speaks, she slowly removes the necklaces from her neck and the rings from her fingers.

Lore   My dear friends in exile and melancholy,
Take pity, be kind, all three of you!
Let me look one last time
At the walls of my city, of my dear country.
These few old jewels and gold
Will make up for the delay.

She puts her jewels into their hands.

It is the final goodbye, the last wish
Of an exiled woman . . . Before the sun sets,
I would like to stop for a while on the hill
Overlooking the river, and let my gaze
Record within me the place I am leaving.
My childhood, my life . . . It is a mad caprice
That makes you smile, but the frivolous souls
Of women take such things or die! Will you let me?

First Reiter (*mocking*)   You want to leave us, is that it?

Second Reiter   Your eyes are too lovely.
Don't look us in the eyes.

Third Reiter   On my soul.
Fritz, I'm like you, I feel a fire inside
Just listening to her.
(*Addressing the* **First Reiter**.) Do you?

First Reiter (*to* **Lore**)   We will wait for you at the foot
Of the rock.

Lore (*bowing her head*)   Thank you.

First Reiter   Take the little path
That turns to the left. It looks out over the river.

Lore *walks slowly towards the left and disappears.*

First Reiter (*watching her go*)   Poor girl; one night has made her poor and a widow.

Second Reiter   Widow of ten husbands.

First Reiter   She has eyes
That make you envy those ten! . . . Well! Let's have a look at these jewels.

All three sit down at the base of the rock and run the jewels between their fingers.

Third Reiter (*fingering the jewels*)   If this is fine gold, it's very heavy.

First Reiter   What are you talking about?
This is real solid gold.
(*Holding up a necklace.*) The price of one of those smiles
She just gave to us for nothing.

Third Reiter (*passing him a ring*)   What about that?

First Reiter (*looking at the ring*)   This big sapphire? One of her kisses from the old
times.

Running his fingers sadly through the jewels.

A whole past of love. Its light is bewitching!

They carry on handling the jewels and estimating their value in low voices. **Lore** *has just appeared half way up the rock. She climbs slowly towards the summit.*

Lore   Too beautiful to die and too beautiful to live!
That voice spoke the truth; the sun
No longer shines for me: the ruby sunsets
And the silver dawns like great fires,
Glow for the nobleman in his castle and the tramp who begs.
Sage and lavender scent the mornings
Of the traveller hurrying towards
Distant villages in the valley; and the birds of the hedges
Charm the vagabond pained by the wounds
In his bare feet as he sits resting on the verge.
But for me, sad child of shame, there are no more
Flowers, or happy mornings, or birdsong. Despised
By all, I wander and roam with the shame
Of my past dragging behind me like a terrible shroud.
The outcast is alone, everywhere and always.
I walk in a desert, where hatred and fear
Keep me alone; in the night I am dead and alive
And the last steps of the abyss into which I am falling
Towards those pale lepers and their rotting bodies,
Are drowned in a horrifying pool of filth
And freezing mud. My whole being braces itself,
But still it faints and does not want to fall in.
(*After a pause.*) Nobody spoke the word that could have saved me.

Walking straight towards the edge.

Because for me there is no pardon and no justice,
I leave you and forgive you, vile, complicit world,
And I come to you, sovereign refuge
Of the unfortunate, to you, old murky Rhine.

She throws herself off the cliff.

The stage goes dark again and everything disappears.

The Narrator   And crossing her bare victim's arms over her heart,
The beauty leaned dreaming over the abyss
And let herself drop into it, her face ecstatic.
The three guards, crouching at the foot
Of the rock, eyed her jewels,
And the river carried the sinner far away.

Curtain.

The Black Maskers

Leonid Andreyev (1908)

Translated by Clarence L. Meader and Fred Newton Scott

Leonid Andreyev (1871–1919) enjoyed enormous success in the 1900s and 1910s, and he was one of the most widely respected authors in Russia at the time. However, his anti-Bolshevik politics in later life and resistance to established schools of thought in both art and politics contributed to his relative obscurity after the 1917 Revolution. According to the biographer and critic Alexander Kaun, Andreyev's 'contempt for mental peace and quiescence, his readiness for interminable battle with established conceptions, his willingness to forgo popularity, and to enjoy the unenviable reputation of a crank and *advocatus diaboli*, make him eligible to the rank of "Man according to Schopenhauer", in the expression of Nietzsche'.[1] Andreyev was attracted to the pessimism espoused by Schopenhauer, which also inspired Nietzsche. He also shared in Nietzsche's struggles with mental health, having been diagnosed with acute neurasthenia that prompted several suicide attempts (he suffered from severe depression, exhaustion, and anxiety, and self-medicated through excessive alcohol consumption). Recent scholarship suggests that his struggles with mental health 'permitted him to tap into the prevailing *hot topic* of the day – Russia's decadent decline' – although it is also the case that his ill-health was overshadowed by its representation in literary criticism, as well as medical discourse referencing the man and his work (several studies turned to his personal life and publications to evidence their theories of degeneration).[2] Caution should therefore be exercised in tracing a line from illness narratives to literary style, not to mention assumptions regarding the relationship between a 'decadent' literature and a 'decadent' society – although his works are, nonetheless, replete with grim hallucinations and an overbearing sense that a black dog bites at its heels.

Andreyev recognised his own work as 'characteristically decadent [. . . even] before Russian decadence had manifested itself in any noticeable way',[3] and this despite the fact that his decadent contemporaries dismissed his *œuvre* as mere 'pseudo-decadence'.[4] Andreyev's plays are shot through with pessimism and morbidity, as with many Russian playwrights of the Silver Age. His works also caught the attention of Russia's leading impresarios, including Stanislavsky, who presented Andreyev's *The Life of Man* in a stripped-back production with the Moscow Art Theatre in 1907. He wrote *The Black Maskers* a year later, which was first performed at the theatre of Komisarzhevskaia in 1908.

The play centres on Duke Lorenzo di Spadaro, who hosts an opulent masque in his castle. Lorenzo's ball is populated by satanic figures, some of whom are covered in thick black fur, and Lorenzo himself is accused of being Satan's vassal. They represent the darker recesses of Lorenzo's psyche, although they also reflect the sense of apocalyptic doom that prompted many of Andreyev's contemporaries in the Russian Silver Age to explore eschatological themes. Religious revival accompanied an occult renaissance between the 1905 and 1917 revolutionary uprisings. As Frederick H. White acknowledges, many playwrights and artists at the time believed, or at least gave the

---

1   Alexander Kaun, *Leonid Andreyev: A Critical Study* (New York: B. W. Huebsch, 1924), 260.
2   Frederick H. White, *Degeneration, decadence and disease in the Russian* fin de siècle: *Neurasthenia in the life and work of Leonid Andreev* (Manchester and New York: Manchester University Press, 2014), 4. White offers many examples of medical 'experts' who studied Andreyev's work to find evidence for their theories of degeneration. This influenced critics to consider plays like *The Black Maskers* as 'a weakness of neurasthenics (ask any doctor)'. White, *Degeneration, decadence and disease*, 262.
3   Kaun, *Leonid Andreyev*, 27.
4   James B. Woodward, *Leonid Andreyev: A Study* (Oxford: Clarendon Press, 1969), 121–2.

impression that they believed, they were 'living in an unreal shadow world full of masks, doubles and devils. Satanism and the demonic as well as searches for a new godhead were pervasive.'[5] Their eschatological interests drew them to the revelatory qualities of revolution and the apocalyptic risks of failed revolutions, although Andreyev's demonic drama foreshadows less the decadence of an inter-revolutionary period than the horrors that beset revolutionary Russia in the years to come. There is more to this play, then, than pathology; it evokes a tormented society fixated on the prospect of its own demise.

---

5   White, *Degeneration, decadence and disease*, 54–5.

Characters

Lorenzo, *Duke of Spadaro*
Ecco, *a jester*
Donna Francesca, *wife of Lorenzo*
Signor Cristoforo, *steward of the wine-cellar*
Signor Petruccio, *overseer*
Gentlemen and Ladies *of the ducal suite*
Maskers, *invited by the Duke*
Black Maskers, *uninvited*
Romualdo, *a singer*
Musicians
Servants
Peasants

Act One

Scene One

A luxurious, newly decorated hall in an ancient feudal castle. The walls are adorned with frescoes and hung with paintings blackened with age. Here and there are weapons and statues. The whole room, though brilliant with gold and with bright-coloured mosaics, is delicately tinted by light falling through coloured glass. At the left and in the rear are three semi-Gothic windows half concealed by heavy, gold-embroidered curtains. The rear wall, turning back at a right angle at the centre of the stage, recedes to a row of paired columns which support the upper part of the building. Behind these columns is a spacious, brightly illuminated entrance-hall. Massive double entrance-doors are seen at the right. Directly in front of the spectator, at the point where the rear wall begins to recede, a broad marble staircase with a massive sculptured balustrade ascends to the height of the columns, then, turning to the right, leads to other apartments. The wall above the columns is pierced by several small windows of coloured glass through which comes a peculiar and brilliant light.

The final, hasty preparations are going on for a masquerade ball. The room is flooded with light from many chandeliers and from strikingly beautiful candelabra and sconces. Several servants in rich but uniform livery hurry from place to place, lighting fresh candles or moving back the heavy armchairs to give room for the dancers. Every now and then certain of them, as if recalling something left undone, rush up-stairs or to the entry doors, the firm, business-like voice of the overseer, **Signor Petruccio,** *redoubling their haste and their emulation. Both the overseer and the servants are in high spirits, and the latter, as they come and go, exchange lively jests and quick, fleeting smiles. The gayest of all, however, is young* **Lorenzo,** *the reigning Duke of Spadaro. Well formed, refined of feature, a little languid in manner, but courteous and kindly toward everyone, he lightly moves about the hall, all aglow with the joy of anticipation, giving orders, jesting, and urging on the servants, now with cheering words and now with gestures of feigned anger. As he goes he casts happy smiles upon his young wife, the beautiful* **Donna Francesca,** *who responds with tender and loving glances. Several ladies and gentlemen, forming the suite of the Duke and Duchess, are also busily engaged, some, like the young Duke, joyfully and eagerly preparing for the reception of the expected guests, others, under cover of the happy confusion, exchanging fond glances, slyly pressing one another's hands, and whispering boldly and quickly into blushing ears. In an upper room somewhere musicians are making ready for the ball, and fragments of musical airs are heard. Suddenly some one begins to sing in a rich baritone, but the song quickly passes over into laughter. Apparently, it is jolly there, too.*

On a rug before a blazing fire the Duke's dog, a huge Saint Bernard, dozes in an attitude of luxurious abandon. Seated near the foot of the stairway, **Ecco,** *the Duke's jester, imitates the Duke's voice and by his orders causes laughable confusion.*

Petruccio   Keep up that speed a little longer, Mario, and you'll be your own grandfather. Hurry, man, hurry!

Mario   Why, Signor Petruccio, the Duke's best horse doesn't get over the ground as fast as I do.

A Servant   When the flies sting.

Another Servant   Or the whip flicks.

Petruccio   Come! lively, there, lively!

Lorenzo   This way! More candles here! Don't you see how dark this corner is? No darkness, Signor Petruccio, no darkness!

Gentleman (*to a lady*)   There! They have driven us out of our last refuge. But I shall kiss you yet.

Lady   In the dark it will be hard to find me.

Gentleman   In the dark I shall spread my arms wide and embrace the whole night.

Another Gentleman   You will make a rich haul, Signor Silvio.

Ecco (*calling out*)   Mario! Carlo! Pietro! Quick! Hold a candle under this gentleman's nose. The darkness frightens him out of his wits.

Francesca (*to the Duke, affectionately*)   My dear! my love! my divinity! How charming your new costume is! You are like a shaft of sunlight flung through the lofty window of our cathedral. Your divine beauty fills me with adoration.

Lorenzo   You are a delicate blossom, Francesca. You are a delicate blossom, and the sun, when it kisses you, is overbold.

He kisses her hand with profound respect and tenderness, but suddenly, in mock terror, calls to the overseer.

But the tower, Petruccio, the tower! If you have forgotten to illuminate the tower I will have you impaled like an unbaptised Turk.

Petruccio   The tower is illuminated, sir.

Lorenzo   Illuminated? How dare you say so? It should blaze, it should sparkle, it should rise toward the dark heavens like a huge tongue of fire.

Ecco   Tut! Tut! Lorenzo. Don't show your tongue to heaven or heaven will answer you with a fig.

Lorenzo   My dear little fellow, you mustn't annoy me with your jokes. I am looking forward to a feast of light, and your barbed shafts wound me to the soul. No darkness, Ecco, no darkness!

Ecco   Then you must light up your wife's tresses. They are too dark, Lorenzo, too dark. And put a torch in each of her eyes. They are too dark, Lorenzo, too dark.

Francesca   Wretch! Here are so many beautiful ladies – can't one of you win the affections of this miserable jester?

First Lady   He's a hunchback.

Second Lady   If he should try to kiss me, his nose would prick me like a sword.

Gentleman   Your heart, madam, would turn the edge of any sword.

Enter a gentleman, tall and thin as a pole, the image of Don Quixote. His moustaches droop and seem to be continually wet. He turns gloomily to the Duke.

Cristoforo   I have a shocking piece of news to impart to you, Signor.

Lorenzo   What is it? You alarm me, Signor Cristoforo.

Cristoforo   I have reason to believe, sir, that we shall run short of both Cyprian and Falernian. These gentlemen (*pointing with his forefinger to the Duke's attendants*) drink wine as camels in the desert drink water.

One of the Suite   Signor Cristoforo, why are your moustaches always wet?

Cristoforo (*with dignity*)   It is my duty, sir, to test all the wines.

Lorenzo (*cheerfully*)   My good friend, you exaggerate the danger. Our cellars are inexhaustible.

Cristoforo (*insistently*)   They drink wine like camels. Your happy mood pleases me, Signor, but you take things too light-heartedly. When your sainted father and I set out to deliver the Holy Sepulchre –

Lorenzo (*gently reproaching him*)   My dear old friend, you surely are not going to spoil, with your mumbling and grumbling, this delightful evening.

Cristoforo (*good-naturedly*)   Well, well, my boy, don't be angry. (*Threateningly.*) Ho, there! Manucci! Filippo! After me!

Exit.

Lorenzo   But the roadway, Signor Petruccio! Heaven punish you! The roadway! You have forgotten to illuminate the roadway, and our friends will not be able to find us.

Petruccio   The roadway is illuminated, Signor.

Lorenzo   Illuminated? Your tongue is like a jaded nag. When the spurs prick its flanks it can only switch its tail. The whole road must sparkle. It must blaze with lights like the road to paradise. Understand me, Sir Overseer. The shades of the cypresses should flee in terror to the mountains where sleep the dragons. Do you lack torches and helpers? Do you lack kegs of pitch?

Ecco   If pitch is lacking, Petruccio, you had better go borrow it in hell. Satan will lend it to you on your personal security.

One of the Servants   He would have fetched some thence before this but that he feared there would not be enough left to keep him warm.

Second Servant   Signor Petruccio is so chilly.

Petruccio   Lively, there, lively!

Francesca (*to the Duke*)   You forget me, Lorenzo. Though you light up everything, yet I, unless you smile upon me, am left in darkness. Do the masks interest you so much?

Lorenzo   So much, my dear, that I am dying with impatience. There will be flowers and serpents, Francesca. There will be flowers, and serpents among the flowers. There will be a dragon, Francesca. A dragon will come crawling to us, Francesca, and you will see real fire issuing from his jaws. It will be great fun. But don't be afraid. It's all in jest. It's all just our friends, and we shall have a glorious laugh over it. Why don't they come?

A Servant (*hurrying in*)   I was watching from the tower, and I saw something moving along the road, Signor. It looks like a black serpent crawling among the cypresses.

Lorenzo (*joyfully*)   They're coming. They're coming.

Another Servant (*running in*)   I was watching from the tower, and I saw a dragon crawling toward us. I saw red fire gleaming from its eyes, and I was frightened, Signor.

Lorenzo (*joyfully*)   They're coming. They're coming. Do you hear, Petruccio?

Petruccio   Everything is ready, Signor.

Third Servant (*running in*)   There is shouting and commotion at the drawbridge, Signor. They are demanding admittance. I heard the clash of weapons, sir.

Lorenzo (*angrily*)   What! The drawbridge not down? Is that the way to receive my guests, Petruccio? To-morrow I discharge you, if you –

Petruccio   Pardon me, sir. I will run.

Runs out.

Lorenzo   They have come! Smile, Francesca! They have come!

Ecco (*laughs very loudly*)   Yes, let's laugh, Lorenzo. We must limber up our jaws.

Yawns.

Lorenzo   But the musicians! Good Heavens! Where are the musicians? Has that dunce forgotten all my directions?

Francesca   Don't be angry, my dear. The musicians are in readiness.

Lorenzo   But why are they not here?

Francesca   See, now, my love, you compel me to let out the secret. They intended to surprise you. The musicians also are to appear in masks.

Lorenzo   And I shall not recognise them? Oh, that is charming! And who planned this surprise? Ah, it was you, it was you, Signora. I can read it in your sly, smiling eyes. But the music! Surely they have not forgotten to learn the piece I composed for them. Oh, this fat rascal of a Petruccio! I shall certainly have to impale him.

Ecco   How indiscreet of you, Lorenzo! Petruccio will steal the stake and run away with it.

Lorenzo   Oh! Now I think of it, Ecco, just a word with you before they come. My dear fellow, you may mock me as much as you please; I understand your humour and I like it. But don't, I beg of you, offend my guests. You must not be malicious, Ecco, even in sport. You have a tender heart, my little hunchback, and you are not ill-natured. Why, then, do you sting people with your jests? Laugh. Entertain my guests. Make yourself agreeable to the ladies – and here you may go far – but do not irritate any one. Today is my day, Ecco.

A Servant (*flinging open the doors*)   They are at the door, Signor.

Lorenzo   I'm coming. I'm coming. Call the musicians!

Commotion in the hall. Several **Maskers** *appear. The costumes are such as are common at masquerades – harlequins, pierrots, Saracens, Turkish men and women, and animals and flowers. But all the faces are concealed under heavy, closely fitting masks. The* **Maskers** *enter in profound silence and respond to the Duke's courteous greetings with silent bows.*

Lorenzo (*bowing low and courteously*)   I thank you, ladies and gentlemen. I am happy to greet you in my castle. Pardon the carelessness of my overseer in failing to lower the drawbridge and thus causing you some delay. I am greatly mortified, ladies and gentlemen.

A Masker (*in a muffled voice*)   We arrived just the same. We got in, did we not, gentlemen?

Second Masker   We got in.

Third Masker   We got in.

Strange, muffled laughter from behind the heavy masks.

Lorenzo   I am delighted to find you in such good spirits, ladies and gentlemen. From this moment my castle is yours.

A Masker   Yes, it is ours. It is ours.

The same strange, muffled laughter.

Lorenzo (*looking about gaily*)   But I do not recognise any one. It is amazing, gentlemen, but I do not recognise a single soul. Is this you, Signor Basilio? It seems to me that I recognise your voice.

A Voice   Signor Basilio is not here.

Another Voice   Signor Basilio is not here. Signor Basilio is dead.

Lorenzo (*laughing*)   That's a good joke. Signor Basilio dead? Why, he is as much alive as I am.

A Masker   Are you, then, alive?

Lorenzo (*impatiently, but with great courtesy*)   Let us leave Death in peace, gentlemen.

A Voice   Ask Death to leave you in peace. What need of peace has he?

Lorenzo   Who said that? Was it you, Signor Sandro? (*Laughing.*) I recognise you, sir, by your melancholy. But cheer up, my gloomy friend. See how many lights there are, how many beautiful, living lights.

A Masker   Signor Sandro is not here. Signor Sandro is dead.

The same strange, muffled laughter. Other **Maskers** *arrive.*

Lorenzo   Yes, yes. Now I understand. (*Laughing.*) All of us are dead. Signor Basilio is dead; Signor Sandro is dead; I am dead. Excellent! I congratulate you, gentlemen, on your extremely interesting jest. Still, I should like to know who you are – Ah, here come others! Greetings, my dear guests – What a strange costume! Why are you all in red, and what is the meaning of this hideous black snake that is twined about you? I trust it is not alive, Signora. If it were I should pity your poor heart into which it has so ruthlessly struck its fangs.

The Red Masker (*with a muffled laugh*)   Do you not recognise me, Lorenzo? ·

Lorenzo (*joyously*)   Is it you, Signora Emilia? But no, Signora Emilia is not so tall as you, and her voice is fuller and softer.

The Red Masker   I am your heart, Lorenzo.

Lorenzo   Exquisite! I am sincerely delighted, my friends, that I invited you for this evening. You are so witty. However, you mistake, madam. This is not my heart. There is no serpent in my heart.

Another Masker   Is this not your heart, Lorenzo?

Lorenzo (*starting back, but controlling himself*)   You frighten me, sir, coming so unexpectedly from behind. What? This hairy black spider; this repulsive monster on thin, wavering legs; those dull, greedy, cruel eyes – this my heart? No, Signor, my heart is full of love and welcome. Within my heart all is as radiant as is this castle, which greets you so joyously, my strange guests.

The Spider   Lorenzo, Lorenzo, let us go and catch flies. In a spider-web in the tower yonder something has long been entangled and awaits you. Let us go, Lorenzo. Would you not like some fresh blood?

Lorenzo (*laughing*)   In my castle there is no spiderweb. In my tower there is none of that darkness which is necessary to such loathsome creatures as you, my strange guest. But who are you?

The Red Masker   Lorenzo, the serpent is restless. It is trying to sting me, Lorenzo. Oh, the pain, the terror of it! Stroke its head, Lorenzo. It has such a beautiful smooth head, and you see it is not alive. Soothe it, Lorenzo.

Muffled laughter.

Lorenzo (*falling in with the jest and cautiously stroking the serpent*)   When the devil tempts he takes the form of a serpent. But you, of course, are not the devil. You are only a mock serpent, only a mock serpent. (*Hastily.*) But, gentlemen, is it not time to dance? The musicians, I presume, have long been waiting impatiently. Petruccio!

A Masker (*approaching him*)   What does your Grace command?

Lorenzo   Pardon me, sir. I did not call to you. I was summoning my overseer. Petruccio!

The Masker   I am Petruccio.

Lorenzo (*laughing*)   Oh, so it is you, you fat old rascal. You, too, have taken a notion to join the sport. And I didn't recognise you. Well, that is very neat. Come, now, tell me – But where are you? Petruccio! Petruccio! Really, I shall have to impale this fat rascal. Hello, there, somebody! Manucci! Pietro!

The First Masker   Did you call me, sir?

The Second Masker   Did you call me, sir?

Lorenzo (*perplexed*)   No, I did not call you. (*Grasping the situation and laughing.*) Ah, yes, I see. My good fellows, how dare you mingle with the guests?

The First Masker   They told us to.

The Second Masker   They told us to.

Lorenzo (*good-humouredly clapping one of the* **Maskers** *on the shoulder*)   Quite right. I was only fooling. Let us all be merry on this glorious night – But isn't it odd that I do not recognise any one – positively not a soul –? Why, I've lost my servants again. Mario! Pietro –! Now, really, Signor, isn't that strange? I have lost all my servants.

A Masker (*turning to the others*)   Gentlemen, Lorenzo has mislaid his servants.

Loud laughter, the **Maskers** *bowing with mock courtesy.*

A Voice   But where is your suite, Lorenzo?

Lorenzo (*looking about and smiling*)   I see nothing but masks. Here's an interesting situation, gentlemen. Mine being the only real face, I am the only person about whom there can be no mistake.

Renewed laughter.

A Voice   We are now your suite, Lorenzo.

Second Voice   We are now your suite, Duke. What are your instructions?

Laughter.

Lorenzo (*very affably, but with dignity*)   It is delightful, gentlemen, to find you in such merry vein. I am overjoyed at your charming jest. But I should be deeply offended if you really took my servants' place – Mario!

Other **Maskers** *come up. On most of them the tightfitting masks are replaced by painted faces. The women, however, as before, wear masks of coloured silk. The painted faces of the newcomers are hideous and revolting. Among them are corpses, cripples, and deformed persona. A grey, helpless creature with long legs moves about, frequently coughing and groaning. Seven humpbacked, wrinkled old women run in, in Indian file, capering joyfully and beating castanets.*

Lorenzo (*bowing courteously*)   I have pleasure, my dear guests, in welcoming you to my castle. From this moment it is entirely at your service. Ah, what a charming procession! Tell me, my beauties, where is your bridegroom, the devil?

First Old Woman (*running up to* **Lorenzo**)   He is at our heels.

Second Old Woman (*running up to* **Lorenzo**)   He is at our heels.

Tall Grey Creature (*bending down to the Duke and coughing*)   Why did you call me from my bed, Lorenzo?

Lorenzo (*lightly*)   And where is your bed, Signor?

Tall Grey Creature   In your heart, Lorenzo.

Lorenzo (*cheerfully*)   How they do slander my poor heart! I am pleased to – (*Staggering back.*) What an amazing disguise, Signor! I actually took you for a corpse. Pray tell me the name of the talented artist who so skilfully altered your features.

The Masker   Death.

Lorenzo   Capital! But if you will permit me to say so, my dear guest, I am sure I recognise in your make-up the beloved features of my friend, Signor Sandro di Grada. Heavens, but you frightened me, my dear fellow! These masks, these curious masks! Do you know, I can't make out at all who they are. Perhaps you can help me, Signor.

The Masker   It is dark, Lorenzo.

Lorenzo   But I ordered an abundance of lights. We will have more of them. Petruccio! Petruccio!

The Masker   It is cold, Lorenzo.

Lorenzo   Cold? Why, to me it seems as hot here as hell itself. However, if you are cold, my dear Sandro, pray come to the fire. Have a goblet of wine. Ho, there, Petruccio! Lazybones!

Several **Maskers**, *alike in appearance, run up at the same time and answer almost in one voice.*

The Maskers   At your service, Signor.

Lorenzo (*not understanding*)   Petruccio!

The Maskers (*together*)   At your service, Signor. At your service.

Lorenzo (*laughing*)   Ah, I see! A moment ago I lost my servants, and now I have lost my overseer. (*In comic terror.*) But here is Signor Sandro come shivering from his grave. Who will give him wine? Pardon me, Signor – Why, he is already gone! Poor fellow! He wants to warm himself. How tired I am! I should like a drop of wine myself. Signor Cristoforo! Has no one seen Signor Cristoforo?

A tall, thin **Masker** *approaches.*

The Masker   Your orders, sir?

Lorenzo   Is that you, my honest friend? I recognise you by your stature. Bring me some wine. This receiving of my guests has wearied me.

The Masker   Something is wrong with our wine, Lorenzo. It has turned as red Satan's blood, and it crazes the brain like the poison of a serpent. Do not drink it, Lorenzo.

Lorenzo (*laughing*)   What could happen to our fine old wine? You have tasted too much of it and your head is muddled.

The Masker (*insistently*)   I have already seen several drunken guests, Lorenzo. If it is honest wine, why should they be drunk?

Lorenzo   Wine, you babbler, wine!

Drinks the wine, but at the first draught he throws away the goblet.

What is this you have given me? It seems as if the fires of hell were licking my throat and burning their way to my very heart. Cristoforo – ! Where is he? Pardon me, gentlemen, but really something incomprehensible has happened to our wine – Ah, more maskers! I am glad to greet you in my castle, my dear guests.

While **Lorenzo**, *weariedly bowing ever lower, greets the strange* **Maskers** *that are coming in, a subdued hum of conversation fills the hall.*

First Masker   Whence do you come, Signor?

Second Masker   From the night. And you, Signor, if you please?

First Masker   I also am from the night.

They laugh. Two other **Maskers** *converse.*

First Masker   He has drunk all my blood. There is not one healthy, living spot left on my body. It is covered with blood and wounds.

Second Masker   He kills those whom he loves.

First Masker   You know, of course, what is to happen today.

They move away. Other **Maskers** *converse.*

Various Maskers
    – It was idle for Lorenzo to light up his castle so brilliantly. Did you notice as we rode along that something was moving in the shadows of the cypresses?
    – I saw nothing but darkness.
    – But are you not afraid of darkness?
    – Why, I do not think there is anything in it for us to be afraid of. What can the darkness do to us? But are you not sorry for this insane Lorenzo?
    – I don't know. Something, I assure you, was moving there.
    – See how happy Lorenzo is. Isn't it delightful to have such a cheerful and nimble servant?

They laugh. The masked musicians take their places in the balcony. **Ecco** *moves about among the legs of the dancers, trying to peer under their masks and arousing laughter by his unsuccessful attempts.*

Ecco   Are you not from the swamps, Signor? It seems to me you are very like the ague[6] which for two months shook me as a dog shakes a rabbit.

---

6   Ague: fever-induced shivering, sometimes associated with malaria.

The **Tall Grey Creature** *strikes a careless blow and* **Ecco** *falls.*

Ecco   That's a strange sort of joke! Here am I, the jester, on the verge of tears, while you, at whom I should laugh, are smiling. Oh! who pinched me? Was it you, Signora?

A Beautiful Masker   Yes, it was I, Ecco.

Ecco   I observe, Signora, that a hump on the breast deforms a character no less than a hump on the back.

The **Beautiful Masker** *swiftly and silently strikes the jester a blow with her dagger. The glittering edge glides across his neck and the jester runs whimpering up the staircase and thence clambers out onto one of the marble projections. Laughter.*

The musicians begin a wild melody in which are heard malicious laughter, cries of agony and despair, and some one's low, sad plaining. The dance of the **Maskers** *is also strange and wild.*

Lorenzo   I am glad that you are merry, my friends. Though for my part I am a little weary – But what sort of music is this? Heavens! how wild it is and how it pierces one's ears. Luigi, are you drunk or crazy? What are you playing there with your band of disguised brigands. Pardon me, my dear guests, this donkey Petruccio has spoiled everything.

A Masker in the Orchestra   We are playing what you gave us, sir.

Lorenzo (*nettled*)   You lie, Luigi. Lorenzo could not compose such a hellish discord. I hear in it the wails of martyrs under merciless torture. I hear in it the laughter of Satan.

The Old Women (*running up with castanets*)   The bridegroom is coming. The bridegroom is coming. The bridegroom is coming.

Lorenzo   Pardon me, my charming jesters, but I must first admonish this bold-faced rascal, Luigi.

A Masker in the Orchestra   Luigi is not here, Signor.

Lorenzo   Then who is speaking? Is that you, Stampa?

The Masker   No, it is another. We are playing only what you gave us, Signor.

Lorenzo (*laughing*)   Ah, I see. The tones are masked. Capital! Do you hear, ladies and gentlemen? Today the very tones are masked. Really, I was not aware that tones could put on such repulsive masks. Isn't it droll?

A Voice   And you had never learned that, Lorenzo? How little you know.

Another Voice   It's certainly your own music, Duke.

A Third Voice   But where are you yourself, Lorenzo?

Laughter. The music continues. The **Old Women** *with the castanets run forward.*

The Old Women. The bridegroom is coming. The bridegroom. The bridegroom is coming.

Lorenzo (*bowing low*)   I crave your pardon, my dear sir, for not greeting you as I should, but there are so many persons here and I recognise no one of them – positively not one. Just conceive of it – I do not even recognise my own music. It's extremely amusing, isn't it?

A Masker   But do you recognise yourself, Lorenzo?

Lorenzo   Myself? (*Laughing*) To be sure. You see that I wear no mask – But what is this?

A strange procession moves slowly past the Duke. A young, proud, and beautiful queen is led in by a half-drunken groom, who embraces her. Before them walks a peasant nurse carrying in her arms a misshapen infant, half animal, half man.

Lorenzo (*in great agitation*)   What is the meaning of this, Signors? Even under the disguise of masks such a union seems to me unseemly and repulsive. And what is this that is borne before them? What a disgusting mask!

A Masker   The groom had intercourse with the queen and this is their charming son. Make way for the queen's son!

The Groom (*drunkenly*)   Hey there! Knights! Crusaders! Out of the way! Drive them off, my queen, or they will harm our precious son.

Laughter.

Voices   Way for the queen's son!

Lorenzo (*turning away much agitated*)   I am not at all pleased with this jest, Signors – Hello, Ecco, you rascally jester, why have you climbed up there? Why are you not entertaining the company with your pleasantries?

Ecco (*weeping*)   I am afraid of your guests, Lorenzo. They have hurt me. Send them away, Lorenzo.

Lorenzo (*with rising anger*)   Who has dared to affront you? It cannot be. My honoured guests are too kind and courteous to injure any one. It is more likely that you, you rascal, having given offence by your malicious wit, are now shielding yourself from punishment.

Ecco (*weeping*)   Your guests are fine people, Lorenzo. My hump is swimming in blood. It is like a hilly island in the sea. Haven't you a little costume for me, Lorenzo? I, too, wish to put on a mask.

Lorenzo   Come here.

The jester, glancing about timorously, comes down to **Lorenzo**.

Ecco   What do you wish? Speak quickly or I will run away. I am all in a tremble.

Lorenzo   I also am somewhat fearful, my dear Ecco. I don't quite understand what is going on. Who are these persons? I don't recognise one of them, and I think there are more than I invited. It's strange. Can't you recognise anybody, Ecco? Their faces, to be sure, are covered, but you are so good at recalling their bearing, voice, and figure. You, perhaps, have recognised some one.

Ecco   Not a soul. Let me go, Lorenzo.

Lorenzo (*sadly*)   Do you, then, desert me, my dear Ecco?

Ecco   I am going to put on a mask.

Lorenzo   Very well, my little hunchback. Go, if you are frightened. But send Donna Francesca to me. Do you know where she is?

Ecco   She is up-stairs. Send them away, Lorenzo. I will run to summon her.

He goes up-stairs.

Lorenzo (*addressing a newly arrived and very beautiful* **Masker**)   Greetings, Signora. You are as entrancing as a vision. You are as delicate as a silvery moonbeam, and I reverently bend my knee before you.

He sinks on one knee and respectfully kisses her hand, then rises.

I see only the graceful outline of your figure and your little foot, but permit me, my divinity, to be so bold as to look into your eyes. How they shine! Even through the meshes of this black and hateful mask I see how beautiful they are. Who are you, Signora? I do not know you.

The Masker   I am your falsehoods, Lorenzo.

Lorenzo (*laughing*)   Can a lie, then, be as beautiful as you are, Signora? But you mistake. There are no lies in me. I hate a lie, my lady. If you knew Lorenzo's thoughts, his clear, pure thoughts – if you knew his soul, which sings in the heavens as the lark sings in spring above the flooding Arno[7] – (*Frightened*) Ah, what's this?

Something formless and shapeless, with many arms and legs, creeps up. It speaks with many voices.

The Thing   We are your thoughts, Lorenzo.

Lorenzo   A bold jest! Still, you are my guests. I invited you –

The Thing   We are your overlords, Lorenzo. This castle is ours.

Lorenzo (*clasping his head*)   Oh, this horrible music! It is enough to drive one mad. Luigi, or somebody there – I do not recognise any one – I beg of you, I command you – play what I gave you. Unmask the tones. Don't you remember how beautiful the melody was that I composed? A little sad it was, gentlemen, I confess. In truth, I often yield myself to a tender and languorous melancholy. But it was so full of harmony, so pure, so pellucid. If, perchance, you have forgotten it, Luigi, listen – I will recall it to you.

He begins singing a lovely melody. After the first two measures, however, he takes up the air that the musicians are playing and breaks off in alarm.

How absurd! You put me out, gentlemen. My head is somewhat dizzy. Really, something was wrong with the wine. How absurd, gentlemen! My brain seems to have turned to melted lead.

Loud laughter.

---

7   Arno: a river in Tuscany, Italy.

A Voice   Why did you break off, Lorenzo?

Second Voice   Lorenzo is drunk. Lorenzo, Duke of Spadaro, is drunk.

Laughter.

Second Voice   We were ready to hear you, Lorenzo; we know what a great artist you are.

Third Voice   Sing, Lorenzo; we insist.

Lorenzo (*with dignity*)   My friends – (*Frightened.*) Ah, who are you? Who touches me on the shoulder? Madam, the guests are all assembled, and you are an intruder. I do not know you.

A Beautiful Masker   It is I, my love.

Lorenzo   Pardon me, madam, but only my wife, Donna Francesca, may address me thus.

The Masker (*laughing softly*)   Do you not know me, Lorenzo?

Lorenzo   Something about you, my charming masker, reminds me of my wife. But this black mask – Permit me to look into your eyes. Out of a million women I should know my beloved by her eyes. (*He gazes into her eyes, then laughs joyfully.*) Francesca, my love, how you frightened me! Why are you masked? You know –

He leads her to one side and, pressing her tightly to him, speaks almost in a whisper.

My dear, I am so weary, and my heart pains me as if a serpent were stinging it. My thoughts are in confusion. You have seen that frightful monster – look! Over yonder! It's in the corner now. It says it is my thoughts. But, Francesca, my dear, my beloved, that is not true, is it?

The Masker   It is only a mask, Lorenzo.

Lorenzo (*doubtfully*)   Do you really think so, Signora? And will they go, and shall we be left alone?

The Masker   Yes, we shall be left alone. (*Passionately.*) And I shall hold you so tightly, Lorenzo, that you will think I have never embraced you before.

Lorenzo (*absently*)   Yes? I am very happy, my lady – But these masks – this horrible Signor Sandro is painted so like a corpse as to deceive any grave-digger. It seemed to me that I saw worms. I would not put on so frightful, so revolting a mask even in jest.

The Masker (*frightened*)   Signor Sandro? Why, Signor Sandro is really dead. My dear, you have made a mistake.

Lorenzo (*slowly*)   Why do you mock at me, Francesca? If he were dead I should have had notice of his death.

The Masker   And so you did, Lorenzo. You have forgotten, and you are weary. Your hands are cold. I must kiss your hand, my love, even though they are watching us.

She kisses his hand. Another beautiful **Masker** *approaches from behind and speaks in a loud voice.*

The Second Masker   Lorenzo, did you send for me?

Lorenzo (*horrified*)   Francesca's voice!

The Second Masker   Eco said that you wished to see me.

Lorenzo   Ecco? (*Slowly pushing away the* **Masker** *whom he had embraced and looking at her in horror.*) But who are you, Signora? And how dared you deceive me? I have done you honour – I have embraced you. (*He pushes her away gently.*) Leave me.

The First Masker (*wringing her hands*)   Lorenzo! Lorenzo! Would you drive me away? What ails you, Lorenzo?

The Second Masker (*impatiently*)   Did you send for me, Lorenzo? Who is this lady who presumes to speak to you so affectionately?

Lorenzo   Francesca! Francesca!

In perplexity he looks now at one and now at the other. Approaching the **Second Masker** *and knitting his brows in an expression of horrified inquiry, he gazes into her eyes.*

Lorenzo   Your eyes, your eyes – show me your eyes. Yes, it is you, Francesca. It is your soft and tender gaze. It is your beautiful soul. Give me your hand. (*To the* **First Masker**, *with contempt.*) And you, madam, leave me.

The Second Masker (*pressing close to the Duke*)   Lorenzo, your maskers frighten me. Our castle is overrun with monsters. I saw Signor Sandro. He is horrible.

Lorenzo (*clasping his head*)   Signor Sandro? Why, he is dead. You told me so yourself.

A third equally beautiful **Masker** *approaches from behind and speaks in a loud voice.*

Masker   Lorenzo, my dear, did you send for me? Ecco said that you wished to see me. Who is this lady with you? And what is the meaning of this unseemly familiarity, Lorenzo?

Lorenzo (*stepping back with a laugh in which is heard a note of insanity*)   What a capital joke, madam, what a delicious farce! Now it is my wife who is lost. Laugh, my dear guests. I had a wife. They called her Donna Francesca, and I have lost her. What a strange jest!

The three Maskers (*together*)   Lorenzo, my beloved!

Lorenzo (*laughing*)   Do you hear, gentlemen?

General unrestrained laughter.

Voices   Lorenzo has lost his wife. Weep, gentlemen. Lorenzo has lost his wife. Give Lorenzo another wife.

On all sides are heard plaintive female voices: 'Here I am, Lorenzo. Here I am, Lorenzo. Take your Francesca.' *From somewhere comes a single terrified voice:* 'Save me, Lorenzo, I am here.'

Loud laughter.

The seven old women, with the air of coy and embarrassed brides, seem about to throw themselves on **Lorenzo**'s *neck.*

Voice   We will give Lorenzo a wife. Gentlemen, Duke Lorenzo is now contracting a new marriage. The wedding march, musicians!

The **Musicians** *play wild strains remotely resembling wedding music, but the music is that which is played in hell at the masquerade wedding of Satan. The* **Red Masker** *with the serpent approaches* **Lorenzo**.

The Red Masker   Do you recognise your heart now, Lorenzo? (*Plaintively.*) Caress the poor serpent, caress the poor serpent. It has drunk all my blood.

The Spider   Now do you recognise your heart, Lorenzo? Let us go up into the tower, my friend. Something is entangled in the spider-web there and waits for you. But is your sword sharp, Lorenzo? Is your sword sharp?

Lorenzo   Hence, hence! Brood of darkness, I know you not.

Running a few steps up the staircase, and raised thus alone above the throng of **Maskers**, *he tries to cry out, but suddenly presses his hand to his heart, and, smiling sadly, comes down again, the same winning, candid, noble, and handsome figure as before.*

Lorenzo   Pardon me, my dear friends, for my touch of ill-humour. These choice jests, these adroit tricks of yours have just a little dashed my spirits – And I have lost my wife – Her name was Donna Francesca. Permit me now – since the hour of departure draws nigh – permit me to call your attention to some real music – not the hideous discords with which this disguised brigand of a Luigi has, in his desire to contribute to the general gaiety, so tortured our ears, but some music of my own. I am a very poor composer, gentlemen. It is rare that these earthly ears of mine are ravished by celestial melodies. But you will not criticise me too harshly. In the virgin purity of the tones you will find a restful calmness and the reflection of some one's heavenly vision – And I have lost my wife, gentlemen, I have lost my wife. Her name was Donna Francesca.

The Maskers   We are waiting for your music, Lorenzo. All the world knows the enchanting music of Duke Lorenzo. But the hour of departure is still remote.

Lorenzo   I am at your service, my dear guests.

He confers with the **Musicians**. *A little before this the first of the* **Black Maskers** *has appeared in the hall – a strange, deformed creature like a living fragment of darkness. Glancing around timidly and suspiciously, wondering at everything new, strange, and unfamiliar, the* **Black Masker** *steals guiltily along the wall and awkwardly conceals itself behind the other* **Maskers**. *Every one whom it approaches starts back perplexed and alarmed.*

A Voice   Who is this? This is not a masker.

Second Voice   I don't know. Who invited you, sir?

The **Black Masker** *makes no answer, but, shrinking into itself, quietly hides behind the others. Two* **Maskers** *converse.*

First Masker (to *the other in a low voice*)   How many of us were there?

Second Masker   A hundred.

First Masker   But now there are more. Who is this? Don't you know?

Second Masker   Not I. But I am afraid to speak of it. It seems that they fly toward the light.

First Masker   Crazy Lorenzo! He lighted up his castle too brilliantly.

Second Masker   Lights are dangerous in the night.

First Masker   To those who are abroad?

Second Masker   No, to him who lights them.

Lorenzo   My friends, I beg your attention. You see this masked gentleman. His name is Romualdo and he is an admirable singer. He will now render for you a little ballad which I made bold to compose. Have you your notes, Romualdo?

The Masked Singer   I have, sir.

Lorenzo   And the words? Consult your notes frequently. In one place, my friend, you often go wrong.

The Masked Singer   I have the words also, sir.

Lorenzo   Luigi, you villain, if you make a mistake in a single note I will have you hanged from the castle wall to-morrow.

A Masker in the Orchestra   You will have no occasion to waste rope on me, sir.

Lorenzo   Attention, ladies and gentlemen, attention. (*Much excited*) Now, Romualdo, do your best, my friend. Do not disgrace me, and to-morrow I will give you a costly belt.

The accompaniment begins with a beautiful, soft, and tender harmony, pure and clear as a cloudless sky or as the eyes of a child; but with each successive measure which the masked artist sings the music becomes more fragmentary and more restless and soon passes over into wild cries and laughter, expressive of tragical but incoherent emotion. It closes with a solemn and melancholy hymn.

The Masked Singer (*singing*)   'My soul is an enchanted castle. When the sun shines into the lofty windows, with its golden rays it weaves golden dreams. When the sad moon looks into the misty windows, in its silvery beams are silvery dreams. Who laughs? Who laughs so tenderly at the mournful dirge?'

Lorenzo   Right, right, Romualdo.

The Masked Singer (*singing*)   'And I lighted up my castle with lights. What has happened to my soul? The black shadows fled to the hills and returned yet blacker. Who sobs? Who groans so heavily in the black shadows of the cypresses? Who came at my call?'

Lorenzo (*in perplexity*)   That is not there, Romualdo. What kind of music is that?

The Masked Singer (*singing*)   'And terror entered my shining castle. What has happened to my soul? The lights go out at the breath of the darkness. Who laughs? Who laughs so horribly at insane Lorenzo? Have pity on me, O Monarch. My soul is filled with terror. O Monarch – O Lord of the World – O Satan!'

The Maskers (*laughing*)   Have pity on him, Satan.

Lorenzo   That is false, singer. I, Lorenzo, Duke of Spadaro, Knight of the Holy Ghost, could never have called Satan the monarch of the world. Give me the notes. My sword shall teach you how to read. (*Snatches the notes and reads with growing horror.*) 'And my soul is filled with terror, O Monarch – O Lord of the World – O Satan!' That is false. Someone has imitated my handwriting, gentlemen. I never wrote this. I swear by almighty heaven, sirs, I swear by the sacred memory of my mother, I swear by my word of honour as a knight. There is some base deceit here. The words have been altered, gentlemen.

The Maskers   We have no need of your oaths, Lorenzo. Go to the church if you want to repent. We are the masters here. Continue, singer.

Lorenzo (*smiling feebly*)   Pardon me, gentlemen, I had for the moment forgotten that for me everything is changed – faces, tones, even words. But who would have thought, my dear guests, that words could assume such revolting masks. Go on with your jest, singer.

The Masked Singer (*singing*)   'In the black depths of my heart I shall erect a throne to you, O Satan. In the black depths of my thought I shall erect a throne to you, O Satan. Divine, immortal, almighty, from now on and for ever hold sway over the soul of Lorenzo, happy, insane Lorenzo.'

Applause. Laughter.

Voices
 – Bravo, Lorenzo! Bravo, bravo!
 – Lorenzo is the vassal of Satan.
 – We kneel to you, Lorenzo.
 – Lorenzo, Duke of Spadaro, is a vassal of Satan.
 – Bravo! Bravo!

Lorenzo (*crying out*)   In God's name, gentlemen, we are all deceived. This is not my singer. This is not Romualdo but some impostor. Satan has sent him here. Something frightful has happened, gentlemen.

A Voice   He sang your own song, Lorenzo.

Second Voice   Out of your own mouth he confessed to Satan.

Lorenzo (*pressing his hand to his heart*)   This is a horrible falsehood, gentlemen. Just imagine, my dear guests – how could I, Duke Lorenzo, Knight of the Holy Ghost, son of a crusader –

A Voice   But did your mother tell you whose son you are, Duke Lorenzo?

Laughter. **Lorenzo**, *extending his arms, tries to say something, but his words are inaudible. Pressing his hands to his head, he runs swiftly up the staircase. Cries:* 'Way for the queen's son!' *Two* **Black Maskers** *appear one after the other.*

A Voice   Who is this? Our numbers increase.

A Frightened Voice   Uninvited guests are coming. Uninvited guests are coming.

Third Voice   They fly to the light. Off with your mask, sir. (*He tries to pull the black mask from the face of the stranger and springs back in terror, crying.*) They are not masked, gentlemen.

General confusion. Everything is enveloped in darkness. The wild music, however, continues, gradually receding.

Curtain.

Scene Two

From somewhere in the distance come sounds of music, which, mingling with the howling and whistling of the wind that rages about the castle, fill the air with a wild, tremulous melody.

An ancient library in the castle tower. A low, massive oak door, partly open, through which steps are seen leading down and a little beyond other steps leading upward. The heavy ceiling is vaulted and there are small windows in deep stone recesses. Here and there on the walls and hanging from the ceiling are spider-webs. Everywhere are large old books on the floor, in heavy, iron-bound chests, and on small wooden stands. A portion of the wall, hollowed out in niches, is also used to hold books. Some of the niches are draped with heavy curtains.

Beside one of the open chests, which is full of papers yellowed with age, **Lorenzo** *is seated on a low stool. Near him, on a support, stands a wrought-iron lantern which, by reason of its crossbars, throws here dark shadows and there bright lines of light. For some time there is profound silence. All that can be heard is the far-off music and the rustling of the sheets of paper as* **Lorenzo** *turns them over.* **Lorenzo** *is dressed as at the ball.*

Lorenzo (*raising his head*)   What a frightful wind there is today! For three nights now it has been raging and grows steadily more violent. How horribly like the music of my thoughts! These poor thoughts of mine! How like frightened creatures they beat about within this tight box of bone! Once Lorenzo was young, but now, though only a little time has passed – though the sun has encircled the earth but twice – lo, he is old, and the weight of terrible experience, the horrible truth of things human and divine, has bowed his youthful back. Poor Lorenzo! Poor Lorenzo! (*He reads. Breaking off for a moment.*) If all that is in these yellowed papers is true, who then is ruler of the world, God or Satan? And who am I that call myself Lorenzo, Duke of Spadaro? Oh, the horrible reality of human life! My young soul is smitten with sorrow. (*He reads, then carefully lays aside the sheets and speaks.*) So it is true, mother; it is true. I thought, my mother, that you were a saint. I swore by your memory, and my oath was as solemn as if I had sworn upon my knightly sword; and yet you, my saintly mother, were the paramour of a drunken, thieving groom. And my noble father, returning from Palestine to die in his ancestral home, learned of this and pardoned you, and bore the terrible secret with him to grave. Whose son am I, O my saintly mother – the son of a knight, who gave his life's blood to the Lord, or the son of a filthy groom, an abominable traitor and thief, who robbed his master at his orisons?[8] Poor Lorenzo! Poor Lorenzo!

He falls into deep thought. Swift footsteps are heard along the staircase, and **Lorenzo** *rushes into the room, his head between his hands in the same attitude in which he left the hall. He takes his hands from his face, sees the* **Lorenzo** *who is seated, and cries out in a frightened voice.*

The Second Lorenzo   Who is this?

The First Lorenzo (*rising in alarm*)   Who is this?

The **Second Lorenzo** *throws himself upon the other and hurls the lantern to the floor. The room is now faintly illuminated by the light from the open door. There is a brief, muffled struggle and then the two figures separate.*

The Second Lorenzo   Your jest is overbold, sir. Remove your mask, I command you, else I will remove it for you by force. I gave you my castle but not myself, and by assuming my mask you insult me. There is but one Lorenzo, but one Duke of Spadaro, and that is I. Off with your mask, sir!

He advances toward the other.

The First Lorenzo (*in a trembling voice*)   If you are only a frightful apparition, I conjure you, in the name of God, vanish. There is but one Lorenzo, but one Duke of Spadaro, and that is I.

The Second Lorenzo (*wildly*)   Off with your mask, sir! I have borne too long with your unseemly jests. My patience is at an end. Either remove your mask or draw your sword. Duke Lorenzo knows how to punish insolence.

The First Lorenzo   In God's name!

The Second Lorenzo   In the devil's name, you mean, unhappy man. Your sword, sir, your sword, else I shall run you through on the spot like a guilty dog.

The First Lorenzo   In God's name!

The Second Lorenzo (*furiously*)   Your sword, sir, your sword!

From the dimly lighted stage comes the whistling and the clash of meeting rapiers. The two **Lorenzos** *engage each other savagely, though the* **First Lorenzo** *is obviously the inferior. There are brief, muffled exclamations:*

'In God's name!'
'Off with your mask!'
'You have killed me, Lorenzo.'

---

8 Orison: a prayer.

He falls and dies. **Lorenzo** *sets his foot upon the corpse and, wiping his sword, speaks with unexpected sadness and tenderness.*

Lorenzo   I am sorry for you, Sir Impostor. Your strength of wrist, your deep breathing, showed me that you were young like myself. But your misfortune, unhappy sir, lay in this, that Duke Lorenzo wearied of laughing at the amiable quips of his guests. You went to an obscure death, young man, the hapless victim of a masquerading joke; but still I pity you, and if I knew where your mother is I would bear to her your parting words. Farewell, Signor.

He goes out. For some time there is silence. Then all is veiled in darkness, and the sounds of wild music grow louder and draw nearer.

Curtain.

Scene Three

The ball continues. There seem to be more **Maskers***. The hall is more crowded, and the* **Maskers** *are restless as if the strange, mysteriously altered wine were having its effect upon the guests. The music, though it has grown a little languorous, is as wild as before. A mournful and lovely melody springs up, as it were accidentally, in the chaos of wild and turbulent cries, but is immediately overwhelmed and swept away upon the wind like a withered leaf which, torn from its branch, flutters in circles before it sinks to rest. Part of the* **Maskers** *continue to dance, but the greater number, perplexed and restless, move to and fro, gathering for a moment in groups to interchange brief, excited remarks. The* **Black Maskers** *wander about singly in the throng. Hairy and black from foot to crown, some resembling orangutangs and others those uncouth hairy insects which in the night-time fly toward the light, they move along the walls with a guilty, embarrassed, and somewhat absent air and hide in the corners. But curiosity overcomes their shyness, and, creeping cautiously about, they examine various objects, holding them close to their eyes. They touch the white marble columns with their hairy black fingers. They take in their hands the costly goblets, only to drop them again, as it were, helplessly. The* **Maskers** *who arrived before them are manifestly afraid of them.*

Voices   Where is Lorenzo?

  – Where is Lorenzo? We must find Lorenzo. Did no one notice where the Duke went? We must tell him now or it will be too late.

  – They fly toward the light.

  – It is plain that they are here for the first time. See how they look at everything, with what curiosity they touch things. Who invited them?

  – They were not invited. They came of their own accord along the lighted road.

  – But perhaps they are some of our friends.

  – No, no, they are strangers.

  – It is all due to the light in the tower. How dreadful!

  – Crazy Lorenzo! Crazy Lorenzo! Crazy Lorenzo!

  – The drawbridge should be raised. Then they cannot enter.

  – Call Lorenzo.

*A **Black Masker** touches, out of curiosity, the sleeve of one of the other **Maskers**, who springs back affrighted.*

The Masker   What do you wish, sir? I do not know you. Who are you? Who invited you here?

The Black Masker   I do not know who I am. Someone lighted up the tower, and we came. It's dark out there and very cold. But who are you? I do not know you, either.

*He tries to embrace the **Masker**, but the latter shrinks from him.*

The Masker   Keep your hands from me, sir, or I will hew off your fingers.

*The **Black Masker** moves unsteadily towards the fire burning on the hearth and sits cross-legged to warm himself. His fellows join him and in a black ring encircle the fire, which immediately begins to die out.*

First Black Masker   It's cold, it's cold.

Second Black Masker   It's cold.

Third Black Masker   Is this what they call fire? How beautiful it is! Whose house is this? Why didn't we come here before?

First Black Masker   Because we were then unborn. The light begat us.

Second Black Masker   Why does the fire go out? I love it so, and yet it goes out. Why does the fire go out?

A Masker   Duke Lorenzo is a traitor. He has played us false. He said the castle was ours. Why, then, did he invite these creatures?

Second Masker   He did not invite them. They came of themselves. But this castle is ours, and we will have the drawbridge raised. Ho! Servants! Servants of the Duke Lorenzo! This way!

No one comes.

Third Masker   The servants have run away. Call Lorenzo. Call Lorenzo.

The Old Women (*running up with castanets*)   The bridegroom is coming. The bridegroom is coming. The bridegroom is coming.

Voices   Lorenzo! Lorenzo! Lorenzo!

Lorenzo appears, smiling, on the staircase. His clothes are torn. On his bared breast is a large blood-red spot, but he seems not to be aware of it and bears himself with his former dignity and with the refinement and reserve of a prince regent.

Lorenzo   Kindly pardon me, my friends, for presuming to leave you for a moment. You can't imagine, my dear guests, what an amusing and diverting trick has been played upon me. I have just met a very clever gentleman who had donned the mask of Duke Lorenzo. You would have been amazed at the striking resemblance. This skilful artist had stolen not only my dress but even my voice and my features. Really, it's amusing.

He laughs.

A Masker   There is blood on you, Lorenzo.

Lorenzo (*glancing at himself indifferently*)   It is not my blood. I think, (*Rubbing his forehead thoughtfully.*) I killed that jester. Did you not hear falling bodies, gentlemen?

A Masker   Duke Lorenzo is a murderer! Whom did you kill, Lorenzo?

Lorenzo   Pardon me, gentlemen, but really I do not know whom I did kill. He lies in the tower, and if you like you may take a look at him. He is lying there. But why has the music ceased? And why, my dear guests, are you not dancing?

A Masker   The music has not ceased, Lorenzo.

Lorenzo   Oh really? I thought it was the wind, merely a violent wind. Dance my friends. Your unbounded joy delights me. Petruccio! Cristoforo! More wine for my dear guests. (*Sadly.*) Ah, to be sure, (*he laughs*) I have lost them all – Petruccio, Cristoforo, and Donna Francesca. So my wife was called – Donna Francesca. A charming name, isn't it? Donna Francesca –

The number of the **Black Maskers** *increases. One of them mounts the stairs and addresses himself to the Duke.*

The Black Masker   Did you kindle the light?

Lorenzo   Who are you, sir? You have a strange, coarse voice, and I think I did not invite you. How did you gain admittance?

The Black Masker   Did you kindle the light?

Lorenzo   Yes, my charming stranger. I had my castle lighted up. The lights shine far, do they not?

The Black Masker   You roused the whole night. Everything is astir there, and now the night is coming hither. No harm in our coming, was there? Is your name Lorenzo? Is this your house? Is this your light?

He seeks to embrace **Lorenzo**, *who violently thrusts him away.*

The Maskers (*from below*)   Be on your guard, Lorenzo. Lorenzo, your castle is in danger. They have come uninvited. Have the drawbridge raised and all the doors tightly barred.

A Voice   The drawbridge is already raised, but they are clambering over the walls.

Another Voice   All the darkness of the night is transformed into living creatures, and from every side they are coming hither. Bar the doors.

A Masker (*from below*)   Lorenzo, you invited us, and we are your guests. You must protect us. Summon your armed guards and kill these creatures. Otherwise they will kill both you and us.

A Third Voice   Look! For every one of them a light goes out. They devour the light. They put the light out with their black bodies.

First Voice   Who are they? They love the light and yet they put it out. They fly to the light and the light goes out. Who are they?

Lorenzo   What a delightful jest, Signors! It's very clever of you. But the lights are actually going out, and it is becoming strangely cold here. May I trouble some of you to call my servants? They will bring fresh lights. I really do not know where they are.

The closed doors burst open, as if suddenly yielding to a strong pressure, and let in a throng of **Black Maskers,** *and at the same instant the light grows markedly fainter. The* **Black Maskers,** *roaming about the hall with the same embarrassed but persistent curiosity, gather in a black throng around the fireplace, completely extinguishing the already enfeebled blaze.*

The Black Maskers   It's cold, cold, cold.

Voices   Relight the candles. They are going out. Who opened the doors? Bring torches. Torches!

In the confusion that ensues several of the guests try to close the doors, but give back before the pressure of the continually increasing throng of **Black Maskers.** *Others, with no greater success, attempt to light the extinguished chandeliers, which flare up but immediately go out again. Now and then, a* **Masker** *appears with a blazing torch, the red, flickering light filling the hall with a fantastic dance of shadows.*

Lorenzo (*watching the scene with pleasure*)   A charming sight. A more interesting conflict between light and darkness it has never been my good fortune to witness. A thousand thanks to him who devised it. I am his devoted, life-long servant.

Voices   The torches are going out. Bring torches.

A Masker   We must put out the lights in the tower. This insane Lorenzo will ruin us all.

Second Masker   Someone has already gone to the tower.

The Spider (*speaking to a* **Black Masker** *toward whom he has for some time been making his way*)   Are you from Satan?

The Black Masker   Who is Satan?

The Spider (*incredulously*)   Why, don't you know Satan? Who sent you here?

The Black Masker   I don't know. We came of our own accord.

He tries to embrace the **Spider.** *The latter, frightened, runs away on wobbling legs.*

Lorenzo   Luigi, you villain, why are you and your orchestra silent? Play, I beg of you, that song of mine – Do you remember it? Pardon my weak voice, gentlemen; I must refresh the memory of this forgetful singer. Listen, Luigi.

He runs over the opening bars of a simple, touching air, such as mothers sing when they lull their children, and strangely, with low and tender harmonies, the strains of the orchestra answer to the song. All else is silent.

The **Black Maskers,** *in awkward and ungainly attitudes, listen to the music, gaping with vacant curiosity. Only at the door, which the* **Maskers** *hold shut by the main strength of their shoulders, there is a knocking and scratching and a low, plaintive moaning.* **Lorenzo,** *closing his eyes and swaying slightly, sings in a low voice. Suddenly, behind him, along the stairway, echoes the trampling of many feet, distinctly audible in the silence. Several* **Maskers** *run down the staircase past* **Lorenzo,** *jostling him.*

Lorenzo (*gently reproaching them*)   Gentlemen, you put me out.

One of the Maskers (*panting*)   Murder! Murder! There has been a murder in the tower.

Voices   Who is murdered?

First Masker   Lorenzo himself – Lorenzo, the Duke of Spadaro, lord of this castle – is murdered.

Second Masker   We saw his corpse. The unhappy Duke lies in the library, pierced by a rapier thrust from behind. His slayer is not only a murderer, but a traitor.

Lorenzo   That is false, gentlemen. I struck him in the heart. I slew him in honourable combat. He defended himself savagely, but the Lord God strengthened my hand, and I slew him.

Voices   Vengeance, gentlemen! To arms, to arms! The Duke of Spadaro is treacherously slain.

First Masker (*pointing to* **Lorenzo**)   And there is his murderer. Off with your mask, sir!

Lorenzo   My mask? (*With dignity.*) It is true, gentlemen, that I killed someone in the tower – some brazen jester – but it was not the Duke Lorenzo. I am Duke Lorenzo.

Voices (*shouting*)   Off with your mask, murderer!

Meanwhile the influx of the **Black Maskers** *and the quenching of the lights continue. Now and, then another torch replaces one that has gone out. The ensuing words of* **Lorenzo** *and the* **Maskers** *are interrupted by frequent cries of* 'Bring torches, the lights are going out.'

Lorenzo   Why do you think that I am masked, gentlemen? (*Feeling his face.*) This is no mask. I assure you, gentlemen, this is my own face.

Voices   Off with your mask, murderer!

Lorenzo (*flaring up*)   I beg you to give over this unbecoming jest. I swear on my honour that this is the face that God gave me when I was born, and not of those repulsive masks that I see on you, gentlemen. A mask cannot smile as I smile in answer to your daring jests.

He tries to smile, but his lips only twitch convulsively. For a moment, with teeth bared, he presents the appearance of a frightful, laughing mask, but instantly his face becomes motionless, turns pale, and stiffens.

Lorenzo (*horrified*)   What is this? What has happened to my face? It does not obey me. It will not smile, but grows rigid. (*Piteously.*) Perhaps I am going insane. Just look at me, gentlemen. This is surely not a mask. It is a face – a living, human face.

Laughter and shouts: 'Off with your mask, murderer! Look, look! Lorenzo is turning to stone.'

Lorenzo (*his face turned to stone*)   All is lost, gentlemen. I tried to smile and could not. I tried to weep and could not. I wear a mask of stone.

He grasps his face in a fury, trying to tear it off.

I'll tear you off, accursed mask, I'll tear you off together with the flesh and blood. Help me, Donna Francesca. Cut the edge here a bit with your dagger and it will at once fall away and let you see the face of your Lorenzo. Bring your consecrated sword, Cristoforo. Save your master, whom God has abandoned. One moment, gentlemen, one moment – I will –

He utters a wild cry and falls. At the same instant there is a crash of breaking window-frames, the windows are burst open, and through them pour in the **Black Maskers**. *The hall is dark save for the tremulous light of two remaining torches, and presently one of these goes out. A commotion arises on the darkened stage. There are wild cries of terror and despair and vain efforts to escape. Several of the* **Black Maskers** *mount the musicians' balcony, seize the horns, and trumpet wildly.*

A Voice   Do you hear? They are blowing the trumpets. They are summoning their kin.

Second Voice   That is their music.

Third Voice   Save yourselves, they are coming through the windows!

First Voice   The tower is full of them. They are pouring down from it like a black torrent. Bring torches.

Fourth Voice   There are no more torches. This is the last.

Many Voices   Save yourselves, save yourselves!

Third Voice   They hold all the exits.

A Female Voice   He is embracing me. I am stifling. I shall die. Save me! Among so many knights is there none to protect me?

A Voice   To arms!

Third Voice   Swords are powerless against them.

Fourth Voice   There is no way of escape. We are lost! Crazy Lorenzo! He has ruined us all!

The Black Maskers (*roaming about, one by one*)   It's cold, cold. Where's the light? Where's the fire? They have deceived us!

A Voice (*in rage and despair*)   You have devoured the light, you brood of darkness!

The Black Maskers   It's cold, cold. Where is the light? Where is the fire?

They crowd around the last torch, which one of the **Maskers** *holds high in his uplifted hand, seeking to keep it alight. The torch goes out. Darkness.*

Voices   Crazy Lorenzo! Crazy Lorenzo! Crazy Lorenzo!

Curtain.

Act Two

Scene One

A corner of the chapel in the feudal castle.

The walls are draped in black in sign of mourning. The tall, dust-laden windows of coloured glass admit a feeble, softly tinted light. On a black dais, in a massive black coffin, lies the body of **Lorenzo***, Duke of Spadaro. At each corner of the coffin is a huge wax candle. On the dais at the head of the coffin, in the soft glow of the candles, stands* **Duke Lorenzo***, dressed entirely in black, his hand resting on the bier.*

From the courtyard of the castle comes at intervals the whining and barking of hunting-dogs. Now and then a prolonged and mournful blare of trumpets carries abroad the sad news of the death of the Duke of Spadaro. In the intervals of silence the solemn notes of an organ and the voice of a priest can be heard at one side beyond the glass doors leading to the other half of the chapel. Mass is being conducted there uninterruptedly.

Lorenzo (*to the one lying in the coffin*)   The whole neighbourhood has by now been informed of your death, Duke Lorenzo, and in tears is calling for vengeance on your murderer. Lie still, Signor. Those who loved you are now coming to pay their respects to your dust. The peasants will come, and your servants, and your inconsolable widow, Donna Francesca. But I beseech you, Lorenzo, lie quiet. I have already had the honour of running my sword through your unworthy heart, but if you stir, if you dare to speak or cry out, I will tear your heart clean from your breast and throw it to your hunting-dogs. In the name of our former friendship, I beseech you, Lorenzo, lie quiet.

He arranges the shroud with tender solicitude and kisses the corpse on the forehead. At this moment in the corner of the chapel, in the folds of the black drapery, is heard a deep sigh and the plaintive tinkling of bells.

Who's there? Oh, is that you, my little Ecco, hidden in the corner and softly tinkling your little bells? Who let you in?

Ecco   Why did you die, Lorenzo? Foolish Lorenzo! Why did you die?

Lorenzo   I had to die, Ecco.

Ecco   Then I shall die with you, Lorenzo. Your servants use me ill. Your dogs' teeth are sharp. All day I lay hid in the tower, waiting for the door of the chapel to open. Do not drive me away, Lorenzo.

Lorenzo   You shall stay here, jester.

Ecco   What a long, white nose you have, Lorenzo. It must be embarrassing to have such a nose and to be compelled to hold it up like that. I would laugh if it were not so frightful.

Lorenzo   That is death, Ecco. But hide yourself, someone is coming.

Ecco *conceals himself. Several* **Peasants** *enter and bow low at a little distance from the coffin, not venturing to come nearer.*

Lorenzo (*impressively*)   Duke Lorenzo, open your heart and return to life for a moment. Your good peasants have come to bid you farewell. Come nearer, my friends. Duke Lorenzo in his lifetime was a kind master, and now that he is dead he will not harm you. Draw nearer.

The **Peasants** *approach, though it is apparent that they are still afraid.*

First Peasant   God forgive you, Duke Lorenzo, as I forgive you. Many a time you and your hunters have trampled down my fields of grain, and what the hoofs of your horses left untouched your kind overseer took for himself, depriving me and my family of bread. Yet you were a good master, and I pray God to forgive you your sins.

Lorenzo (*to the one lying in the coffin*)   Quiet, sir, quiet. I understand how it is with you: you cannot hear unmoved this bitter truth about your evil deeds. But do not forget that you are dead. Lie quiet, sir, lie quiet.

A Peasant Woman   May God forgive you, Duke Lorenzo, as I forgive you. You took my little daughter from me for your ducal pleasure, and she was ruined. But you were young and handsome, and you were a good master to us. I pray God to forgive you your sins.

She weeps.

Lorenzo (*to the one lying in the coffin*)   Quiet, sir, quiet. I remember how you loved the blue corn-flowers amid the ripened grain. Does not this remind you of someone's blue eyes, of someone's golden hair?

Second Peasant   On the very eve of your departure for Palestine, Duke Lorenzo, to deliver the Holy Sepulchre, my son was killed in your service. A poor service you rendered to the Lord, Duke Lorenzo, and you shall have no forgiveness either on earth or in heaven.

Lorenzo (*setting his teeth*)   Did you hear, sir? (*To the* **Peasants***.*) Return in peace to your homes, my friends. Duke Lorenzo has heard you, and he will humbly bear your every word to the throne of the Almighty.

The **Peasants** *withdraw.*

Lorenzo (*to the one lying in the coffin*)   Lorenzo, insane Lorenzo, what have you done to me?

Enter **Signor Cristoforo**, *slightly tipsy. He kneels unsteadily and for some time is silent.* **Ecco** *peeps from his hiding-place, then conceals himself again.*

Lorenzo   He is listening, Signor Cristoforo.

Cristoforo (*swaying to and fro*)   Duke di Spadaro! Lorenzo! Boy! How lonely I am without you. Forgive me, my poor boy. When your noble father and I returned from Palestine and you were born – and a little, red chap you were – I swore to your father that I would always protect you. And I have protected your wines. Pardon me, Lorenzo, but they drink like camels. Today, however, having opened all the cellars, I knocked out the heads of the casks and slit all the skins and said: 'Drink, you camels, you asses, you accursed sponges. I shall gird on my sword and go seek the murderer of my boy, of my dear Lorenzo.'

He wipes his eyes with his fist and staggers to his feet.

Lorenzo (*with dignity*)   The Duke thanks you, Cristoforo. You are drunk, my old friend, but at your words the lips of his wound have opened and two crimson drops have welled up from the depths of his heart. They are yours, Cristoforo. Go.

Cristoforo *withdraws.* **Ecco** *creeps out, tinkling his bells.*

Ecco   Have you nothing for me, Lorenzo? Give me at least one little drop of blood from your heart. I am tired of being ill-tempered and deformed.

Lorenzo   I will give you more than that, Ecco. Come and kiss me.

Ecco   I am afraid.

Lorenzo   He loved you, little coward.

Ecco   If you were alive, Lorenzo, I should be glad to kiss you, but I am afraid of corpses. Why did you die, Lorenzo? It was unkind of you.

He seats himself on the floor, curling his legs under him as if getting ready for a long and interesting conversation.

You see, Lorenzo, we must go away. You look upon me as a jester and do not take me seriously, but once when you were playing with me you touched me with your sword, and now I am just as much a knight as you are, Lorenzo. So listen to me. Cease being dead, take your sword, and we will go away together like two knights.

Lorenzo (*smiling*)   Whither, my doughty knight?

Ecco   To the Lord God! (*With growing animation.*) He knows you, Lorenzo, and, as for me, you will tell him that I am your brother, a little hunchback. And when he has sanctified our swords – Oh, oh, Lorenzo, there come your ruffians! I am afraid; I will hide myself.

He conceals himself. A band of drunken, boisterous **Servants** *come in, reeling and jostling one another. Several keep their hats on.*

Lorenzo (*angrily*)   Off with your hats, you villains! Lie quiet, sir, lie quiet.

Pietro   Bah! He's already beginning to stink. Whoever wishes can go and kiss his hand. I won't.

Mario   I'd rather kiss Donna Francesca. Of all the ladies I have seen, she pleases me best. You see, gentlemen, the inclination is inherited; my uncle kissed Duke Lorenzo's mother, so I want to kiss his wife.

Laughter.

Lorenzo   I implore you, sir, be quiet. I see how the black blood surges in your wound, but it is another's blood, Lorenzo.

Lorenzo   Pietro, you have stolen one of my golden spurs. Tomorrow I shall flay you for it.

Pietro   And I'll lop off your nose.

Lorenzo   Away with you, you villains; be off!

He half draws his sword. The **Servants** *look about in fright.*

Pietro   Did you say that, Mario?

Mario   Sh! I heard the voice of the dead Duke, old Henry. Let's be off.

Manucci   I'll have the hide of you yet.

Mario   Come, let's be off.

They go out.

Lorenzo (*to the one lying in the coffin, contemptuously*)   And these, sir, are your servants, to whom you intrusted your castle, your treasures, and your wife, the beautiful Donna Francesca. Let us have no charges of disloyalty or treason, unhappy Duke. Do not insult me with lying evasions nor stain your honourable grave with sin. (*Greatly agitated.*) Be calm, sir, be calm. I hear Donna Francesca coming. I recognise her step, and I implore you, sir, in the name of God, lie quiet. Summon your strength, sir.

Silence. The mournful notes of the requiem from behind the wall grow louder.
Lorenzo, *bending forward and laying his hand upon his heart, awaits the appearance of* **Donna Francesca**. *She enters alone, clad in deep mourning. She kneels. Silence. During the following scene* **Ecco** *comes partly out from the black drapery and weeps bitterly, softly tinkling his bells.*

Lorenzo (*unable to control himself*)   I love you, Francesca.

Francesca (*in a low voice*)   I love you, Lorenzo.

Lorenzo (*sadly*)   But you see that I am dead, Francesca.

Francesca   To me, Lorenzo, you will always be alive.

Lorenzo (*sadly*)   You will forget me, Donna Francesca.

Francesca   I shall never forget you, Lorenzo.

Lorenzo (*sadly*)   You are young, Donna Francesca.

Francesca   In a single night my heart has grown old, Lorenzo.

Lorenzo (*sadly*)   Your face is beautiful, Donna Francesca. (*Gently reproachful.*) Bitter tears have not dulled the bright gleam of your eyes, O Donna Francesca! Bitter tears have not washed the delicate roses from your checks, O Donna Francesca! Your black mourning does not conceal the grace and beauty of your form, O Donna Francesca, O Donna Francesca!

Francesca   The light has gone out of my eyes, Lorenzo. My face has withered as a leaf withers at the cruel touch of the sirocco, and my form is bowed to the earth in bitter and overwhelming grief.

Lorenzo   That is not true, Francesca.

Francesca   I swear it, Lorenzo.

Lorenzo (*his voice trembling*)   Lie still, sir, lie still. I see how your heart heaves, Lorenzo. I see how your tortured heart quivers at the pitiless words of love, and I pity you, Lorenzo. Go, Donna Francesca. Leave me with my dead friend. Your beautiful grief tears at our hearts, and I implore you in the name of God to leave us.

Donna Francesca *weeps.*

Lorenzo (*in an agony of grief*)   O Donna Francesca! O my love! O light of my youth! (*Covering his face with his hands, he weeps silently.*) Draw nearer, Francesca. Kiss him. I will not look.

Francesca *sobbing convulsively, kisses the dead* **Lorenzo***.*

Lorenzo (*covering his face with his hands*)   Kiss him more ardently, Donna Francesca, for you will never see him again. Kiss him more ardently. God placed a sword in my hand, and with it I punished the insane Lorenzo. But still he was a knight. He was a Knight of the Holy Ghost, Francesca. And now leave us.

Ecco*, frightened, conceals himself.* **Donna Francesca***, in tears, descends from the dais, kneels again, and withdraws. Silence. The last mournful strains of the funeral dirge are heard.*

Lorenzo (*to the one lying in the coffin*)   I thank you for obeying my behest and lying quiet. I saw how hard it was for you, and again I thank you, Lorenzo. Now we are alone – now and forever. Let us go, Lorenzo; let us go into the unknown future.

The stage is suddenly dark.

Curtain.

Scene Two

The same hall as in Scene One. It is toward evening. Through the half-open window mountain peaks are seen glowing in the last rays of the setting sun. A fire burns in the fireplace. A number of candles are burning, but two **Servants***, moving along the wall, continue to light others. Silence.*

Pietro   Why have they ordered so many candles to be lighted? Is anyone expected today? I have heard nothing of it.

Mario   Hold your tongue, stupid. You talk as if you didn't know.

Pietro (*gruffly*)   How should I know? They call me in when they need me, but as soon as anything goes wrong they shout: 'Begone!'

Mario   Everybody knows. The townspeople of Spadaro came up to the castle today. So they know, too. You're the only one that hasn't heard.

Pietro   I don't care to hear. Only tell me, why so many lights?

Mario   Because Duke Lorenzo has so ordered.

Pietro   But why did he so order?

Mario   Because today Duke Lorenzo is expecting guests.

Pietro   Well, I said myself that there were to be guests. You might have told me in the beginning.

Mario (*sighing*)   You're stupid, Pietro. There will be no guests today. It's only that Lorenzo expects them.

Pietro   How can he expect them if they are not coming?

Mario   He imagines that they are coming. Do you understand, stupidity? He only imagines it. Probably you, when you are drunk, imagine things also. Why did you cry out yesterday in your drunken sleep?

Pietro   I dreamt that Signor Cristoforo was beating me with his cane.

Mario   There, now. You see, don't you?

Pietro   Well, is the Duke, then, drunk?

He laughs.

Petruccio, *the overseer, enters.*

Petruccio   Lively, now, you lazybones, lively! You, there, Pietro, what are you yawning about?

Mario   My dear Signor Petruccio, you are so wise that even Signor Cristoforo listens to you. Explain to this fool what has happened to our Duke.

Petruccio   That, my fine fellows, is none of your affair.

Pietro   There, you've got your explanation. Which of us is the fool now?

Petruccio (*gazing at the ceiling*)   Both of you. The Duke is simply indisposed. He has delirium.

Pietro   But why so many lights?

Petruccio   Because – Clear out!

Enter **Cristoforo**. **Pietro** *bows low before him.*

Petruccio   Good evening, Signor.

Cristoforo   Ah, Petruccio, Petruccio, when will you become thin so that you may contain less wine?

Petruccio   If I become any thinner I shall be like a long drain-pipe, which, letting everything flow through, contains naught.

Cristoforo (*threatening him with his finger*)   Take care, take care, Signor Overseer. (*Sighs.*) Well, drink all you like, Petruccio. No one is left to save the wine for. Poor Lorenzo, poor Lorenzo! Little did I think, when we returned from Palestine with his father, that so horrible a fate was in store for the proud family of the Dukes of Spadaro. What has come over him? Where hovers his immortal soul? I looked him in the eyes today with a gaze that might have pierced the head of a wine-cask, but he merely smiled at me and, in a voice that would have brought tears to the eyes of a heathen Turk, said gently: 'Who are you? I don't know you. Take off your mask, Signor.'

Petruccio   Indeed, indeed! but that is amazing, Signor Cristoforo.

Cristoforo   'My boy', I said to him, 'Duke Lorenzo, just stop and think. If this were a mask, then what a horrible mask I should be wearing.' (*Wiping away his tears.*) 'My boy', I said, 'Duke Lorenzo, just touch with your finger this scar that I received in defending the Holy Sepulchre. Do masks have such scars?'

Mario   Really, really! Holy Virgin!

Cristoforo   And Lorenzo put his finger on the scar and said: 'What a wretched mask, Signor; it is apparently made of two pieces sewed together.' Poor Lorenzo, poor Lorenzo!

Ecco *appears and shrinks into a corner, making himself as small as possible. He sighs deeply.*

Petruccio   You see that Ecco, too, is sad, Signor. It's an ill thing in a house when the jester takes to sighing like a half-frozen dog. Man cannot live without laughter, Signor Cristoforo. When laughter dies the man dies too. Laugh, Ecco. Even if you utter no word, at least laugh, and you will cheer my soul.

Ecco (*with a deep sigh*)   I cannot, Signor Petruccio.

Cristoforo   Don't you find my queer moustachios very amusing?

Ecco (*with a deep sigh*)   Very, Signor Cristoforo.

Cristoforo   Then why don't you laugh?

Ecco   I cannot, Signor Cristoforo.

Petruccio   There, you see for yourself. Laughter is dead. Poor Lorenzo!

Cristoforo   Yes. Poor Lorenzo!

All the candles are now lighted and the **Servants** *withdraw.*

Petruccio   Mario, go tell Donna Francesca that the candles are lighted and all is in readiness – for the reception of the guests.

Cristoforo   What guests, pray, can there be, Signor Overseer?

Petruccio (*with a gesture of despair*)   And you, Pietro, go and see that the drawbridge is lowered.

Cristoforo   What for?

Petruccio   The Duke so ordered.

Cristoforo   Lorenzo? Why do you take orders from him?

Petruccio   If, Signor Cristoforo, you had heard his voice and seen his gesture of command, you would have obeyed him too.

Cristoforo   I? Never.

Ecco   You would have obeyed, Signor Cristoforo, as I obeyed. What was I? A little, malicious dwarf found in the castle moat. When he so willed, I became his laughter. And what shall I now become? It is not for you to judge, gentlemen. I shall be whatever my master, Lorenzo, bids.

Petruccio   His tears?

Cristoforo   His fears?

Ecco (*sighing*)   No, his fire. I was his tears. I do not know, Signor Cristoforo, if I was his fears, but now I shall become his fire. He said to me, as he said to you: 'Who are you, sir? I do not know you. Take off your mask.' And I fell to weeping, gentlemen, and replied: 'Very well, Lorenzo. If you bid me, I will take off my mask.'

Cristoforo   No, Ecco, you were better when you smiled.

Enter **Signora Francesca** *with her suite of ladies and gentlemen. They move silently and sadly about the hall, embarrassed by its emptiness and the brilliant lights.*

A Gentleman (*in a low voice*)   It seems an eternity since I kissed you last, Leonora.

Leonora   And it will be an eternity before you kiss me again, sir.

The Gentleman   How cruel you are, my goddess. As if one eternity were not enough.

Francesca   I beg of you, ladies and gentlemen, to do me a favour. You are no doubt aware that the Duke, my husband, is somewhat indisposed. He is expecting guests, though none are invited, and since he will probably assume, my dear friends, that you are his guests, I beg of you not to express surprise or alarm. The Duke's memory is somewhat impaired, so that he forgets even persons who are dear to him. Divert him, gently and cautiously, from his illusions. I count on your tact and kindness, my friends. Announce to Duke Lorenzo (*covering her face with her hands*) that the guests are arriving.

Ecco (*sighing*)   I was his laughter. I was his tears. What shall I now become?

He rises and starts to go out.

Cristoforo   Where are you going, Ecco?

Ecco   Where the will of my master may lead me.

Francesca   Signor Petruccio, I trust that you have not forgotten the musicians. Have they learned the music that Duke Lorenzo composed for them?

Petruccio   The musicians only await your instructions, madam.

Voices   Silence! Silence! Duke Lorenzo! Duke Lorenzo!

On the brilliantly illuminated staircase appears **Duke Lorenzo**. *He wears the same costume as at the ball, even to the torn doublet, which exposes the spot of blood on his breast over his heart. His face is very pale. He pauses and, looking radiantly about the brilliantly lighted hall, bows with an air of gracious hospitality.*

Lorenzo   I am delighted to welcome you, my dear guests. From this moment my castle is at your disposal. I am merely your servant. Petruccio, is the roadway lighted?

Petruccio   It is lighted, sir.

Lorenzo   Do not forget, my friend, that the whole night is watching us. We will show it, sir, what is meant by a bright and living fire. (*He comes down.*) What charming masks! I am happy, my friends, to be honoured by your presence. I am infinitely charmed by your inexhaustible cleverness and wit. Who are you, sir? I do not know you. Please remove your mask, that I may extend to you a friendly greeting.

Cristoforo (*on the verge of tears*)   It is I, Lorenzo. I am Cristoforo. Do you not know me?

Lorenzo (*with touching candour*)   Why, how should I know you, sir, when you wear so frightful a mask? I knew a Signor Cristoforo. He was my friend from the cradle, and I loved him, but you I do not know. Remove your mask, my dear sir, I beseech you.

Cristoforo   I were better thrown to the dogs. I can bear no more.

Francesca   Signor Cristoforo!

Lorenzo   What ails the gentleman? Why does his mask change so oddly? I am extremely sorry, sir, and I should be infinitely pleased to learn who you are, but, pardon me, I do not recognise you. And who is this funny fat gentleman with the red nose? What a comical mask!

Petruccio   I have just had the honour, sir – I am Petruccio, your overseer.

Lorenzo   You mean you are wearing the mask of Petruccio.

Petruccio   Yes, the mask of Petruccio.

Lorenzo (*laughing*)   A bad bargain, my dear sir. You made a poor choice. My overseer is a great rascal and a knave, and his red nose did not come from praying.

Cristoforo   My poor boy!

Lorenzo   Ah, now I think of it, has any one of you gentlemen seen a masker in red entwined with a serpent that stings her in the heart? Right in this spot. They say (*laughing*) – they say (*laughing*) that it is my heart. A capital joke! As if everyone did not know that Lorenzo, Duke of Spadaro, has no serpent in his heart.

One of the Guests (*incautiously*)   You have wounded yourself on something, Duke Lorenzo. There is blood on your doublet.

Lorenzo (*eagerly*)   Oh, that? Thereby hangs a very strange story, gentlemen. It sounds like a fairy-tale. While I was in the tower, some stranger who had concealed his face under a hideous mask, extinguished the light, fell upon me in the darkness, and stabbed me in the back. As you see, gentlemen, the dagger entered under the left shoulder-blade and came out here at the breast. It was a skilful, if treacherous, stroke. My heart was pierced straight through.

Francesca (*endeavouring to distract* **Lorenzo**'s *attention from the wound, which, throwing open his doublet, he eagerly displays*)   Lorenzo!

Lorenzo   See, ladies and gentlemen, what a masterstroke!

Francesca   Look at me, Lorenzo. Why do you not smile upon me? I am sad when you do not smile. It is as if the sun had set for ever.

Lorenzo   You are charming, Signora. I see only your supple figure and your tiny foot, but permit me, my divinity, to make so bold as to peep into your eyes – How they shine! Even through the openings of this ugly black mask I can see how beautiful they are. Who are you, madam? I do not know you.

Francesca   God in heaven! Do you not recognise me, Lorenzo?

Lorenzo (*with the same touching candour as before*)   Take off your mask, madam, I beseech you. Your question is a strange one. Take off your mask, madam, and I will greet you willingly and cordially. By your stature I should take you to be Signora Emilia; but no. (*He shakes his head.*) Signora Emilia is not so shapely. Who are you?

Francesca (*weeping*)   I am your wife, Lorenzo, your wife, Donna Francesca. My love, do you not remember that name – Francesca?

Lorenzo (*knitting his brows*)   Francesca? Did you say Francesca? Yes, that was my wife's name. True, that was my wife's name. But I have lost my wife. Have you not heard, madam? There is no Donna Francesca anymore.

Francesca   Remember how you loved me, Lorenzo. Look into my eyes. You said that among a thousand women you would recognise me by the eyes alone. Listen to my voice, Lorenzo – you are not looking at me.

Lorenzo (*gently reproachful*)   Your voice is tender and kind, my lady. I hear in it the utterance of a virgin heart. Why do you inflict this painful jest upon me? You are cruel, my dear lady. You should not mock Lorenzo or twist the dagger in his bosom. I have lost my wife. Her name was Donna Francesca, and I have lost her.

Francesca   If you do not believe me, my love, at least give me leave to touch with my lips your blood-stained wound. By the tenderness of her kiss you will recognise your Francesca.

She bends forward to kiss the wound.

Lorenzo (*with an expression of extreme pain and horror, thrusting her away*)   What are you about, madam? You are drinking my blood. Have mercy on me, I beg of you. You have fastened yourself on my heart and you are drinking my blood. You hurt me. Leave me, pray.

Donna Francesca *weeps.* **Lorenzo**, *shrinking from her with an expression of suffering and extreme terror, tries to cover the wound, but his hands tremble.*

Lorenzo (*covering the wound and making an effort to smile*)   A bitter jest, my friends. You saw how this vampire fastened herself upon my heart?

Cristoforo (*angrily*)   You are crazy, Lorenzo, this is your wife!

A gentleman   He has insulted you, Donna Francesca.

Francesca (*ceases weeping and speaks angrily*)   It is you who insult him, sir! Lorenzo, Duke of Spadaro, cannot insult a woman even though he be insane.

Lorenzo (*to Petruccio, in a low voice*)   What is the trouble, Signor? What has disturbed this charming masker?

Petruccio   I do not know.

Francesca   Call the musicians, Petruccio.

Lorenzo (*joyfully*)   Yes, yes, call the musicians.

Francesca (*tenderly*)   I beg you to be attentive, my dear Lorenzo. Signor Romualdo will now sing for us the charming song that you dedicated to me in the bright days of our love.

Lorenzo   You are jesting again, madam. I never loved you.

Francesca (*greatly distressed*)   Do not listen to him, my friends. I beg you to be seated, Duke, and, if you will permit me, I will sit beside you. Signor Romualdo, show the Duke the song which he wrote with his own hand in the bright days of our love. Do you recognise your handwriting, my dear Lorenzo?

Lorenzo (*courteously*)   Show it to me, Signor. Yes, that is my writing, and a capital joke it is, too. (*Glancing at* **Francesca**.) But here is written: 'To my love, to my bride, the charming Donna Francesca.' (*Suspiciously.*) How did this sheet come into your hands, madam?

Francesca (*hastily*)   Signor Romualdo, I beg you to begin. We are listening.

Strains of soft and beautiful music flooded with sunshine and with the charm of youth and love.

Romualdo (*singing*)   'My soul is an enchanted castle. I have lighted my castle with lights. I have lighted my castle with lights.'

Lorenzo (*searching his memory*)   I seem to have heard those words before. Continue, Signor.

Romualdo (*singing*)   'And the sun entered my charming castle. The black shadows fled affrighted, and an infinite joy, the revellings of a bright and happy soul, gave wings to my thoughts, O Donna Francesca! O Donna Francesca!'

Lorenzo   The singer speaks falsely, my friends. I never wrote that.

Romualdo (*singing*)   'And on wings of fancy my flaming spirit ascended to heaven. And on wings of fancy my flaming spirit ascended to heaven.'

Lorenzo (*rising and halting* **Romualdo** *with an angry gesture*)   Stop, singer. Do not listen to him, my friends. He lies. He is deceiving you. I remember the words. Luigi, you villain, obey me. If you err even in a single note I will have you hanged tomorrow from the castle walls. Attention, ladies and gentlemen.

Through the windows the far-off mountain tops stand out from the darkness as if touched by the red glow of sunset. From somewhere behind the **Musicians** *comes the wild music that was played at the ball, but no one hears it.*

Lorenzo   Right, right, Luigi. (*Singing.*) 'I, the insane Lorenzo, have lighted up my tower and hither will come those whom I invited not. And the lights in the tower will go out, and my soul will be shrouded in darkness and will rejoice in thee, my lord, my master, ruler of the world – Satan.'

Cries of indignation and horror. Many, terrified, leave their places and crowd about the columns.

A Voice   He is calling upon Satan.

Second Voice   He says that Satan is lord of the world. Sacrilege! Sacrilege! Sacrilege!

Cristoforo   Awake, madman, you are the son of a crusader.

A Lady (*to a gentleman*)   Look, the sun is setting a second time!

Voices   The sun! the sun! Look, the sun has appeared again!

Cristoforo (*stamping his foot*)   Even though you are insane, even though you are my master, Duke Lorenzo, I throw down my gauntlet to you.

The others seize him. The light outside grows stronger and seems to be mixed with flame and blood. The mountains are no longer visible.

Voices   Look! Look! See what is happening to the sky.

Francesca   Duke Lorenzo is mad, Signor Cristoforo, and cannot do you the honour of crossing swords with you, but in the name of his son, whom I bear in my bosom, I accept your challenge.

She takes up the glove.

Voices   The Duchess expects a son. Donna Francesca expects a son. Poor Lorenzo! Poor Lorenzo!

Lorenzo (*recovering from a profound reverie*)   What has happened? I thought I heard the sound of a naked sword. Who dares to draw his sword in the presence of

Duke Lorenzo? I showed you honour, my friends, and invited you to my festival. You outrage my hospitality.

Voices   Look! Something has happened to the sky. There is a fire somewhere. See, the heavens are ablaze! What has happened? There is a fire somewhere.

Lorenzo (*looking through the window and speaking with elation*)   That is the beginning of my holiday, my friends. To our joyful banquet will come one more guest. I commend him to your attention. His eyes are fire, his bright locks are clouds of gilded smoke, his voice is the roar of the impetuous flame that devours stone, and his godlike visage is flame and fire and boundless, pellucid light. Such a masker, ladies and gentlemen, you have never seen!

The light outside becomes stronger. Frightened cries. Commotion. Voices.

Voices   Satan! Satan! He calls on Satan. See, the heavens are on fire, the earth is ablaze! Save yourselves! He is summoning Satan.

Lorenzo (*raising his voice*)   Who dares to speak here the foul name of Satan? I thought I heard a strange song. Some madman, deserving of curses and death, called out in tremulous prayer the name of Satan.

Cristoforo   It was you, Lorenzo. You are the vassal of Satan.

Lorenzo   I? Oh, no, sir. You imagined it. These charming masks beget so many ridiculous misunderstandings. Some jester, assuming my voice and features, has long been deceiving you with a base falsehood.

Cristoforo   But you yourself called on the name of Satan.

Lorenzo   Oh, no, my friends. (*Falling on his knees and speaking with solemnity.*) He whom I have invited to my festival and who now deigns to appear – uncover, gentlemen – is the Lord God, the ruler of heaven and earth. On your knees, knights and ladies.

Nearly all kneel. Several weep. Low exclamations: 'God in heaven! God in heaven!' **Ecco**, *the jester, rushes in, all ablaze, and runs frantically about the hall. The* **Servants**, *shouting, pursue him.*

Lorenzo   To me, Ecco; I am here.

Mario   Seize the villain. He has fired the tower.

Pietro   He has strewn fire about and the castle is burning on all sides. Save yourselves, ladies and gentlemen. In a moment the fire will seize upon the staircase.

Manucci   We must kill him. Strike him! Strike him!

Lorenzo (*to whose knees presses the blazing and almost blinded jester*)   Back! Who dares touch the messenger of God? Back, sirs!

He draws his sword.

Ecco (*trembling*)   Is it you, Lorenzo? I am blinded. The fire has burned out my eyes. Do not drive me away, Lorenzo.

Lorenzo   Brother, you shall greet our great Master along with me.

The window-glass crashes. Above appear tongues of flame commingled with volumes of black smoke. Panic and flight. Shouts.

Voices   Save yourselves! Save yourselves!

Francesca   Fly, Lorenzo, fly!

Lorenzo   Your heart has stopped beating, Ecco. Hold fast to life for at least a moment. He comes, Ecco.

Ecco (*trembling*)   Is he coming? Do you see him?

Lorenzo   I hear him, Ecco.

Ecco   I am dying, Lorenzo. But do you tell him that I am your little brother.

Lorenzo   I will tell him.

Ecco (*growing calmer*)   You know – they gave me some bells – I forgot to cut them off – I am dying, Lorenzo.

Francesca   Fly, Lorenzo!

Cristoforo   Do you not see, madam, that he is mad? If you will permit me, I will take him in my arms, as I did when he was a child, and carry him away.

He approaches **Lorenzo**, *but, encountering the point of his sword, steps back.*

Lorenzo   Stand back, sir.

Cristoforo   Well, come on, then.

He draws his sword.

Francesca   Go, Signor Cristoforo. Do not dare to touch that which belongs to God alone.

Cristoforo   Well, be it so. But I shall not leave without you, my lady.

Francesca   I leave you, Lorenzo. In the name of your unborn son, I leave you and renounce the happiness of dying with you. But I shall tell your son, Lorenzo, how the Almighty called you to himself, and he will bless your name.

The fire breaks through everywhere.

Cristoforo   Quick, madam, quick!

Francesca   Farewell, my Lorenzo; farewell, my beloved; farewell.

Lorenzo   Farewell, Signora. I regret that you wear a mask. Your voice and your words remind me of Donna Francesca. I beg of you, Signora, bear to her my last farewell.

Francesca   Farewell.

Cristoforo   Come! Away! Away!

He takes **Donna Francesca** *in his arms and, making his way through the clouds of smoke, carries her out. There remain only* **Lorenzo** *and* **Ecco**, *the latter having fallen at* **Lorenzo**'s *feet. The fire spreads over everything. Outside the broken windows and the ruined doors, in the midst of the black volumes of smoke, appear the* **Black Maskers**. *One can see their ineffectual efforts to enter the castle, their silent struggle with the fire, which lightly and buoyantly tosses them back. Again and again they rush forward, only to fall back writhing with pain.*

Lorenzo   Up, Ecco, the Lord is coming.

He touches **Ecco**, *but the jester falls lifeless from him. The flames now completely surround them. The* **Black Maskers** *have disappeared. The crackling and roaring of the triumphant fire is heard.*

Lorenzo (*solemnly*)   I greet thee, O Lord. While I still lay in the cradle my father touched me with his sword and consecrated me a Knight of the Holy Ghost. Do thou touch me, O Lord, if I am worthy of thy accolade. (*Falling on his knees.*) But this truth, I aver, O Lord, is known to all people in the world: Lorenzo, Duke of Spadaro, has no serpent in his heart!

The fire envelops him. Everything falls in ruins.

Curtain.

EROTICISM AND IDOLATRY

La Gioconda

Gabriele D'Annunzio (1898)

Translated by Arthur Symons

Gabriele D'Annunzio (1863–1938) had a professional and an amorous relationship with the influential Italian performer Eleonora Duse, and dedicated the play to her. *La Gioconda* is one of four plays dedicated to her. More specifically, it is dedicated to her hands, which would seem a strange dedication were it not for the fact that the play's ill-fated protagonist, Silvia Settala (played by Duse in one of many collaborations between the artist lovers), has her hands crushed by a statue made by her husband – Lucio Settala – that depicts the transcendent beauty of his model and mistress: Gioconda Dianti. In a fit of rage prompted by a belief that Lucio may no longer love her, Gioconda casts down her own icon '*as if she is invaded by a turbid destructive will, as by a demon*', only for the statue to be saved once Silvia dives beneath it, breaking both its fall – and her hands. There is no *deux ex machina* in this work, as there is in Pierre Quillard's symbolist play *La Fille aux Mains coupées* (*The Girl with Cut-off Hands*, 1886), which, while stylistically very different, bears several thematic similarities with D'Annunzio's drama.[1] Instead, the remainder of the play depicts Silvia as a pitiable 'mutilated woman' who is no longer capable of embracing her daughter, and whose amputated hands seem intended to position and shame her as a half-formed creature. These very same appendages, in Duse's hands, were also symbolic of the destruction of the gestural apparatus for which the great actress was famed.

D'Annunzio's play, understood as a work that appeals to a decadent sensibility, needs to be understood in the context of a specific cultural discourse concerned with Italian literature and culture in the second half of the nineteenth century: *Decadentismo*, through which texts canonized as *Decadenti* came to be read and understood. The discourse of *Decadentismo* approaches decadence largely in a broad and pejorative sense as identifying an 'epochal *crisis* of values, rather than signs of a *critique* of those values'.[2] This 'crisis' was linked to the perception of decline and decay across multiple areas – social, political, national, moral, physiological, and so on, as well as declining standards in the quality and integrity of art and literature – that were seen to be at odds with Italian renewal (although some, like Gian Pietro Lucini, saw decadence as a necessary part of the process of renewal). Walter Binni and, more influentially still, Benedetto Croce in the early twentieth century strived to distinguish notions of epochal crisis from a historically bound movement in literature marked by its distinction from a nascent modernism inspired by various European trends. For Croce, the literature exemplified by D'Annunzio in the late nineteenth century was complicit in the decline of literary values and the blocking of civilisational progress because of its reactionary

---

1   Quillard's verse drama focuses on a young girl – referred to simply as The Girl – who is meant to look like she has been sculpted from marble. Her hands are willingly severed by a servant after what seems to be an ecstatic encounter with her father, only to have them regrow as she is cast adrift at sea, journeying toward a transcendent, ethereal world. A similar story is also depicted in Giambattista Basile's *Pentamerone* (1634–36) and Grimm's *The Girl without Hands* (1812), and precedents can be found throughout Europe, the Middle East, Japan, Africa, and North and South America. See Julie Dashwood, 'The Metamorphosis of a Fairy-Tale: Quillard, D'Annunzio and *The Girl With Cut-Off Hands*', in *Romancing Decay: Ideas of Decadence in European Culture*, ed. Michael St. John (Aldershot: Ashgate, 1999), 118–27 (120).

2   Mario Moroni, 'Sensuous Maladies: The Construction of Italian *Decadentismo*', in *Italian Modernism: Italian Culture between Decadentism and Avant-Garde*, ed. Luca Somigli and Mario Moroni (Toronto: University of Toronto Press, 2004), 65–85 (69), original emphasis.

aristocratic sensibility, and because of the aestheticism and imperialism that D'Annunzio vaunted most explicitly at the time, which he deemed irrational and overpowering. The crushing of Silvia's hands in *La Giaconda* epitomises the kind of submission to aestheticism that bore the brunt of Croce's critique, with the playwright apparently falling foul of an 'irrational' moral fault that relishes sacrifice, neurosis, and suffering in the name of art.

Scholars have since highlighted a more dialogical relationship between *Decadentismo* and post-First World War poetry and literature. A failure to recognise this dialogism has resulted in 'a moral judgment on the validity of certain literary experiences which has traditionally functioned to repress them (as in the case of D'Annunzio)'.[3] Croce's criticisms of D'Annunzio's aestheticism played an important role in turning many in the next generation of authors against D'Annunzio, which has led to a too-easy dismissal of his poetic studies of eroticism and the death drive in plays like *La Giaconda* that find female characters with the most depth and intensity 'stealing the scene' from more two-dimensional male counterparts.[4] Nonetheless, there is good reason why a contemporary audience might be uneasy about accommodating D'Annunzio's sadistic eroticism in a twenty-first century repertoire. He is also better-known in Italy today as an eccentric nationalist who played an important role in the rise of fascist sentiment in Italy. D'Annunzio made it his mission to break up 'the decadent old forms of Italian society in order to make the nation anew',[5] but his embrace of decadence as a poetic and theatrical style also complicates his self-fashioning as a beacon of renewal: at once forward-looking in wanting to reshape the nation, and at the same time relishing retreat into the decadent worlds he imagined for both page and stage.

It would be egregious to omit from an anthology of decadent plays a work and an author who together represent the darker side of decadence. *La Gioconda* is a seductive, engrossing play, but the power of its seduction must be read alongside the context in which it was produced, the means and ramifications of its seductiveness, and the legacy of a poet, novelist and playwright who at one time was among the most influential leaders in a fascist nation. The play's eroticism, and its relationship to both his private life with Duse and positioning of himself as an idol in the Italian imaginary, make it an essential calling point in any study of decadent drama that takes seriously the complicated and at times unpalatable qualities of a decadent sensibility as imagined by one of its most notorious exemplars.

---

3 Luca Somigli and Mario Moroni, 'Modernism in Italy: An Introduction', in Somigli and Moroni, *Italian Modernism*, 3–31 (7).

4 Lucia Re, 'D'Annunzio, Duse, Wilde, Bernhardt: Author and Actress between Decadence and Modernity', in Somigli and Moroni, *Italian Modernism*, 86–129 (103).

5 Lucy Hughes-Hallett, *The Pike: Gabriele D'Annunzio: Poet, Seducer and Preacher of War* (London: Fourth Estate, 2013), 62.

Cosa bella mortal passa, e non d'arte

Leonardo da Vinci

For Eleonora Duse of the beautiful hands

Characters

Lucio Settala
Lorenzo Gaddi
Cosimo Dalbo
Silvia Settala
Francesca Doni
Gioconda Dianti
Little Beata
La Sirenetta

Place

At Florence, and on the coast of Pisa, at the present time.

Act One

A quiet, foursquare room, in which the arrangement of everything indicates a search after a singular harmony, recalling the secret of a profound correspondence between the visible lines and the quality of the inhabiting mind that has chosen and loved them. All around seems to have been set in order by the hands of one of the thoughtful Graces. The aspect of the place evokes the image of a gentle and secluded life.

Two large windows are open on the garden beneath; through one of them can be seen, rising against the placid fields of the sky, the little hill of San Miniato,[6] and its bright Basilica, and the convent, and the church of the Cronaca, 'la Bella Villanella', the purest vessel of Franciscan simplicity.

There is a door opening into an inner room, another leading out. It is the afternoon. Through both windows enter the light, breath, and melody of April.

Scene One

Silvia Settala *and the old man* **Lorenzo Gaddi** *are seen on the threshold of the first door, side by side, as they both come into the fresh spring atmosphere.*

Silvia Settala   Ah, blessed be life! because I have always kept one hope alight, today I can bless life.

Lorenzo Gaddi   New life, dear Silvia, good brave soul, so good and so strong! The storm is over. Lucio has come back to you, full of gratitude and of tenderness, after all the evil. It is as if he were born again. Just now he had the eyes of a child.

Silvia Settala   All his goodness comes back to him when you are with him. When he calls you Maestro his voice becomes so affectionate that it must make your heart beat, the father's heart that you have for him.

Lorenzo Gaddi   Just now he had the same eyes that I saw in him when he came to me for the first time and I put the clay into his hands. His eyes were gentle and wondering; but from that moment his thumb was full of energy, a revealing thing. I have kept his first sketch. I thought of giving it to you on the day of your betrothal. I will give it to you in token of your new happiness.

Silvia Settala   Thanks, Maestro.

Lorenzo Gaddi   It is the head of a woman crowned with laurels. I remember there was rather a bad model there. As he worked, he hardly looked at her. Sometimes he seemed absorbed, sometimes anxious. There came out of his hands a sort of confused mask, through which one half saw I know not what heroic lineaments. For some moments he remained perplexed and discouraged, almost ashamed, at the sight of his work, not daring to turn to me. But suddenly, before letting it out of his hands, with a

---

6   San Miniato: town in Tuscany, Italy.

few touches he set a crown of laurel about the head. How it delighted me! He wanted to crown in the clay his own unaccomplished dream. The end of his day's work was an act of pride and of faith. I loved him from that instant, for that crown. I will give you the sketch. Perhaps, if you look at it closely, you will discover the ardent face of Sappho, that ideal figure which, only a few years later, he was able to bring to perfection, in a masterpiece.

Silvia Settala (*listening eagerly*)   Sit down, sit down, Maestro; stay a little longer, I beg of you. Sit here, by the window. Stay a few minutes longer. I have a thousand things to tell you, and I do not know how to tell you one of them. If I could overcome this continual tremor! I want you to understand.

Lorenzo Gaddi   Is it joy that makes you tremble?

He sits down near the window. **Silvia**, *leaning back against the window-sill, remains with her face turned towards him; her face is seen against the blue air, the little hill standing out in the background.*

Silvia Settala   I do not know if it is joy. Sometimes everything that has been, all the evil, all the sorrow, and even the blood, and the wound, all melts away, vanishes, is wiped out into oblivion, is there no more. Sometimes everything that has been, all that horrible weight of memory, thickens and thickens, and grows compact and opaque and hard as a wall, like a rock that I shall never be able to surmount. Just now, when you spoke to me, when you offered me that unexpected gift, I thought: 'Ah, now I shall take that gift in my hands, that morsel of clay into which he cast the first seed of his dreams, as into a fruitful soil; I shall take it in my hands, I shall go to him smiling, bearing intact the better part of his soul and of his life; and I shall not speak, and he will see in me the guardian of all his goods, and he will never go away from me any more, and we shall be young again, we shall be young again!' I thought that, and the thought and the act were mingled in one, with an incredible ease. Your words transfigured the world. Then, do you know, a breath passed, a vapour, the merest breathing, a mere nothing, and cast down everything, and destroyed everything, and the anxiety came back, and the dread, and the tremor. O April!

Suddenly she turns to the light, drawing a deep breath.

How this air troubles one, and yet how pure it is! All one's hope and despair pass in the wind with the dust of flowers. (*She leans out, calling.*) Beata! Beata!

Lorenzo Gaddi   Is the little one in the garden?

Silvia Settala   There she is, she is running about between the rose-bushes. She is wild with delight. Beata! She has hidden herself behind a hedge, the rogue. She is laughing. Do you hear her laughing? Ah, when she laughs, I know the joy of flowers when they are filled to the brim with dew. That is how her fresh laughter fills my heart to overflowing.

Lorenzo Gaddi   Perhaps Lucio too hears her, and is consoled.

Silvia Settala (*grave and trembling, leaning towards the* **Maestro**, *and taking his hands*)   You think then that he will really be healed of all his wounds? You think he will come back to me with all his soul? Did you feel that, when you saw him, when you talked with him? What did your heart say?

Lorenzo Gaddi   It seemed to me, just now, that he had the look of a man who begins to live over again with a new sense of life. He who has seen the face of death cannot but have seen in that instant the face of truth also. The bandage is taken off his eyes. He knows you now wholly.

Silvia Settala   Maestro, Maestro, if you deceive yourself, if it is a vain hope, what will become of me? All my strength is worn out.

Lorenzo Gaddi   But what is there now to fear?

Silvia Settala   He wanted to die; but *the other*, the other woman lives, and I know that she is implacable.

Lorenzo Gaddi   And what could she do now?

Silvia Settala   She could do anything, if she were still loved.

Lorenzo Gaddi   Still loved? Beyond death?

Silvia Settala   Beyond death. Ah, if you knew my anguish! It was for her that he wanted to die, in a moment of rage and of delirium. Think how he must have loved her, if the thought of me, if the thought of Beata, could not restrain him! Then, in that awful moment, he was her prey wholly; he was at the height of his fever, of his agony, and all the rest of the world was blotted out. Think how he must have loved her!

The woman's voice is subdued but lacerating. The old man bows his head.

Silvia Settala   Now, who can say what took place in him, after the blow, when the mist of death passed before his soul? Has he awakened without memory? Does he see an abyss between his life as it renews itself and the part of himself that he left behind in that mist? Or else, or else the image has risen again out of the depths, and remains there, against the shadow, dominant, in indestructible relief? Tell me!

Lorenzo Gaddi (*perplexed*)   Who can say?

Silvia Settala (*in a sorrowful voice*)   Ah, now you yourself dare not console me any longer. Then, it is so? There is no help?

Lorenzo Gaddi (*taking her hands*)   No, no, Silvia. I meant: who can say what change is brought about in a nature like his by so mysterious a force? Everything in him speaks of some new good thing that has come to him. Look at him when he smiles. Just now, yonder, before you left him to come out with me, when he kissed those dear hands of yours, did you not feel that his whole heart melted into tenderness and humility?

Silvia Settala (*her face slightly flushed*)   Yes, it is true.

Lorenzo Gaddi (*looking at her hands*)   Dear, dear hands, brave and beautiful, steadfast and beautiful! Your hands are extraordinarily beautiful, Silvia. If sorrow has too often set them together, it has sublimated them also, perfected them. They are perfect. Do you remember the woman of Verrocchio, the woman with the bunch of flowers, with the clustering hair? Ah, she is there!

He perceives, from the look and smile of **Silvia**, *that there is a copy of the bust on a little cupboard in a corner of the room.*

Lorenzo Gaddi   So you have realised the relationship. Those two hands seem of the same blood as yours, they are of the same essence. They live – do they not? – with so luminous a life that the rest of the figure is darkened by them.

Silvia Settala (*smiling*)   Oh, young, always young in soul!

Lorenzo Gaddi   When Lucio comes back to his work, he ought to model your hands the first day. I have a fragment of ancient marble, found in the Oricellari Gardens. I will give it to him, that he may chisel them in that, and lay them up like a votive offering.

Silvia Settala (*a cloud passing across her forehead*)   Do you think he will come back to his work soon? Will he wish to? Have you spoken of it with him?

Lorenzo Gaddi   Yes, just now, when you were not there.

Silvia Settala   What did he say?

Lorenzo Gaddi   Vague, delicious things, a convalescent's dreams. I know them. I too was once ill. It seems to him now as if he has lost hold of his art, as if he had no longer any power over it, as if he had become a stranger to beauty. Then again it seems to him as if his thumbs had assumed a magic force, and that at a mere touch he can evoke forms out of the clay as easily as in dreams. He is somewhat uneasy about the disorder in which he fancies his studio was left, on the Mugnone yonder.[7] He asked me to go and see. Have you the key?

Silvia Settala (*anxiously*)   There is the caretaker.

Lorenzo Gaddi   How long is it since you were there?

Silvia Settala   Since *this* began. I never had the courage to go back again. I feel as if I should see the stains of blood, and find traces of her everywhere. She is still mistress there. That place is still *her* domain.

Lorenzo Gaddi   The domain of a statue.

Silvia Settala   No, no. Do you not know that she had a key? She came and went there as if it belonged to her. Ah, I have told you, I have told you; she lives, and is implacable.

Lorenzo Gaddi   Are you sure that she came back, after what happened?

Silvia Settala   Sure. Her insolence has no bounds. She is without pity and without shame.

---

7   Mugnone: river in Florence, Italy.

Lorenzo Gaddi   And he, Lucio, does he know?

Silvia Settala   He does not know. But he will surely know it sooner or later. She will find a way of letting him know.

Lorenzo Gaddi   But why?

Silvia Settala   Because she is implacable, because she will not relinquish her prey.

A pause. The old man is silent. The woman's voice becomes harsh and tremulous.

Silvia Settala   And the statue, the Sphinx, have you seen it?

Lorenzo Gaddi (*after a moment's hesitation*)   Yes. I have seen it.

Silvia Settala   Was it he who showed it to you?

Lorenzo Gaddi   Yes, one day last October. He had just finished it.

A pause.

Silvia Settala (*in a trembling voice, which almost fails her*)   It is wonderful, is it not? Tell me.

Lorenzo Gaddi   Yes, it is exquisitely beautiful.

Silvia Settala   For eternity!

A pause burdened with a thousand undefined and inevitable things.

The Voice of Beata (*from the garden*)   Mamma! Mamma!

Lorenzo Gaddi   The child is calling you.

Silvia Settala (*starting up and leaning out of the window*)   Beata! Ah, there she is; my sister Francesca is coming across the garden; she is coming here with Cosimo Dalbo. Do you know? Cosimo has returned from Cairo; he arrived at Florence last night. Lucio will be delighted to see him.

Lorenzo Gaddi (*rising to go*)   Good-bye, then, dear Silvia: I shall see you perhaps to-morrow.

Silvia Settala   Stay a little longer. My sister would like to see you.

Lorenzo Gaddi   I must go. I am late now.

Silvia Settala   When shall I have the gift you promised me?

Lorenzo Gaddi   Perhaps to-morrow.

Silvia Settala   No perhaps, no perhaps. I shall expect you. You must come here often, every day. Your presence does us good. Do not forsake me. I trust in you, Maestro. Remember that a menace is still banging over my head.

Lorenzo Gaddi   Do not fear. Keep up your courage!

Silvia Settala (*moving towards the door*)   Here is Francesca.

Scene Two

Francesca Doni *enters, goes up to her sister, and embraces her.* **Cosimo Dalbo**, *who follows her, shakes hands with* **Lorenzo Gaddi**, *who is on the point of going out.*

Francesca Doni   Do you see whom I am bringing? We met outside the gate. How are you, Maestro? Are you going just as I come in?

She shakes hands with the old man.

Silvia Settala (*holding out her hand cordially*)   Welcome back, Dalbo. We were expecting you. Lucio is impatient to see you.

Cosimo Dalbo (*with affectionate solicitude*)   How is he now? Is he up? Is he quite well?

Silvia Settala   He is convalescent; still a little weak; but getting stronger every day. The wound is entirely closed. You will see him in a minute. The doctor is with him; I will go and tell him you are here. It will be a great delight for him. He has asked after you several times today. He is impatient to see you. (*She turns to* **Lorenzo Gaddi**.) Tomorrow, then.

She goes out with a light and rapid step. The sister, the **Maestro**, *and the friend follow her with their eyes.*

Francesca Doni (*with a kindly smile*)   Poor Silvia! For the last few days, she seems as if she had wings. When I look at her sometimes, it seems to me as if she is going to take flight towards happiness. And no one deserves happiness more; is it not true, Maestro? You know her.

Lorenzo Gaddi   Yes, she is really as your sisterly eyes see her. She comes winged out of her martyrdom. There is a sort of incessant quiver in her. I felt it just now, when she stood near me. Truly she is in a state of grace. There is no height to which she could not attain. Lucio has in his hands a life of flame, an infinite force.

Francesca Doni   You were with him some time today.

Lorenzo Gaddi   Yes, hours.

Francesca Doni   How was he?

Lorenzo Gaddi   Running over with sweetness, and a little bewildered. You will see him presently, Dalbo. His sensitiveness is a danger. Those who love him can do him much good and much harm. A word agitates and convulses him. Watch over all your words, you who love him. Good-bye. I must go.

Takes leave of them both.

Francesca Doni   Good-bye, Maestro. Perhaps we shall see you here again to-morrow. I hope so. You have a horror of my stairs!

She accompanies the old man to the door; then returns to the friend.

Francesca Doni   What a fire of intelligence and of goodness, in that old man! When he comes into a room he seems to bring comfort to all. The sad rejoice and the merry become fervent.

Cosimo Dalbo   He inspires the soul; he belongs to the noblest race of mankind. His work is a continual exaltation of life; it is the continual force of communicating a spark, whether to his statues or to the creatures whom he meets by the way. Lorenzo Gaddi seems to me to deserve a far higher fame than he receives from his contempories.

Francesca Doni   It is true, it is true. If you knew what energy and what delicacy he showed, in that horrible affair! When the thing happened, my sister was not there; she was with our mother, at Pisa, with Beata. The thing happened in the studio, there, on the Mugnone, in the evening. Only the caretaker heard the report. When he discovered the truth, he ran to tell Lorenzo Gaddi before any one else. In the anguish and horror of that winter evening, in the midst of all the confusion and uncertainty, he alone never lost his presence of mind, nor had a single instant's hesitation. He preserved a strange lucidity, by which every one was dominated. He made every arrangement: all obeyed him. It was he who had poor Lucio brought to the house here, half dead. The doctor despaired of saving him. He alone declared, with an obstinate faith: 'No, he will not die, he will not die, he cannot die'. I believed him. Ah, what a heroic night, Dalbo. And then the arrival of Silvia, his telling her himself, forbidding her to enter the room where a mere breath might have quenched that glimmer of life: and her strength, her incredible endurance under watching and waiting for whole weeks, the proud and silent vigilance with which she guarded the threshold as if to hinder the coming of death!

Cosimo Dalbo   And I was far away, unconscious of all, blissfully idle in a boat on the Nile! Yet I had a kind of presentiment, before leaving. That was why I tried every means to persuade Lucio to go with me, as we had often dreamed of doing together. He had then finished his statue; and I thought that his liberty was in that wonderful marble. He said, 'Not yet!' And a few months after he was seeking it in death. Ah, if I had not gone away, if I had stayed by him, if I had been more faithful, if I had known how to defend him against the enemy, nothing would have happened.

Francesca Doni   There is nothing to regret if so much good can come out of so much evil. Who knows in what sadness of despair my sister might have perished, if the violence of that act had not suddenly reunited her to Lucio! But do not think that the enemy has laid down arms. She has not abandoned the field.

Cosimo Dalbo   Who? Gioconda Dianti?

Francesca Doni (*motioning to him to be silent, and lowering her voice*)   Do not say that name!

Scene Three

Lucio Settala *appears on the threshold of the door, leaning on the arm of* **Silvia**; *he is pale and thin, and his eyes look extraordinarily large with suffering; a faint, sweet smile gives refinement to a voluptuous mouth.*

Lucio Settala   Cosimo!

Cosimo Dalbo (*turning and running up to him*)   Oh, Lucio, dear, dear friend!

He puts his arms about the convalescent, while **Silvia** *moves aside, nearer to her sister, and goes out with her, slowly, pausing for a moment to look at her husband before going.*

Cosimo Dalbo   You are well again, are you not? You are not suffering now? I find you a little pale, a little thin, but not so very much. You look as I have seen you sometimes after a period of feverish work, when you have been with your clay for twelve hours a day, consumed with that fire. Do you remember?

Lucio Settala (*looking confusedly about him, to see if* **Silvia** *is still in the room*)   Yes, yes.

Cosimo Dalbo   Then too your eyes looked larger. . . .

Lucio Settala (*with an indefinable, almost childish restlessness*)   And Silvia? Where is Silvia gone? Wasn't she here with Francesca?

Cosmo Dalbo   They have left us alone.

Lucio Settala   Why? She thinks, perhaps. . . . No, I have nothing to tell you, I know nothing now any more. Perhaps you know. For me, no; I don't remember. I don't want to remember. Tell me about yourself! Tell me about yourself! Is the desert beautiful?

He speaks in a singular way, as if in a dream, with a mixture of agitation and stupor.

Cosimo Dalbo   I will tell you. But you must not tire yourself. I will tell you all my pilgrimage; I will come here every day, if I may; I will stay with you as long as you like, only not long enough to tire you. Sit here.

Lucio Settala (*smiling*)   Do you think I am so feeble?

Cosimo Dalbo   No, you are all right now, but it is better for you not to tire yourself. Sit here.

He makes him sit down near the window, and looks out at the hill clearly outlined against the April sky.

Cosimo Dalbo   Ah, my dear friend, I have seen marvellous things with these eyes, and they have drunk light in comparison with which this seems ashen; but, when I see again a simple line like that (look at San Miniato!) I seem to find myself again, after an interval of wandering. Look at that dear hill! The pyramid of Cheops does not make one forget the Bella Villanella; and more than once, in the gardens of Koubbeh and Gizeh, hives of honey, chewing a grain of resin, I thought of a slim Tuscan cypress on the edge of a narrow grove of olives.[8]

Lucio Settala (*half closing his eyelids under the breath of spring*)   It is good to be here, is it not? There is an odour of violets. Perhaps there is a bunch of violets in the room. Silvia puts them everywhere, even under my pillow,

---

8   Herodotus attributed the Great Pyramid of Giza to King Cheops (a Hellenic rendering of Khufu). A grand nineteenth-century palace also stands at Koubbeh in Egypt.

Cosimo Dalbo   Do you know, I have brought you the violets of the desert, between the pages of a Koran. I gathered them in the garden of a Persian monastery, near the Thebaid, on the side of the Mokattam, on an eminence of sand.[9] There, in a cavern dug out of the mountain, covered with carpets and cushions, the monks offer their visitors a tea with a special flavour, Arab tea, perfumed with violets.

Lucio Settala   And you have brought them for me, buried in a book! How happy you were to be able to gather them, so far away; and I might have been with you.

Cosimo Dalbo   There, all was oblivion. I went up by a long, straight stone staircase, that leads from the foot of the mountain to the gate of the Bectaschiti.[10] The desert was all about; vast, hallucinating dryness, in which there was no life but the stirring of wind and the quivering of heat. I could only distinguish here and there, between the sand-heaps, the white stones of Arab cemeteries. I heard the crying of hawks high up in the sky. I saw on the Nile multitudes of boats with great lateen sails, white, slow, going on, going on, like snow-flakes. And little by little I was caught up into an ecstasy that you can never have known, the ecstasy of light.

Lucio Settala (*in a far off voice*)   And I might have been with you, loitering, forgetting, dreaming, drunk with light. You went down the Nile, did you not? in an ancient boat loaded with wine-skins, sacks, and cages. You landed on an island towards evening; you were dressed in white serge; you were thirsty; you drank at a spring; you walked barefoot upon flowers; and the odour was so strong that you seemed to have forgotten hunger. Ah, I thought, I felt, these things from my pillow. And I followed you through the desert, when the fever was at its height; through a desert of red sand, sown with glittering stones that splintered crackling like twigs in the fire.

A pause. He leans forward a little, saying in a clear voice and with open eyes:
And the Sphinx?

Cosimo Dalbo   I saw it first at night, by the light of stars, sunken into the sand that still keeps the violent imprint of whirlwinds. The face and the croup rose out of that quieted storm, all that was human and all that was bestial in it. The face, whose mutilations were hidden by the shadow, seemed to me at that moment exquisitely beautiful: calm, august, cerulean as the night, almost meek. There is nothing in the world, Lucio, so much alone as that; but my mind was, as it were, before multitudes who had slept, and on whose eyelashes the dew had fallen. Then I saw it again by day. The face was bestial, like the croup; the nose and throat were eaten away; the droppings of birds fouled the fillets. It was the heavy wingless monster imagined by the excavators of tombs, by the embalmers of corpses. And I saw, in the sun before me, your Sphinx, pure and imperious, with wings imprisoned alive in the shoulder.

---

9   Thebaid: region in ancient Egypt. The Mokattam: mountain and desert plateau in the south of Cairo.
10   Bectaschiti: most likely a reference to the Bektashi Order, originally an Islamic Sufi mystic order dating back to the thirteenth century. The order underwent a revival in the mid nineteenth century, and was known for its embrace of poetry and the drinking of wine in ritualistic ceremonies.

Lucio Settala (*with a sudden emotion*)   My statue? You mean my statue? You saw it, ah, yes, before you went; and you found it beautiful.

He looks uneasily towards the door, fearing **Silvia** *might hear him, and lowers his voice.*

Lucio Settala   You found it beautiful?

Cosimo Dalbo   Exquisitely beautiful.

Lucio *covers his eyes with both hands and remains for some seconds as if trying to evoke a vision in the darkness.*

Lucio Settala (*uncovering his eyes*)   I no longer see it. It escapes me. It comes and goes in a breath, confusedly. If I had it here before me now it would seem new to me: I should cry out. And yet I carved it, with these hands!

He looks at his thin, sensitive hands. His agitation increases.

I don't know. I don't know. In the beginning of my fever, when I still had the bullet in my flesh, and the continual murmuring of death in my lost soul, I saw it standing at the foot of the bed, lit like a torch, as if I myself had moulded it out of some incandescent material. So for many days and nights I saw it through my eyelids. It grew brighter as my fever increased. When my pulse burned it turned to flame. It was as if all the blood shed at its feet had gone up it and boiled up in it . . .

Cosimo Dalbo (*uneasily, looking towards the door, with the same fear*)   Lucio, Lucio, you said just now that you knew nothing now, that you did not want to remember anything. Lucio!

He gently shakes his friend, who remains rigid.

Lucio Settala (*recollecting himself*)   Do not fear. I have left it all far, far behind me, at the bottom of the sea. The statue was drowned too, with all the rest, after the shipwreck. That is why I can no longer see it except confusedly, as if through deep water.

Cosimo Dalbo   It alone shall be saved, to live for ever; and so much sorrow shall not have been suffered in vain, so much evil shall not have been useless, if one thing so beautiful remains over, to be added to the ornament of life.

Lucio Settala (*smiling again with his faint smile and speaking in his far-off voice*)   It is true. I sometimes think of the fate of one whose ship and all that was in it went down in a storm. On a day as calm as this, he took a boat and a net, and he returned to the place of the shipwreck, hoping to draw something up out of the depth. And, after much labour, he drew on shore a statue. And the statue was so beautiful that he wept for joy to see it again; and he sat down on the sea-shore to gaze upon it, and was content with that gain, and would seek after nothing more: 'well, I forget the rest!'

He rises hastily.

Why has not Silvia come back?

He listens.

Who is laughing? Ah, it is Beata in the garden. Look; San Miniato is all gold; it lightens. Is there a more glorious light at Thebes?

Cosimo Dalbo   The ecstasy of light! I told you: you can know it nowhere else. Circles, garlands, wheels, roses of splendour, innumerable sparkles. . . . The verses of the *Paradiso* recur to one's mind.[11] Only Dante has found dazzling words. In certain hours the Nile becomes the flood of topazes, the 'marvellous gulf'. Like a stone in water, a gesture in the air arouses thousands and thousands of waves. All things swim in light; all the leaves drip with it. The women, who pass along the stream with full wine-skins, actually flame like the angelic host in the song, 'distinct in light and form'.

Lucio, *catching sight of a bunch of violets on the table, takes them up and buries his face in them, to drink in their odour.*

Lucio Settala (*still holding the violets to his nostrils and half-closing his eyes with delight*)   Are the women of the Nile beautiful?

Cosimo Dalbo   Some, in youth, have bodies of marvellous purity and elegance. You, who like firm and active muscles, a certain acerbity in form, long, nervous legs, would find incomparable models there. How often have I thought of you! In the island of Elephantina[12] I had a little friend of fourteen; a girl golden as a date, thin, lithe, firm, with strong, arched loins, straight, strong legs, perfect knees; a very rare thing, as you know. In all that hard slenderness, which gave one the impression of a javelin, sharp and precise, three things delighted me with their infinitely soft grace: the mouth, the shadow of the eyelashes, the tips of the fingers. She braided her hair with fingers rosy-tipped like petals dyed with purple: and to watch her in that act, on the threshold of her white house, was the delight of my mornings. I should like to have taken her away with the statuettes, the scarabæi,[13] the cloths, the tobacco, the scents, the weapons. I have brought you a beautiful bow that I bought at Assouan,[14] and that is a little like her.

Lucio Settala (*with a slight perturbation, throwing back his head*)   She must have been a delicious creature!

Cosimo Dalbo   Delicious and harmless. She was like a beautiful bow, but her arrows were without venom.

Lucio Settala   You loved her?

Cosimo Dalbo   As I love my horse and my dogs.

Lucio Settala   Ah, you were happy there; your life was light and easy. It must have been the island of Elephantina where I saw you come on shore, in a dream. I might have been with you! But I will go, I will leave here. Do you not long to return? I will have a white house on the Nile; I will make my statues with the slime of the river, and set them up in that light of yours that will turn them to gold for me. Silvia! Silvia!

---

11 *Paradiso*: final part of Dante's *Divine Comedy* (1308–21).
12 Elephantine: an island on the River Nile.
13 Scarabæus: ancient Egyptian amulet.
14 Aswan: a city on the River Nile.

He calls towards the door as if seized by a sudden impatience, an anxious will to live.

Would it be too late?

Cosimo Dalbo   It is too late. The great heats are coming on.

Lucio Settala   What does it matter? I love summer heat, sultriness even. All the pomegranates will be in flower in the gardens, and when it rains they will see those large, warm drops that make the earth sigh for pleasure.

Cosimo Dalbo   But the Khamsin?[15] when all the desert rises up against the sun?

Silvia *appears on the threshold, smiling, her whole being visibly animated. She has changed her gown; she is dressed in a clearer, more spring-like colour; and she carries in her hands a bunch of fresh roses.*

Silvia Settala   What do you say, Dalbo, against the sun? Did you call, Lucio?

Lucio Settala (*re-taken by a kind of restless timidity, as of a man who feels the need of self-abandonment, to which he dares not give way*)   Yes, I called you, because I thought you were never coming back. Cosimo was telling me of so many beautiful things. I wanted you to hear them too.

He looks at his wife with surprise in his eyes, as if he discovered a new charm in her.

Were you going out?

Silvia Settala (*blushing slightly*)   Ah, you are looking at my gown. I put it on to see how it looked, while Francesca was there. My sister sends her apologies to you both for having gone without coming to say good-bye. She was in a hurry: her children were waiting for her. She hopes, Dalbo, that you will come and see her soon.

She puts the roses on a table.

Will you dine with us to-night?

Cosimo Dalbo   Thanks. I cannot to-night. My mother expects me.

Silvia Settala   Naturally. To-morrow, then?

Cosimo Dalbo   To-morrow. I will bring my presents for you, Lucio.

Lucio Settala (*with childish curiosity*)   Yes, yes, bring them, bring them.

Silvia Settala (*smiling mysteriously*)   I too am to have a present to-morrow.

Lucio Settala   From whom?

Silvia Settala   From the Maestro.

Lucio Settala   What?

Silvia Settala   You shall see.

Lucio Settala (*with a joyous movement*)   You too shall see all the beautiful things that Cosimo has brought me: cloths, scents, weapons, scarabæi. . . .

---

15 Khamsin: a dusty wind that blows across the Mediterranean and Sahara.

Cosimo Dalbo   Amulets against every evil, talismans for happiness, on Gebel-el-Tair,[16] in a Coptic convent,[17] I found the most powerful of scarabæi. The monk told me a long story of a cenobite[18] who, at the time of the first persecution, took refuge in a vault, and found a mummy there, and took it out of its swathings of balm, and restored it to life, and the resuscitated mummy, with its painted lips, told him the story of its old life, which had been one whole tissue of happiness. In the end, as the cenobite wished to convert it, it preferred to lie down again in its embalmings; but first it gave him the guardian scarabæus.[19] To tell you what use was made of it by the solitary, and through what vicissitudes it passed across the centuries into the hands of the good Copt, would take too long. Certainly, a more powerful one is not in all Egypt. Here it is: I offer it to you, I offer it to you both.

He hands the amulet to **Silvia**, *who examines it carefully and then passes it to* **Lucio**, *with a sudden light in her eyes.*

Silvia Settala   How blue it is. It is brighter than a turquoise. Look.

Cosimo Dalbo   The Copt said to me: 'Small as a gem, great as a destiny!'

Lucio *turns the mystic stone between his fingers, which tremble a little, fumblingly.*

Cosimo Dalbo   Good-bye then: to-morrow! Good night.

Silvia Settala (*picking a rose out of the bunch and offering it to him*)   Here is a fresh rose in exchange for the amulet. Take it to your mother.

Cosimo Dalbo   Thanks. To-morrow!

He salutes them again and goes out.

Scene Four

Lucio Settala *smiles timidly, turning the scarabæus between his fingers, while* **Silvia** *puts the roses in a vase. Both, in the silence, hear the beating of their anxious hearts. The setting sun gilds the room. In the square of the window is seen the pallid sky; San Miniato shines on the height; the air is soft, without a breath of wind.*

Lucio Settala (*looking into the air, and listening anxiously*)   There is a bee in the room.

Silvia Settala (*raising her hand*)   A bee?

Lucio Settala   Yes. Don't you hear it?

Both listen to the murmur.

Silvia Settala   You are right.

---

16 Jabal al-Tair: island in Yemen, also known as the mountain of the birds.
17 Coptic monasticism: derives from St Anthony of Egypt, the first monk.
18 Cenobite: community-driven monastic tradition.
19 Scarabæus: ancient Egyptian amulet.

Lucio Settala   Perhaps you brought it in with the roses.

Silvia Settala   Beata picked these.

Lucio Settala   I heard her laughing, just now, down in the garden.

Silvia Settala   How pleased she is to be home again!

Lucio Settala   It was a good thing to send her away then.

Silvia Settala   She is stronger and lovelier for having breathed the odour of the pines. How good the spring must be at Bocca d'Arno![20] Would you not like to go there for a while?

Lucio Settala   There, by the sea. . . . Would you like it?

Their voices are altered by a slight tremor.

Silvia Settala   It has always been a dream of mine to pass one spring there.

Lucio Settala (*choked with emotion*)   Your dream is mine, Silvia.

The amulet falls from his hands.

Silvia Settala (*stooping quickly to pick it up*)   Ah, you have let it fall! They would say it is a bad omen. See. I put it on Beata's head. 'Small as a gem, great as a destiny!'

She lays the amulet delicately upon the roses.

Lucio Settala (*holding out his hands to her, as if imploring*)   Silvia! Silvia!

Silvia Settala (*running to him*)   Do you feel ill? You look paler. Ah, you have tired yourself too much today, you are worn out. Sit here, come. Will you sip some of this cordial? Do you feel as if you are going to faint? Tell me!

Lucio Settala (*taking her hands with an outburst of love*)   No, no, Silvia; I never felt so well. You, you sit down, sit here; and I at your feet, at last, with all my soul, to adore you, to adore you!

She sinks back on the divan and he falls on his knees before her. She is convulsed and trembling, and lays her hand on his lips, as if to keep him from speaking. Breath and words pass between her fingers.

Lucio Settala   At last! It was like a flood coming from far off, a flood of all the beautiful things and all the good things that you have poured out on my life since you began to love me; and my heart overflowed, ah, overflowed so that I staggered under the weight of it, and fainted and died of the pain and the sweetness of it, because I dared not say. . . .

Silvia Settala (*her face white, her voice almost extinct*)   No more, say no more!

Lucio Settala   Hear me, hear me! All the sorrows that you have suffered, the wounds that you have received without a cry, the tears that you have hidden lest I should have shame and remorse, the smiles with which you have veiled your agonies,

---

20 Bocca D'Arno: the mouth of the river Arno in Tuscany, Italy.

your infinite pity for my wanderings, your invincible courage in the face of death, your hard fight for my life, your hope always alight beside my bed, your watches, cares, continual tremors, expectation, silence, joy, all that is deep, all that is sweet and heroic in you, I know it all, I feel it all, dear soul; and, if violence is enough to break a yoke, if blood is enough for redemption (oh, let me speak!) I bless the evening and the hour that brought me dying into this house of your martyrdom and of your faith to receive once more at your hands, these divine hands that tremble, the gift of life.

He presses his convulsed mouth against the palms of her hands, and she gazes at him through the tears that moisten her eyelids, transfigured with unexpected happiness.

Silvia Settala (*in a faint and broken voice*)   No more, say no more! My heart cannot bear it. You suffocate me with joy. I longed for one word from you, only one, no more; and all at once you flood me with love, you fill up every vein, you raise me to the other side of hope, you outpass my dreams, you give me happiness beyond all expectation. Ah, what did you say of my sorrows? What is sorrow endured, what is silence constrained, what is a tear, what is a smile, now, in the face of this flood that bears me away? I feel as if by-and-by, for you, for you, I shall be sorry not to have suffered more. Perhaps I have not reached the depths of sorrow, but I know that I have reached the height of happiness.

She blindly caresses his head, as it lies on her knees.

Silvia Settala   Rise, rise! Come nearer to my heart, rest on me, give way to my tenderness, press my hands on your eyelids, be silent, dream, call back the deep forces of your life. Ah, it is not me alone that you must love, not me alone, but the love I have for you: love my love! I am not beautiful, I am not worthy of your eyes, I am a humble creature in the shadow; but my love is wonderful, it is on high, on high, it is alone, it is sure as the day, it is stronger than death, it can work miracles; it shall give you all that you ask. You can ask more than you have ever hoped.

She draws him to her heart, raising his head. His eyes are closed, his lips tight set, he is as pale as death, drunk and exhausted with emotion.

Silvia Settala   Rise, rise! Come nearer to my heart; rest on me. Do you not feel that you can give yourself up to me? that nothing in the world is surer than my breast? that you can find it always? Ah, I have sometimes thought that this certitude might intoxicate you like glory.

He kneels before her with uplifted face; she with both hands pushes back the hair to uncover his whole forehead.

Silvia Settala   Beautiful, strong forehead, sealed and blessed! May all the germs of spring awaken in your new thoughts!

Trembling she presses her lips to his forehead. Silently he stretches out his arms towards the suppliant. The sunset is like a dawn.

Act Two

The same room, the same hour of the day. A cloudy and changing sky is seen through the window.

Scene One

Cosimo Dalbo *is seated by a table, on which he rests his elbows, putting his hand to his forehead, grave and thoughtful.* **Lucio Settala** *is on foot, restless and agitated; he moves about the room uncertainly, giving way to the anguish that oppresses him.*

Lucio Settala   Yes, I am going to tell you. Why should I hide the truth? From you! I have had a letter, I have opened it, read it. . . .

Cosimo Dalbo   From Gioconda?

Lucio Settala   From her.

Cosimo Dalbo   A love letter?

Lucio Settala   It burnt my fingers.

Cosimo Dalbo   Well? (*He hesitates. In a voice changed by emotion*) You still love her?

Lucio Settala (*with a shudder of dread*)   No, no, no.

Cosimo Dalbo (*looking into the depths of his eyes*)   You no longer love her?

Lucio Settala (*entreatingly*)   Oh, do not torture me. I suffer.

Cosimo Dalbo   But what is it then that distresses you?

A pause.

Lucio Settala   Every day, at an hour that I know, she waits for me, there, at the foot of the statue, alone.

Another pause. The two men seem as if they saw before them something strong and living, a Will, evoked by those brief words.

Cosimo Dalbo   She waits for you? Where? In your studio? How could she get in?

Lucio Settala   She has a key: the key of that time.

Cosimo Dalbo   She waits for you! She thinks, she desires, then, that you should still belong to her?

Lucio Settala   You have said it.

Cosimo Dalbo   And what shall you do?

Lucio Settala   What shall I do?

A pause.

Cosimo Dalbo   You vibrate like a flame.

Lucio Settala   I suffer.

Cosimo Dalbo   You are burning.

Lucio Settala (*vehemently*)   No.

Cosimo Dalbo   Listen. She is terrible. One cannot fight against her save at a distance. That is why I wanted to take you with me, across the sea. You preferred death to the sea. Another (you know who, and your heart bleeds for her) has saved you from death. And now you can live only for her.

Lucio Settala   It is true.

Cosimo Dalbo   You must go away, fly from her.

Lucio Settala   For always?

Cosimo Dalbo   For some time.

Lucio Settala   She will wait for me.

Cosimo Dalbo   You will be stronger.

Lucio Settala   Her power will have increased. She will have more profoundly impregnated with herself the place that is dear to me for the work's sake that was achieved there. I shall see her from far off like the guardian of a statue into which I put the most vivid breath of my soul.

Cosimo Dalbo   You love her.

Lucio Settala (*despairingly*)   No. I do not love her. But think: she will always be the stronger: she knows what conquers and what binds me; she is armed with a fascination from which I cannot free my soul except by tearing her out of my heart. Must I try again?

Cosimo Dalbo   Ah, you are raving!

Lucio Settala   The place where I have dreamed, where I have worked, where I have wept with joy, where I have cried on glory, where I have seen death, is her conquest. She knows that I cannot keep away from it or renounce it, that the most precious part of my substance is diffused there: and she waits for me, certain.

Cosimo Dalbo   Does she then exercise an inviolable right there? Can no one forbid her entrance?

Lucio Settala (*with a profound emotion*)   Turn her out?

Cosimo Dalbo   No: but there may be another way, less hard, the simplest way: ask her for the key which she has no right to retain.

Lucio Settala   And who is to ask her for it?

Cosimo Dalbo   Any one of us, I myself, respectfully, in the name of necessity.

Lucio Settala   She would refuse, she would look upon you as a stranger.

Cosimo Dalbo   You yourself then.

Lucio Settala   I? I Face her?

Cosimo Dalbo   No, write to her.

A pause.

Lucio Settala (*with the accent of absolute impossibility*)   I cannot. And it would all be in vain.

Cosimo Dalbo   But there is another way: leave that house, clear out everything, take everything somewhere else. You will thus avoid the intolerable sadness of memory. How is it you do not realise that change is necessary, if your life is to renew itself, so that the companion you have found again may help you in your work? Would you have her sit where the other had been? Would you have her always see before her eyes the vision of that horrible evening?

Lucio Settala (*smiling, disheartened and bitter*)   Well, yes, you are right: we will leave here, we will go somewhere else, we will choose a beautiful solitary place, we will shake off the dust from old things, open all the windows, let in the pure air, take a heap of clay, a block of marble, set up a monument to liberty.

He breaks off. His voice becomes singularly calm.

One morning, Gioconda will knock at the new door; I shall open to her: she will come in: without surprise I shall say to her, 'Welcome'. (*Unable to restrain his bitterness.*) Ah, but you are like a child! The whole thing seems to you no more than a key. Call in a locksmith, change the lock, and I am saved.

Cosimo Dalbo (*tenderly and sadly*)   Do not be angry. At first I thought you had simply to rid yourself of an intruder. Now I see that my advice was childish.

Lucio Settala (*imploringly*)   Cosimo, my friend, do understand me!

Cosimo Dalbo   I understand, but you deny it.

Lucio Settala (*again carried away by excitement*)   I deny nothing. I deny nothing. Would you have me cry to you that I love her?

Looks about him in an aimless bewilderment. Passes his hand across his forehead with an air of suffering. Lowers his voice.

You should have let me die. Think, if I who was intoxicated with life, if I who was frantic with strength and pride, if I wanted to die, be sure I knew there was an insuperable necessity for it. Not being able to live either with or without her, I resolved to quit the world. Think: I who looked on the world as my garden, and had every lust after every beauty! Be sure, then, I knew there was an insuperable necessity, an iron destiny. You should have let me die.

Cosimo Dalbo   You have forgotten the divine miracle, cruelly.

Lucio Settala   I am not cruel. Because I was in horror of that cruelty towards which the violence of evil drew me, because I would not trample upon a more than human virtue, because I could not endure the sweetness of a little unconscious voice questioning me, because I wished to keep myself from the worst of all (do you understand?) I made my resolve. And because I am in horror of beginning over again, therefore I hate myself; because today I am like one who has taken a narcotic in despair, and who wakes up again, after a sound sleep, and finds the same old despair by his bedside.

Cosimo Dalbo   The same! And your first words are still in my ears: 'I know nothing now, I don't remember, I don't want to remember any more.' You seemed as if you had forgotten all, as if you reached out after some new good thing. The sound of your voice is still in my ears as you called to Beata's mother, getting up hurriedly, impatient, as if with an ardour that permits no delay. I still see the way you looked at her, when she entered, tremulous as hope. And, surely, that night you must needs have knelt to her, and she must have wept over you, and both together must have felt the goodness of life.

Lucio Settala   Yes, yes, it was indeed so: adoration! All my soul was prostrate at her feet, knowing all that is divine in her, with an intoxication of humility, with a fervour of unspeakable gratitude. I was carried away. You spoke of the ecstasy of light: I experienced it in that moment. Every stain was wiped out, every shadow cleared away. Life had a new splendour. I thought I was saved for ever. (*He breaks off.*)

Cosimo Dalbo   But then?

Lucio Settala   Then I knew that there was something else that must be abolished in me: the force that flows incessantly to my fingers, as if to reproduce.

Cosimo Dalbo   What do you mean?

Lucio Settala   I mean that I should perhaps have been saved, if I had forgotten art also. Those days, there in my bed, as I looked at my feeble hands, it seemed to me incredible that I should ever create again; it seemed to me as if I had lost all my power. I felt completely estranged from the world of form in which I had lived . . . *before I died.* I thought: 'Lucio Settala, the sculptor, is dead.' And I dreamt of becoming the gardener of a little garden.

He sits down, as if quieted, half closing his eyes, with a weary air, a scarcely visible smile of irony.

To prune roses, water them, pick the caterpillars off them, clip the box with shears, train the ivy up the walls, in a little garden sloping to the waters of oblivion; and not regret that one has left on the other shore a glorious park, populous with laurels, and cypresses, and myrtles, and marbles, and dreams. You see me there, happy, with shining shears, dressed in twill.

Cosimo Dalbo   I do not see you.

Lucio Settala   It is a pity, my friend.

Cosimo Dalbo   But who forbids your return to the great park? You can return to it by the alley of cypresses, and find your tutelar genius at the end of the way.

Lucio Settala (*leaping to his feet, like one who again loses self-control*)   Tutelar! Ah, you seem to heap one word on another, like bandages on lint, for fear of feeling the pulsation of life. Have you ever put your finger on an open artery, a torn tendon?

Cosimo Dalbo   Lucio, your anger grows on you every minute. You have something wry and acrid, a kind of exasperation which hinders you from being just. You are not yet out of convalescence, you are not yet well. A sudden shock has come to disturb the placid work that nature was carrying out in you. Your new-born strength festers. If my advice were worth anything, I would bid you go at once to Bocca d'Arno, as you proposed. There, between the woods and the sea, you will find once more a little calm, and you will think over what your attitude must be; and you will find too the goodness that will give you light.

Lucio Settala   Goodness! goodness! Do you think then that light must come from goodness and not from that profound instinct which turns and hurries my spirit towards the most glorious images of life? I was born to make statues. When a matrimonial form has gone out of my hands with the imprint of beauty, the office assigned to me by nature is fulfilled. I have not exceeded my own law, whether or not I have exceeded the laws of right . . . Is it not really true? Do you admit it?

Cosimo Dalbo   Proceed.

Lucio Settala (*lowering his voice*)   The sport of illusion has mated me with a creature who was never meant for me. She is a soul of inestimable price, before whom I kneel and worship. But I am not a sculptor of souls. She was not meant for me. When the other appeared before me, I thought of all the blocks of marble hidden in the caves of far mountains, that I might arrest in each of them one of her motions.

Cosimo Dalbo   But now you have obeyed the commandment of Nature, in creating your masterpiece. When I saw your statue I thought that you were free from her. You have perpetuated a frail sample of the species in an ideal and indestructible type. Are you not therefore satisfied?

Lucio Settala (*more excitedly*)   A thousand statues, not one! She is always diverse, like a cloud that from instant to instant seems changed without your seeing it change. Every motion of her body destroys one harmony and creates another yet more beautiful. You implore her to stay, to remain motionless; and across all her immobility there passes a torrent of obscure forces, as thoughts pass in the eyes. Do you understand? do you understand? The life of the eyes is the look, that indefinable thing, more expressive than any word, than any sound, infinitely deep and yet instantaneous as a breath, swifter than a flash, innumerable, omnipotent: in a word, *the look*. Now imagine the life of the look diffused over all her body. Do you understand? The quiver of an eyelid transfigures a human face and expresses an immensity of joy or sorrow. The eyelashes of the creature whom you love are lowered: the shadow encircles you as the waters encircle an island: they are raised: the flame of summer burns up the world. Another quiver: your soul dissolves like a drop of water; another: you are lord of the universe. Imagine that mystery over all her body! Imagine through all her limbs, from the forehead to the sole of the foot, that flash of lightning, like life! Can one chisel the look? The ancients made their statues blind. Now, imagine, her whole body is like the look.

A pause. He looks about him suspiciously, in fear of being heard. He comes nearer to his friend, who listens with increasing emotion.

Lucio Settala   I have told you: a thousand statues, not one. Her beauty lives in every block of marble. I felt this, with an anxiety made up of regret and fervour, one day at Carrara, when she was with me, and we saw, coming down the mountain-side, those great oxen with yokes, drawing the marble in waggons. An aspect of her perfection was enclosed for me in each of those formless masses. It seemed to me as if there went out from her towards the raw material a thousand lifegiving sparks, as from a shaken torch. We had to choose a block. I remember, it was a calm day. The marble shone in the sun like the eternal snows. We heard from time to time the rumbling of the mines that tore asunder the bowels of the silent mountain. I shall never forget that hour, though I were to die over again. She went into the midst of that concourse of white cubes, stopping before each. She leant over, observed the grain attentively, seemed to explore the inner veins, hesitated, smiled, passed on. To my eyes her garments were no covering. There was a sort of divine affinity between her flesh and the marble that she leant over until her breath touched it. A confused aspiration seemed to rise to her from that inert whiteness. The wind, the sun, the grandeur of the mountains, the long lines of yoked oxen, and the ancient curve of the yokes, and the creaking of the waggons, and the cloud that rose from the Tirreno,[21] and the lofty flight of an eagle, everything I saw exalted my spirit into a limitless poetry, intoxicated with a dream that I had never equalled. Ah, Cosimo, Cosimo, I have dared to throw away a life on which there gleams the glory of such a memory. When she laid her hand on the marble that she had chosen, and turning to me said 'This', all the mountains, from root to summit, breathed beauty.

An extraordinary fervour warms his voice and quickens his gestures. The listener is carried away by it, and makes no sign.

Lucio Settala   Ah, now you understand! You will never ask me again if I am satisfied. Now you know how furious must be my impatience when I think that she is there now, alone, at the foot of the Sphinx, awaiting me. Think, the statue rises above her, immobile, immutable, in its immunity from all sorrow; and she is there, grieving, and her life is ebbing away, and something of her perishes continually. Delay is death. But you do not know, you do not know . . . . (*He speaks as if about to confide a secret.*)

Cosimo Dalbo   What?

Lucio Settala   You do not know that I had begun another statue?

Cosimo Dalbo   Another?

---

21 Tirreno: Tyrrhenian Sea, part of the Mediterranean Sea.

Lucio Settala   Yes, it was left unfinished, sketched out in the clay. If the clay dries, all is lost.

Cosimo Dalbo   Well?

Lucio Settala   I thought it was lost. (*An irresistible smile shines in his eyes. His voice trembles.*) It is not lost; it still lives. The last touch of the thumb is there, still living. (*He makes the gesture of moulding, instinctively.*)

Cosimo Dalbo   How?

Lucio Settala   She knows the ways of the art, she knows how the clay is kept soft. Once she used to help me. She herself damped the cloths.

Cosimo Dalbo   So she thought of keeping the clay moist while you were dying!

Lucio Settala   Was not that too a way of opposing death? Was not that too an act of faith, admirable? She preserved my work.

Cosimo Dalbo   While the other preserved your life.

Lucio Settala (*gloomily, lowering his forehead, without looking at his friend, in an almost hard voice*)   Which of the two is worth more? Life is intolerable to me, if it was only given back with such a dragging weight on it. I have told you: you should have let me die. What greater renunciation can I make than that I have made? Only death could stay the rush of desire that drives my whole being, fatally, towards its own particular good. Now I live again: I myself the same man, the same force. Who shall judge me if I follow out my destiny?

Cosimo Dalbo (*terrified, taking him by the arm as if to restrain him*)   But what will you do? Have you made up your mind?

Struck by the sudden terror in the voice and gesture of his friend, **Lucio** *hesitates.*

Lucio Settala (*putting his hands through his hair feverishly*)   What shall I do? What shall I do? Do you know a more cruel torture? I am dizzy; do you understand? If I think that she is there, and waiting for me, and the hours are passing, and my strength being lost, and my ardour burning itself away, dizziness clutches hold of my soul, and I am in fear that I shall be drawn there, perhaps to-night, perhaps to-morrow. Do you know what that dizziness is? Ah, if I could reopen the wound that they have closed for me!

Cosimo Dalbo (*trying to lead him towards the window*)   Be calm, be calm, Lucio. Hush! I think I hear the voice . . .

Lucio Settala (*starting*)   Silvia's? (*He turns deathly pale.*) Yes. Be calm. You are in a fever.

He touches his forehead. **Lucio** *leans on the window-sill, as if all his strength is leaving him.*

Scene Two

Silvia Settala *enters with* **Francesca Doni**. *The latter has her arm round her sister's waist.*

Silvia Settala   Oh, Dalbo, are you still here?

She does not see **Lucio**'s *face, which he has turned to the open air.*

Cosimo Dalbo (*composing his countenance, and greeting* **Francesca**)   Lucio kept me.

Silvia Settala   Had he a great deal to tell you?

Cosimo Dalbo   He always has a great deal to tell me, sometimes too much. And he is tired.

Silvia Settala   Did he tell you that we are going to Bocca d'Arno on Saturday?

Cosimo Dalbo   Yes. I know.

Francesca Doni   Have you ever been to Bocca d'Arno?

Cosimo Dalbo   No, never. I know the country about Pisa: San Rossore, Gombo, San Pietro in Grado; but I never went as far as the mouth of the river. I know that the coast is most lovely.

Silvia *gazes fixedly at her husband, who remains leaning motionless against the window-sill.*

Francesca Doni   Delicious at this time of the year: a low, open coast, with fine sand: sea, river, and woods: the scent of resin and sea-grass: sea-gulls, nightingales. You ought to come often and see Lucio while he is there.

Cosimo Dalbo   With pleasure.

Silvia Settala   We can put you up.

She leaves her sister and goes towards her husband, with her light step.

Francesca Doni   Our mother has a simple house there, but it is large, white inside and outside, in a thicket of oleanders and tamarinds, and there is an Empire spinet,[22] which used to belong – fancy to whom? – to a sister of Napoleon, the Duchess of Lucca, the terrible, bony Elisa Baciocchi:[23] a spinet that sometimes wakes and weeps under Silvia's fingers; and there is a boat, if the Napoleonic relic doesn't tempt you, a lovely boat, as white as the house.

---

22 Spinet: a small keyboard instrument.
23 Elisa Baciocchi (1777–1820, also known as Elisa Bonaparte) was Napoleon's sister. She controlled Lucca and Piombino under French occupation, and wielded considerable political power. She also established the Académie des Beaux-Arts (Academy of Fine Arts), connecting the Tuscan city of Carrara with the rest of Europe as one of its most important suppliers of white marble – and marble statues.

Silvia *leans in silence against* **Lucio**'s *shoulder, as if expectant. He remains absorbed.*

Cosimo Dalbo   To live in a boat, on the water, aimlessly, there is nothing so refreshing. I have lived like that for weeks and weeks.

Francesca Doni   We ought to put our convalescent on a boat, and confide him to the good sea.

Silvia Settala (*touching her husband lightly on the shoulder*)   Lucio! (*He starts and turns.*) What are you doing? We are here. Here is Francesca.

He looks his wife in the face, hesitatingly; then tries to smile.

Lucio Settala   There is a shower coming. I was looking for the first drops: the odour of the earth. . . .

He turns towards the window, and holds out his open hands; they tremble visibly.

Francesca Doni   April either weeps or laughs.

Lucio Settala   Oh, Francesca, how are you?

Francesca Doni   Quite well. And you, Lucio?

Lucio Settala   Quite well, quite well.

Francesca Doni   Are you going away on Saturday?

Lucio Settala (*looking at his wife, in a dreamy way*)   Where?

Francesca Doni   Why, to Bocca d'Arno.

Lucio Settala   Ah, yes, true. My memory is quite gone.

Silvia Settala   Do you not feel well today?

Lucio Settala   Yes, yes, quite well. The weather upsets me a little; but I feel well, pretty well. (*In the tone with which he pronounces these simple words there is an excess of dissimulation, which gives him the strangeness of a madman. It is evident that the attention of the three bystanders is intolerable to him.*) Are you going, Cosimo?

Cosimo Dalbo   Yes, I am going. It is time. (*He prepares to go.*)

Lucio Settala   I will go with you as far as the garden-gate.

He leaves the window and goes towards the door, anxiously.

Silvia Settala   Are you going without your hat?

Lucio Settala   Yes, I am hot. Don't you feel how heavy the air is?

He pauses on the threshold, waiting for his friend. A sharp pain suddenly goes through all hearts, striking everyone silent.

Cosimo Dalbo   Au revoir.

He bows in a constrained way, and goes out with **Lucio**. **Silvia** *bends her head, knitting her brows, as if she is thinking out some resolution. Then it seems as if she is lifted on a sudden wave of energy.*

Francesca Doni   Have you seen Gaddi?

Silvia Settala   Not yet. He has not come today.

Francesca Doni   Then you don't know.

Silvia Settala   What?

Francesca Doni   What he has done?

Silvia Settala   No.

Francesca Doni   He went to see Dianti.

Silvia Settala (*with restrained emotion*)   To see her! When?

Francesca Doni   Yesterday.

Silvia Settala   And you have seen him?

Francesca Doni   Yes, I met him. He told me . . .

Silvia Settala   Speak, speak!

Francesca Doni   He went to see her yesterday, about three. He sent in his name. He was admitted at once. She received him smilingly, bowed, never said a word, stood before him, waiting for the old man to speak, listened to him quietly and respectfully. You can imagine what he might have said to persuade her to give back the key, to give up any further attempts, and not trouble a peace bought back at the price of blood, and what sorrow! When he had finished she merely asked: 'Did Lucio Settala send you to me?' On his reply in the negative, she added very firmly: 'Pardon me, but I cannot admit that any one but he has the right of asking what you have asked.'

Silvia Settala (*turning pale and drawing herself up as if for a contest*)   Ah, that is her last word. Well, there is someone else who has an equal right and who will insist on her right. We shall see.

Francesca Doni (*startled*)   What are you thinking of doing, Silvia?

Silvia Settala   What is necessary.

Francesca Doni   What then?

Silvia Settala   Seeing her, facing her, in the place where she is an intruder. Do you understand?

Francesca Doni   You would go there?

Silvia Settala   Yes, I am going there. I know her time. You yourself know it. I will wait for her. She shall see. We shall meet face to face at last.

Francesca Doni   You will not do it.

Silvia Settala   Why not? Do you think I have not the courage?

Francesca Doni   I entreat you, Silvia!

Silvia Settala   Do you think I tremble?

Francesca Doni   I entreat you!

Silvia Settala   Oh, be sure, I shall not lower my eyes, I shall not faint. You ought to know me by now; I have gone through more than one ordeal.

Francesca Doni   I know, I know. Nothing is too much for you. But think: to go there, after all that, in the very place where the horrible thing happened, there, alone, face to face with that woman, who has done you so much injury.

Silvia Settala   Well? what of that? Have I once – once, Francesca! – failed to accomplish what seemed to me necessary? Tell me, have you ever known me refuse a burden? From what torture have I drawn back? I have faced many other sorrows, as you know. You are afraid that my heart will fail me if I set foot where he fell? But I had the courage then to look at him through the crack of the door, when he lay on his bed of death, and there was no one by me to support me; and, before I was allowed to go to his bedside, the surgeon's steel and the blood-stained lint passed through my hands.

Francesca Doni   Yes, yes, true: your strength is great. Nothing is too much for you. But think; this is not the same thing. It is not the same thing to go there, and to find yourself face to face with a woman whom you do not know, capable of anything, obstinate, impudent.

Silvia Settala   I have no fear of her. What she does is base. Because she thinks me weak and submissive, therefore she is bold; because I have so long remained silent and aloof, therefore she thinks she can once more get the better of me. But she is wrong. Then all I cared for was lost, all resistance was useless. Now I have won it back, and I defend it.

Francesca Doni   My God! you are throwing yourself into a hand to hand contest. And if she resists?

Silvia Settala   How resists? I have my right. I can turn her out.

Francesca Doni   Silvia, Silvia, my sister, I entreat you; wait a few days longer, think it over a little before you do this. Do not be rash.

Silvia Settala   Ah, you speak well, you who are happy, you who are safe, you whose life is secure and with nothing to threaten your peace. Wait, think over! But do you know the crisis in which I find myself today? Do you know what I am fighting for? For my own self and for Beata, for existence, for the light of my eyes. Do you see? I cannot again go through a martyrdom in which all my nerves were torn to pieces; in which every torture was tried on me. I have given sorrow all I can give it; I have felt the hard iron on my neck and on my wrists; at the day's end my sleep was taken away by the horror of the day to come, in which I should have to go on living, and, in order to live, squeeze out my heart drop by drop when it seemed empty of everything. Ah, you speak well, you! When you smile in your home your smile returns to you in a hundred rays, as if you lived in a crystal. For me, smiling was one sorrow the more; under it, I clenched my teeth; but Beata never saw a tear in my eyes. That I might fulfil the promise of her name, when there was not a fibre in me that was not wrenched asunder, my hands were always held out to her with flowers. I could not begin over again. I would rather go away myself, and find a little quiet seashore somewhere, and lie down there with Beata and let the sea take us.

Francesca Doni (*throwing her arms around her sister's neck, and kissing her*)   What are you saying? what are you saying? You ought to be afraid of nothing any longer. Does he not love you? Have you not seen all his love come back? That is what matters; all the rest is nothing.

Silvia *closes her eyes for a few instants, and the illusion brightens her face.*

Silvia Settala   Yes, yes, I have seen his love come back. It seems . . . How could I doubt that voice? When I am not there, he calls me, he looks for me; he needs me; it seems as if I am to lead his steps.

She shakes herself, withdraws from her sister's arms, and becomes anxious again.

But today. . . . Did you see him? did you look at him? Today he is not like he was yesterday. A sudden change. . . . Did you look at him when he was at the window, leaning out? Did you hear the sound of his words? Did you see how his arm trembled when he stretched it out? Ah, tell me if you too felt that something had happened, that something had disturbed him.

Francesca Doni   He is still convalescent. Think; a mere nothing is enough to disturb him, the air, the weather . . .

Silvia Settala   No, no, it is not that. And did you not see? Cosimo Dalbo too seemed to be making an effort to hide some shadow. My eyes never deceive me.

Francesca Doni   No, it did not strike me. He was talking with me.

Silvia Settala (*with increasing agitation*)   But Lucio went down to see him out, and he has not yet come back. Or perhaps he went across to the other side. (*Goes to the window, and looks through the curtains.*) Ah, he is still there, at the gate, talking, talking. He seems beside himself. (*Lifts her eyes to the clouds.*) The thunder is coming. (*Looks out again, very intently.*)

Francesca Doni   Call him!

Silvia Settala (*turning, as if seized by a terrible thought*)   I am sure of it, I am sure of it.

Francesca Doni   What are you thinking of now?

Silvia Settala (*pausing, and pronouncing the words distinctly, pale but resolute*)   Lucio knows that she is waiting for him.

Francesca Doni   He knows? How?

Silvia Settala   There is no doubt, there is no doubt.

Francesca Doni   You imagine it.

Silvia Settala   I feel it; I am sure of it.

Francesca Doni   But how?

Silvia Settala   It was bound to come; she was bound to find out the way one day or another. How? A letter, perhaps. He has received a letter.

Francesca Doni   And you were not on the watch?

Silvia Settala (*disdainfully*)   Even that?

Francesca Doni   But perhaps you are mistaken.

Silvia Settala   I am not mistaken. After the old man's visit, she wrote. Delay is no longer possible now, not a day, not an hour. You see the danger. Though he may have come back to me with all his soul, though he may have broken with her entirely, though he may have gone back to another life, another happiness, do you not feel what might still be the fascination for him of a woman who says, obstinate and certain: 'I am here, I wait'? To know that she is there, that she is waiting there every day, that nothing can dishearten her. Do you see the danger? If Lucio knew this morning that she is waiting for him, he must know to-night, and from my lips, that she waits for him no longer. (*An indomitable energy strengthens and lifts her whole being.*) He shall know it tonight; I promise him. (*She stretches out her hand towards the window, with the gesture of one taking an oath.*) Will you come with me?

Francesca Doni (*anxious and entreating*)   Silvia, Silvia, think for one moment! Think what you are doing!

Silvia Settala   I do not ask your aid. I only ask you to come with me as far as the door. For the rest, I alone suffice; it is necessary that I should be alone. Will you? What time is it?

Turns to look at the time; goes towards the table.

Francesca Doni (*stopping her*)   I entreat of you! Listen to me, Silvia! My heart tells me that no good can come of what you are wanting to do. Listen to your sister! I entreat of you.

Silvia Settala (*with a gesture of impatience*)   Don't you know the game I am playing? Let me be. I am going alone. (*Bends over the table, and looks at the time.*) Four o'clock. I have not a moment to lose. Is your carriage there?

The rain falls suddenly on the trees in the garden.

Francesca Doni   See how it is pouring! Don't go out! Put it off till to-morrow. Come, listen. (*Tries to draw her towards her.*) Wait at least till it stops raining.

Silvia Settala   I have not a minute to lose. I must be there before her; she must find me there as if in my own house. Do you understand? Let me go. Quick, my hat, my cloak, my gloves. Giovanna!

She goes into the next room calling to her maid. **Francesca Doni**, *terrified, goes towards the window, on which the rain is beating.*

Francesca Doni   My God! my God! (*Looks into the garden; calls:*) Lucio! Lucio!

Turns towards the door through which her sister has gone out.

Silvia Settala (*coming back, out of breath*)   I am ready. I left Beata there in tears. She wanted to go out with me, Stay, please; go and comfort her. I will go alone. I shall take your carriage. *Au revoir.* (*Is about to kiss her sister.*)

Francesca Doni   You are going, then? You have decided?

Silvia Settala   I am going.

Francesca Doni   I will go with you.

Silvia Settala   Let us go.

Involuntarily she turns and looks around the room, as if to embrace everything that is in it in one look. The curtains tremble, the rain increases. She breathes in the damp fragrance that enters at the window. For one instant the strung bow of her will slackens.

The odour of the earth . . .

She shivers, as she suddenly catches sight of **Lucio**, *who appears on the threshold, feverishly, with bare head, his hair and his clothes wet with rain. They look at one another. An interval of weighty silence.*

Lucio Settala (*in a hoarse voice*)   You are going out?

Silvia Settala   Yes, I am going out.

Lucio Settala   How pale you are! (**Silvia** *puts her hand to her throat*)   Where are you going? It is a deluge. (*He touches his dripping hair.*)

Silvia Settala   I have to go out. I shall not be long. Beata is in there, crying because she wants to come with me. Go and comfort her, tell her that perhaps I will bring her back something beautiful.

Lucio *suddenly takes her hands and looks her fixedly in the eyes.*

Silvia Settala (*mistress of herself, with a clear and firm accent*)   What is it, Lucio?

He casts down his eyes. She withdraws her hands, shaking his as if in a farewell greeting. The temper of her will rings out in her vivid voice.

Silvia Settala   *Au revoir!* Come, Francesca. It is time.

She goes out rapidly, followed by her sister. **Lucio Settala** *remains with bowed head, staggering under a thought that transfixes him.*

Act Three

A high and spacious room, lighted by a glass roof, covered with dark awnings. In the wall at the back there is a rectangular opening, somewhat larger than a door, leading into the sculptor's studio. On the architrave are some fragments of the frieze of the Parthenon; against the two sides are two large winged figures, 'clothed with the wind', the Nike of Samothrace and the other Nike sculptured by Pœonius for the Doric temple of Olympia consecrated to Zeus; the opening is covered by a red curtain.

In the left wall there is a door, hidden by a rich and heavy portière; in the left, a little door is hidden by curtains. Wide divans, covered with cloths and cushions, surround the room. The figures are arranged carefully, as if to induce meditation and reverie: a bunch of corn in a copper vase stand before the Eleusinian bas-relief of Demeter; a little bronze Pegasus on a pedestal of 'verde antico' stands before the Ludovisi Medusa.

The sentiment expressed by the aspect of the place is very different from that which softens the aspect of the room in the other house, over against the mystic hill. Here the choice and analogy of every form reveals an aspiration towards a carnal, victorious, and creative life. The two divine messengers seem to stir and widen the close atmosphere incessantly with the rush of their immense flight.

Scene One

Silvia Settala *stands in the middle of the room, having laid down her hat, cloak, and gloves. She seems trying to remember the things about her, almost to renew her acquaintance with them, to re-establish a communion with them, not to feel estranged from them. She represses her anguish under her sister's eyes.* **Francesca Doni** *is seated, because her knees tremble and her heart beats too loud.*

Silvia Settala (*looking about her*)   It is strange; it seems larger.

Francesca Doni   What?

Silvia Settala   The room. It doesn't seem the same.

She looks about her, as if breathing an unfamiliar air. An interval of silence.

Francesca Doni (*listening*)   Did you shut the door?

Silvia Settala   Yes, I shut it.

Francesca Doni   We shall hear her open it.

Silvia Settala   Are you afraid? It is not time yet. In a minute you must go.

Francesca Doni   Where?

Silvia Settala   Will you wait for me in the carriage, in the street?

Francesca Doni   No, it is impossible. I want to be here, to be near you. Could I not hide myself?

Silvia Settala   Hide yourself, here? No. I must be alone.

Francesca Doni   Have pity on me! I shall die of suspense.

Silvia Settala   Wait. There ought to be a secret door here.

Guided by memory, she goes towards the wall where there is the hidden door; looks, finds it, opens it. A wave of light falls over her.

Do you see! It goes from here into the model's room, then into a corridor. At the end of the corridor there is a door, which leads to the Mugnone. Will you go out that way?

Francesca Doni   Yes, but let me stay in the room or the corridor and wait. I will wait till you call.

Silvia Settala   You promise to wait till I call?

Francesca Doni   Yes, I promise.

Silvia Settala   Do not fear. See, there is the sun on the window.

Both look out through the half open door. The inner light shines on their faces. A luminous streak extends over the floor.

Francesca Doni   It is not raining now. Look at all the primroses on the roadside.

Silvia Settala   Go and wait on the roadside, in the open air. Go.

Francesca Doni   There is an old sick horse, with his legs in the water. Do you see? And the swallows skim across it. I think . . .

She starts and turns suddenly, gazing at the motionless folds of the portière.

Silvia Settala   What is it?

Francesca Doni   I thought I heard . . .

Both listen.

Silvia Settala   No, you are mistaken. It is still early. And then the door on the stairs makes a great noise when it closes. Did you not hear it when we came in? The walls tremble.

Francesca Doni (*imploringly*)   Silvia!

Silvia Settala   What is it now?

Francesca Doni   Listen. There is still time. Come away, come away at least for today! Try, at least. She will know you have been here. We will speak to the caretaker again. You ought to leave some sign here, forget a glove, for instance. She will understand, she will not return.

Silvia Settala   A glove enough? Ah, how easy everything is for your heart!

She looks around her again, with a secret despair.

There is nothing left of me, here.

The sister remains by the half open door, her figure partially lit up by the vivid reflection. **Silvia** *moves some paces into the room. An interval of silence.*

Silvia Settala　Everything seems larger, higher, darker.

Francesca Doni　It is the shadow that deceives you. There is not much light. Draw back the awning over the sky-light.

Silvia Settala　No, it is better like this.

She looks in every corner, as if seeking a trace.

Tell me . . . (*Her voice chokes with emotion.*) That night they came for you, and you hurried here. You were here at the very beginning . . . (*Hesitates.*) Where was he? Do you remember exactly where?

Francesca Doni　There, in the studio, under the statue. No, do not go!

Silvia *turns towards the red curtain that hangs between the two Victories. At her feet, like a dividing line, stretches the thin zone of the sun.*

Silvia Settala (*in a low voice*)　The statue is there.

Francesca Doni　Do not go!

Silvia *remains for some instants motionless and silent before the closed curtain, from which she is separated by the shining zone.*

Francesca Doni　Do not go!

Silvia *steps across the sunlight, almost violently, as if to overcome an obstacle; with a rapid movement she raises the curtain, slips between the folds, and disappears. The curtain falls behind her, heavy and thick. There are a few instants of silence, in which nothing is heard but the rapid breathing of the sister. Suddenly, within the purple depths, appears the white face of* **Silvia**, *which seems irradiated with the light of the masterpiece. Her bare hands, as they put aside the curtains, seem to shine against the depths of colour. Her eyes are intent, widened by wonder, dazzled, not by a vision of death, but by an image of perfect life. The water gathers tremulously in her eyes. Two marvellous tears form little by little, shine, and slowly run down her cheeks. Before they reach her mouth she stops them with her fingers, diffuses them over her face, as if to bathe in lustral dew; for it is not by the remembrance or the trace of human bloodshed that she is moved, but by the sight of a thing of beauty, solitary and free. She has received the supreme gift of beauty: a truce to anguish, a pause to fear. The sublime lightning-flash of joy has shone through her wounded soul for an instant, rendering it crystalline as tears. These tears are but the soul's mute and ardent offering before a masterpiece.*

Francesca Doni　Silvia, Silvia, you are weeping.

Silvia Settala (*in a subdued voice, with a gesture of silence*)　Hush!

She moves away from the curtain, asking in a subdued voice:

Have you seen? have you seen?

Francesca Doni (*misunderstanding, with a start*)   Who? Her? Is she there?

Silvia Settala   No, the statue.

The sister nods her head, with a gesture expressing rapt admiration. The sound of a heavy door closing is heard. Both start.

Silvia Settala   She is here. Go, go.

Francesca Doni (*holding out her arms towards her with a last agonised entreaty*)   Oh, my sister!

Silvia Settala (*recovering her former energy*)   Go! Do not fear.

She pushes her sister out through the door, and closes it. The zone of sun disappears; the room returns to an even shadow.

Scene Two

Silvia Settala *is standing with her face turned towards the door, her eyes turned, almost rigid in expectation. Through the profound silence is heard distinctly the turning of the key in the lock.* **Silvia**'s *attitude does not change. A hand lifts the portière.* **Gioconda Dianti** *enters, closing the door behind her. At first she does not perceive the adversary, since she comes from the light into the shadow and a thick veil covers her whole face. When she perceives her, she stops, with a choked cry. Both remain for some instants facing one another without speaking.*

Silvia Settala (*with a firm and clear accent, but without resentment or menace*)   I am Silvia Settala.

Her rival is silent, still veiled. A pause.

Silvia Settala   And you?

Gioconda Dianti (*in a low voice*)   Do you not know, Signora?

Silvia Settala (*still restraining herself*)   I know only that you have entered here, as into a place that belongs to you. You find me here, as in my own house. One of us two, therefore, usurps the right of the other; one of us two is the intruder. Which? (*A pause.*) I perhaps?

Gioconda Dianti (*always hidden under the veil, and in a low voice, as if to lessen her audacity*)   Perhaps.

Silvia Settala *turns paler and staggers a little, as if she had received a blow.*

Silvia Settala (*resolutely, quivering with disdain*)   Well, there is a woman who has drawn a man into her net with the worst allurements; who has torn him away from the peace of home, the nobility of art, the beauty of a dream which he had nourished for years with the flowers of his force; who has dragged him into a turbid and violent delirium, where he has lost all sense of goodness and justice; who has inflicted on him the sharpest torments that the cruelty of a torturer sick with *ennui* could desire; who has exhausted and withered him up, keeping a perverse fever continually alight in his veins; who has rendered life intolerable to him; who has armed his hand and turned it against his own life; who in short, has known that he was lying wounded to death on a far-off bed, for days and days, while a ceaseless fight went on about him against death; and who has not had remorse, nor pity, nor shame, but has gone back to the sinister place before the blood was wiped off the floor, meditating another attack upon her prey, awaiting him again at the journey's end, calculating one by one the effects of her temerity and of her tenacity, promising herself the pleasure of another ruin. There is a woman who has done this, who has said: 'A strong and noble life flourished freely in the world; I have seized it, bent it back, beaten it down, then shattered it at a blow. I thought I had destroyed it for ever. And lo! it flourishes again, is renewed, re-arises, can put forth fresh flowers! About it the wounds close, the pains are calmed, hope springs up again, joy can smile! Shall I endure this wrong? Shall I let myself be thus deluded? No, I will begin again, I will hold on, I will overcome all resistance, I will be implacable.' There is a woman who has promised this to herself, who has gripped her will like an axe, who is prepared to deliver fresh blows smiling. Do you know her? She has entered here with her face covered, she has spoken in a dull voice, she has let fall a cold word, calculating always on her own audacity and on the other's submissiveness. Do you know her?

Gioconda Dianti (*without changing her manner*)   She whom I know is different. Only because she is sad in your presence, does she speak in a low voice. She respects the great and sorrowful love that has given you life; she admires the virtue that exalts you. While you were speaking, she understood that it was only in order to comfort an unutterable despair that your words had created a figure so different from the real person. There is nothing implacable in her; but she herself obeys a power that may be implacable.

Silvia Settala (*bitter and haughty*)   I know that you are practised in all tongues.

Gioconda Dianti   Of what avail is this harshness? Your first words had another sound; and it seemed, when you asked me a question, that you wanted simply to know the truth.

Silvia Settala   And what then is your truth?

Gioconda Dianti   The truth that matters, between us, is one only: truth of love. You know it. But I fear to wound.

Silvia Settala   Do not fear to wound.

Gioconda Dianti   The woman against whom you made such accusations was ardently loved, and – suffer me to say it! – with a glorious love. She did not abase but exalt a strong life. And since the last voice that she heard, a few hours before the terrible deed was accomplished, the last was of love, she believes that she is still loved. And this is the truth that matters.

Silvia Settala (*blindly*)   She is wrong, she is wrong . . . You are wrong! He loves you no longer, he loves you no longer; perhaps he has never loved you. His was not love but a poisoning, but sharp slavery, madness, and thirst. When he suffered on his pillow, remembrance passed through his eyes from time to time like a flash of terror. Weeping at my feet, he has blessed the blood that was poured out for his ransom. He does not love you, he does not love you!

Gioconda Dianti   Your love cries out like a drowning man.

Silvia Settala   He does not love you! You have been a gad-fly to him, you have made him frantic, you have driven him to his death.

Gioconda Dianti   Not I, not I, have driven him to his death, but you yourself. Yes, he wished to die, that he might cast off a fetter, but not that which bound him to me: another, yours, that which was set upon him by your virtue or your rule, and which made him suffer intolerably.

Silvia Settala   Ah, there is nothing that you dare not travesty! From him, from his own mouth, in an hour when his whole soul had risen up into the light, from him I heard it: 'If violence is enough to break a yoke, let it be blessed!' From him I heard it, when all his soul opened again to the truth.

Gioconda Dianti   But here, a few hours before he gave way to the horrible thought, here (all these things are witnesses to it) he said to me the most ardent and the sweetest words of all his love; here he once more called me life of his life, here he told me once more his dream of forgetfulness, of liberty, of art, of joy. And here he told me of the insupportableness of his yoke, the inevitable weight of goodness, more cruel than any other, and the horror of daily suffering, the repugnance at returning to the house of silence and tears, the repugnance at length become unconquerable.

Silvia Settala   No, no. You lie.

Gioconda Dianti   To escape that anguish, one evening when all seemed to him sadder and more silent than ever, he sought death.

Silvia Settala   You lie, you lie! I was far away.

Gioconda Dianti   And you accuse me of having inflicted an infamous torment upon him, of having been his torturer! Ah, your hands, above all, your hands of goodness and pardon, prepared for him every night a bed of thorn, on which he could not lie down. But, when he entered here where I awaited him as one awaits the creating God, he was transformed. Before his work he recovered strength, joy, faith. Yes, a continual fever burned in his blood, kept alight by me (and this is all my pride); but the fire of that fever has fashioned a masterpiece.

Points towards her statue, hidden by the curtains.

Silvia Settala   It is not the first; it will not be the last.

Gioconda Dianti   Truly, it will not be the last; because another is ready to leap forth from its covering of clay, another has palpitated already under the life giving thumb, another is half-alive, and waits from moment to moment for the miracle of art to draw it wholly forth to the light. Ah, you cannot understand this impatience of matter to which the gift of perfect life has been promised!

Silvia Settala *turns towards the curtain, takes a few steps, slowly, as if involuntarily, as if in obedience to a mysterious attraction.*

Gioconda Dianti   It is there; the clay is there. That first breath that he infused into it, I have kept alive from day to day, as one waters the furrow where the seed lies deep. I have not let it perish. The impress is there, intact. The last touch, which his feverish hand set upon it at the last hour, is visible there, energetic and fresh as yesterday, so powerful that my hope in the midst of all the agony of sorrow is set there with a seal of life, and takes strength from it.

Silvia Settala *pauses in front of the curtain, as before, and remains motionless and silent.*

Gioconda Dianti   Yes, it is true, you watched by the bedside of the dying man, intent upon a ceaseless strife to win him back from death; and for this be envied, and for this be praised to all eternity. You had strife, agitation, effort: you had to accomplish a thing which seemed superhuman, and which intoxicated you. I, shut out, far off, in solitude, could only gather and bind up, knitting my will together, my sorrow in a vow. My faith was equal to yours; truly, it was leagued with yours against death. The last creative spark of his genius, of the divine fire that is in him, I have not let it go out, I have kept it alive, with a religious and uninterrupted vigilance. Ah, who can say to what height, the preserving force of such a vow may attain?

Silvia Settala *is about to turn violently, as if to reply, but restrains herself.*

Gioconda Dianti   I know, I know: it is simple and easy enough, what I have done; I know: it is no heroic effort, it is the humble duty of a menial. But it is not the act that matters. What matters is the spirit in which the act is accomplished; the fervour of it is all that matters. Nothing is more sacred than the work that begins to live. If the spirit in which I have watched over it can reveal itself to your soul, go and see! That the work may go on living, my visible presence is needful. Realising this necessity, you will understand how in replying 'Perhaps' to a question, I wished to respect a doubt which might be in you, but which was not in me, which is not in me. You cannot feel at home here as in your own house. This is not a house. Household affections have no place here; domestic virtues have no sanctuary here. This is a place outside laws and beyond common rights. Here a sculptor makes his statues. He is alone here with the instruments of his art. Now I am nothing but an instrument of his art. Nature has sent me to him to bring him a message, and to serve him. I obey; I await him to serve him still. If he entered now, he could take up the interrupted work which had begun to live under his fingers. Go and see!

Silvia Settala *stands before the curtain, without advancing. An increasing shiver shakes her whole body, betraying her inner agitation; while the words of her rival become more and more sharp and stinging, definite, and at last hostile. Suddenly she turns, panting, impetuous, resolved upon the last defence.*

Silvia Settala   No. It is useless. Your words are too clever. You are practised in all tongues. You transform into an act of love and faith what is only an act of policy or of treachery. The work that was interrupted should have perished. With the same hand that had impressed the sign of life upon the clay, with the same hand he grasped the weapon and turned it against his heart. He did not doubt that he had set the deepest of gulfs between himself and his work. Death has passed there, and has severed every bond. What was interrupted should be lost. Now he is born again, he is a new man, he aspires towards other conquests. In his eyes there is a new light; his strength is impatient to create other forms. All that is behind him, all that is on the other side of the shadow, has no longer any power or value. What does it matter to him that an old piece of clay should fall into dust? He has forgotten it. He will find fresher pieces, into which to infuse the breath of his new birth, and to model into the image of the idea that now inflames him. Away with the old clay! How could you profess to think that you were necessary to his art? Nothing is necessary to the man who creates. All converges in him. You say that Nature sent you to him to bear him a message. Well, he has received it, he has understood it, and he has responded to it with a sublime expression. What other could he derive from you? What other could you give him? It is not given to man to attain twice the same summit, to accomplish twice the same prodigy. You are left there, on the other side of the shadow, far off, alone, on the old earth. He goes towards the new earth now, where he shall receive other messages. His strength seems virgin, and the beauty of the world is infinite.

Gioconda Dianti (*taken aback by the unexpected vigour which repels her becoming more acrid, more haughty than ever, and with an air of defiance*)   I am living and am here; and he has found in me more than one aspect, and the words still intoxicate me that he said when he spoke to me of his vision, different every morning when I come before him. Up to yesterday, certainly, he did not know that I was waiting for him; and his unconsciousness has deceived you. But today he knows. Do you understand? He knows that I am here, that I await him. This morning a letter told him, a letter which came into his hands, which he has read. And I am certain – do you understand? – I am certain that he will come. Perhaps he is on the way, perhaps he is near the door. Shall we wait for him?

An extraordinary change comes over the face of **Silvia**. *It seems as if something strange and horrible enters into her. She is like one suddenly caught in the coils, writhing in the fascination of the serpent, blindly. The ancient fatality of deceit suddenly assails the soul of the pure woman, conquers and contaminates it. At the last words of the enemy she breaks into an unexpected laugh, bitter, atrocious, provocative, that renders her unrecognisable.* **Gioconda Dianti** *seems overcome by it.*

Silvia Settala   Enough, enough. Too many words. The game has lasted too long. Ah, your certainty, your pride! But how could you believe that I should have come here to contest the way with you, to forbid your entrance, to face your audacity, if I had not had a certainty far more sound than yours to warrant me? I know your letter of yesterday, it was shown to me, I know not if with more astonishment or disgust.

Gioconda Dianti (*overcome*)   No, it is not possible!

Silvia Settala   Yes, it is so. As for the answer, I bring it. Lucio Settala has lost the memory of what has been, and asks to be left in peace. He hopes that your pride will prevent you from becoming importunate.

Gioconda Dianti (*beside herself*)   He sends you? he himself? It is his answer? his?

Silvia Settala   His, his. I would have spared you this harshness if you had not forced me. Will you go now?

Gioconda Dianti (*her voice hoarse with rage and shame*)   I am turned out?

Fury suffocates her, and gives her a frantic vigour. The vindictive and devastating wild beast seems to awaken in her. Through her flexible and powerful body passes the same force which contracts the homicidal muscles of feline animals in ambush. The veil, which she has kept on her face like a dark mask, renders more formidable the attitude of one ready to do injury in any way and with any weapon.

Turned out?

Silvia Settala *stands convulsed and livid before the furious woman, and it is not the spectacle of that fury which terrifies her, but something which she sees within herself, something horrible and irreparable: her lie.*

Gioconda Dianti   Ah, you have brought him to this! How? how? Binding the soul like the wound with cotton-wool? doctoring him with your soft hands? He is unmade, finished, a useless rag. I understand; now I understand. Poor thing! poor thing! Ah, why is he not dead, rather than the survivor of his soul? He is finished, then, a poor beggar whom you lead by the hand in the empty streets. All is destroyed, all is lost. He will never lift his head again, his eye is darkened.

Silvia Settala (*interrupting her*)   Be silent, be silent! He is living and strong; never had he such light in himself. God be praised!

Gioconda Dianti (*frantically*)   It is not true. I, I was his strength, his youth, his light. Tell him! Tell him! He has become old; from today he is limp and soulless. I carry away with me (tell him!) all that was most free, ardent, and proud in him. The blood that he poured out there, under my statue, was the last blood of his youth. What you have re-infused into his heart is without flame, is weak, is vile. Tell him! I carry away with me today all that was his power and his pride and his joy and his all. He is finished. Tell him!

Fury blinds and suffocates her. It is as if she is invaded by a turbid destructive will, as by a demon. All her being contracts in the necessity of accomplishing an immediate act of destruction. A sudden, thought precipitates that instinct towards an aim.

And that statue which is mine, which belongs to me which he has made out of the life that I have shed from me drop by drop, that statue which is mine . . .

She rushes like a wild beast towards the closed curtain, raises it and passes through.
. . . well, I will shatter it, I will cast it down!

Silvia Settala *utters a cry, and rushes forward to prevent the crime. Both disappear behind the curtain. The rapid breathing of a brief struggle is heard.*

Silvia Settala (*crying out*)   No, no, it is not true, it is not true! I lied!

*The despairing words are covered by the sound of a mass that inclines and falls, the fracture of the falling statue; then follows another lacerating cry from **Silvia**, torn by agony from her very vitals.*

Scene Four

Francesca Doni *appears, mad with terror, running towards the cry, which she recognises; while Gioconda Dianti is seen between the curtains, still veiled, in the attitude of one who has committed a murder and seeks to escape.*

Francesca Doni   Assassin! Assassin!

She stoops to succour her sister, while the other rushes out.

Francesca Doni   Silvia, Silvia, my sister, my sister! What has she done to you, what has she done to you? Ah, the hands, the hands . . .

Her voice expresses the horror of one who sees something frightful.

Silvia Settala   Take me away! Take me away!

Francesca Doni   My God, my God! They were underneath! My God! They are crushed! Water! water! There is none here. Wait.

Silvia Settala   Ah, what agony! I cannot bear it: I am dying. Take me away!

She appears between the red curtains, her face inexpressibly contracted by agony, while her sister bends to support her two hands wrapped in a piece of wet cloth, taken from the clay, through which the blood oozes.

Silvia Settala   What agony! I cannot bear it any longer.

She is about to faint, when all at once **Lucio Settala** *rushes into the room like a madman. She trembles, fixing on him her great eyes full of tears, in which her despairing soul dies.*

Silvia Settala   You, you, you!

Francesca Doni (*still supporting the two poor crushed hands that drench the cloth in which the incurable wreck is hidden*)   Support her, support her! She is falling.

Lucio Settala *supports the poor bleeding creature, almost fainting, in his arms. But, before losing consciousness, she turns her glazing eyes towards the curtains as if to indicate the statue.*

Silvia Settala (*in a dying voice*)   It . . . is safe.

Act Four

A ground floor room, white and simple, with two side walls making an angle, almost entirely open to the light, which comes through a sort of large window, after the manner of a tepidarium. The blinds are raised, and through the window-panes can be seen oleanders, tamarinds, rushes, pines, golden sands dotted with dead seaweed, the sea calm and dotted with lateen sails, the peaceful mouth of the Arno, beyond the river the wild thickets of Gombo, the Cascine di San Rossore, the far off marble mountain of Carrara.[24]

A door, leading to the interior, is on the third side. By the side of the door, on a bracket, is the Lady with the bunch of flowers, the famous figure of Andrea del Verrocchio,[25] *a new guest, come from the other house, like a faithful companion, whose beautiful hands are always flawless, as they make a graceful gesture towards the heart. On the other side is an old spinet, of the time of Elisa Baciocchi, Duchess of Lucca, with its case of dull wood inlaid with bright wood, borne by little gilded Cariatides*[26] *in the Empire style, with its four pedals united in the form of a small harp.*

It is an afternoon in September. The smile of vanishing summer seems to lay an enchantment over everything. In the deserted room the soul of music sleeping in the forgotten instrument makes itself felt, as if the hidden strings were touched by the calm rhythm of the neighbouring sea.

Scene One

Silvia Settala *appears on the threshold, from the inner room; she pauses; takes several steps towards the window; looks into the distance, looks about her with infinitely sad eyes. In her way of moving there is a sense of something wanting, calling up a vague image of clipped wings, a vague sentiment of strength humbled and shorn, of nobility brought low, of broken harmony. She is dressed in an ash-coloured gown, with a hem of black, like a thread of mourning. Long sleeves hide her arms without hands, which she sometimes lets drop by her side, and sometimes sets together, drawn a little back, as if to hide them in the folds, with a movement of shame and sorrow.*

From outside, between the thick oleanders, appears a girlish figure, **La Sirenetta***, half fairy and half beggar girl, peering in. She glides towards the window with a furtive step, holding up in one hand a fold of her apron filled with seaweed, shells, and starfish.*

---

24 Gombo: region in Tuscany, Italy. San Rossore: parkland on the Pisan coast. Carrara: Tuscan city, known for its production of white marble.
25 Andrea del Verrocchio (1435–88): Italian sculptor and painter.
26. Caryatid: sculpted figure of a woman that serves as a supporting structure.

Silvia Settala (*catching sight of her, and going towards her with a smile*)   Oh, la Sirenetta! Come, come.

La Sirenetta (*coming forward to the window*)   Do you remember me?

She remains outside so that her face is seen through the shimmer of the glass, which seems to continue about her the incessant, tremulous radiance of the sea. She is young, slender, graceful; her yellow hair is in disorder, her face the colour of ruddy gold, her teeth white as the bones of the cuttle-fish, her eyes humid and sea-green, her neck long and thin, with a necklace of shells about it; in her whole person something inexpressibly fresh and glancing, which makes one think of a creature impregnated with sea-salt, dipped in the moving waters, coming out of the hidingplaces of the rocks. Her petticoat of striped white and blue, torn and discoloured, falls only just below the knees, leaving her legs bare; her blueish apron drips and smells of the brine like a filter; her bare feet, in contrast with the brown colour that the sun has given her flesh, are singularly pallid, like the roots of aquatic plants. And her voice is limpid and childish; and some of the words that she speaks seem to light up her ingenuous face with a mysterious happiness.

Do you remember me, pretty lady?

Silvia Settala   I remember you; I remember you.

La Sirenetta   Do you remember me? Who am I?

Silvia Settala   Are you not la Sirenetta?

La Sirenetta   Yes, you have remembered me. When did you come back?

Silvia Settala   Not long ago.

La Sirenetta   You will stay?

Silvia Settala   A long time longer.

La Sirenetta   Till the winter, perhaps.

Silvia Settala   Perhaps.

La Sirenetta   And your little girl?

Silvia Settala   I expect her today. She is coming.

La Sirenetta   Beata! Isn't she called Beata?

Silvia Settala   Yes Beata.

La Sirenetta   You called her that, Beata, not Beatrice. When she was here, she asked me every day for starfish, stars of the sea. Did she tell you? She made me sing. Did she tell you?

Silvia Settala   Yes, she told me. She remembers you. She likes you.

La Sirenetta   She likes me! I know. She gave me some of her bread every day.

Silvia Settala   You shall have it every day, if you like. Bread and food, Sirenetta, morning and night, whenever you like. Remember.

La Sirenetta   Morning and night I will bring you a starfish. Will you have one? A pretty one, larger than a hand?

Silvia Settala *troubled, draws back her arms with an instinctive movement.*

Silvia Settala   No, no, keep it for Beata.

La Sirenetta (*surprised*)   Won't you have it?

Silvia Settala   Tell me instead what you do with your life, tell me how you spend the day. Is it true that you talk with the sirens of the sea? Tell me all about it, Sirenetta,

La Sirenetta   Seven sisters were we,

> Our mirror the fountain head,
> All of us fair to see.
> 'Flower of the bulrush makes no bread,
> Hedgerow mulberry makes no wine,
> Blade of grass no linen fine',
> The mother to the sisters said;
> All of us fair to see,
> And our mirror the fountain-head.
> The first was fain to spin,
> And wished for spindles of gold;
> The second to weave threads in,
> And wished for shuttles of gold;
> The third to sew at her leisure,
> And wished for needles of gold;
> The fourth to cook for her pleasure,
> And wished for platters of gold;
> The fifth to sleep beyond measure,
> And wished for dreams of gold;
> The sixth to sleep night away,
> And wished for coverings of gold;
> The last to sing all day,
> To sing for evermore,
> And wished for nothing more.

She laughs with a quick glittering laugh that seems to tinkle against her shining teeth.

Do you like this story?

Silvia Settala (*charmed by the grace of the simple creature*)   Is that all? Why don't you go on?

La Sirenetta   If you sit here, I will put you to sleep as I put your child to sleep on the sands. Are you not sleepy now? Sleep is good, in September.
September bears to the plain
The windy breath of the mountain rain;

And puts the summer to sleep again.
Amen.

Silvia Settala   No. Go on with your story, Sirenetta.

La Sirenetta   The olive darkens for shedding,

Sorrow speeds the wedding,
Oil and tears wait for the treading.

Silvia Settala   Go on with your story, Sirenetta.

La Sirenetta   Where had we got?

Silvia Settala   'And wished for nothing more!'

A pause.

La Sirenetta   Ah, here it is:

'Flower of the bulrush makes no bread,
Hedgerow mulberry makes no wine,
Blade of grass no linen fine',
The mother to the sisters said;
All of us fair to see,
And our mirror the fountain-head.
And so the first one spun
Her own heart's woe for the morrow;
And so the second wove,
And wove the cloth of sorrow;
And so the third one sewed
A poisoned shirt to wear;
And so the fourth one cooked
A dish of heart's despair;
And so the fifth one slept
Under the coverings of death;
And so the sixth one dreamt
In the arms of death.
The mother wept full sore,
And sighed away her breath;
But the last, that only sang
To sing, to sing all day,
To sing for evermore,
Found her a happy fate.

She lowers her voice and makes it secret and remote.

The sirens of the bay
Called her to be their mate.

A pause.

Silvia Settala   Then it is true that you talk with the sirens?

La Sirenetta (*putting her forefinger to her lips*)   Mustn't ask!

Silvia Settala   Is it true that no one knows where you sleep at night?

La Sirenetta (*with the same gesture*)   Mustn't ask!

Silvia Settala   Shall I give you shelter, here in the house?

La Sirenetta (*looking intently in her face, as if she had not heard the question*)   Your eyes are sad. I did not know what troubled me when I looked at them. Now I see: you have a great sorrow in your eyes. Some one of yours is dead,

Silvia Settala   You alone can comfort me.

La Sirenetta   Who of yours is dead?

Silvia Settala   Mustn't ask!

La Sirenetta   Now I see you: you are not the same. I was thinking of a swallow, last September, who had lost his longest feathers, and was nearly drowned in the sea. What have they done to you? Something wicked has been done to you.

Silvia Settala   Mustn't ask!

Instinctively she hides her arms without hands in the folds of her garment, with a sorrowful movement, which does not escape the notice of the bewitching creature; who suddenly, as if intentionally, drops the end of her apron, so that her little sea treasure falls and is scattered over the ground.

La Sirenetta (*stooping and choosing*)   Will you have a starfish, a pretty one, bigger than a hand? Look!

She shows the mutilated woman a large sea-star with five rays.

La Sirenetta   Take it! I give it to you.

The mutilated woman shakes her head in sign of refusal, pressing her lips together, as if to keep down the knot that tightens in her throat.

La Sirenetta   Can't you? Are your hands sick, tied up?

The mutilated woman nods her head. **La Sirenetta**'s *voice becomes tremulous with pity.*

La Sirenetta   Did you fall into the fire? Were you burnt? Do they still hurt? Or are they getting better?

Silvia Settala (*in a scarcely audible voice*)   I haven't any hands.

La Sirenetta (*rising in affright*)   You haven't any! They have cut them off? No hands?

The mutilated woman nods her head, frightfully pale. The other shivers with horror.

La Sirenetta   No, no, no! It isn't true.

She keeps her eyes fixed on the folds of the garment in which the mutilated woman hides her arms.

La Sirenetta   Tell me it isn't true.

Silvia Settala   I haven't any hands.

La Sirenetta   Why? Why?

Silvia Settala   Mustn't ask!

La Sirenetta   Ah, what a cruel thing!

Silvia Settala   I gave them away.

La Sirenetta   You gave them away? To whom?

Silvia Settala   To my love.

La Sirenetta   Ah, what a cruel love! How beautiful they were, how beautiful! Do you think I don't remember? I have kissed them; many many times. I have kissed them with this mouth. They gave me bread, a pomegranate, a cup of milk. They were as beautiful as if the dawn had made them with a breath, as white as the flower of the foam, more delicate than the embroidery that the wind makes on the sand; they moved like the sun in the water, they talked better than the tongue or the eye, they said kind words, what they gave turned to gold. I remember them! I see them, I see them. One day they were playing with the warm sand: the sand ran between the fingers as through a sieve, and they were pleased at playing; and Beata looked at them and laughed; and I looked at them and had the same pleasure. One day they peeled an orange; and made it into many pieces, and touched me with one of them, and it was as sweet as a honeycomb. One day they wrapped a handkerchief about the little one's foot, and she was crying because a crab had nipped her, and the pain stopped all at once, and the little one began to run along the shore. One day they played with those lovely curls, and of every curl they made a ring for every finger, and then began over again, and then began over again; and Beata fell asleep with the dew on her lips.

Silvia Settala (*in a choking voice*)   Don't say any more! don't say any more!

La Sirenetta   Ah, what a cruel love!

A pause. She remains pensive.

And where are they? Far away, all alone, in the earth, deep down. Did they bury them? Where? In a pretty garden?

A pause. The mutilated woman shuts her eyes and leans her head against the window, in which the quiver of the sea is reflected.

La Sirenetta   Did you see them taken away? How white they were! They have wrapped them up in strong ointment. And the rings? With all the rings? There was one with a green stone, and one with three pearls, and one of gold and iron twisted, and a smooth one, a shining hoop, and only that one was on the third finger.

A pause. An indefinable expression appears on the face of the mutilated woman, as she lets her arms drop by her sides, while the rigidity of her whole body slackens.

La Sirenetta   What are you thinking about? Dreaming of them? If they should grow warm again. . . .

The mutilated woman opens her eyes and starts, as if suddenly awakened. Her arms quiver.

La Sirenetta   What is the matter?

Silvia Settala   It is strange. Sometimes it really seems to me as if I have them again, I seem to feel the blood rise to the tips of my fingers. When you spoke, I had them: they were more beautiful, Sirenetta!

La Sirenetta   More beautiful?

Silvia Settala   You will comfort me, Sirenetta. I cannot take your starfish, but I can see your eyes and hear your voice. Keep near me, now I have found you again I would like to have you for a sister.

La Sirenetta   I would like you to have my hands, if they were not so rough and dark.

Silvia Settala   Your hands are happy hands: they touch the leaves, the flowers, the sand, the water, the stones, children, animals, all innocent things. You are happy, Sirenetta: your soul is born again every morning; now it is little as a pearl, and now it is large as the sea. You have nothing and everything; you know nothing and everything.

La Sirenetta (*turning suddenly and interrupting her*)   Did you feel the gust? Look, look how many swallows on the sea! There are more than a thousand: a living cloud. Look how they shine! Now they are off; they are going on a long journey, to a far away land; the shadow walks over the water with them; some feathers are falling: evening will come on; they will meet the ships on the high sea; they will see the fires, hear the songs of the sailors; the sailors will see them pass; they will pass close to the sails; one of them will strike against the sails, and fall on the deck, tired. One night, a cloud of tired swallows fell upon a ship like a flock of starlings on the deck and quite covered it. The sailors never touched them. They never moved, for fear of frightening them; they never spoke, so that they might go to sleep. And as they were all over the stock of the anchor and the bar of the rudder, that night the ship went drifting under the moon. But at dawn . . . Ah, who is calling to you?

She interrupts her dream, hearing a strange voice among the oleanders; and prepares to fly.

Good-bye, good-bye.

Silvia Settala (*anxiously*)   It is my sister. Do not run away, do not go, Sirenetta. Stay here near. Beata is coming.

La Sirenetta   Good-bye, good-bye. I will come back.

Runs towards the sea, vanishing into the sunlight.

Scene Two

Francesca Doni *appears between the oleanders, followed by the old man,* **Lorenzo Gaddi**.

Francesca Doni   Do you see who I am bringing you?

Silvia Settala (*anxiously*)   And Beata? And Beata?

Francesca Doni   She is coming presently. I left her with Faustina. I came beforehand, so that she should not come to you unexpectedly.

Silvia Settala   Dear Maestro, how pleased I am to see you!

The old man instinctively stretches out his hands toward her. She bends slightly and offers him her forehead, which he touches with his lips.

Lorenzo Gaddi (*concealing his emotion*)   How happy I am to see you again, dear Silvia, and to see you up and well again! The sea helps you. The sea is always the great comforter. At Forte dei Marmi,[27] yonder, I thought much of you.

Silvia Settala   Is Forte dei Marmi far from here?

Lorenzo Gaddi (*pointing to the distant shore*)   Yonder, under Serravizza, on this side of Massa.[28]

They look out of the window into the distance.

Francesca Doni   How well one can see the mountains of Carrara today! You can count the peaks one by one. I never remember a clearer day than this. Who was with you, Silvia? La Sirenetta? I thought I saw her running towards the sea. And then here are her traces: sea-weed, shells, starfish.

She points to the childish treasures scattered over the ground.

Silvia Settala   Yes, she was with me just now.

Lorenzo Gaddi   Who is la Sirenetta?

Francesca Doni   A little wandering mad creature.

Silvia Settala   A seer, who has the gift of song; a creature of dream and truth, who seems a spirit of the sea. You should know her and love her as I do. When you know her and hear her speak, you find out many deep things. Truly she will seem to you perfect: he always gives and never asks.

Lorenzo Gaddi   She is like you in that.

Silvia Settala   Alas, no. I should like to have been like her in that; but the light died away before the deceit of life. What blindness! I asked so much, that to obtain it, I

---

27 Forte dei Marmi: Tuscan town by the sea.
28 Serravizza: Tuscan town, near to the Apuan Alps. Massa: another Tuscan town, ten kilometres north west of Serravizza.

stooped to tell a lie: I came out mutilated, maimed, in punishment for my lie. I had stretched out my hands too violently towards a good thing that fate denied me. I do not lament or weep. Since I must live, I will live. Perhaps one day my soul will be healed. I felt some hope arise in me, as I listened to the voice of that simple and guileless creature who can teach eternal things. She has promised to bring me a starfish every morning.

She tries to smile. The sister stands near the window and seems to be looking intently at the distant mountains; but there is a shadow of sadness over her gentle face.

Silvia Settala   Look, Maestro, at the lady with the bunch of flowers. She has come with me. Now, if I look at her, there is something mournful in her for me: all the same I could not separate myself from her. Do you remember, Maestro, that day in April, that garlanded head?

Lorenzo Gaddi   I remember, I remember.

Silvia Settala   The new life!

Lorenzo Gaddi   There was an omen in everything.

Silvia Settala   When I see the camels pass loaded with faggots, there, on the other side of the Arno, in the thickets of Gombo, I think of the arrival of Cosimo Dalbo, of the joy of that evening, of the scarabæus that I put in the midst of a bunch of roses that Beata had picked. (*Turns towards her sister.*) O Francesca, I speak, and all the while my heart troubles me so that I can resist no longer. Where is Beata?

Francesca Doni (*wrung with pain*)   You want to see her now? You are strong?

Silvia Settala   Yes, yes, I am strong, I am ready. Suspense is worse.

Francesca Doni   Then I will go and bring her to you,

Silvia Settala (*unable to contain her anxiety*)   Wait a minute. Will you not stay with us here to-night, Maestro? I should be glad.

Lorenzo Gaddi   Well, yes, I will stay.

Silvia Settala   We can put you up. I will have your room got ready. Wait, Francesca, a minute.

She is convulsed with emotion, which she can no longer restrain. She goes towards the door like one who runs away to hide the tears that are about to break forth.

Francesca Doni   Shall I come, Silvia?

Silvia Settala (*with a choking voice*)   No, no.

Goes out.

Francesca Doni   Ah, the curse, the curse! Do you see her? While she was in bed, under the bedclothes, bound up, bleeding, all the horror of the thing did not appear. But now that she is on her feet again, now that she moves, walks, sees her friends, returns to her old ways, is about to use the gestures that she used to use! Think of it!

Lorenzo Gaddi   Yes, it is too frightful a fate. I remember what you said to her so tenderly, as you looked at her, on that day in April: 'You seem as if you had wings!' The beauty and lightness of her hands gave her the aspect of a winged thing. There was in her a kind of incessant quiver. Now it is as if she dragged herself along.

Francesca Doni   And it was a useless sacrifice, like all the others; it has done nothing, changed nothing: that is where it is so frightful a fate. If Lucio had stayed with her, I believe she would have been happy to have been able to give that last proof, to have been able to sacrifice for him her living hands. But she knows now all the truth, in all its nakedness. Ah, what an infamous thing! Would you have believed that Lucio was capable of it? Tell me.

Lorenzo Gaddi   He too has his fate, and he obeys it. As he was not master of his death, so he is not master of his life. I saw him yesterday. He had written me at Forte dei Marmi to ask me to go to the quarry and send him a block. I saw him yesterday in his studio. His face is so thin that it seems burnt up in the fire of his eyes. When he speaks, he becomes strangely excited. It troubled me. He works, works, works, with a terrible fury: perhaps he is seeking to rid himself of a thought that gnaws him,

Francesca Doni   The statue is still there?

Lorenzo Gaddi   It is still there, without arms. He has left it so: he would not restore it. So, on the pedestal, it looks really like an ancient marble, dug up in one of the Cyclades. There is in it something sacred and tragic, after the divine immolation.

Francesca Doni (*in a low voice*)   And that woman, the Gioconda, was there?

Lorenzo Gaddi   She was there, silent. When one looks at her, and thinks that she is the cause of so much evil, truly one cannot curse her in his heart; no, one cannot, when one looks at her, I have never seen so great a mystery in mortal flesh.

A pause. The old man and the sister remain in thought, for some instants, with bowed heads.

Francesca Doni (*sighing because of the anguish that oppresses her*)   My God, my God! And now it is time to bring Beata to her mother, and they will see one another again, after all that has happened; and the little one will learn the truth, will know the horrible thing. How is one to hide it, from her, remembering all her caresses, and mad for them! You saw her, you heard her, of old. . . .

Silvia Settala *reappears on the threshold. Her eyes are burning and all her body is contracted by a spasmodic force.*

Silvia Settala   I am here, Francesca; I am ready. The room is ready, Maestro, if you would like to go to it.

Lorenzo Gaddi (*going towards her, and in a voice trembling with emotion*)   Courage! It is the last ordeal.

He goes out by the door. The mutilated woman goes towards her sister, breathlessly.

Silvia Settala   Now go, go! Bring her. I will wait here.

The sister puts her arms round her neck and kisses her in silence. Then she goes out towards the sea, and disappears rapidly among the oleanders.

Scene Three

Silvia Settala, *breathlessly, looks through the midst of the boughs lighted by the oblique rays of the sun. The hour is exquisitely peaceful. The light is more limpid than the windows of the white room; the sea is tranquil as the flower of the flax, so motionless that the long reflections of the mirrored sails seem to touch the bottom; the stream seems to create that immense repose, pouring out the perennial wave of its peace; the health-giving woods, penetrated with fluid gold, rejoice marvellously, almost as if they lost their roots that they might swim in the delight of their odour; the marble Alps in the distance trace a line of beauty on the sky, in which they seem to reveal the dream arising out of their imprisoned populace of sleeping statues.*

La Sirenetta *reappears in the silence, through which her pure voice is heard.*

La Sirenetta   Are you alone?

Silvia Settala (*agitated*)   Yes. I am waiting.

La Sirenetta (*coming close to her*)   Have you been crying?

Silvia Settala   Yes, a little.

La Sirenetta (*with infinite pity*)   You seem as if you had been crying for a year. Your eyes are burning. Your heart hurts you too much.

Silvia Settala   Don't speak. I cannot crush my heart,

She presses herself against the trunk of the nearest oleander, convulsed, no longer able to endure the agony of waiting.

She is coming now, she is coming now.

She moves away from the tree and re-enters the room, as if seized with terror, like one seeking refuge.

The Voice of Beata (*from among the oleanders*)   Mamma! Mamma!

The mother starts, and turns, frightfully pallid.

The Voice of Beata   Mamma!

The child rushes towards her mother with a cry of joy, her face lit up, heated, her hair in disorder, panting after a long run, carrying an untidy bunch of flowers. As she runs in, the bunch falls. The mutilated woman stoops towards the little arms that clasp her neck, and offers her death-like face to the furious kisses.

Silvia Settala   Beata! Beata!

Beata (*panting*)   Ah, how I have run, how I have run! I ran away from them, all alone. I ran, I ran. They didn't want to let me come. Ah, but I ran away from them, with my bunch of flowers.

Covers her mother's face with fresh kisses.

Silvia Settala   You are all damp with sweat, you are hot, burning . . . My God!

In her rush of tenderness she instinctively makes a movement as if to wipe the child's face; but stops and hides her arms in the folds of her garments; and a shiver of visible horror runs through her.

Beata   Why don't you take me up? Why don't you put your arms round me? Take me up, take me up, mamma!

She rises on tiptoe, to be caught into her mother's embrace. The mother takes a step backwards, blindly.

Silvia Settala   Beata!

Beata (*following her*)   Don't you want me? don't you want me?

Silvia Settala   Beata!

She tries to feign a smile with her ashen lips, distorted by unspeakable sorrow.

Beata   Is it for fun? What are you hiding? O, give, give me what you are hiding!

Silvia Settala   Beata! Beata!

Beata   I have brought you flowers, such a lot of flowers. Do you see? do you see?

As she turns to pick up the fallen bunch, she perceives her little wild friend, and remembers her.

Beata   Oh, Sirenetta! Are you there?

La Sirenetta *is there, before the window, standing, a silent witness, with her eyes fixed on the sorrowful mother. As the repeated breath of the wind passes between the fronds of an arbutus[29] and makes it tremble, so the sorrow of the mother seems to invest and penetrate that slender body which the oblique rays of the sun ring with bands of gold.*

Beata   Do you see what a lot? All for you!

The child picks up the bunch.

Take it!

She runs towards her mother again, who steps back.

Silvia Settala   Beata! Beata!

Beata (*astonished*)   Don't you want them? Take them! Take them!

Silvia Settala   Beata!

She falls on her knees, overcome with sorrow, as if stricken by an unendurable blow, falls on her knees before her frightened child; and a flood of tears, that bursts from her eyes like blood from a wound, bathes her face.

---

29 Arbutus: shrub with red berries.

Beata   You are crying? You are crying?

Frightened she throws herself upon her mother's breast, with all her flowers. **La Sirenetta**, *who has also fallen on her knees, lays her forehead and the palms of her hands upon the ground.*

The End.

Ardiane and Barbe Bleue or, The Useless Deliverance

Maurice Maeterlinck (1899)

Translated by Bernard Miall

The Flemish playwright, poet, and essayist **Maurice Maeterlinck** (1862–1949) enjoyed considerable fame in his own day, winning the Nobel Prize for Literature in 1911. He is best-known today for his plays, which, in the words of Patrick McGuinness, gave the symbolist movement 'something that it had been seeking for more than a decade: a theatre' – and this despite the reservations that many symbolists held about the prospect or desirability of a symbolist theatre.[1] This includes Maeterlinck, who began his career as a playwright by arguing that most great plays were essentially unstageable, including the best works of Shakespeare.[2] However, while it is true that many, like Mallarmé, found in Maeterlinck a champion of a dematerialised theatre – Mallarmé indirectly launched Maeterlinck's career after giving a copy of his first play, *La Princesse Maleine* (1889), to Octave Mirbeau, who wrote a laudatory review that compared the young playwright to Shakespeare – others, like Rainer Maria Rilke, thought him to be a pioneer of contemporary stagecraft.[3] Maeterlinck was also a playwright of 'total theatre', taking a keen interest in direction and acting, as well as design (he was particularly inspired by the Pre-Raphaelites), and he frequently amended his plays after attending first performances.[4] Hence, it is more appropriate to approach Maeterlinck's plays on the basis of a productive tension between an apparent dismissal of theatre, and an imaginative attempt to claim it back.[5]

The 'static theatre' with which Maeterlinck has become so closely associated – a theatre of inaction, silence and loaded eventlessness – only tells part of the story of his dramatic output. His early plays, like *L'Intruse* (*Intruder*, 1890) and *Les Aveugles* (*The Blind*, 1890), certainly fit the bill of a static theatre, but throughout his career as a playwright Maeterlinck experimented with different forms and styles of theatre that are not so easily compartmentalised. His famous proposition that he wrote theatre not for actors, but marionettes or shadows, also needs to be read in the light of a commitment to experimentation and innovation. We might read his interest in shadows and marionettes not as a definitive call for his works to be realised as puppet plays (much as they work well as puppet plays), but as a state to which the actor should aspire (just as we might read the British scenographer Edward Gordon Craig's influential essay 'The Actor and the Über-Marionette' (1907) in a similar light, however staunchly he seems to repudiate the living actor's body).[6]

As McGuinness recognises, 'there are as many Maeterlincks as there were avant-garde writers and artists to read and interpret him. He fits as well into a "yellow book"

1   Patrick McGuinness, *Maurice Maeterlinck and The Making of Modern Theatre* (Oxford: Oxford University Press, 2000), 1.

2   Maurice Maeterlinck, *Maeterlinck: Introduction à une psychologie des songes (1886–1896)*, ed. Stefan Gross (Brussels: Labor, 1985), 83.

3   Rainer Maria Rilke, 'Maurice Maeterlinck', *Synthèses*, 195 (August 1962): 60–73.

4   See Katherine Worth, *Theatre in Focus: Maeterlinck's Plays in Performance* (Cambridge: Chadwyck-Healey, 1985), 12.

5   See Patrick McGuinness, 'Mallarmé, Maeterlinck and the Symbolist Via Negativa of Theatre', in *Against Theatre: Creative Destructions on the Modernist Stage*, ed. Alan Ackerman and Martin Puchner (Basingstoke and New York: Palgrave Macmillan, 2006), 149–67 (150).

6   Edward Gordon Craig, 'The Actor and the Über-Marionette', in *The Twentieth Century Performance Reader*, ed. Teresa Brayshaw and Noel Witts, 3rd edn (London and New York: Routledge, 2014), 144–52.

vision of the 1890s [. . .] as he does into what Artaud called, in 1923, "la poésie archi-actuelle" ("ultra-contemporary poetry")'.[7] *Ardiane and Barbe Bleue* (1899) lends itself to the *Yellow Book* camp, but not because it harkens back to his days as a poet associated more with decadence than symbolism in the 1880s. This music-drama does not so much stage an 'opulent sickliness', as McGuinness describes his early poetry collection *Serres chaudes* (*Hothouses*, 1889);[8] rather, it stages the precarity of an opulent domain – at once ethereal and eerie, seductive and disturbing – teetering on the precipice of doom, succumbing to the subversive life force of a heroine. This marks it as a transitional work for Maeterlinck as he branched out from symbolism to explore other styles and genres. Characters from Maeterlinck's earlier works also appear in *Ardiane and Barbe Bleue* as Bluebeard's captive wives: Mélisande (*Pelléas et Mélisande*, 1893), Alladine (*Alladine et Palomides*, 1894), Ygraine and Bellangère (*La Mort de Tintagiles*, 1894), and Sélysette (*Aglavaine et Sélysette*, 1896). Ultimately each character chooses to remain in the darkness of Bluebeard's castle. Only Ardiane leaves for the world beyond, suggesting that *Ardiane and Barbe Bleue* served as a vehicle for Maeterlinck to wrestle with his origins – and future – as a playwright.

Ardiane and Barbe Bleue was written for the actress and singer Georgette Leblanc in 1899, although the composer Paul Dukas did not finish his score until 1907. Maeterlinck's text is loosely based on Charles Perrault's folkloric tale *Barbe-bleue* (*Bluebeard*, 1697), and legend has it that Bluebeard himself is a mythologisation of the fifteenth-century French nobleman Gilles de Rais, whose taste for murderous debauchery is depicted in Joris-Karl Huysmans's *Là-Bas* (1891), although Gilles de Rais – companion-in-arms to Joan of Arc – is better-known as a monstrous child killer. Ardiane appears fated to be Bluebeard's sixth wife in Maeterlinck's play, although Maeterlinck makes several important changes to the folklore. In the folkloric tale she discovers the bloodied corpses of Bluebeard's wives on the other side of the door, but in Maeterlinck's play she finds the wives alive in the darkness. Ardiane also releases Bluebeard after he is taken captive by a mob, before leaving his castle and its tyrannical occupant. These twists are important, as it complicates figurations of victimhood in the original source material. At the end of Maeterlinck's play it is Bluebeard who is bound and at the mercy of Ardiane. Neither husband nor wife are 'obedient' to one another. Ardiane gains her freedom by transgressing the threshold of a forbidden door and 'discovering' knowledge she had already intuited, charging the ensuing encounters with Bluebeard's wives with a strange homoeroticism. The play offers a decadent reimagining of folkloric morality, then, not least in its conclusion. The 'shrinking heroines' associated with symbolist drama remain captive and attached to their condition, whereas Ardiane – who Katherine Worth describes as the play's 'New Woman' – escapes in search of a new destiny.[9]

7   McGuinness, *Maurice Maeterlinck*, 2–3.
8   McGuinness, *Maurice Maeterlinck*, 33.
9   Worth, *Theatre in Focus*, 45.

Characters

Ardiane[10]
Sélysette
Mélisande
Ygraine
Bellangère
Alladine
A Nurse, *foster-mother to Ardiane*
Barbe Bleue
Peasants, *the crowd*

---

10 Ardiane is an alternative spelling of Ariadne, the mythological daughter of King Minos and Pasiphae.

Act One

A vast, resplendent hall, of semi-circular form, in the castle of **Barbe Bleue**. *At the remoter end, in the centre of the semi-circular wall, is an enormous door; on either hand of this are three smaller doors, of ebony, with locks and ornaments of silver; each door is set within a niche, and all these niches are enclosed by a semi-circular colonnade of marble, the pillars of which support the balcony overhead. Above these doors, but set further back, are six great windows, to which the aforesaid balcony gives access; these may be gained from either side of the hall, by two flights of stairs, which follow the curve of the walls, and lead up to the semi-circular gallery.*

It is evening; the great windows are open, and the candelabra lit. Without, below the windows, is an invisible, excited crowd, whose cries, now uneasy, now terrified, now threatening, together with the sound of sudden movements, the trampling of feet, and the murmur of persons speaking, are heard with great distinctness. During the first bars of the overture the curtain rises, and the voices of the hidden crowd are at once heard above the music.

Voices in the Crowd   So . . . she was in the chariot? Did you see?
All the village lingered there,
There, to see her. . . . Is she fair?
She looked at me. . . . And me. . . . And me.
O miserable child! . . . Yet all the while
She seemed to smile.
Whence hath she come? . . . From very far away,
To know not . . . what awaits her here today.
Their journey hath endured for thrice ten days. . . .
He cannot see us . . . shout, that he may know. . . .

All together.

Back! Back! . . . Advance no nearer! Never go
Up to the castle! . . . It is death, death, death!

Isolated voices.

She does not understand. . . . I hear they say
No less than twenty men pursued her way,
That dwelt about her home. . . . You wonder why?
Because they loved her. . . . Many used to cry
Along the roads. . . . Why has she come, O why?
They tell me that she knew. . . . He shall not have her, no!
She is too fair for you! . . . He shall not have her, no! . . .
O see them, see them, there they go!
Where are they going? . . . They are coming through,
By the red gate. . . . It is not true . . .
I see their torches in the avenue!
There the great chariot goes between the trees!

He is afraid. . . . He shall not have her, no!
He is mad, mad, mad! He is mad! He has done enough!
It is too much! . . . So she will be the sixth!
O murderer, butcher! . . . Death to the butcher, death!
Fire, fire! . . . Bring fire! . . . I have brought my hay-fork, see!
And I my scythe! – They are entering the yard . . .
Hey, let me see! . . . Take care! . . . The gates are barred!
Wait for them here . . . They say she knows it all!
What does she know? . . . She knows what I know too.
What do you know? . . . I know they all are dead!
Not dead, not dead? . . . I buried them myself!
But I one evening once as I went by
Heard singing voices. . . . So did I. . . . And I . . .
Ay, they come back, they say. . . . But he
Brings down misfortune on our heads. . . . O see,
The windows! . . . They are closing of themselves!
Now . . . they are going in! They are going in . . .
Nothing to see! . . . Death to him! Death! Death! Death!

And at this moment the six great windows above the interior balcony close of their own motion, stifling little by little the voices of the crowd. Soon nothing is heard but an indefinite murmur which is almost silence. Shortly afterwards **Ardiane** *and the* **Nurse** *enter by a side door.*

The Nurse   Where are we? . . . Listen! . . . Ah! . . . that muttering there!
It is the peasants: they were eager, yes,
To save us: yes, they ran along the roads,
But never dared to speak: they made us signs,
They made us signs that meant we should return. . . .

She goes forward to the great door at the end of the hall.

They are here, behind this door! . . . I hear them: some
Tramp to and fro. . . . Now let us try to flee. . . .
He leaves us here alone: we can escape,
Perhaps. . . . I tell you plainly, he is mad!
O, it is death! For all they say is true,
He has killed five women.

Ardiane   No, they are not dead . . .
Yonder I heard it spoken of at times,
In the far place whereto his savage love,
That yet was tremulous, came to seek me out,
As of a thing incomprehensible.
I was suspicious of the truth, and here
Am sure. He loves me: I am beautiful:
So shall I learn his secret. But ere all
We must be insubordinate. When the future
Is threatening to us and inscrutable

That is ere all our duty. For the rest,
They were mistaken; and if they are lost
They were lost by hesitation.
Here are we,
Within the outer hall whence opens out
The chamber where his love awaits me.
Here
Are keys he gave me of the treasure-chests
Of bridal raiment, and the silver keys
Are ours to use: the golden is forbid.
That is the only one of import. These,
The six, I cast away: the last I keep.

She throws away the keys of silver, which tinkle and ring on the marble flags.

The Nurse (*who hastily picks them up again*)   What are you doing? He has given you
The treasures, all the treasures that they open!

Ardiane   Open them you, then, if it give you pleasure;
For me, I seek for the forbidden door.
Open the others if you will; but all
That is permitted us will tell us nought.

The Nurse (*looking at the keys and then about the hall*)   The doors are yonder, set
within the marble,
And we may know, since all have locks of silver,
They answer to the keys: but first of all,
Which one shall I unclose?

Ardiane   What matter which?
They are but there to turn aside our minds
From that we need to know. . . . I do not find,
Although I seek for it, the seventh door. . . .

The Nurse (*trying the lock of the first door*)   Is this the key of the first? . . . Or this?
. . . Or this?
Not yet, not yet. . . . Ay, but the third goes in,
Dragging my fingers after it! Beware! . . .
Fly! . . . The two panels both have come to life!
They are gliding back like curtains! . . . What is this?
Beware, beware! . . . It is a hail of fire,
That beats upon my hands, that wounds my face!
O!

The **Nurse** *springs backward, for while she is speaking the two leaves of the door glide of their own motion into lateral recesses, and suddenly disappear, disclosing a vast heap of amethysts piled up to the top of the doorway. Then, as though delivered suddenly from centuries of constraint, countless gems and jewels of every size and form, but all of the one substance, amethyst – necklaces, bracelets, rings, aigrettes,* *buckles, girdles, collars, diadems – fall like a crumbling mass of violet flames, and rebound as far as the further side of the hall; and, while the first to fall spread themselves over the marble flags, others, more and more numerous and more and more resplendent, begin to fall from all the mouldings of the enchanted vaultings, and flow therefrom continually with an incessant sound of living jewels.*

The Nurse (*fascinated, bewildered, gathering up jewels with both her hands*)   Gather them up, O stoop, gather them up!
Take the most beautiful! Enough are here
To glorify a kingdom! Still they fall!
They pierce my hair, they stone my hands! O look!
Unheard-of gems are raining from the vaults,
Miraculous violets, purple, lilac, mauve!
Plunge your arms into them and hide your face,
And I will fill my mantle full with them!

Ardiane   These amethysts are noble. Open now
The second door.

The Nurse   The second? I dare not! . . .
Yet I would know if . . .

She inserts the key in the lock of the second door.

O, beware, beware!
The key already turns! And they have wings,
The doors: the walls too tear themselves asunder!
O!

The scene is the same as on the opening of the first door, but this time is seen the accumulated wealth, the rebounding irruption, the dazzling and musical fall of a blue rain of sapphires.

Ardiane   These are fine sapphires. Open now the third.

The Nurse   Wait, wait until I see that I have here
Indeed the most magnificent. My cloak
Will break beneath the weight of blue, blue sky!
O see them overflow! on every hand
They pour, pour, pour! – a violent torrent here,
And yonder in a stream of azure blue!

Ardiane   Come, come, Nurse, quickly, for the chance to sin
Is rare and fugitive. . . .

The Nurse (*opens the third door, when the same thing befalls, save that this time follows the pale invasion, the milky rush, of a deluge of pearls, a shower less heavy, but more illimitable than those preceding*)   I will but take
A handful of them, so they may caress
The sapphires.

Ardiane   Open now the fourth door.

The Nurse (*opens the fourth door, when as before there is a shower of jewels, but this time of emeralds*)   O, these are greener than the Spring that runs
Along the poplars thick with drops of dew
That catch the lovely sunlight in my home!

Shaking her mantle, which overflows with amethysts, sapphires, and pearls.

Away, away, ye others! give you place
For the most beautiful – for I was born
Under the boughs, and love the light of leaves.

Ardiane   Open the fifth door.

The Nurse   O, not even these?
You do not love them?

Ardiane   What I love is fair
Beyond all fairness of miraculous gems.

The Nurse (*opening the fifth door, to set free a blinding irruption, a living incandescence, a sinister deluge and cascade of rubies*)   O, these are terrible: I will not touch!

Ardiane   Now we approach the end: the threat lies here.
Open the sixth.

The Nurse   It is the last key.

Ardiane   Open it quickly.

The **Nurse**, *hesitating, opens the sixth door. All passes as before: but the radiance is this time intolerable. Cataracts of enormous diamonds of the first water pour into the hall; myriads of sparks, flashes, flecks of fire, and prismatic rays mingle, are extinguished, blaze forth again and multiply, outspreading as they fall.* **Ardiane**, *startled, gives a dazed cry. She stoops, picks up a diadem, a necklace, and handfuls of the glistening splendour, and therewith she decks at random her hair, her arms, her throat, her hands. Then, flashing before her eyes and raising before her face diamonds that shed a brilliance upon her.*

Ardiane O, my flashing diamonds!
For you I never sought, but on my way
I greet you! O immortal dew of light!
Stream o'er my hands, illuminate my arms,
Dazzle my very flesh! O, you are pure,
And you are tireless, and you never die:
And that which in your fires eternally
Trembles, like to a populace of spirits,
That have constrained and wear the stars of Heaven,
It is the passion of that Radiance
Which, penetrating all things, knows no rest,
And finds no more to conquer, save itself!

She approaches the door, and looks up at the vaulted arch.

Rain on, O supreme heart of summer, rain.
O shards of light, O limitless soul of flame!
Yea, wound my eyes, yet shall you never tire
Those eyes of gazing!

Leaning yet further back.

O, what is it there?
O Nurse, where are you? For the splendid rain
Hangs motionless, suspended in a bow,
A diamond rainbow of prismatic fire! . . .
O see the seventh door, with golden bars,
With golden lock and hinges!

The Nurse   Come away!
No, never touch it! No, withdraw your hands!
Withdraw your eyes, lest of itself it open!
Come, let us hide! These diamonds – after them
Or fire will come, or death!

Ardiane   Go back, go back!
Hide you yourself behind a marble shaft:
I will alone go forward.

She steps into the recess under the vaulted doorway, and inserts the key in the lock. The door divides into two panels, and disappears: nothing is visible save an opening full of darkness: but the sound of singing, muffled and remote, rises from the depths of the earth, and spreads through the hall.

The Nurse   Ardiane!
What are you doing? Is it you that sings?

Ardiane   Listen!

Distant Voices   Orlamonde's five daughters,
When the faery died,
Orlamonde's five daughters
Sought to win outside.[11]

The Nurse   They are . . . the other women!

Ardiane   Yes.

The Nurse   O, shut the door! Their singing fills the hall:
It will be heard, heard everywhere!

Ardiane (*trying to close the door*)   I cannot!

Distant Voices   They lit their five lanterns,
Through all the towers they sought,

---

11 Maeterlinck named his chateau in Nice Orlamonde, after a name in Maeterlinck's *Quinze Chansons* (1896).

And in four hundred chambers;
The day, they found it not.

The Nurse   Now it is louder, always louder! Come!
Come, let us close – help me – the outer door. . . .

They try to close the door that concealed the diamonds.

The Nurse   This too resists! We cannot shut them in!

Distant Voices   Then they found an echoing deep,
And let it them enfold:
And upon a stubborn door
Found a key of gold.

The Nurse (*bewildered, and also entering the recess*)   Be silent, silent! . . . We shall
all be lost! Stifle that voice!

Stretching out her mantle.

The doorway – ah, my cloak
Will cover it. . . .

Ardiane   I see beyond the sill
Steps. I am going down to where they sing.

Distant Voices (*always louder*)   Through the chinks they see the ocean:
Ah, they fear to die!
They strike the door they dare not open,
And the hours go by.

At the last words of the song **Barbe Bleue** *enters the hall. For a moment he stops
short, gazing; then he draws near to the women.*

Barbe Bleue   You too!

Ardiane (*who starts, leaves the doorway, and advances, glittering with diamonds,
towards* **Barbe Bleue**)   I above all.

Barbe Bleue   I thought that you
Were stronger, wiser than your sisters were.

Ardiane   How long did they avoid the thing forbid?

Barbe Bleue   This, for some days; that, a few months; and one,
The last of all, a year.

Ardiane   It was the last,
Only the last, that there was need to punish.

Barbe Bleue   It was a very little thing to ask.

Ardiane   You asked of these more than you ever gave.

Barbe Bleue   The happiness I willed for you you lose.

Ardiane   The happiness I would lives not in darkness.
When I know all to pardon will be mine.

Barbe Bleue (*seizing* **Ardiane** *by the arm*)   Come! Come!

Ardiane   Where would you, then, that I should go?

Barbe Bleue   Where I shall lead you.

Ardiane   No.

Barbe Bleue *strives to drag her away by force. She gives a long cry of pain. This cry is answered at first by a low murmur from without. The struggle between the two continues for a few moments, and the* **Nurse** *gives vent to despairing outcries. Suddenly a stone, hurled from without, shatters one of the windows, and the crowd is heard, excited and enraged. Other stones fall; the* **Nurse**, *running to the great door at the end of the hall, raises the bars and shoots the bolts. A sudden rush from outside splinters the door and forces it in; and the peasants, infuriated but hesitating, crowd upon the threshold.* **Barbe Bleue**, *releasing* **Ardiane**, *draws his sword and prepares for the onset. But* **Ardiane**, *tranquil, advances towards the crowd.*

Ardiane   What would you? He has not done me any ill.

She gently disperses the peasants, and carefully closes the door, while **Barbe Bleue**, *with lowered eyes, gazes at the point of his sword.*

Curtain.

Act Two

At the rising of the curtain the scene is a vast subterranean hall, with a vaulted roof supported by many columns; it is plunged in almost total darkness. From the extreme right, almost in the wings, there runs back a narrow, winding subterranean passage, also with a vaulted roof; it debouches into the great hall towards the front of the stage by a roughly-arched opening.

At the further end of this passage **Ardiane** *and the* **Nurse** *are seen, descending the last few steps of a stairway;* **Ardiane** *carries a lamp.*

The Nurse   Hush! Do you hear? He shuts the iron door
Over our heads! Why would you not give way?
We never shall behold the day again.

Ardiane   Fear not; he is wounded, he is overcome;
But knows it not as yet. With supplication
He will re-open it: but let us seek
First if we cannot of ourselves win free.
Meanwhile his wrath all that his love refused
Has granted: we shall find what here is hid.

She advances, holding the lamp high above her head, to the mouth of the passage, and there bends forward, seeking to penetrate the darkness of the hall. At the first ray of light which pierces the obscurity is heard the sound of hushed and fearful flight. **Ardiane** *turns towards the* **Nurse** *to call her.*

Ardiane   Come! They are here!

She enters the hall, which the lamp illuminates pillar by pillar.

Where are you?

A terrified moan replies. **Ardiane** *directs the rays of her lamp toward the part from which it seems to proceed, and perceives the forms of five women, motionless with fright, who are huddled together in the shadows of the remotest pillars.*

Ardiane (*in a muffled, voice, still half fearful*)   They are there!
Nurse, nurse, where are you?

The **Nurse** *hastens toward* **Ardiane**: **Ardiane** *gives her the lamp, and takes a few hesitating steps toward the five.*

Ardiane   Sisters, O my sisters!

The five start.

They live! They live! They live!
Behold me here!

She runs to them with open arms, clasps them with hesitating hands, strains them to her breast, and kisses them and caresses them, feeling about her with uncertain *gestures, in a kind of impassioned and convulsive tenderness, while the **Nurse**, lamp in hand, stands still a little apart.*

Ardiane   O, I have found you! . . . They are full of life,
They are full of sweetness! . . . When I saw the hall
Open in darkness from the passage end,
I thought to find . . . ah me! . . . dead bodies here. . . .
And lo . . . I kiss these loveliest lips in tears!
Have you not suffered? O, your lips how fresh,
Your cheeks how like the cheeks of children! See,
Your naked arms are supple, ay, and warm;
Your round round breasts are throbbing through their veils!
Why do you tremble? . . . O, how many you are!
Now I clasp shoulders; now my arms entwine
Hips, and my touch on whom I know not rests. . . .
On every hand my lips meet lips, my breast meets breasts.
O this that bathes you all, this hair!
You must be fair, so fair!
Waves, faintly warm, are parted by my hands,
My arms are lost amid rebellious strands. . . .
Have you a thousand tresses? . . . and are they
Like night, or like the day?
I see no longer what I do,
But I am kissing, kissing all of you,
And one by one I gather all your hands!
It is the least of you I find the last:
O never tremble! See, I hold you fast,
My arms enfold you close to me!
Nurse, nurse, what are you doing there?
Behold me like a mother here,
Feeling in darkness, and my children . . . they
Await the dawn to clear.

*The **Nurse** draws near, bearing the lamp, and its light falls on the group of women. The captives are then seen to be clad in rags, their hair in disorder, their faces emaciated and their eyes dazzled and alarmed. **Ardiane**, for a moment astonished, takes the lamp from the **Nurse**, in order the better to light them, and to regard them more closely.*

Ardiane   O, you have suffered here!
And O, how gloomy does your prison seem!
Great clammy drops are falling on my hands,
And my lamp's flame is flickering all the while!
How strange your eyes are when you look at me!
And you draw back as I approach – but why?
What, are you still afraid?
And who is that who seeks to fly?
Is it not she, the youngest of you all,

She that I kissed but now?
O, has my long long sister's kiss
Done to you any harm?
Come to me, come then! Do you fear the light?
Tell me, what is her name?

Two or Three Timid Voices   Sélysette.

Ardiane   Sélysette – a smile?
It is the first that I have seen this while!
Your wide eyes falter as though they saw the Dead,
Although in truth they look on life instead:
And O, these delicate bare arms that tremble,
Both waiting to be loved! Come, my arms too
Are waiting, though I tremble not as you!

Embracing her.

You have been in this tomb how many days?

Sélysette   We count the days but ill here, oftentimes
Deceive ourselves, but none the less I think
I have been here for upwards of a year.

Ygraine *advances: she is paler than the others.*

Ardiane   It is a long while since you saw the light!

Ygraine   I used not to unclose my eyes; I wept
So long alone.

Sélysette (*looking fixedly at* **Ardiane**)   How beautiful you are!
How could he bring himself to punish you
As he used us? You also in the end
Have disobeyed him?

Ardiane   No, it was not so!
No, I obeyed more swiftly than the rest,
But other laws than his.

Sélysette   Why have you come?
O why have you come here?

Ardiane   To set you free.

Sélysette   How should we be set free?

Ardiane   But follow me:
No more than that. . . . What used you here to do?

Sélysette   We prayed, sang, wept, and then we waited always.

Ardiane   You never sought escape?

Sélysette   We could not flee,
For all the ways are shut, and flight forbid.

Ardiane   That we shall see. . . . But she that looks at me
Between the tangles of her fallen hair
That seems to wrap her round in frozen flame –
What is her name?

Sélysette   Her name is Mélisande.

Ardiane   Come hither, Mélisande! And she whose eyes,
Wide, eager eyes, are following my lamp?

Sélysette   Bellangère.

Ardiane   And that other, who is hid
Behind the heavy pillar?

Sélysette   She has come
From very far away, poor Alladine!

Ardiane   Why do you call her poor?

Sélysette   Because she came
Last of us all, and speaks another tongue.

Ardiane (*holding out her arms to* **Alladine**)   Come, Alladine! . . . You see that I speak hers,
When I embrace her thus.

Sélysette   She has not yet
Ever ceased weeping.

Ardiane (*looking at* **Sélysette** *and the others with astonishment*)   Why, but you yourself,
Can you not laugh yet – laugh and clap your hands?
And all the rest are silent! What is this?
What are you? Will you live in terror thus
Always? I do not see you smile at all,
While with your eyes – incredulous eyes! – you watch
My every gesture. Will you not believe
The joyful news? O, do you not regret
The light of day, the birds among the boughs,
The high green gardens blowing overhead?
Do you not know the world is in the Spring?
I yester-morning, wandering by the way,
Drank in the light, the sense of space of dawn,
So many flowers beneath my every step,
I knew not where to set my careless feet!
Have you forgot the sunlight and the dew,
Dew in the leaves, and laughter of the sea?
The sea but now was laughing as it laughs

On days whereon it knows the wind of joy,
And all its thousand ripples approved my feet,
Its ripples singing on the sands of light. . . .

At this moment one of the drops of water which drip incessantly from the roof falls upon the flame of the lamp which **Ardiane** *holds before her, as she turns towards the mouth of the subterranean passage, and the light flickers and is extinguished. The* **Nurse** *gives a cry of terror, and* **Ardiane** *stops, dismayed.*

Ardiane (*in the darkness*)   O, but where are you?

Sélysette   Hither: take my hand.
Stay by me: water, stagnant and profound,
Lies yonder.

Ardiane   What, and you can see it still?

Sélysette   Yes, we have lived so long in darkness here.

Bellangère   Come hither: it is lighter here by far.

Sélysette   Yes, let us all go thither to the light.

Ardiane   Then is there in this deepest darkness light?

Sélysette   Yes, there is light. Do you not see it there,
A wide, pale glow illumining the depth
Beyond the further arches?

Ardiane   Where?

Sélysette   O blind!
O, let me kiss you. . . .

Ardiane   Yes, there is indeed
A faint light, growing wider. . . .

Sélysette   O no, no!
It is your eyes, your lovely astonished eyes
That widen!

Ardiane   O, whence is it?

Mélisande   We do not know.

Ardiane   But we must know!

She goes toward the back of the scene, and moves to and fro, feeling along the wall with her hands.

Here is the wall . . . and here . . .
But higher . . . here . . . it is no longer stone!
Help me to mount upon this mass of rock!

She climbs, supported by the others.

Here it is like an altar. Here the roof

Is moulded in a pointed arch. . . . And here –
O, O, enormous bolts and iron bars!
You have sought to push them? Have you?

Sélysette   Never! No!
No, never touch them: for they say the sea
Washes the walls – great waves will tumble in!
It is the sea that makes it glimmer green!

Ygraine   We have so often heard it: have a care!

Mélisande   O, I see water tremble above our heads!

Ardiane   No, no, it is the light that seeks you out!

Bellangère   She is trying to force it open!

The terrified women recoil, and take refuge behind a great column, whence they follow with widened eyes **Ardiane**'s *every movement.*

Ardiane   My poor sisters!
Why, if you love your darkness, do you seek
Deliverance from any quarter? Why,
If you were happy, did you use to weep?
O, the bars rise! They rise! And now the doors
Are going to open! Wait!

And indeed the heavy panels of a sort of great interior shutter are seen, while yet she is speaking, to open, but as yet only a very faint, diffused, and sombre light illuminates the round aperture perceived under the vaulted ceiling.

Ardiane (*continuing her search*)   No light as yet,
No real light! But now I pass
My hands across. . . . What is it? Glass?
Or maybe marble. . . . One would say
This were a window, sealed away,
Blackened with pitch. . . . My nails are broken! Nay,
Where are your distaffs?[12] Mélisande,
Sélysette, give me in my hand
A distaff: nay, a stone,
A single pebble of the thousands strown
Over the floor. . . .

Sélysette *runs to* **Ardiane**, *holding up to her a stone, which she takes.*

Ardiane   Behold before your eyes
The key of your sunrise!

She strikes a violent blow upon the glass. One of the square panes is shattered into fragments, and a great dazzling star seems to burst forth in the darkness. The women give a cry of almost delighted terror, and **Ardiane**, *now beside herself, and wholly*

---

12 Distaff: a spindle for spinning wool or flax.

submerged in a more and more intolerable radiance, breaks all the remaining panes
with heavy, hurried blows, in a kind of ecstatic delirium.

Yet another pane!
Now, and now again!
Till they fall, great and small, shattered, down to the last of all!
All the panes in ruin crack,
And O the flames are driving back
My hands, my hair!
I can see nothing now of what is there!
Nor do I longer dare
To raise my lids, for now it seems
They are mad with fury, the dazzling beams!
Stir not from where you were!
I can no longer stand upright,
But shut my eyes behold the sight
Of bright long strings of pearls, my eyelids lashing!
I know not what assails me, o'er me dashing:
Is it the skies or else the seas,
Is it the light or else the breeze?
All my tresses bright have grown a torrent of light,
And miracle all over me is flashing!
I see no longer, but I hear
A myriad rays of light beating on either ear!
But how to hide my eyes I do not know,
For no shade now my two hands throw;
My eyelids dazzle me; my arms, that try
To cover them, do cover, but with light!
Where are you? Hither, all of you! for I
Am helpless to descend; I cannot see aright;
I see not, know not, where to press
My feet amid the surf of fire that sway my dress!
Come hither, hither all, or I shall fall
Into your darkness!

At this cry **Sélysette** *and* **Mélisande** *leave the shadows wherein they had taken refuge,*
and run to the window, their hands pressed upon their eyes, as though to pass through
flame; and thus, groping in the light, they mount beside **Ardiane** *on the mass of rock.*
The others follow them, and do as they; and thus all crowd together in the stream of
blinding radiance, which forces them to lower their heads. Then passes a moment
of dazzled silence, during which is heard the murmur of the sea without, the caress of
the wind among grasses, the song of birds, and the bells of a flock of sheep going by
in a distant pasture.

Sélysette   I can hear the sea!

Mélisande   And I can see the sky. . . .

Covering her eyes with the bend of her arm.

One cannot look!

Ardiane   My eyes are growing calmer 'neath my hands.
Where are we?

Bellangère   Trees are all that I would see.
Where are they?

Ygraine   O, but how the world is green!

Ardiane   We are midway upon the cliff-side here.

Mélisande   Down there – the village! Do you see the village?

Bellangère   We cannot reach the village: all around
Is water, and the bridges all up-drawn.

Sélysette   Where are there people?

Mélisande   There is a peasant there –
Yonder.

Sélysette   He saw – is looking at us now. See, I will make a sign to him. . . .

She waves her long hair.

He saw!
He saw my hair, he takes his bonnet off!
He makes the sign of the Cross!

Mélisande   A bell, a bell!

Counting the strokes.

Seven, eight, nine!

Bellangère   Ten . . . and eleven . . . twelve!

Mélisande   So it is noon. . . .

Ygraine   Who is it singing so?

Mélisande   Why, those are birds! Do you see them?
There they are!
There are thousands in the lofty poplar trees
That grow along the river.

Sélysette   Alladine!
Where is she, O where is she, Alladine?
For I would kiss her.

Mélisande   Alladine is here,
And I, I kiss her.

Sélysette   You – O Mélisande,
You are so pale!

Mélisande   You also, you are pale!
No, do not look at me!

Sélysette   And see, your dress
Is all in tatters: I can see you through it. . . .

Mélisande   And yours; for your uncovered breasts appear,
Parting your tresses. . . . Do not look at me.

Bellangère   How long our tresses are!

Ygraine   How pale our cheeks!

Bellangère   The sun shines through our hands. . . .

Mélisande   O, Alladine!
She is sobbing!

Sélysette   I am kissing, kissing her. . . .

Ardiane   Ah yes, kiss one another: do not yet
Look in each other's faces: more than all
You shall not think that light will make you sad.
You shall by your intoxication profit
To issue from the tomb. Here steps of stone
Descend the cliff-side. Though I do not know
Whither they lead, yet they are full of light,
And the free winds of heaven assail them. Come!
Follow me all! A thousand thousand rays
Are dancing, dancing on the crests of the sea!

She goes out through the opening and disappears in the light without.

Sélysette (*who follows, drawing the others after her*)   Come, yes, O come, my poor,
my happy sisters!
Let us too dance, dance, dance the dance of the light!

They all climb the great stone and disappear, singing in the brilliance of outer day.

The Receding Voices   Orlamonde's five daughters
(The faery's days were o'er),
Orlamonde's five daughters
Found at last the door.

Curtain.

Act Three

The curtain rises on the same scene as in the First Act. The scattered jewels are still glistening in the niches, and on the marble floor. Between the pillars of the semi-circular colonnade are open coffers, overflowing with costly raiment. It is now night without, and under the hanging candelabra, the tapers of which are lit, **Alladine,** **Sélysette, Mélisande, Ygraine** *and* **Bellangère** *are standing before the great mirrors, and each is giving the touches of completion to the dressing of her hair, or adjusting the folds of her glittering attire, or decking herself with jewels and flowers, while* **Ardiane,** *passing from one to the other, assists and advises them all. The great windows are open.*

Sélysette   Though from the spell-bound castle we as yet
Discover no escape, yet wherefore fear,
Since he is here no longer?
(*Embracing* **Ardiane**.) We are happy,
And still, because you tarry with us, free.

Mélisande   Where has he gone?

Ardiane   I know no more than you.
Yet gone he has. It may be he is troubled:
It may be for the first time disconcerted.
It well may be the anger of the peasants
Left him uneasy; he has felt their hate
Brim over: who shall say he has not gone
To search out guards or soldiers to chastise
The mutinous, and so return a master?

Mélisande   You will not go away?

Ardiane   How should I go,
When all the castle moats are brimming full,
When all the drawbridges are hoisted high,
When all the doors and gates are locked and barred,
When all the walls are inaccessible?
Though none are seen to guard them, none the less
The doors are not abandoned; all our steps
Are closely spied; he must have given out
Mysterious orders. But on every side
The peasants wait and watch upon the roads.
Meanwhile, my sisters, the eventful hour
Draws nigh; we must be very beautiful.
But is it so that you prepare yourselves?
Your hair was full of miracle, Mélisande!
Below, it lit the darkness of the vaults,
Steadfast it smiled upon the night of the tomb,

And now you have extinguished every flame!
Again I come to liberate the light!

She removes **Mélisande**'s *veil, cuts with her scissors the fillets that constrain her
tresses, and all her hair suddenly flows downwards, streaming resplendent over her
shoulders.*

Ygraine (*turning about to look at* **Mélisande**)   O!

Sélysette (*also turning*)   I can hardly think it still is she!
She is so beautiful!

Ardiane   And you, and you!
Those loveliest arms, where are they, **Sélysette**?
What have you done?

Sélysette   Within my silver sleeves,
Here are my arms.

Ardiane   I cannot see them, no,
Not as I saw them but a while ago,
Saw those arms I worshipped so,
The while I watched you, saw you dress,
Every strand and every tress;
They seemed as they were raised above
Your head to reach, to appeal for love.
My loving eyes caressed your every gesture:
I turned about, and when I turn again
I see their shadow merely through their vesture
That shone but now so bright. But now these twain
Twin rays of happiness I liberate!

She detaches the sleeves.

Sélysette   My poor bare arms! O, they will shake with cold!

Ardiane   No, for they are too beautiful! And you,
(*Turning to* **Ygraine**.) Ygraine, where are you? For there shone but now,
Deep in this mirror, shoulders, and a throat,
That flooded it with happy, tender light:
Come, I must liberate you all! My sisters,
In truth I do not wonder any more
He never loved you as he should have loved,
Or that he coveted a hundred, yet
Possessed no woman.

Removing the mantle that **Ygraine** *has thrown over her shoulders.*

Ardiane   O two fountain-heads
Of beauty into darkness cast away!
This above all: fear nothing! And to-night
Let us be beautiful!

*The **Nurse** haggard and dishevelled, enters by a side door.*

The Nurse   O, he is here!
He is returning!

The Others   Who? Who? He? To-night?

Ardiane   Who told you?

Sélysette   Were you able to go out?

Ardiane   Have you seen any one?

The Nurse   Yes, yes, a guard!
He has seen you, he admires you!

Ardiane   I have seen
No creature since the hour he went away.
All gates, all doors of their own motion close,
Though none knows how; the palace seems deserted.

The Nurse   They hide, I say they hide,
And we are all espied
Forever here.
It was the youngest spoke to me;
He is returning; he must be,
He said, quite near.
The peasants are in arms. The peasants know!
They are rising! All the village is below,
Lurking among the hedges! Hark! A cry!

She mounts by one of the curving lateral stairways to the windows of the gallery.

There are torches in the copses going by!

*The women, terrified, give a cry of horror, and run to and fro through the hall, seeking a point of exit. The **Nurse** endeavours to stop them.*

The Nurse   Seek not to fly: you know the doors are shut.
Where would you go? Stay here, stay here, and wait!

Sélysette (*also mounting to the windows*)   O, the great chariot! It is stopping!

All mount the stairs to the windows, crowding together on the interior balcony, and leaning out into the night.

Mélisande   See!
Now he steps out! I see him! And he makes
Signs, signs of anger!

Sélysette   All around him stand
His negroes!

Mélisande   And they all have naked swords
That glitter in the moon!

Sélysette (*taking refuge in* **Ardiane**'s *arms*)   O Ardiane!
O Ardiane, I am frightened!

The Nurse   Do you see?
The peasants are appearing! There they come!
See, there again! And O, they have their scythes,
Their pitch-forks!

Sélysette   They are going to fight!

Murmurs, cries, uproar, tumult, blasphemy, and the clashing of arms in the distance without.

Mélisande   They fight!

Ygraine   One of the negroes there has fallen!

The Nurse   O,
The peasants, they are terrible! Their scythes!
They are so huge! And all the village there!

Mélisande   O look, the negroes are deserting him!
They fly, they fly! They are hiding in the woods!

Ygraine   And he is flying also! Now he runs!
Now he is making for the castle court!

The Nurse   The peasants after him!

Sélysette   O, they will kill him!

The Nurse   They are going out to help him! See the guards!
They have opened wide the castle gates!
They run!
They run to help him!

Sélysette   One, two, three, four, five . . .
Now six . . . now seven. . . . There are only seven!

The Nurse   O look, the peasants are surrounding them!
They are there in hundreds!

Mélisande   O, what are they doing?

The Nurse   I see them dancing round about a man:
The rest have fallen!

Sélysette   And the man is he!
I caught a sight of his blue mantle then:
He is lying on the grass!

The Nurse   Now they are still!
Now they are raising him!

Mélisande   O, is he hurt?

Ygraine   He staggers!

Sélysette   He is bleeding! I saw blood!
Ardiane!

Ardiane   Come away then, look no more!
Hide your head here in my arms!

The Nurse   They are bringing ropes!
They are disputing! Now they tie his limbs!

Mélisande   Where are they going? For they carry him. . . .
They are dancing, they are singing!

The Nurse   Hither, see!
They are coming hither: see them on the bridge!
The gates are open. They are halting. O,
They mean to cast him in the moat!

Ardiane and the others (*terrified, crying aloud, and rocking to and fro in
desperation at the windows*)   No, no!
Help, help him! Do not kill him! Help him, help!
No, no, not that! Not that! Not that! Not that!

The Nurse   They do not hear. . . . The others thrust them on. . . .

Ardiane   He is saved!

The Nurse   And now they are before the gate,
And now they seek to break into the yard!

Cries from the **Crowd**, *who have caught sight of the women at the windows. They
then sing.*

The Crowd   Open! Open! Open! Open the door!
Open wide the door!
Open in God's name!
The candle gutters o'er,
The wick has no more flame!

The Women   We cannot! . . . It is barred! . . . They break it in!
Hear it give way! They all are coming in!
And now they struggle up the flight of steps
Before the door below. Beware! Beware!
They are all drunken!

Ardiane   I am going now
To unbar the door below. . . .

The Women   O Ardiane!
(*Terrified and imploring.*) No! They are drunken! Bolt it, Ardiane!
They are at the door!

Ardiane   Fear nothing: stay you there.

Do not come down, for I will go alone.

The five women descend the stairs which lead down from the windows, and recoil towards the nearer end of the hall, and there remain, grouped rigidly together in an attitude of terrified attention. **Ardiane**, *followed by the* **Nurse**, *goes to the great central door, under the colonnade, and throws back both leaves of it. There is a sound of trampling feet, of shouting, singing, and laughter. The foremost members of the crowd appear, amid the red glare of the torches, as it were framed in the doorway, which they entirely fill, but without crossing the threshold. They are folk of brutal appearance, savage or hilarious according to disposition; their clothes are torn and disordered after their struggle. They are carrying* **Barbe Bleue**, *who is tightly pinioned, and pause for a moment, disconcerted at the appearance of* **Ardiane**, *who is standing before the grave, unperturbed, and imperial. At the same time, further back among those peasants who are crowded together on the flight of steps, and cannot see what is passing, there are cries, sudden thrusts and pushes, shouts, and laughter that lasts a moment and is then extinguished by the perplexed and respectful whisperings of those about the door. At the moment of the invasion of the doorway by the crowd, the five women silently and instinctively fall on their knees at the end of the hall remoter from the door.*

An Old Peasant (*removing his bonnet and rolling it in his hands*)   Well, lady, can a man come in?

One of those that carry Barbe Bleue   You see,
He'll do you no more ill!

A Third Peasant   He's heavy. . . . Ouf!

The First Peasant   Where would you have us put him?

Another Peasant   Over there
Down in the corner.

They lay **Barbe Bleue** *down.*

There now, there he lies
Now he will never stir again! No more!
Much evil has he done us!

Another Peasant   Have you got
Somewhat to kill him with?

Ardiane   Yes, never fear. . . .

The Peasant   Will you have some one help you?

Ardiane   No, no need. . . .
We shall do well.

A Peasant   But look you have a care:
Beware lest he escape you!

Baring his chest.

See you now,
What he has done to me!

Another Peasant (*baring his arm*)   Now see my arm!
It came in here, and then out there it went.

Ardiane   You are all brave folk, but do you leave us now.
We shall avenge ourselves, and well; but now
Leave us, I pray, for night is growing late,
And see to all your wounds.

The Old Peasant   Now show respect,
Because we are not savages, to ladies.
We shall not make a sound. . . . It is not, lady,
Words, merely – but you are too beautiful. Good-bye, good-bye.

Ardiane (*closing the door*)   Good-bye; you have my thanks.

She turns and sees the five women on their knees at the other end of the hall.

You were on your knees!

Approaching **Barbe Bleue**.

Ardiane   And you are wounded? Yes!
The blood is flowing here – 'tis in the neck –
'Tis nothing; no, the wound is shallow. This,
Here on the arm – but hurts upon the arm
Are seldom very grave – but as for this –
The bleeding will not stop: the hand is pierced.
First we must dress it.

While **Ardiane** *is speaking the five women draw nigh, one by one, and without speaking kneel or lean about* **Barbe Bleue**.

Sélysette   His eyes are open now.

Mélisande   How pale he is! He must have suffered!

Sélysette   O!
Those peasants are so terrible!

Ardiane   Some water!

Nurse   Yes, I will go and seek some. . . .

Ardiane   Have you linen?

Mélisande   Here is my kerchief.

Sélysette   He is stifling! O,
Would you not have me hold his head up?

Mélisande   Stay,
See, I will help you.

Sélysette   No, for Alladine
Is helping me.

Alladine *indeed is helping her to raise* **Barbe Bleue**'*s head, and she furtively kisses his forehead, sobbing the while.*

Mélisande   O softly, Alladine!
What are you doing?

Sélysette   How his forehead burns!

Mélisande   His beard is shaven, and he is not now
So terrible. . . .

Sélysette   Have you not some water? See,
His face is covered all with dust and blood.

Ygraine   He breathes with effort. . . .

Ardiane   Yes, it is these cords,
They stifle him. The bonds are drawn so tight
A rock would crumble in them. . . . Have you not,
Some one, a knife?

Ygraine   Two knives were on the table. . . .
Here is the larger.

She gives it to **Ardiane**.

The Nurse (*who has returned with the water – terrified*)   You are going to . . .

Ardiane   Yes.

The Nurse   But he is not – you see . . . he looks at us!

Ardiane   Raise well the cord, so I may do no hurt. . . .

One by one she cuts the bonds which imprison **Barbe Bleue**. *When she comes to those that pinion his arms behind his back the* **Nurse** *seizes her hands to check her.*

The Nurse   Wait till he speaks . . . we do not know at all. . . .

Ardiane   Have you another knife? This blade is broken. . . .
The cords are very hard.

Mélisande (*giving her the knife*)   Here is the other.

Ardiane   Thank you!

She cuts the last turns of the cord. Silence: the beating of their hearts is heard. **Barbe Bleue**, *feeling himself free, rises slowly to a sitting posture, his arms still benumbed, and moves his hands to make them supple. He then regards each of the women about him fixedly, and in silence. Then, leaning against the wall, he stands upright and remains motionless, looking at his injured hand.*

Ardiane (*drawing near to him*)   Good-bye.

She kisses him upon the brow. **Barbe Bleue** *makes an instinctive movement to detain her. She gently frees herself, and proceeds toward the door, followed by the* **Nurse**.

Sélysette (*running after her and stopping her*)   Ardiane, Ardiane!
Where are you going?

Ardiane   Far away from here,
Down yonder, where I am awaited still . . .
Do you come with me, Sélysette?

Sélysette   I too?
But when will you return?

Ardiane   I shall not.

Mélisande   O!
Ardiane!

Ardiane   Are you coming, Mélisande?

Mélisande *looks to and fro from* **Ardiane** *to* **Barbe Bleue** *and does not reply.*

Ardiane   O see the open door, the far blue hills!
Ygraine, are you not coming?

Ygraine *does not turn her head.*

Ardiane   Now the moon,
The stars, illumine every road. And you,
Bellangère, do you come?

Bellangère (*shortly*)   No.

Ardiane   Alladine,
Do I go forth alone?

At these words **Alladine** *runs to* **Ardiane**, *throws herself into her arms, sobbing convulsively, and holds her in a long and feverish embrace.*

Ardiane (*embracing her in turn, and softly disengaging herself, in tears*)   You too
remain, Alladine! O be happy! And farewell. . . .

She goes out hastily, followed by the **Nurse**. *The five women look at one another and at* **Barbe Bleue**, *who slowly raises his head.* **Bellangère** *and* **Ygraine** *shrug their shoulders, and go to close the door. Silence.*

The curtain falls.

Kerria Japonica

Izumi Kyōka (1923)

Translated by M. Cody Poulton

In his own time **Izumi Kyōka** (1873–1939) – who went on to inspire key writers associated with decadent literature in Japan, like Mishima – was considered a novelist first and a playwright second. However, since the 1950s and especially the 1960s he has become better-known in Japan as a playwright. Importantly, as Cody Poulton points out – who also translated the version of *Kerria Japonica* that appears in this volume – the drama was traditionally viewed as a 'blueprint' for performance in late-nineteenth and early-twentieth-century Japan, with the playwright being accorded lower status relative to the craft and manipulation of puppets in *bunraku* or actors in *kabuki* theatre (although both literary fiction and drama, at least relative to poetry, were considered relatively frivolous forms of expression at the time).[1] This hierarchy started to change by the time of the Taishō period (1912–26), the period in which *Kerria Japonica* was written, but the recognition and praise accorded to playwrights as artists in their own right took time to bed in, with Kyōka's original plays only really starting to gain recognition after popular Kabuki as well as directors like Yukio Ninagawa helped to revive interest in his dramatic works in the mid to late twentieth century (in Ninagawa's case since 1975).

The interplay between *Kerria Japonica*'s humorous and erotic qualities lends it a 'perverse difficulty',[2] which is part and parcel of what makes its depiction of uncommon pleasures so compelling. This is a writer who, after all, wanted to offer his audience 'pleasure and delight', as Kyōka puts it, permitting them 'to experience emotions and aesthetic sensations beyond the range of the ordinary'.[3] Kyōka may have been commenting on his own literary fiction here, but much the same could be said of his drama, especially once staged in front of an audience, and regardless of whatever literary quality some of his best-known plays possess. These plays also invite us to stretch 'the range of the ordinary' into some surprising and arresting directions. To be seated before a character gnawing on a rotten carp in *Kerria Japonica* surely presents a different kind of emotional and aesthetic range compared with imagining this scenario in the secluded comfort of a domestic setting. Moreover, if a taste for the uncommon is a key facet of the decadent sensibility, as David Weir suggests,[4] then in this instance it finds itself indebted to Japanese culture more than European influences that would later come to inform experimentation with decadence in Japanese literature and theatre.

There are parallels to be drawn between Kyōka's idiosyncratic decadence and the work of his more familiar European counterparts, particularly with regard to celebrating transgression and the uncommon, but these parallels need to be situated in the historical and cultural context of his plays first and foremost. Even the water from which the carp is plucked in *Kerria Japonica* brims with symbolism and associations specific to Japanese folkloric and literary traditions: synonymous with death (according to folklore the land of the dead was said to be at the bottom of the ocean, or at the water's edge),

---

1 M. Cody Poulton, 'Drama and Fiction in the Meiji Era: The Case of Izumi Kyōka', *Asian Theatre Journal* 12, no. 2 (Autumn 1995): 280–306 (281).

2 We are borrowing the term 'perverse difficulty' from Juliet Carpenter. See Juliet Carpenter, 'Izumi Kyōka: Meiji-Era Gothic', *Japan Quarterly* 31, no. 2 (1984): 154–8 (154).

3 Kyōka qtd. in Carpenter, 'Izumi Kyōka', 155.

4 David Weir, 'Afterword: Decadent Taste', in *Decadence and the Senses*, ed. by Jane Desmarais and Alice Condé (Cambridge: Legenda, 2017), 219–28 (221).

and recurrent as a motif throughout Kyōka's prolific career.[5] Add to examples like this Kyōka's fascination with *kabuki*, and we find that the work's decadent qualities are as much thematic as stylistic, and rooted in traditions and associations specific to Japanese folklore and literature.

Most of Kyōka's plays contain elements of symbolism and the supernatural. They are full of strange creatures and flights of fancy linked to his favouring of a premodern sensibility instead of the modernising impulses that tended to underpin Meiji art and literature at the turn of the twentieth century. This makes *Kerria Japonica* particularly interesting as a work of Kyōka's, as it is entirely concerned with human relationships – albeit unconventional relationships that still 'display touches of the grotesque and decadent that can be found in his wildest fantasies', as Poulton points out.[6] It is also worth highlighting the play's subversion of traditional gender roles in Japan at the time. Kyōka's embrace of the premodern brought with it a traditional belief that female roles should be played by male actors, but his depiction of the relationship between the Lady and the Puppeteer also pokes its nose at heteronormativity, which 'was an integral part of the process of modernization'.[7] *Kerria Japonica* revels in the transgressive quality of a relationship that is heterosexual without being heteronormative – even if Kyōka's own convictions about archaic theatre traditions attenuate the extent to which we might view his work as 'progressive'.

5   Charles Shirō Inouye, 'Water Imagery in the Work of Izumi Kyōka', *Monumenta Nipponica* 46, no. 1 (Spring 1991): 43–68.

6   M. Cody Poulton, '*Kerria Japonica*', in *The Columbia Anthology of Modern Japanese Drama*, ed. J. Thomas Rimer, Mitsuya Mori and M. Cody Poulton (New York: Columbia University Press, 2014), 29–45 (29–30).

7   Nina Cornyetz, 'Heterosexualizing the *Bishōnen*: Ambivalence in Izumi Kyōka's *Yōken kibun*', *The Journal of Japanese Studies* 47, no. 2 (Summer 2021): 381–409 (402).

How like a lovely woman fresh from her bath (her dark eyebrows, faint mountain crescents) are the white blooms of the kerria rose, strikingly pale against their deep, green leaves damp with rain!

Characters

An Artist, *Shimazu Tadashi, forty-five or forty-six years old*
A Lady, *Nuiko, Viscountess Koitogawa, formerly the daughter of the proprietor of the restaurant Yukari, age twenty-five*
A Travelling Puppeteer, *Heguri Tōji, age sixty-nine*
A Young Boy and Girl, *festival pages*
A Shopkeeper, *of a general store*
A Groom
Fourteen or fifteen **Villagers**

Time

The present. A morning in late April.

Place

A back alley in Shuzenji hot spring. Later, also in Shuzenji, a shortcut in the woods to the road to Shimoda.

Scene One

A general store. On one side are three double-petalled cherry trees in full bloom. Inside the closed glass doors of the store are a variety of products for sale: cotton batting, paper, bolts of cloth, dried shiitake mushrooms, patent medicines, soft drinks, and the like. In the earthen entrance, with its door open, are some chairs and a table laid with beer, juice, a keg of saké covered in straw matting, and a bottle of shōchū. *Right beside the store is a rice paddy.*

To the other side of the store is a hedge of cedar over a low stone wall, beneath which flows a small stream. Saffron flowers and weeds grow in the wall. Behind the hedge is a willow in fresh green leaf, its branches drooping over the path. A purple magnolia in blossom would also look good in the background. There is a path between the store and the hedge. The rice paddy, which has not yet been tilled, is covered with green waterweeds. Here and there bloom milk vetch and mustard blossoms. Following the path along the hedge, farther on is a bamboo grove and a tall zelkova tree, in whose shadows the path disappears up the mountain.

The **Puppeteer** *is seated, his back to the audience, at the squalid-looking table at the earthen storefront. As he speaks, he rubs his upper lip.*

The Puppeteer   Master – Kind master! Pour me another, won't you?

The Shopkeeper (*enters the storefront from behind the glass partition*)   Why, there ain't no need to be calling me 'kind'! A simple sir will do me fine. (*Smiles wryly.*) Don't you think the sun's high enough yet, old man? How do you expect to make a living if you drink like that?

The Puppeteer   Hah, hah, hah. I've done with work for the day already. Pardon me for saying so, but once I'm through here, I'll just stagger off to my little nest in the woods.

The Shopkeeper   You needn't tell me how unsteady your legs will be, but it's a bit too early to be heading back to that nest of yours! – I have to mind the store today on me own, but this side of the bridge to the public baths don't see much traffic compared to the crush of visitors in Shuzenji. Now's when you ought to be making money.

The Puppeteer   Right you are. First the locals, then the pilgrims from all over the country – aunties and grannies, grandpas with their grandkids, swarms of them, black as the smoke rising from the ritual bonfires, undaunted by cloudbursts like the monsoons of summer. – And then, the boom! boom! of festival drums have drowned out the tinkle-tinkle coming from the little sideshow tents – why would anybody want to come way over here? Cross the bridge, and so long customers! Hah, hah! – I can ply my trade come evening and make some money, but I've earned enough right now for a drink or two, and I don't need no more than that. – And if worse comes to worst, well then, just let me die here.

Bows deeply, bumping his head hard against the glass pane.

– Kind master, pour me another drink!

The Shopkeeper   You're just like a dying sailor begging Davy Jones to give him water. Maybe that's where the expression 'bottomless cup' came from. . . . Drink as much as you like. It's my business, after all.

Wipes the neck of the bottle.

– Just don't go smashing the merchandise there, old man.

The Puppeteer   Let me die in peace.

Gulps down the drink and laps up what's left on the palm of his hand.

Besides, it's the anniversary of the Saint's death. – Reverend Kōbō, come pick me up and take me away in your automobile with its shiny gold trim!

The Shopkeeper   It won't be the saint that comes and takes you away, but the town hall, and there'll be hell to pay for that. Easy with the alcohol there.

Starts to go inside.

The Puppeteer (*shouting*)   Kind master, pour me another!

The Shopkeeper   It's the Feast of Saint Kōbō, so I won't have my spuds turn into stones on account of you.[8] . . . I hate to be stingy, so be my guest, drink as much as you like. But are you sure you finished the last drop of the one I just gave you?

The Puppeteer   So far, I knocked back five cups. I drank to the snow . . . and now I drink to the blossoms. . . . Kind master, three cherries grow under your eaves. . . . Young trees but in full bloom. . . . There ain't another house in Shuzenji that can boast such blossoms. – And it costs me nothing to look at 'em. The drink costs me dear, but still this is a fine sight. Damn, that's good!

The Shopkeeper   Don't spout nonsense. You're drunk, old man. . . .

The Puppeteer   Why, just the occasional cup or two is a libation for the cherries, to ensure they blossom better. A blessing from Saint Kōbō himself!

The Shopkeeper   Cut the cheap compliments. – It's awful how nobody passes this way. . . . Just two children a while back, in a procession over the mountain from Tatsuno, and nobody else since then, not even a horse and his groom. – It's such a bore having to mind the shop. – Ah, I can hear the drums!

The drums are the kind held up on a pole by two musicians who beat them in turn on both sides. The sound – boom! baboom! boom! – can be heard dimly in the distance.

The Puppeteer   The pipes and flutes, men in formal jackers and *hakama*. – An escort of firemen and pages. In fore and aft, monks burning incense and chanting sutras. The procession of young men in court caps from the Inner Sanctum. carrying

---

8   Saint Kōbō (Kūkai, 774–835) was the founder in Japan of Shingon (Mantrayana) Buddhism, an esoteric sect. He is reputed to have established springs, wells and reservoirs all over Japan, including Shuzenji hot spring. A folktale has him turning potatoes into stones, to punish stingy farmers who refused to give him alms.

the portable shrines. – Hail to the Great Teacher, Diamond of Universal Light! Both right and left of the path are thick with men and women. Offerings fall like rain. . . . The young ladies of town have come to pray in their best kimonos with their flowing sleeves. An old lady leaps out of the Vajra Bath stark naked![9] – Ah, hah, hah, hah! Bet Saint Kōbō would've been pleased if it were a young 'un instead!

The Shopkeeper   Shut up! You'll pay for such profanity.

Goes inside.

The Puppeteer   Hail to the Great Teacher, Diamond of Universal Light!

Sipping his saké slumps down.

Enter the **Lady***, Nuiko, holding a handbag and a folded umbrella downward by the handle. Her hair is held up with a comb, and her obi is simply tied. She is wearing wooden clogs. She gazes at the last, double-petalled cherry in blossom.*

The Lady   My, how lovely! – Such work for such beauty – (*Pause.*) . . . You ought to be thanked for it. – You really are so lovely. Such blossoms!

So speaking, she follows the path along the little stream. Gazing at the saffron flowers growing on the wall, her attention is turned to the water.

Why, it's a carp! Such a big one! – Dear me! He's dead.

A longish pause. As the **Lady** *steps aside to avoid the carp, she stops in front of the puppet that the* **Puppeteer** *has left propped up against the wall. It is a beautiful and elegant figure of a shirabyōshi dancer, attached by strings to bamboo sticks.[10] The* **Lady** *studies it carefully, saying nothing. The sound of rain.*

The Lady   Ah, it's started to rain. (*The Japanese umbrella she opens has the insignia of an inn, the Igiku, or Well-Side Chrysanthemum.*) There are dewdrops on the doll's eyelashes, as if she were weeping . . .

She holds the umbrella over the puppet as if to protect it.

The **Puppeteer** *sticks his head out of the shop curtain to stare at the* **Lady**. *His mouth is large, his brow is furrowed, his face wrinkled and flushed with liquor and pockmarked with a grizzled five o'clock shadow. Covered in a headscarf, he looked mild mannered, but now he is without it, and with his boxy forehead and grey hair, he is a fright to behold.*

Enter the **Artist***, wearing a thin cape and fedora. His face is long and narrow, elegantly thin, his hooded eyes a little sleepy looking. He sports a slender and well-trimmed moustache that is dappled with grey. His complexion is a little pallid, his expression mild, yet dignified. He is shod in borrowed clogs from the inn he is staying at, and heedless of the rain, he carries only a walking stick. He stops to gaze at the cherries. The* **Puppeteer** *turns back and flops down at the table.*

---

9   Varja bath (*tokko no yu*) is the hot spring created by Kūkai when he struck his *vajra* staff against a rock.

10 *Shirabyōshi* refers to a type of female dancer in the Middle Ages who danced in a man's cap and costume.

The Artist (*as if unconcerned about the* **Lady***'s presence*)   A puppet, I see.

The Lady   Sir? – Excuse me, but she doesn't belong to me.

The Artist (*only now seeming to have noticed her*)   Excuse me, Madame. Actually, I never thought it was yours. It's just a strange sight to see in this day and age. – In Tokyo, you hardly see such a thing nowadays, not even in the little shrine or temple fairs off the beaten track. . . . This would be Lady Shizuka, right? Turn her around and there's bold Benkei, with his halberd. . . . Turn Benkei around and you've got yourself an octopus, sporting a red bandanna, who'll dance you a jig.[11] But this one doesn't seem rigged out for such tricks. (*Nonchalantly leans in under the umbrella that the* **Lady** *is holding.*) Nope, this one is just the dancing girl. Ah, but she's a real work of art. – Take a look, see how fine the workmanship is! . . . Who's the owner? Who'd leave a lovely thing like this out in the rain?

The Lady   The puppeteer, I believe, is over there. – (*Modestly indicating and lowering her voice.*) . . . The old man's been drinking.

The Artist   I bet he's a master. . . . Shall we have him perform a bit for us?

The Lady   Please don't, sir. . . . He's had rather a lot to drink, it seems.

The Artist   I see. It would be a bother if the man's as drunk as he looks. Ah, but this puppet is truly a work of art! If you'll excuse me, Madame. (*Half muttering.*) Maybe we'll meet again on my way back.

Coolly saunters off in the direction of the mountain path.

The Lady (*following a few steps behind him*)   Sir! Uh, sir . . . Which way would you be going?

The Artist (*again, as if noticing her for the first time. Speaking softly*)   Please. (*Pause.*) . . . Don't call me 'sir'. The town's in such pandemonium that I thought I'd take myself to the mountains for a bit. – Excuse me, Madame. (*Gazing at her with his sleepy eyes.*) I failed to notice you before, but would you be staying at the same inn as me?

The Lady   Yes, near you. . . . In back, downstairs. Uh . . .

The Artist   Is that so? Then, you'll excuse me.

Again, makes to go.

The Lady (*following a step behind*)   Sir, on your way here, did you happen to run into a manservant wearing a jacket with the inn's insignia?

The Artist   Yes I did.

The Lady   Did he say nothing?

---

11 Lady Shizuka was the mistress of Minamoto Yoshitsune (1159–89), the famous general in the war between the Genji and Heike clans, and Benkei was his loyal retainer. Yoshitsune was eventually hunted down and killed on the orders of his brother Minamoto Yoritomo (1147–99), who became the first shogun of the Kamakura period. Many tales and plays hail Yoshitsune's exploits.

The Artist (*slowly crossing his arms*)   Well . . . just as I was about to cross the bridge over to the Kikuya and Nodaya inns, on the railing, attached to a long pole, was a straw raincoat. Seems they were selling a lot of them in the market for the Saint's Day. It was an advertisement of sorts for it, but it looked for all the world like a scarecrow. I stood there looking at it and had to laugh. – I look like a scarecrow myself mind you. (*Smiles.*) Thought of buying one, but it'd have just weighed me down. That was when the manservant from the inn passed me.

The Lady   Then what happened?

The Artist   Ah, yes. (*Uncrosses his arms.*) . . . 'The lady went that way', said the man, then passed me. . . . I see, he must have been talking about you. I suppose he thought we were a couple and went out together. – If you'll excuse me.

The Lady   Well, sir. We're separate now, but late last night we arrived together, you know.

The Artist   With you?

The Lady   Yes.

The Artist   I knew nothing about that.

The Lady   In Ōhito . . . We came in separate cars, but at the same time . . .

The Artist   I shared a car. – Ah, come to think of it . . . there was someone I think who called for the cab, with the most modish hairstyle parted on the side . . . (*Half to himself.*)

The Lady   A woman . . . (*Breathing heavily.*) That woman, as soon as she got to the inn, sir, she shaved her eyebrows.[12] (*Looks up, suddenly embarrassed.*) Her hair was done up in curls, like this.

The Artist   Ah hah. (*Growing more suspicious, yet acting nonchalant.*)

The Lady   Sir. (*Holding out her umbrella, hangs her head. Snow could not be whiter than the nape of her neck.*) None other than I was the lady the manservant from the inn was talking about. (*Rather excitedly.*) He meant your wife.

Pause.

The Artist (*quietly*)   . . . Meaning?

The Lady   Last night, as soon as I arrived at the inn with you, I told the innkeeper I'm with Mr. Shimazu. You see, I, uh, . . . (*Haltingly, pausing a moment.*) I know you from your photographs, your exhibitions. – 'I'm Shimazu's wife', I told the innkeeper. 'I followed him on the same train in secret, so he wouldn't see me', I said. Of course, what I said didn't make much sense, but I said it. . . . And the reason I gave was my husband was having an affair and was meeting a woman there.

---

12 Although outlawed as a practice in 1870, shaved eyebrows traditionally indicated that a woman was married.

The Artist *I* was.

The Lady Yes, you being my, uh, husband.

The Artist That was quite impertinent of you!

Smiles wryly.

The Lady Please forgive me, sir. – 'Book me next door to him in secret, so I can spy on him. I'll make myself look different in case we run into each other in the hallway and I get caught', I said. . . . And right then and there, in front of the mirror stand, I shaved my eyebrows, rearranged my hair, shook off my *haori*, and retied my obi this way (*lissomely turns around and gazes at the bow*) loosely, telling him, 'For heaven's sake, keep this a secret.' Then in the register, after your name I wrote 'his wife'.

The Artist (*frowns slightly, but then generously*) One comes to a place like this for rest, so I'll indulge a prank like that, I suppose. . . . Well, you'll have to excuse me –

The Lady Please, sir, don't be angry with me.

The Artist What? Have somebody's beautiful wife play a joke on me? – You never know, I might be pleased. – But I really must go.

The Lady What'll I do? Sir, this was no joke I was playing.

The Artist What do you mean by that?

Speaking sharply for the first time.

The Lady (*upset, trembling slightly*) I beg you, look. I have something to show you.

Pulling forcefully at the sleeve of his cape, she draws him back toward the edge of the stream.

Look there.

She points at the dead carp. It still is invisible to the audience.

The Artist That is awful! How frightful!

The Lady Sir, I feel like that carp. I'm at death's door myself.

*The **Artist** says nothing. Pause.*

The Lady There are men after me. If they find me, they'll have to take me away. – I happened to recognise you and followed you as far as the inn, then I took it in my mind to do something unpardonable. I was desperate and made up my mind to die. – Anyway, I shaved my eyebrows, changed the way I look, and pretended to be your wife. I was lost, at my wit's end, at that busy inn. Please forgive me. . . . Never in my dreams would I ever play a trick on you.

The Artist I suppose there's nothing I can do.

The Lady (*reluctantly, as if unsatisfied with his response*) Can you forgive me? . . . I know this sounds as if I'm taking advantage of your kindness, but would you please let me join you on your walk? I'll even follow behind you. If you grant me this wish, no one will notice me, I'm sure. – Sir! (*Ever so slightly coquettish.*) Please, let me come with you.

The Artist (*firmly*)   You'd be in the way.

The Lady   Ah . . . but, no. You see, even if I went with you, I'd go only so far as it took to make up my mind to become like that thing there. (*Points at the dead fish.*)

The Artist   We can't have that happen to you! I have no idea what your situation may be, but you mustn't end up like that.

The Puppeteer (*lying face down, then bolting up suddenly*)   Master! Gimme another drink! Master!

The Artist (*hearing, but trying to pay him no attention*)   I consider it my duty to see that at the very least you do not turn out that way. – If you'll excuse me.

Steps away and heads toward the path into the mountains.

The Lady (*as the* **Artist** *disappears into the trees, she hastily runs after him, then holds back, watching him go*)   Nothing lasts, does it?

She looks around, ashamed of her own voice. She opens her umbrella, though there is no rain, as if to hide her embarrassment, then dejectedly heads into the grove of trees along the same path the **Artist** *took.*

The Puppeteer   Master! Another drink!

The Shopkeeper   Tch! You are a troublemaker, aren't you? (*Pours him another.*)

The Puppeteer   But this drink – hah, hah, hah – I dedicate to the moon. When the clouds come out, the full moon hides his face. (*Drains the glass in one gulp.*) Aaah, whew! . . . The bill, sir. . . .

Sloppily pulls out a change purse from a string around his neck and tosses down some coins.

For Saint Kōbō and the moon as well. These coins, too, shine like the diamonds of universal dharma. Oof!

Stands. He is tall, staggering on a pair of scrawny shins poking through torn gaiters. The **Shopkeeper**, *paying him no mind, clears off his table and goes indoors.* Oof! (*Tipsily staggers over to the puppet.*) My dear Lady Shizuka!

Suddenly respectful, he practically collapses to the ground to prostrate himself before the doll. Pause. His drunken eyes take in the dead carp.

Ah, brother, you lie there still. Did an otter bite you? A weasel take a nip out of you? Somebody's surely taken a chunk out of you – look at them teeth marks – and now the maggots are making off with what's left. Any stray cat or dog that saw you here would have taken one sniff and left you to rot. Even a dog wouldn't eat you. You had it in you to become a dragon, but some ill karma fell on you that your carcass should be exposed here, food for the worms. Poor thing! – Let me give you a proper funeral.

Pulls out the bloated, rotten corpse of the carp. Now the audience can see it.

But I don't know what to say for your last rites. How 'bout this: 'A curse on all who think ill of you! Go haunt the lot of them, even charge an admission fee! Amen!'

Wraps the carcass in the headscarf tied around his neck with his change purse, straps it to his waist, and kneels down again.

Ah, Lady Shizuka!

Unties the ragged cloth around his throat and wraps it over his mouth, like a gag. He has done this so as not to offend the beautiful woman with his breath, stinking of stale alcohol. He raises the doll on its bamboo pole high over his shoulder and heads toward the mountain path.

Oof! (*Tipsily staggers from side to side.*)

*The **Lady** steps out slightly from the shadow of the trees watching this scene.*

The Puppeteer   Oof! (*Staggers.*) Oof! (*Staggers.*)

The Lady (*slowly steps from the shadows and crosses the **Puppeteer**'s path, as if turning back the way she came, and accosts him*)   Grandpa, grandpa!

*The **Puppeteer**, tall and red faced, looks eerily at her as if he were possessed.*

The Lady (*boldly strides up to him*)   I no longer have any wishes for this world, nothing holding me back, so please, if there's anything I can do to make your wish come true, I'll do it for you. Please make me a wish, grandpa.

*The **Puppeteer**, still silent and gazing at her as if to consume her with his eyes, eventually picks up a rope lying under a bale of rotten straw by the roadside. He approaches her, with it dangling, swinging limply from his hand.*

The Lady   Ah! (*She steps back. The **Puppeteer** sneers at her.*) I thought it was a snake! – Oh, so what if it is a snake? What are you going to do? What will you do to me?

*Saying nothing, the **Puppeteer** merely stretches out his wrinkled hand and beckons her. Beckoning her, he backs again into the shadows of the trees.*

The Lady   What will you do to me? What are you planning to do?

She follows him into the trees.

For a while the stage is empty. Five white ducks waddle through the rice paddy in a line hunting for grub. It is, as it were, a portent of spring's passing.

The Groom (*leading a horse, emerges from the trees, gazing back the way he came. There are two sacks of rice on the horse's back, donations to the temple. The sacks bear labels on which are written: 'White Rice. Hail to the Great Teacher, Diamond of Universal Light!'*)   There was a sight to chill your blood! Why, makes me wonder whether now, even in the noonday sun, this rice I'm carrying hasn't turned to sand.

Wets his brows with spittle and fishes out a few grains from one of the sacks.

Still safe. (*Listens to the beating of festival drums.*) – Thanks be to Saint Kōbō! Still, it was awful! Damned devils, they were, scared the life out of me!

The stage revolves.

Scene Two

On one side a steep hill where alternate rows, two to three feet wide, of mustard flowers and barley grow. On the brow of the hill bloom bushes of Kerria japonica, a wild rose. Below in a ravine where the foot of the mountain has deeply eroded away, is an expanse of grass where mulberry saplings grow here and there, small and spindly as stalks of rattan.

On the other side is a wooded mountain with strands of evergreen oak, some trees tall, others shorter, their boughs so thick they seem black with leaf, roiling like eddies of black clouds, in stark contrast to the brightness of the scene on the other side.

A narrow path wends its way down the hanamichi *and between the hills. In the distance looms the Izu mountain chain.*

Alone, halfway up the slope between the kerria roses growing on the cliff and the mustard flowers below, the **Artist** *quietly takes a swig from a flask of whisky. – The call, far off, of a bush warbler. Two, three sharp cries of a cockerel, then farther away, the belling of a deer. He stands there for some time, seemingly surprised. Then, as if spying on someone, he hides himself among the leaves and flowers.*

The **Lady** *enters. In one hand she holds her umbrella; in the other she clings to one end of the rope. She is leading the* **Puppeteer,** *his headscarf tied like a monkey's bit. Strapped crosswise to his back is a black, Western-style umbrella and, vertically, his Shizuka doll. His arms, which hold the puppet's bamboo staff, are tied behind his back with the* **Lady's** *rope. Head down, his shoulders slumped, it is as if he were being led to slaughter. Still drunk, stumbling on unsteady legs, he steps forth into the shadows of the deep ravine at the foot of the mountain. The* **Lady** *releases the rope, and it falls to the ground. In fact, he wasn't bound at all, it only appeared that way. He props his puppet against the trunk of a mulberry and kneels in prayer. Thus, at some distance from the* **Lady,** *he unties the headscarf.*

The Puppeteer   Lady, honour your promise and grant me what I beg of you.

He rises on his hands and legs and grovels face down in the grass.

The Lady   Are you sure, grandpa?

The Puppeteer   Could I make up such a lie? Please, thrash me as hard as you can.

The Lady   Strike you? Are you sure?

The Puppeteer   Thrash me till you draw blood, till I can't breathe no more. I beg you!

The Lady   Really hit you? You're sure, are you?

The Puppeteer   Please, don't trifle with me! I can't wait no longer.

The Lady   . . . I won't trifle, in case later you resent what I do. – Well, in that case, since I made a promise, I'll really beat you. Bear with it.

She strikes him three, four times with her Japanese umbrella, then five, six more times to follow.

The Puppeteer   No good! No good at all!

The Lady (*whipping him*)   Like this? – Like this?

The Puppeteer   Too weak! (*Twisting around to look at her.*) Let me really have it! Like you were giving me what for.

The Lady   Like I, uh, was giving you what for –

The Puppeteer   That's why it's not good enough! Hang on a sec.

He removes his padded vest together with his worn and filthy crested jacket, baring his skinny, wrinkled back. He totters to his feet and embraces the tree with his back toward her. He turns around and glares at her.

Rip off the parchment so the staff and ribs are exposed. If you just continue swatting me the way you were, you won't even scratch me.

The Lady (*sighing*)   Ah!

The Puppeteer   You'll never be able to put any muscle into it if you keeping thinking I'm just some old, drunken beggar. Surely, lady, there's somebody you hate in this world, someone you'd like to thrash the living daylights out of. A mother-in-law, a father-in-law, a brother-in-law, some relative, some stranger, even a friend. You needn't hold back.

The Lady   Ah!

The Puppeteer   Think of those bastards and give me what for. All right? Are you ready?

The Lady   Ah!

The Puppeteer   Pull yourself together!

The Lady   Ah, all right, then!

Growing aroused, she begins ripping the parchment off the umbrella, and in so doing, she cuts herself. Her fingers and arms grow pink with the flow of blood to her extremities. – She grasps the umbrella again.

– You beast! You beast! You beast! You beast, you!!

The Puppeteer   Unh. (*Groaning faintly.*) Unh, yeah, right there, uh huh, that's better now.
Oh, yeah.

The Lady   Is that how you like it? Huh? You beast!

The Puppeteer   No, it ain't enough for you just to whack me 'cross the rump or back that way. Smack me 'cross the head, box my ears, as hard as you can!

The Lady   You beast! You beast! You beast!

Losing all control of herself, as if possessed, she leaps and dances around, her hair flying, her face growing pale. Beating and thrashing him for all she is worth, she begins to run out breath.

Ah! For pity's sake, I can't take it anymore!

The Puppeteer   Can't take it anymore? Good! That's the spirit! Keep it up!

The Artist (*following the embankment, descends into the ravine. Though calm, he hastens to stop them*)   – Madame!

The Lady   Why, sir!

On seeing him, her frail arms freeze, her legs turn to jelly, and she sinks down and falls half into a faint.

The Artist   This is whisky. – To revive you. – What on earth has been going on here?

In shock, the **Puppeteer** *writhes around on the ground. The* **Artist** *observes him.*

The Artist   I've no idea what this is about, but I do know anything taken too far is wrong.

The Lady (*gasping for breath*)   What have I done? I've exposed you to something so base, something no human should ever see, let alone do. Oh, what am I to do?

Begins weeping hysterically.

The Artist (*at a loss to stop her, he rubs her hands, her back, in an effort to soothe her*)   Please, calm yourself.

The Puppeteer (*wraps his bloody flesh in his jacket and, panting, bows on hand and knee in the grass*)   Ah . . . This must be, er, er, your husband, Would it, ma'am?

The Artist   I'm no one to this lady, particularly. Call me an acquaintance.

The Puppeteer   Then let this old man tell the gentleman – her acquaintance, if you will – what's happening here. Yes, er, forgive me my impertinence – this ain't an easy story to listen to. . . . In short, this dried-up, decrepit ruin, slimy and black as a strip of eel jerky, was once a young man, and long ago committed a great sin. All for a woman. I was a snake that wound itself around an angel on some high balcony. No, rather, I was a lizard who'd gobbled up a frog in a pond. I'm at a loss for metaphors. . . . I sucked the very lifeblood out of her. – And when I awoke from my dream, the sin I committed terrified me. There was nowhere I could go. . . . Exposing myself to the elements, risking life and limb to lose myself, to disappear, I met a travelling monk on the pilgrim's road in Shikoku – surely it was Saint Kōbō himself – who left me this mysterious gift. This doll attached to this bamboo pole is the image of a lovely woman. I'm sure she's offended every time the old man gets drunk, so I bite on this kerchief to protect her from the fumes from my foul-smelling mouth. . . . This beautiful young lady is a goddess for these ancient eyes, so every time I see her I'm reminded of my old sin. Were someone able morn and night to punish me, to beat and torture me, then perhaps I could rid myself of at least some of the sin I've piled up. I'm not afraid neither of going to hell in the afterlife. My load of suffering in this life is not enough, so I long for nothing else in all the world. I'd have old wives and women, the kind who'd lie with me in seedy flophouses or under the verandas of village shrines, kick and beat me, but it was never enough. It was a beautiful lady who lost her precious life, all due to the recklessness of this here beggar. So, if I'm not punished at the hands of a young and beautiful woman like her, my flesh and blood scarcely feel a thing. – And when such a wish, the veritable prayer of a ghost or vengeful spirit, comes from someone with my face, anybody in his right mind would run away. . . . You'd have to be a saint or a genius, a fearless hero or a man of peerless virtue, to listen to a tale like mine! – This ruin you see before you was born sixty-nine years ago, and it's forty-one years to the month and day today that he made this vow. – And here it was just now that this beautiful lady accosted this beggar, called to me, promising me she'd grant me any wish I had, whatever it might be. I may be no expert, but it's my trade, after all, and I made the most fearsome face I could, but I could see she was afraid of nothing, no ghost or demon crying for vengeance. I told her my wish, a wish I'd borne so long, that I wanted to be exposed like some common criminal on the execution ground. And so we came here, on the roadside to be sure, but in a hidden place in a gully where the mountain has washed away, where I could submit to this blessed beating, this exquisite torture. . . . Master. – Thank you, lovely lady, thank you most kindly!

The Lady (*for the first time, calm*)   Does it hurt you, sir?

The Puppeteer   Why, lady, this pain brings as much joy to this besotted face as the caress of a spring breeze, or the sweet nectar proffered by Kannon herself from the tresses of a willow.[13] . . . And that it was a beauty, like you, ma'am – better yet, somebody like one of them Buddhist she-demons – makes me worship you even more, like you was some kind of angel or goddess. Surely, thanks to the pain you inflicted on me, my flesh and bones have grown soft and supple, my blood courses fast like I was twenty years old again, and I can live another blessed day with joy in my heart.

The Artist (*cocking his head as he listens, he casually lights up a gold-tipped cigarette*)   Old man, care for a smoke?

The Puppeteer   Why, sir, if saké is holy water, then tobacco is incense burned for a dead man.

The Artist   Have a smoke, then.

Holds out a cigarette case encrusted with pearls.

The Puppeteer   Now don't it shine like Saint Kōbō's staff? 'Tis a sin.

---

13 Kannon is the bodhisattva Avalokitesvara, sometimes called the goddess of mercy.

Crawls out and lights one of the gold-tipped cigarettes.

There'll be hell to pay for this. 'Tis a sin, to be sure. I'll fly up on a waft of this here purple smoke and sail off to paradise.

The Lady   I have to leave now, sir. . . . Are you sure all you wanted was to be beaten?

The Puppeteer   Even if the Katsura River turned round and flowed back the other way, I'd tell you no lie.

The Lady   Ask me a favour. I feel I still owe you.

The Puppeteer   Had I anything left to ask, it'd be for you to beat and punish me again, another time, three times more.

The Lady   Anything else?

The Puppeteer   My utmost desire would be for you, my lovely lady, to beat me day after day and day and night, till my body was pummelled to dust. – But I've sobered up now. Enough of this nonsense. – By day I avoid others, but just like the badgers and otters and goblins, none can begrudge my coming on this mountain trail to Shuzenji, bedding down in a flophouse in Tatsuno along the way, to enjoy a dip in Saint Kōbō's springs. – Today, I'll let my feet take me somewhere down the road to Shimoda. I spoke of clouds and water, but Heaven's River[14] and the runoff in a ditch each have their separate courses, so here's where you and I must part and I'll never see the likes of you again. May the two of you prosper till the end of time. – Lady Shizuka, aye, I'll keep you company.

The Lady   Sir, wait. (*Having made an important decision, she steels herself.*) I'll follow you down that muddy course for ten years, a hundred even, to make your wish come true each morn and night.

*The **Puppeteer**, by his visage, wordlessly expresses shock.*

The Lady   Master – I left home. I'm the wife of another man. So he won't drag me back, I'd hide myself anywhere, no matter how out of the way it was. As it is, I've nowhere to go. – When I saw that dead carp in the ditch, how dreadful it was, I made up my mind I'd drink poison or drown, commit suicide somehow, no matter how ugly my corpse would look. But maybe it was just out of impatience with me that you said you'd never let me end up that way. . . . In any case, because of what you said to me back then, I decided not to kill myself.

Sir – I am the wife of Koitogawa, a family with a title but no money.

The Artist   Ah, the viscount's?

The Lady   What should I say? Why . . . it was some years ago, back when you had just returned from Europe. With your friends and fans, you used to come often, to Nihonbashi . . . (*Gazes at the **Artist** ecstatically.*) – Have you forgotten me? I'm Nui, the daughter at the Yukari Restaurant.

14 The Milky Way

The Artist   Ah, so you're O-Nui? . . . The little sister, right? I heard folks say how pretty the younger one was.

The Lady (*wistfully*)   Yes, master. I'm sure my mention made no more impression on you than someone commenting on how cold it was on a chilly day. I was so shy about being seen by you that I wouldn't even dare stray past the threshold of a room you were in, but I stayed close enough that I never missed a single word of what you had to say at any of your parties. When you held court in the room downstairs, I'd lie face down on the floor above and listen in. And when you were in the room at back, I'd hide out in the bathhouse in the courtyard behind, pressed naked against the wall, listening. Whatever room they put you in, like a mouse, I'd find a spot to hide myself, my heart like a moth drawn to the light of your heart. Nobody, not the hardworking maids nor even my worldly sister, ever guessed how I felt about you. My heart was true. My gestures, my whole demeanour, betrayed nothing; I never spoke a word of this to anyone. Only love shames one. That's why from that time on – I wonder if I wasn't even hysterical – people said I was a little strange. . . . Please, sir, understand what I say. . . . I truly went a little crazy. When you married, for a whole year all I could do was weep; my hair grew long and wild. It wasn't as if they locked me up, but I just lay there like an empty shell while they tended to me. It annoyed me that I couldn't die. . . . I felt wretched that I couldn't simply disappear, and so somehow I went on living.

– When I came to my senses, I was already twenty-three. My mother, who had so spoiled me in that big house, had passed away. When blind love dies, the world grows dark. Having been able to have my way so long made me feel obligated to crush that selfish nature of mine. Still, I stayed selfish. – I turned down all the suitors that my brothers and sisters and relatives picked out for me – keen merchants, savvy businessmen, every one – and married into the family I did.

There was the mother-in-law and two sisters-in-law, one divorced – three women. It's the family tradition, they said, for a wife to serve her husband, so I had to go fetch the water from a well, the house being located in the suburbs. . . . I cut vegetables. Evenings I went out with the mother-in-law to shop for groceries – I didn't mind those household chores. For savories for supper and sweets for snacks, the boys from the restaurant brought them by bicycle, all the way from my home in Nihonbashi, cases of food, pails of fish, every single day. My mother-in-law would berate the chef, saying the fish wasn't fresh or the omelette hadn't set, that they were feeding us the restaurant customers' leftovers, and sometimes she'd even kick the trays of dishes. At first, knowing I was still so inept, I swallowed my anger, my bitterness, but when this went on for a year, two years, I learned how they really felt. – My husband, for starters . . . well, they all had their eyes on my money, that is, my share of the family business. The monthly interest – how shall I say it? – it was enough for living costs, but it was never enough for them. Every time a niece had a suitor, or a cousin got married, I lost some heirloom, like a formal kimono or ornaments for my hair. My brocades and white underthings, my black satin and crepe – every single bolt of cloth for my kimonos was sold for summer and year-end gifts, presents to pay off the people they knew with some favour or other. The chest of drawers I brought with me when I married was practically empty by then. . . .

And what did my husband do for a living? He wrote poetry, both classical and in the modern style; he wrote plays; he sent letters to the editors of newspapers.

The Artist   It must have been hard on you. But surely he still has prospects.

The Lady   But no! His prospects were my inheritance, and they bullied me unless I brought my inheritance to them. If I coughed or complained of a headache, all the in-laws would huddle together and mutter lines like you'd hear in a play or movie, that it was 'that lung disease' and for the sake of the family they had no choice but to send me back home. – 'Put up with it! Put up with it!' was all my husband ever said, but I'd have died before I'd finished putting up with what they had in store for me. Finally I came down with a cold that kept me in bed for three days. Then in the hall on the way to get some water to drink, I heard my mother in-law say, 'Now's our chance. . . . What say we send her home?' That cut me to the quick.

The Artist   Cruel, for sure.

The Lady   Cruel? Was that all it was? – I was so mad, my cold cleared up completely and I said to my husband, 'Even if I have to fight for it, I'll go home and bring you back my inheritance. But I want you to do something for me, just once – take your mother and throw her out of my room, then grab your one sister by her ponytail and slap the other one hard across the face!' . . .

The Puppeteer (*slithering out*)   That's the spirit! That's the spirit!

The Artist   Hah, hah, hah! Bet that made you feel better! Hardly meek, mind you.

The Lady (*furious, then smiling as if all were forgotten*)   Hardly.

The Artist   Not then, anyway.

The Lady   'You're a demon!' my husband suddenly shouted, and he flung me out of the room, grabbed me by the hair and slapped *me* hard across the face. That night was last night? No, the night before last – had I left that night it would have been too obvious. Sir, if I was as good as a goldfish or quiet as a houseplant, then the house where I was born or one of my relatives would surely take me back, but I have my pride. . . . Ready to die because there was no place for me, I've found a place to go now. (*With resolution.*) I'll follow this old gentleman. – This man understands the sin of making a woman suffer, and now he wants to pay for it by being beaten night and day. I'll become all the women of this world to avenge ourselves on this one man. He worships this doll of Lady Shizuka as if she were human. He'll offer me the pride and blessing of having been born a woman, and in return, he can have my weak and discarded body, like the carcass of that dead carp he saved from its fate.

The Artist (*sometimes nodding, sometimes cocking his head doubtfully*)   Madame. I mean, O-Nui.

The Lady (*happy, laughs guilelessly*)   Ye-es!

The Artist   Is there nothing I can do to change your mind?

The Lady   No, sir. Unless you take me by the hand, back to the inn . . .

The Puppeteer   That's right! That's right!

*The **Artist** is silent.*

The Lady (*turns around*)   Sir.

The Artist   Madame, you are ill, you're sick. But I'm no doctor and I cannot tell you what to do. – I can't fathom your reasoning, but then again, I don't claim to understand the ways of other people. I've nothing to teach you. Whether it's right or wrong to take you back with me, I can't say at the moment. I'm not leaving you out of cowardice. I'm preoccupied with my own work right now and haven't the freedom to pass judgement on you. – I'm sorry to say I'm weak, and I can do nothing for you. But if you could wait for a month or even a fortnight, then I'd find it in me to do something.

The Lady   Master, in the course of just one night I've changed the way I look. My destiny can't wait any longer.

The Artist   Understood. (*As if no longer able to look her in the eye, he turns to the **Puppeteer**.*) Old man, promise to keep her company.

The Puppeteer   I'll be her dog –

*He picks up the **Lady**, then gets down on all fours. The **Lady** mounts his back. The **Artist** takes her hand so she will not fall.*

The Puppeteer   I'll be her horse and take her where she wants to go.

The Artist   Madame. . . . May all go as you desire.

The Lady   Please give us your whisky, sir. . . . Then be witness to our union.

*Saying nothing, the **Artist** takes out the bottle, pours a cup, and offers it her. The **Lady** drinks the cup in one gulp, then takes a deep breath.*

The Lady   Grandpa, we need something to go with the toast.

The Puppeteer   I could sing a ditty in place of a formal speech . . .

The Lady   No, bring out that rotten carp you rescued.

The Puppeteer   Surely not!

The Lady   Take it out. Have you a knife?

The Puppeteer   I always carry a knife, to fend off dogs and whatever else may come my way.

From a bowl wrapped in his waist he pulls out a rusty blade.

The Artist   Surely, Madame!

The Lady   We'll be travelling together. – I'll have to get used to eating this sort of fare. . . .

The Puppeteer   Now you're talking! I'll have some, too.

Shocked, the **Artist** *turns his head away. From far off, voices chant 'Hail to the Great Teacher, Diamond of Universal Light! Hail to the Great Teacher, Diamond of Universal Light!' A young* **Boy** *and* **Girl** *enter, in procession.*

The Children (*innocently*)   Hail to the Great Teacher, Diamond of Universal Light!

The two **Children** *at first enter slowly, the* **Girl** *with her hair tied in a ponytail with purple cloth, the* **Boy** *with his hair formally tied back with a long white ribbon. Then, noticing the* **Puppeteer**, *the* **Lady**, *and the* **Artist**, *they suddenly become afraid and hastily race past them, running down the* hanamichi. *As if they have come to an understanding, the* **Lady** *and the* **Artist** *both turn and look their way. The* **Puppeteer** *also gazes after them, beckoning. The scene created by this ensemble is truly eerie. The two* **Children** *return, as if pulled back.*

The Artist   Fine children! We need your services.

The Lady   Aren't they sweet?

The Artist (*removes his cloak and lays it on the grass*)   Madame, please seat yourself down next to grandpa here.

The Lady   Surely we don't deserve this.

The Artist   Of course you do. But if you're sick, then maybe I've fallen a bit ill myself. – Now, seal your oath with a toast.[15]

The **Lady** *and the* **Puppeteer** *sit down side by side. The two* **Children**, *as if in the service of demons, take turns pouring the whisky. Silence. A cloud passes over, darkening the stage. A bush warbler cries impatiently. Distant sounds of court music. Then, gradually, the cries of 'Hail to the Great Teacher, Diamond of Universal Light!' draw nigh, and some dozen or so* **Villagers**, *old and young, men and women, enter chanting.*

Villager 1   Hey! Why are you children here?

Villager 2   You're Saint Kōbō's emissaries. That's why we keep a respectful distance from you.

Villager 3   We follow you reverently. – You mustn't play tricks on us.

Villagers 4, 5, 6 (*in turn*)   Come! Come! (*Surrounding the* **Children**.) Hail to the Great Teacher, Diamond of Universal Light! . . .

Thus they exit the wings.

The Lady (*takes the cloak, brushes off the dust, and drapes it over the* **Artist***'s shoulders*)   It was only once – perhaps you don't remember? You were drunk and put your hand on mine. This one. . . . Please take my hand, once more, in memory of me. I wish for no more.

---

15 In a traditional Japanese wedding, rather than using rings, a marriage is sealed by an exchange of cups of saké.

Kneels on the grass and bows to him.

Dear sir. If only it could be otherwise.

The Artist   And if I could do anything else.

The Lady   Grandpa, let's be going.

The Puppeteer   Aye, aye. . . . Farewell, sir!

The Lady   Let's go!

As they start off, it begins to rain in earnest.

The Artist   Wait!

Rushing after them, he holds out an open umbrella.

The Lady   Sir, what about you?

The Artist   A little rain won't hurt me.

The Lady   Thank you kindly. (*Takes the umbrella.*) Oh, to hell with them!

She kicks off her clogs and, barefoot, hikes up the skirt of her kimono, exposing fetching scarlet petticoats underneath. She pulls hard on the **Puppeteer**'s *hand.*

The Puppeteer (*follows on tottering legs*)   Hail to the Great Teacher, Diamond of Universal Light!

The Lady (*halfway down the* hanamichi, *she turns back. The* **Artist** *sees her off*)   Master! . . . Farewell! Pay my respects to the world.

The Artist   Take care of yourself.

Wrapping the **Puppeteer**'s *wrinkled arm around her own, the* **Lady** *leads him, holding high the umbrella, toward the curtain at the end of the* hanamichi. *The* **Artist** *watches them. From offstage, the* **Puppeteer**'s *voice is heard chanting, 'Hail to the Great Teacher, Diamond of Universal Light!' Then we hear the* **Lady** *also chant, 'Hail to the Great Teacher, Diamond of Universal Light!'*

The Artist   Ah, are we in hell? Or surely, this is a dream. No, it's real. – (*Sees the* **Lady**'s *clog.*) Should I throw it all away, I wonder? My name, everything?

Takes the clog in his hands, looking distressed.

But no, I've got my work.

Throws the clog away.

The sound of the rain stops. The vespa bell of Shuzenki Temple rings.

Curtain.

The Dove

Djuna Barnes (1923)

Some of the most interesting plays that we might read in terms of both decadence and queerness were written by women who reclaimed figurations of lesbian desire from the male gaze, gay or otherwise. The 'specifically *female* homoerotic aesthetic' in work by Michael Field is an example.[1] We close this volume with another: North American playwright **Djuna Barnes'** brilliant one-act drama *The Dove* (1923), which was performed at the Bayes Theater in New York City in 1926 as part of a one-act play competition under the direction of a Provincetown Players actor, Samuel A. Elliot, Jr. (Barnes (1892–1982) was closely affiliated with the Provincetown Players, which directed three of her earlier one-act plays).[2] Rather than romanticising gay identity, Barnes – who was bisexual – presents a layered exploration of queerness that undermines the objectifying gaze of the male author, while at the same time refusing to gloss more pessimistic aspects of lesbian experience. The play may have been written in the roaring 1920s, but in *The Dove* even those marginalised by bourgeois morality seem to have absorbed something of its consciousness. Equally, the play is full of witticisms and humour, acting as an effective foil for its darker underbelly.

Barnes has been criticised by various scholars for not being sufficiently pro-lesbian.[3] However, as Ery Shin asks, 'why must queer writers invent only winning queer characters and adopt only socially conscientious attitudes toward the queer? We hardly expect straight writers to create only well-adjusted straight men and women'.[4] One reading of *The Dove*'s *dénouement* would be to see it as a refusal of a progressive social conscientiousness in favour of a darker queer pessimism, so long as we read the sound of an offstage gunshot that closes the play as proving fatal to the Dove, who is desired by the two sisters, Amelia and Vera. One might therefore be tempted to understand the play as a pessimistic rumination on lesbian desire, although the Dove's fate remains ambiguous. We only know for sure that a painting of two courtesans beloved by Vera and Amelia has been shot, which is important given their erotic objectification of the much younger Dove (the term's Christian sense connoting virginal innocence, and its pre-Christian sense being more suggestive of female sexuality and lustfulness,

1   Sarah Parker, 'Bittersweet: Michael Field's Sapphic Palate', in *Decadence and the Senses*, ed. Jane Desmarais and Alice Condé (Cambridge: Legenda, 2017), 121–40 (129).

2   The three plays staged by the Provincetown Players include *Three from the Earth* (1919), *An Irish Triangle* (1920) and *Kurzy of the Sea* (1920). Barnes took a trip to Paris in 1920, and time spent away from the company may be why *The Dove* was not staged by the Provincetown Players. See Cheryl J. Plumb, *The Dove*, in *Modern Drama by Women 1880s–1930s*, ed. Katherine E. Kelly (London and New York: Routledge, 1996), 299–302 (300). Note that Barnes referred to her own work as 'baroque' rather than 'decadent'. See Kate Armond, *Modernism and the Theatre of the Baroque* (Edinburgh: Edinburgh University Press, 2018), 12.

3   For instance, see Karla Jay, 'The Outsider among the Expatriates: Djuna Barnes' Satire on the Ladies of the Almanack', *Silence and Power: A Reevaluation of Djuna Barnes*, ed. Mary L. Broe (Carbondale: Southern Illinois UP, 1991), 184–93 (193).

4   Ery Shin, 'The Apocalypse for Barnes', *Texas Studies in Literature and Language* 57 no. 2 (Summer 2015): 182–209 (183).

5   Anne B. Dalton, '"*This* is obscene": Female Voyeurism, Sexual Abuse, and Maternal Power in *The Dove*', *Review of Contemporary Fiction* 13, no. 3 (Fall 1993): 117–39 (126). Dalton references Barbara Walker, *The Women's Dictionary of Symbols and Sacred Objects* (San Francisco: Harper & Row, 1988), 399.

associated in the Indian context, for instance, with a dove-goddess whose name means 'lust').[5] This leaves open the possibility that the explosive ending is less fatal than based on a cryptic release – both sexual and, quite possibly, actual if we understand The Dove's exit to be a flamboyant repudiation of the sisters' closeted lives.[6]

Where Ennoïa's recurrent resurrection is both the source of her power over men and perpetual torment by them, *The Dove* lends itself to a wider range of interpretations and possibilities that are not so easily compartmentalised. Artifacts and objects are destroyed – shot through, or transfigured from china into chiffon and lace, 'including the carefully crafted artifact of the public self' – presenting what Ann Larabee describes as 'a liberating drama of disintegration, providing a new ground for self-creation'.[7] This is Barnes the anarchist, Barnes the New Woman, and it is also Barnes the decadent, presenting decadence at its most radical: decadence as an art of subversive ruination, in which acts of disobedience and dissent are attuned to possibilities that might rise from, or thrive within, the ashes.

---

6 This is a reading forwarded by Kelly in her Introduction to *Modern Drama by Women 1880s–1930s*, 1–16 (13). An alternative reading finds Dalton considering the play as an autobiographical working through of Barnes' own sexual abuse at the hands of her father and quite possibly her grandmother as well. See Dalton, '*This* is obscene.'

7 Ann Larabee, 'The Early Attic Stage of Djuna Barnes', in *Silence and Power*, 37–44 (44).

Characters

Amelia Burgson } *sisters*
Vera Burgson }

The Dove, *a young girl living with the Burgsons*

Time

Early morning

Place

The Burgson apartment, a long, low rambling affair at the top of a house in the heart of the city.

The decoration is garish, dealing heavily in reds and pinks. There is an evident attempt to make the place look luxuriously sensual. The furniture is all of the reclining type. The walls are covered with a striped paper in red and white. Only two pictures are evident, one of the Madonna and Child, and one of an early English tandem race. There are firearms everywhere. Many groups of swords, ancient and modern, are secured to the walls. A pistol or two lie in chairs, etc. There is only one door, which leads out into the back hall directly back centre. **Amelia Burgson** *is a woman rather over the normal in height, with large braids of very yellow hair, done about a long face. She seems vitally hysterical.* **Vera Burgson** *is small, thin and dark.* **The Dove** *is a slight girl barely out of her teens; she is as delicate as china with almost dangerously transparent skin. Her nose is high-bridged and thin, her hands and feet are also very long and delicate. She has red hair, very elegantly coiffured. When she moves (seldom) the slightest line runs between her legs, giving her the expectant waiting air of a deer. At the rising of the curtain* **The Dove**, *gowned in white, is seated on the divan polishing the blade of an immense sword. Half reclining to her right lies* **Vera** *in a thin yellow morning gown. A French novel has half fallen from her hand. Her eyes are closed.*

The Dove   Yes, I'm hurrying.

Vera   That's best, she will be back soon.

The Dove   She is never gone long.

Vera   No, never very long – one would grow old waiting for the day on which she would stay an hour – a whole hour.

The Dove   Yes, that's true.

Vera (*wearily*)   She says we live dangerously; (*laughs*) why, we can't even keep the flies out.

The Dove   Yes, there are a great many flies.

Vera (*after a pause*)   Shall I ever have a lover, do you suppose?

The Dove (*turning the sword over*)   No, I suppose not.

Vera   Yet Amelia and I have made it our business to know – everything.

The Dove   Yes?

Vera   Yes. We say this little thing in French and that little thing in Spanish, and we collect knives and pistols, but we only shoot our buttons off with the guns and cut our darning cotton with the knives, and we'll never, never be perverse though our entire education has been about knees and garters and pinches on hindquarters – elegantly bestowed – and we keep a few animals – very badly – hoping to see something first-hand – and our beds are as full of yellow pages[8] and French jokes as a bird's nest

---

8   In the late nineteenth century yellow was regarded as the primary colour of decadence, deriving from the yellow covers of illicit French novels and inspiring the title of *The Yellow Book*, a literary and artistic periodical published between 1894 and 1897.

is full of feathers – God! (*She stands up abruptly.*) Little one, why do I wear lace at my elbows?

The Dove   You have pretty arms.

Vera   Nonsense! Lace swinging back and forth like that, tickling my arms, well, that's not beauty –

The Dove   I know.

Vera (*returning to her couch*)   I sometimes wonder what you do know, you are such a strange happening anyway. Well then, tell me what you think of me and what you think of my sister, you have been here long enough. Why do you stay? Do you love us?

The Dove   I love something that you have.

Vera   What?

The Dove   Your religious natures.

Vera   Good heavens!

The Dove   You misunderstand me. I call that imagination that is the growth of ignorance, religion.

Vera   And why do you like that?

The Dove   Because it goes farther than knowledge.

Vera   You know, sometimes I wish –

The Dove   Yes?

Vera   That you have lived all we pretend we have.

The Dove   Why?

Vera   I don't know, but somehow someone like you should know – everything.

The Dove   Do I seem so young?

Vera   I know, that's what's so odd. (*Impatiently.*) For heaven's sake, will you stop polishing that infernal weapon!

The Dove (*quietly*)   She said to me: 'Take all the blood stains off first, then polish it.'

Vera   There you are; she is quite mad, there's no doubt. Blood stains! Why, she would be afraid to cut her chops with it – and as for the rest of her manifestations – nonsense!

The Dove   She carries a pistol with her, just to go around the corner for a pound of butter.

Vera   It's wicked! She keeps an enormous blunderbuss in the corner of her room, but when I make up her bed, all I find is some Parisienne bathing girl's picture stuck full of pin holes –

The Dove   I know, she sits beside me for hours making those pin holes in the borders of everything in sight.

Vera (*with a strange anger*)   Why do you stay?

The Dove   Why should I go?

Vera   I should think this house and two such advanced virgins as Amelia and myself would drive you to despair –

The Dove   No, no, I'm not driven to despair –

Vera   What do you find here?

The Dove   I love Amelia.

Vera   Another reason for going away.

The Dove   IS it?

Vera   Yes, it is.

The Dove   Strange, I don't feel that way about it.

Vera   Sometimes I think –

The Dove   Yes?

Vera   That you are the mad one, and that we are just eccentric.

The Dove   Yet my story is quite simple.

Vera   I'm not so certain.

The Dove   Yet you have heard it.

Vera   There's more than one hears.

The Dove   I was born on a farm –

Vera   So you say.

The Dove   I became very fond of moles – it's so daring of them to be in the darkness underground. And then I like the open fields, too – they say there's nothing like nature for the simple spirit.

Vera   Yes, and I've long had my suspicions of nature.

The Dove   Be that as it may, my brothers were fond of me – in a way, and my father in – a way – then I came to New York –

Vera   And took up the painting of china –

The Dove   Exactly. I was at that for three years, then one day I met you walking through the park, do you remember? You had a parasol, you tipped it to the back of your head, you looked at me a long time. Then I met Amelia, by the same high fence in the same park, and I bowed to her in an almost military fashion, my heels close together –

Vera   And you never did anything wild, insane –

The Dove   It depends on what you call wild, insane –

Vera (*with great excitement*)   Have you ever taken opium or hasheesh?

The Dove (*as if answering*)   There are many kinds of dreams – in one you laugh, in another you weep –

Vera (*wringing her hands*)   Yes, yes, once I dreamed. A dream in the day, with my eyes wide open. I dreamt I was a Dresden doll[9] and that I had been blown down by the wind and that I broke all to pieces – that is, my arms and my head broke all to pieces – but that I was surprised to find that my china skirt had become flexible, as if it were made of chiffon and lace.

The Dove   You see, there are many dreams –

Vera   Have you ever felt that your bones were utterly sophisticated but that your flesh was keeping them from expressing themselves?

The Dove   Or vice versa?

Vera   Yes, or vice versa.

The Dove   There are many kinds of dreams –

Vera   You know, I'm afraid of you!

The Dove   Me?

Vera   Yes, you seem so gentle – do we not call you The Dove? And you are so little – so little it's almost immoral, you make me feel as if –

The Dove   As if?

Vera   Well, as if your terrible quality were not one of action, but just the opposite, as if you wanted to prevent nothing.

The Dove   There are enough people preventing things, aren't there?

Vera   Yes – that's why you frighten me.

The Dove   Because I let everything go on, as far as it can go?

Vera   Yes, because you disturb nothing.

The Dove   I see.

Vera   You never meddle –

The Dove   No, I never meddle.

---

9   Dresden doll: also known as a parian doll, with a delicate porcelain head and (contrary to Vera's description of china skirts) a body comprised of fabrics, largely manufactured in Germany between 1860 and 1880.

Vera   You don't even observe as other people do, you don't watch. Why, if I were to come to you, wringing my hands saying, 'Amelia has shot herself', I don't believe you would stand up.

The Dove   No, I don't suppose I would, but I would do something for all that.

Vera   What?

The Dove   I should want to be very sure you wrung your hands as much as possible, and that Amelia had gotten all there was to get out of the bullet before she died.

Vera   It's all very well, but why don't you do something?

The Dove   A person who is capable of anything needs no practice.

Vera   You are probably maligning yourself, you are a gentle creature, a very girl –

The Dove   If you were sensitive, you would not say that.

Vera   Well, perhaps. (*She laughs a hard laugh.*) What can you expect of a lumber dealer's daughter?

The Dove   Why are you so restless, Vera?

Vera   Because I'm a woman. I leave my life entirely to my imagination and my imagination is terrific. I can't even turn to religion, for the *prie-dieu*[10] inclines me to one thing only – so there you are!

The Dove   You imagine – many things?

Vera   You know well enough – sitting here day after day, giving my mind everything to do, the body nothing –

The Dove   What do you want, Vera?

Vera   Some people would say a lover, but I don't say a lover; some people would say a home, but I don't say a home. You see I have imagined myself beyond the need of the usual home and beyond the reach of the usual lover –

The Dove   Then?

Vera   Perhaps what I really want is a reason for using one of these pistols!

She laughs and lies back. **The Dove**, *having risen, goes up behind* **Vera** *and places her hand on her throat.*

The Dove   Now you may use one of those pistols.

Vera (*startled, but making no attempt to remove* **The Dove**'*s hand*)   For such a *little* thing?

The Dove (*dropping her hand, once more taking up her old position, sword on knee*)   Ah!

---

10 *Prie-dieu*: a prayer desk for private worship.

Vera   Why do you say that?

She is evidently agitated.

The Dove   I suppose I shall *always* wait.

Vera   What is the matter?

The Dove   Always, always!

Vera   What is the matter?

The Dove   I suppose I'm waiting for the person who will know that anything is a reason for using a pistol, unless one is waiting for the obvious, and the obvious has never been sufficient reason.

Vera   It's all hopeless, I am hopeless and Amelia is hopeless, and as for you –

She makes a gesture.

The Dove   I've never held anything against hopelessness.

Vera   Now what do you mean?

The Dove   It doesn't matter.

Vera (*after a long pause*)   I wish you danced.

The Dove   Perhaps I do.

Vera   It might make me happier.

The Dove (*irrelevantly*)   Why don't people get angry at each other, quite suddenly and without reason?

Vera   Why should they?

The Dove   Isn't there something fine and cold and detached about a causeless anger?

Vera   I suppose so, it depends –

The Dove   No, it does not depend, that's exactly it; to have a reason is to cheapen rage. I wish every man were beyond the reach of his own biography.

Vera   You are either quite an idiot, or a saint.

The Dove   I thought we had discussed that.

Vera (*dashed but not showing it*)   Yes, a saint.

The Dove (*continuing*)   I'm impatient of necessary continuity, I'm too sensitive, perhaps. I want the beautiful thing to be, how can logic have anything to do with it, or probable sequence?

Vera   You make my hair stand on end!

The Dove   Of course, that's logical!

Vera   Then how is it you like Amelia? And how do you stand me?

The Dove   Because you are two splendid dams erected about two little puddles.

Vera   You're horrid!

The Dove   Only horrid!

Vera   Yes, I'm really afraid of you.

The Dove   Afraid?

Vera   For instance, when you're out of this room all these weapons might be a lot of butter knives or pop guns, but let you come in –

The Dove   Well?

Vera   It becomes an arsenal.

The Dove   Yet you call me The Dove.

Vera   Amelia called you The Dove, I'd never have thought of it. It's just like Amelia to call the only dangerous thing she ever knew The 'Dove'.

The Dove   Yes, there's something in that.

Vera   Shall I sing for you?

The Dove   If you like.

Vera   Or shall I show you the album that no one ever sees? (*She laughs*) If we had any friends we would have to throw that book in the fire.

The Dove   And you would have to clear the entry –

Vera   True. It's because of that picture of the Venetian courtesans that I send Amelia out for the butter, I don't dare let the grocer call.

The Dove   You have cut yourselves off – just because you're lonely.

Vera   Yes, just because we are lonely.

The Dove   It's quite wonderful.

Vera   It's a wonder the neighbours don't complain of Amelia's playing that way on the violin.

The Dove   I had not noticed.

Vera   No, I presume not, but everyone else in the house has. No nice woman slurs as many notes as Amelia does!

At this moment **Amelia** *enters the outer room. She is wearing a cloak with three shoulder-capes, a large plumed hat, and skirt with many flounces.*

Amelia (*from the entry*)   You should come and see Carpaccio's *Deux Courtisanes Vénitiennes* now,[11] the sun is shining right in on the head of the one in the foreground.

She begins to hum an Italian street song.

Well, I have brought a little something and a bottle of wine. The wine is for you, my Dove – and for you, Vera, I've a long green feather.

Pause in which **The Dove** *continues to polish the blade of the sword.* **Vera** *has picked up her book.*

Amelia (*advancing into the room, shrugging*)   It's damp! (*Seeing* **The Dove** *still at work.*) What a sweet, gentle creature, what a little Dove it is! Ah, God, it's a sin, truly it's a sin that I, a woman with temperament, permit a young girl to stay in the same room with me!

The Dove (*in a peaceful voice*)   I've loaded all the pistols –

Vera (*with suppressed anger*)   Shined all the swords, ground all the poniard[12] points! Attack a man now if you dare, he'll think you're playing with him!

Amelia (*in an awful voice*)   Vera! (*She begins pacing.*) Disaster! Disaster! – wherever I go, disaster! A woman selling fish tried to do me out of a quarter and when I remonstrated with her, she said with a wink: 'I, too, have been bitten by the fox!'

The Dove   If you'll sit down I'll make some tea.

Amelia   No, no, we'll have a little lunch soon, only I never can get the corks out of bottles.

The Dove   I can.

Vera   Rubbish!

She gets up and goes out.

Amelia   Well, has anything happened since I went out?

The Dove   No.

Amelia   No, no it never does. (*She begins to walk about hurriedly.*) Aren't there a great many flies in here?

The Dove   Yes, the screens should be put up.

Amelia   No, no, no; I don't want anything to be shut out. Flies have a right to more than life, they have a right to be curious.

The Dove   A bat flew into the room last night.

---

11 *Two Venetian Ladies* (about 1490): painting by Vittore Carpaccio, possibly a single panel from a larger piece, the whereabouts of which is unknown. The two women in the image could be courtesans, or possibly siblings given their resemblance. They seem overcome by boredom, and are surrounded by a menagerie of birds and dogs – one of which is biting a crop.
12 Poniard: a small dagger.

Amelia (*shuddering*)   Some day I shall look like a bat, having beaten my wings about every corner of the world, and never having hung over anything but myself –

The Dove   And this morning, early, before you got up, the little seamstress' monkey walked in through the window –

Amelia (*stopping short*)   Are we to become infested?

The Dove   Yesterday the mail-man offered me some dancing mice, he's raising them.

Amelia (*throwing up her hands*)   There! You see! (*Pause.*) Why should I wear red heels? Why does my heart beat?

The Dove   Red heels are handsome.

Amelia   Yes, yes, that's what I say. (*She begins to dance.*) Little one, were you ever held in the arms of the one you love?

The Dove   Who knows?

Amelia   If we had not been left an income we might have been in danger – well, let us laugh. (*She takes a few more dance steps.*) Eating makes one fat, nothing more, and exercising reduces one, nothing more. Drink wine – put flesh on the instep, the instep that used to tell such a sweet story – and then the knees – fit for nothing but prayers! The hands – too fat to wander! (*She waves her arm.*) Then one exercises, but it's never the same; what one has, is always better than what one regains. Is it not so, my little one? But never mind, don't answer. I'm in an excellent humour – I could talk for hours, all about myself – to myself, for myself. God! I'd like to tear out all the wires in the house! Destroy all the tunnels in the city, leave nothing underground or hidden or useful, oh, God, God!

She has danced until she comes directly in front of **The Dove**. *She drops on her knees and lays her arms on either side of* **The Dove**.

Amelia   I hate the chimneys on the houses, I hate the doorways, I hate you, I hate Vera, but most of all I hate my red heels!

The Dove (*almost inaudibly*)   Now, now!

Amelia (*in high excitement*)   Give me the sword! It has been sharpened long enough, give it to me, give it to me!

She makes a blind effort to find the sword; finding **The Dove**'s *hand instead, she clutches it convulsively. Slowly* **The Dove** *bares* **Amelia**'s *left shoulder and breast, and leaning down, sets her teeth in.* **Amelia** *gives a light, short, stifled cry. At the same moment* **Vera** *appears in the doorway with the uncorked bottle.* **The Dove** *stands up swiftly, holding a pistol. She turns in the doorway hastily vacated by* **Vera**.

The Dove   So!

She bows, a deep military bow, and turning goes into the entry.

The Voice of the Dove   For the house of Burgson!

A moment later a shot is heard.

Amelia (*running after her*)   Oh, my God!

Vera   What has she done?

Amelia (*reappearing in the doorway with the picture of the Venetian courtesans, through which there is a bullet hole – slowly, but with emphasis*)   This is obscene!

Curtain